80E 19.95

QUESTIONING MEDIA ETHICS

Editor

Bernard Rubin

PRAEGER PUBLISHERS
Praeger Special Studies

New York　•　London　•　Sydney　•　Toronto

PN
4756
. Q4

PRAEGER PUBLISHERS
PRAEGER SPECIAL STUDIES
383 Madison Avenue, New York, N.Y. 10017, U.S.A.

Published in the United States of America in 1978
by Praeger Publishers,
A Division of Holt, Rinehart and Winston, CBS, Inc.

89   038   987654321

© 1978 by Praeger Publishers

Library of Congress Catalog Card Number: 78-64408

Printed in the United States of America

For all whose ideas and works enhance the First Amendment.

CONTENTS

LIST OF ABBREVIATIONS AND ACRONYMS   viii

INTRODUCTION   ix

PART I: ALTERNATIVES

1   THE SEARCH FOR MEDIA ETHICS   3

Bernard Rubin

Snakes and Ladders   3
Standardizing Ethics   6
    The *News-Journal* Approach   7
    More Ethical Dilemmas   9
    Realism about "Freebies"   12
Media Ethics and Public Opinion   14
    Why the General Public Waits   14
    Critical Advice   16
Choices Forced   18
Ethical Cases in Point   19
    The Santa Clara Exclusive   19
    Post Scripts   20
    To Get the Story   22
    Privacy or Publicity   23
The News Councils   27
    National News Council Cases   29
    The Panax Controversy   30
Horizons   31
    Crisis Reportage   32
    Press Claims for Rights Disallowed the General Public: The
      Gilmore Case and the Texas Controversy   34
Notes   37

2   JOURNALISTIC ETHICS: SOME PROBINGS BY A
    MEDIA KEEPER   40

James C. Thomson, Jr.

Bit of History   42
Some Problems of Definition   44
Some Observed Responses   47
Some Possible Solutions   50

Notes   54

Appendix I Code of Ethics or Canons of Journalism   55

Appendix II A Statement of Principles   56

Appendix III Code of Ethics   58

3   THIS ABOVE ALL   61

Nora Beloff

The Technocrats   62

The Proprietors   67

Union Power   73

Constraints by Government   75

Conclusion   79

Notes   80

4   THE FAIRNESS DOCTRINE   81

Everett C. Parker

PART II: COVERING PUBLICS

5   HOW THE PRESS TREATS WOMEN   89

Joan Behrmann

Foremothers and the Press   90

The Women's Movement in the Press   94

IWY, ERA, and Other Women's Issues   97

The "Women's Section"   100

Women as News-Story Subjects   102

Ms., Miss, Mrs., or Hey You?   103

Sisters under the Headline   105

Say Che-e-e-ese-cake   110

Equal Pay? Equal Status?   111

On the Job—and Getting to It   117

Cooperation for Change   122

Notes   124

Bibliography   128

6   ETHICAL PROBLEMS IN TELEVISION ADVERTISING TO CHILDREN   133

F. Earle Barcus

The Ethical Issues   134

Whether to Advertise   135

How Much to Advertise   137

What to Advertise   139

Medicine and Drugs   139

Food   140

How to Advertise 141
   Format and Techniques 144
   Source Effects 144
   The Use of Premiums 146
Summary and Conclusions 146
Notes 147

7   FOR A "BLUNDERING INQUISITOR": THE PRESSURES AND HAZARDS OF THIRD WORLD COVERAGE 149

William Worthy

Notes 167
Editor's Note 167

8   SMALL-TOWN JOURNALISM HAS SOME BIG ETHICAL HEADACHES 171

Loren Ghiglione

9   LEGAL-ETHICAL INTERACTIONS IN JOURNALISM 180

Richard P. Nielsen

Actions Restricted by Law 180
   The Protection of Confidential Sources 180
   Reporting of Trials 182
   Libel 183
   Access to Government Information 185
   Access to Corporate Information 185
   Reporting Classified Information 186
   Restrictions in Government Areas and Institutions 187
   Extra Restrictions for Broadcasters 188
   Monopoly 190
Actions Ignored by Law 192
   Conflict of Interest—Ownership 192
   Conflict of Interest—Moonlighting 193
   Conflict of Interest—Gifts 194
   Self-Censorship—Political 195
   Distortion—Political 196
   Self-Censorship and Distortion—Economic 197
   Self-Censorship and Distortion—Military/Police 198
   Checkbook Journalism 199
   Advertising as News 200
   Secret Sources 201
Conclusion 202
Bibliography 204

PART IV: MANUFACTURING MEDIA IMAGES—MOTION PICTURES AND TELEVISION

10 MEDIA ETHICS: HOW MOVIES PORTRAY THE
   PRESS AND BROADCASTERS   209

Roger Manvell

The Delicate Balance   209
Journalism as Entertainment: The News "Story" and Its
   Purveyors   211
Front Page Cynicism   212
Dangerous Estate   217
The Newsperson as Humane Citizen   222
The Newsperson as Fighter for Justice   224
The Cinema and Other Media   227
Bibliography   231

11 THE FOURTH ESTATE AND THE SEVENTH ART   232

Deac Russell

Notes   245
Bibliography   246
Notes to the Filmography   247
Filmography—American Films Featuring the Press and
   Journalists—1903–1969   249
Selected Recent Films   281
A Note on Television   281
Miscellany   282

12 MAIMONIDES MEETS THE COOKIE MONSTER   283

Robert Rutherford Smith

The Ethics of Everyman   284
The Eighteenth-century Solution   286
The Shortcomings of Legalism   287
The Phenomenological Reform   288
Situation Ethics: The Third World of Morality   290
Television: Twenty-one-inch Morality   291
Four Possible Explanations   294
Who's to Blame?   300
Notes   301

ABOUT THE AUTHORS   303

LIST OF ABBREVIATIONS AND ACRONYMS

AP	Associated Press
AAUW	American Association of University Women
ABA	American Bar Association
ACT	Action for Children's Television
APME	Associated Press Managing Editors
ASNE	American Society of Newspaper Editors
CBBB	Council of Better Business Bureaus
CMMC	Council on Media, Merchandising, and Children
EEOC	Equal Employment Opportunity Commission
ERA	Equal Rights Amendment
FCC	Federal Communications Commission
FOIA	Freedom of Information Act
FTC	Federal Trade Commission
IDC	Institute for Democratic Communication
IPI	International Press Institute
IWY	International Women's Year
NAB	National Association of Broadcasters
NAD	National Advertising Division
NLRB	National Labor Relations Board
NNC	National News Council
NOW	National Organization for Women
OPC	Overseas Press Club
TVN	Television News Inc.
UPI	United Press International
WICI	Women in Communications Inc.

INTRODUCTION

In April 1976 twenty-two nationally prominent media practitioners and critics met at Boston University at the invitation of the director of the recently founded Institute for Democratic Communication (IDC). They were asked to spend two days analyzing mass media problems in our society and to conclude by suggesting what a research and community service organization could do to protect the First Amendment.

The communications experts generally agreed that three areas deserved full research attention immediately: ethics and mass media enterprises; relations between giant corporations and the mass media; minority group coverage by and participation in the mass media.

I set the goals of the IDC in accordance with that good advice and organized research teams. The plan was to devote at least a full year of research to each of the three subjects. Each research team would be composed of professionals who would work independently of one another, examining topics most closely connected to individual interests and experiences. Each contributor would provide an article that best illustrated a significant segment of the subject.

Questioning Media Ethics is the second research report resulting from that plan.* It aims to deal with major illustrative issues, cases, and arguments. The authors bring a variety of perspectives to bear. Rather than preaching on abstract ethical values, they deal with the real world and reach conclusions about the professional necessity that ethical standards be raised.

This book tries to emphasize key issues, without pretending to cover the entire area of media ethics. The contributors concentrate on matters in their fields. For example, an eminent film historian and a talented film curator discuss the image of the press that motion picture producers have manufactured. Similarly, a publisher of a small-town newspaper active in national news organizations, considers his headaches; a leading political correspondent worries about protecting reporters from big labor unions and their employers in the interests of safeguarding press freedoms; a director of one of the most highly regarded university organizations dedicated to raising media standards ponders his goals and media developments. A media critic explores how the search for ethics is going, given the professional confusions

---

Big Business and the Mass Media was published in 1977.

about political consequences and editorial guidances under the Bill of Rights. One of the nation's outstanding theologians argues for his interpretation of fairness. A brilliant woman reporter details how the media organizations of the nation have discriminated against half of the population. A critic of television turns his sights on the ethical imperatives of that medium. A communications-law specialist traces sample cases he considers of value. The key researcher on television's effects on children reflects on his basic findings. An angry journalist records his battles with the State Department over its passport regulations, which made travel illegal for those anxious to cover the Cuba and China stories in the 1950s and early 1960s. He also reflects on the attitudes of colleagues who backed off from confrontation with this problem.

This study was made possible by a research grant from the Shell Oil Company, which had no role whatsoever beyond providing financial assistance. More corporations should take the lead and assist scholars with support for objective research.

My colleagues in the Fourth Estate question media ethics, as do the publics we serve. Our hope is to learn how to perpetuate and improve democracy.

I would like to express my appreciation to Jean Reinhard and Paul Ford for assisting and for their good cheer.

Bernard Rubin
Director,
Institute for Democratic Communication
School of Public Communication
Boston University

Part I Alternatives

1 THE SEARCH FOR MEDIA ETHICS

Bernard Rubin

SNAKES AND LADDERS

No ethical standards are built into the mass media. The ethics of each responsible communicator contribute to the making of professional codes of conduct to which most media people can subscribe. All professional codes are essentially moral guides to help those who seek solutions to perplexing problems that constantly arise. No statement of professional ethics is aimed at a particular circumstance or chain of reports about any one situation. On the contrary, all constructive codes are useful because they consist of practical, general rules that can be transgressed only at the greatest personal and public risk. The individual communicator always has to face up to the ethical imperatives in deciding how to deal with a detail or a whole story. No formulation of collective wisdom substitutes for the individual searching into his own conscience.

Ethics, so far as mass media professionals are concerned, are anything but abstract. The generalities of the codes do not encompass worries about how many angels can dance on the head of a pin. They deal with the amount of pain that a communications pinprick or hammerblow can inflict, the value of stinging some official of a private or public institution into necessary action.

A publisher can get down to ethical basics merely by looking at the employment data of the newspaper to ascertain how many minority group members are on a staff. Blacks have been frustrated by the inappropriate, inadequate, or nonexistent coverage of their interests by most metropolitan newspapers. So long as that community (or any other) depends upon a white-dominated press—upon a press guilty of the most flagrant avoidance of its responsibilities to train and to hire

3

blacks, Mexican-Americans, American Indians, and other minority representatives—its news and its hopes will be buried. Such a deliberate neglect of professional obligations to serve all the public must lie heavy on the head of any publisher who finds the paper's employment data contrary to the general good.

An owner or manager of a television station knows whether he has made only token response to the democratic goals of fair opportunity and employment. If minority persons are placed on camera as readers ("anchorpersons") and have no editorial say or chances to exercise reportorial initiatives, that constitutes tokenism verging on fraud.

A 1977 survey showed that 2.5 percent of the nation's 40,000 newsroom employees were black, up from the estimated 1 percent in 1972. Only about 2 percent of news executives are drawn from minority groups.[1]

Roger Wilkins, the sagacious and seasoned New York *Times* reporter, attended a television conference of outstanding black journalists in December 1977, almost ten years after the Kerner Commission (National Commission on Civil Disorders) reported to President Johnson that two separate Americas were developing rapidly. A decade after that group urged that more blacks be employed by the news media, the newsrooms were still virtually white havens. Wilkins noted on the show "Black Perspectives on the News" that the leading black journalists compared their situation with Jackie Robinson's entry into major league baseball in 1947.[2] Thirty years after the first black participation in the big leagues; thirty years after Hutchins' Commission (Commission on the Freedom of the Press) called for new training programs; twenty years after Congress created the United States Commission on Civil Rights as a clearinghouse for information; almost ten years after the Kerner Commission's report, some of the most prestigious black journalists in the nation were still waiting for the color bar to be smashed completely and were drawing new strength from Jackie Robinson's experiences. That is as good, or bad, a commentary on the situation as any.

The Freedom House Coalition, a social service agency association, blasted the metropolitan Boston news media in its May 1977 review of the background to three years of school desegregation. "We have concluded that each of you have conspired against the black community (some individually, others collectively). . . . In so doing you have made us the victim, the villain." One of the charges in the four-page statement was that the media did not report that the Boston School Committee "willingly and intentionally" discriminated against the black community in the course of its allegedly "balanced reporting."[3]

The ethics of covering women's activities as if nearly all stories must contain some bizarre details is deplorable. Many stories of the struggles over the Equal Rights Amendment contain camouflaged facts.

With alarming regularity, the scandals involving nursing homes that mistreat the enfeebled aged, usually for considerable financial rewards to the proprietors, are grist for a sensation-seeking press corps. The headlines and stories satisfy a small coterie of reporters and publishers who know how easily the public is beguiled into thinking that a favorite newspaper is committed to "investigative reporting." The majority of media professionals recognize the needs to do less boasting and more in-depth work that brings the facts out *before* the inmates of mismanaged nursing homes are victimized. Reportage that could reduce the number of these scandals that the public reads about with almost clockwork regularity would reflect well upon the ethics of the Fourth Estate.

Other ethical problems are less dramatic although no less important. For example, the coverage of inner-city subjects is becoming less and less interesting to suburbanites, most of whom left to escape urban crime, disorder, and dilapidation. Most suburbanite job holders continue to work in the cities, and virtually all depend upon the commerce and industry of the cities. For news of the suburbs a great many turn to local newspapers that cater to their desires to escape minority problems, deterioration of urban neighborhoods, urban school health, police and welfare problems, and big-city financial crisis. A substantial number of the suburban "newspapers" have become merely blown-up real estate and general advertising sheets. News is almost a frivolous by-product of the local concentration on weddings, confirmations, and how much inflation has changed the values of homes. Big-city newspapers, which do not emphasize selfish localism or inflate the egos of the readers, are finding it increasingly difficult to compete with these suburban papers. So they fight back by giving up and devoting more staff time and column space to pleasing material for suburbanites. Thus the already deplorable lines of communication between the inner-city residents and the suburbanites are further weakened. Inexorably, news media panderings to marketplace-produced schizophrenia further separates the haves from the have-nots.

Meeting the desires of suburbanites, who are mainly white and middle-class, the electronic and print media pay a price. The wiser newspeople know that distinctions and divisions between communities are not healthy for a democracy; that the problems of the inner cities are biologically connected to the suburbs; that the viruses of decay, of crime, of repressed anger, which build into revolt, cannot be contained—the symptoms and the sicknesses can appear anywhere. Watching how competition corrupts the news-delivery processes, media people are vexed.

There is even wider agreement on the importance of adequate coverage of overseas news. Yet most Third World problems are invisible today. Poorly covered are sub-Saharan starvation; massacres in Bangladesh; the plights of refugee "boat people" in Southeast Asia; the struggles for freedom by blacks throughout Africa. There are hardly any black correspondents assigned overseas by radio, television, or print media. Most of the major news organizations have no resident correspondents based in important Third World countries. Africa and Asia, in particular, are deemed to be primarily feature-material areas. When a story arises in a particular place, "stringers" are relied on until an experienced reporter can be flown in. As long as the story lasts, and it usually has to be either highly dramatic or terribly catastrophic, the work is forwarded to home offices. An experienced reporter who has spent years in a huge nation can do a better job than the itinerant journalist who dashes from here to there; yet news organizations in New York have reporters based permanently in Chicago, but not in Asia or Africa. Inevitably—necessity being the mother of invention—concoction must occur when one culture seizes from another whatever it can get under the circumstances. If the American press has not yet handled the subject of race relations competently at home, what are we to imagine of its coverage of a racial clash in Vietnam or Malaysia? But the financial support necessary for even minimal overseas coverage is more than the great media organizations care to bear. The ethical consequences of current practices are of even less interest to non-news and editorial people in the comptrollers' offices than to editors and publishers.

STANDARDIZING ETHICS

Worried about improprieties that have become too identified with the profession, many media people have become convinced of the necessity for written codes of standards. It is agreed that honesty is essential; yet even honesty is subject to interpretation, if special circumstances warrant. For example, is "checkbook journalism" honest? Should the enormously profitable television networks allow reporters to pay people in order to get stories?

The debate as to whether employers, fellow employees, or members of the public have a right to know whether a reporter is or ever has been connected with the Central Intelligence Agency while ostensibly working full-time for a news organization has been going on for some time. Some publishers, radio and television executives, politicians, and private citizens consider such a liaison status so patriotic that they believe the identity of newspeople so engaged should be secret. Others of equally high standing take the position that failures to disclose that information constitute dishonesty in a society with a free press.

Having played devil's advocate with the foregoing examples, the author honestly admits a personal distaste for the infiltration of the press by government agencies acting covertly. For more than three decades such behind the screens C.I.A. connections with college and university professors, who recruited for the Agency and provided reports on campus activities of dissidents, have sullied the academic environment. An American campus is a very fragile place. So long as it is free it grows stronger and more responsible. Impose clandestine controls that impede free thought and research only at the risk of seeing the domestic college and university scene take on the colorations of institutions in authoritarian societies. It is said that few if any college and university presidents want to know the names of C.I.A. linked professors on their campuses. Knowledge requires some form of response, be it support or rejection of those concerned.

Is it any less honest for a university teacher to fail to notify his dean or president that he is working secretly for the government, that it is for a working reporter to so report to his editor, station manager and colleagues? Is it honest for a college president or a publisher to want to learn nothing in order to be free to do nothing? Is it ethical or honest for a teacher to keep students and colleagues in the dark about such a liaison at the same time he poses as a researcher bound only to his search for truth?

Unfortunately, the word *honesty* in the codes of ethics is often constricted to use in connection with acceptance of favors or money. The professional need to keep *honesty* and *integrity* synonymous is too often overlooked.

Let us consider codes handed down from employers or professional associations.

The News-Journal Approach

The executive editor and vice president of the News-Journal Company (Wilmington, Delaware), Mr. Frederick W. Hartmann, decries journalistic hypocrisies. He wrote the author alluding to types of newspersons who overlook or condone ethical mischief. "While the editor-in-chief attends a conference that deals with lofty and ethical ideals, his travel writer is off on a freebie junket to southern France and his theatre reviewer is accepting free tickets to the Broadway play that has come to town."[4] Hartmann's newspapers have a policy about professionalism and ethics, first promulgated in 1971 and revised twice, with the latest version published in 1977. It applies to all news and editorial department employees.

A key feature is the emphasis upon "individual judgment and integrity" held to be "keystones ... because it would be impossible to spell out every single question that might arise." Another is the insistence that "our management and employees must remain free of obligation to any special interests. This means avoiding all possible conflicts of interest or the appearance thereof."

To keep the newspeople free of taint, the code forbids acceptance of favors and favoritism. Employees are forbidden to accept "gifts of money or items of value." Anything worth more than a few dollars is covered. "Free admissions to any event that is not free to the public are prohibited. If the public pays, the News-Journal pays. Whenever possible, arrangements will be made to pay for the use of press boxes or press rooms and for the admission of photographers."

News-Journal news and editorial employees are forbidden to work for a rival news organization, print or electronic, in the company's circulation area; "do public relations, writing, photography or similar work for any organization that comes within the normal range of News-Journal coverage"; be in policy-making positions in "major outside organizations," including state or local school boards, symphony orchestra board, medical center board, and so on, if they "fall in the normal range of News-Journal coverage"; participate in public demonstrations in the News-Journal coverage area; "work for a political party or candidate" or a governmental agency," because politics and government are of "prime news interest and are woven through almost all areas of coverage."

The basic premise behind the strictures that prohibit participation by the employees can be summed up in the policy contention, "People who report the news should not be involved in making that news."[5]

The insistence upon journalistic independence is laudable, but extensions of that insistence into the areas of politics and community work, denying newspeople opportunities to carry on citizenship activities, may be going too far in the name of objectivity. The music editor might find it difficult to criticize the Delaware Symphony if serving on its board. A specialist on medical stories may not find it appropriate to serve on the board of the Wilmington Medical Center. The publication of such affiliations, however, might suffice to alert the readership about possible bias when a story about a specific organization appeared. It is possible that such inflexible, broad prohibitions about civic-related memberships may do more to stymie the socially responsible members of the staff than to prevent those who are determined to be slanted in their coverage. The basic rights and interests of the individual citizen should not be sacrificed to blanket prohibitions.

Still, the News-Journal code of ethics is a step in the right direction. It shows how much depends upon individual integrity, for all the legislated prohibitions. It strikes the right note when it demands that every member of the news and editorial staff be independent and conscious of maintaining public trust.

More Ethical Dilemmas

The individual reporter's independence is the key to ethical work. The selfsame independence that turns the low-minded or weak-willed to unethical behavior permits the great majority of reporters to attain professional excellence. That excellence includes high ethical standards, *selfimposed* by each individual.

Many journalistic leaders consider all written restrictions undesirable. For example, Robert Manning, the editor-in-chief of *The Atlantic Monthly,* looks to other means.

> I think that journalism should resist all written or codified restrictions, employ its own self-policing mechanisms, among them the reasonable cautions imposed by the knowledge that if one goes "too far" he must take the consequences imposed by (1) the courts and (2) the willingness of readers or listeners to continue patronizing the medium involved. I personally would refrain in my journal from the excesses indulged in before and during the Sam Sheppard trial, but I would resist attempts by others to prohibit me from committing those excesses as a matter of course.[6]

Manning's reference to the Sheppard trial is extremely relevant. Dr. Sheppard stood trial in Ohio in 1954 on the charge of murdering his wife. Many reporters covering the trial produced chilling examples of unethical work for the sake of sensational reports about "Dr. Sam." Much of the racy commentary was *not* based on evidence heard by the jurors listening to sworn witnesses. Radio, television, and newspapers across the nation created their own images of "Dr. Sam"—images that titillated mass audiences and were often downright distortions. These circumstances led to the Supreme Court reversal of his conviction in 1966. Mr. Justice Clark said the original trial judge had failed to protect Sheppard's right to a fair trial: "The fact is that bedlam reigned at the courthouse during the trial and newsmen took over practically the entire courtroom, hounding most of the participants at the trial, especially Sheppard. . . . Having assigned almost all of the available seats in the courtroom to the news media, the judge lost his ability to supervise the environment." The sensationalist press concentrated on lurid material extraneous to the evidence and often without foundation. Clark cites stories alleging that Sheppard "must be guilty since he had hired a prominent criminal lawyer; that Sheppard was a perjurer; that he had sexual relations with numerous women. . . . " Some of this "deluge of publicity reached at least some of the jury."[7]

No matter how much we sympathize with Manning's views, there is an obvious need to take every step possible to discourage replays of the distressing Sheppard trial. In 1977 the search for the "Son of Sam" killer of young people in New York City gave one segment of the press an opportunity to discard most ethical standards in order to attract circulation. The accused, one David Berkowitz, was the center of circus-like coverage by press organizations across the United States. A long police search for a culprit, pent-up public fears, and the disturbed character of the accused, offered irresponsible press chieftains a great way to sell newspapers. Rupert Murdoch, the Australian press magnate who had recently bought the New York *Post* and altered its format, went all out with multipage sensational coverage. At a magazine publisher's conference in Los Angeles in late 1977, Murdoch, who also publishes *New West* magazine, was asked if his coverage gave credence to the proposition that Berkowitz had been convicted by the press. He said, "Yes, and that's bad." He said he was partly to blame, along with the mayor and police commissioner of New York City, for the "communal hysteria." Murdoch declared, "If you lived in New York, where there was this tremendous interest in the case, there was nothing else to do but write about it."

The extremely colorful and sometimes lurid *Post* coverage wasn't unique, unfortunately. Despite the ethical importance of avoiding statements that suggest confessions in this type of case especially, the temptations appear to have been too much for many editors and reporters. Examples of headlines: "Son of Sam Had Planned Bloodbath" (Atlanta *Constitution,* August 12, 1977); "A Paunchy Loner Confesses to Being Son of Sam Killer" (Miami *Herald,* August 12, 1977).

Television reports of the developments in the case were sometimes equally offensive. Geraldo Rivera of ABC News used the words "fiend" and "murderer" to describe the suspect. *Time,* in its August 22, 1977 issue, used the headline, "After the capture the twisted killer's life unfolds." Writing for the professional journalists' magazine *Quill,* Jim Frisinger concluded a survey of press treatment of this case on a hopeful note. He commended the San Francisco *Chronicle* and the Boston

Globe for providing accounts that did no damage to the right of the accused to a fair trial.[8]

A vexing dilemma faced by honest newsmen involves the need both to protect individual privacy and to disseminate as much reliable information as possible. One situation that ended well shows the difficult choices that have to be made by ethical defenders of the public's right to know.

WABC-TV sent a camera team into Saint Michael's Home (Staten Island, New York City) in 1976 to interview adolescent wards of the state for a report about criminal abuse of children. After the filming an appeal was made to the Appellate Division of the State Supreme Court in Manhattan to stop the televising of the report in order to protect the privacy of the youngsters. Their names and their faces, it was argued, should not be specifically identified. That is an important protection for children since it was possible to indiscriminately disclose the identities of those already victimized by alleged criminal abuse. The court ruled against prior restraint in favor of First Amendment rights. However, the presiding judge, in a post-decision conference, urged broadcasters to devise a way to protect privacy. WABC-TV wisely altered the film so that the faces of the children were out of focus. Viewers were informed of this action.[9]

Another problem faced by media people anxious to maintain the highest ethical standards is that the codes drawn up by the leading professional associations tend to be so general that the room for interpretation necessity is enormous. The clearest provisions deal with gifts. For example, the standards of practice adopted by Sigma Delta Chi, The Society of Professional Journalists, in 1973, flatly states that "nothing of value should be accepted." Secondary employment and any political or community organizational work that "compromises integrity" should be avoided. Private sources should not be used as the basis for news unless the claims to news value of their communications can be substantiated. Journalists are advised to strive to make public records open to public inspection and to get as much public business conducted in public as possible. Also cited is the "newsman's ethic of protecting confidential sources of information." Other sections of the code of practice cover accuracy, objectivity, and fair play. Journalists are urged to be unselfish, to avoid conflicts of interest, to seek news that serves the public interest, to hold truth to be the ultimate goal, to be objective, to separate clearly opinion from news reports, to offer informed analysis, to "at all times ... respect dignity, privacy, rights, and well-being of people encountered, not to "pander to morbid curiosity about details of vice and crime," to be "prompt and complete" in correcting errors.[10]

The "Code of Professional Standards for the Practice of Public Relations" of the Public Relations Society of America (adopted and effective as of April 29, 1977) is similar. Its point ten, which states, "A member shall not intentionally injure the professional reputation or practice of another public relations practitioner," offers an additional guideline. The code calls for reporting by any member of evidence that any other member "has been guilty of unethical, illegal or unfair practices."[11]

The similarities between these codes are significant, as are what both omit. More case study guides are needed. Perhaps appendices are in order for both guides, analyzing cases revealing how ethical integrity of individuals and organizations, in difficult situations, was found to be commendable, debatable, or condemnable.

The Gannett Co., Inc. (publishers of the Rochester *Times-Union* and many other newspapers) code, adopted by its board of directors on March 22, 1977, is a bit more arresting on the subject of conflict-of-interest clauses and related matters. "The Gannett Company expects its officers and employees to conduct themselves in such a manner that there will be no embarrassment to the company or to the individual concerned if he or she is called upon to explain an action to one's peers, the stockholders or the public." Regarding corporate ethics, there is the interesting provision, well-justified in the light of the reports of U.S. corporations' bribery of public officials and many other influentials—from Indonesia to Watergate, from Tokyo to the Hague—"Commercial bribery ... will not be tolerated.... The company will not contribute to political parties nor to any candidates for public office."[12]

Realism about "Freebies"

Many journalists are cynical about their colleagues' abilities to retain professional objectivity in an environment allowing them to accept gifts or favors—"freebies." We live in a society where money talks very loudly, and most of us are judged less for our ethical behavior than for our ability to acquire possessions, influence, or power. Although newspeople go out into the world and report its developments realistically, they are expected to rise above the prevailing level of seedy corporate and community behavior, to resist the free lunch, stock market tip, sports event tickets, vacation accommodations, travel tickets.

A recent study by Professors Keith P. Sanders and Won H. Chang of the University of Missouri School of Journalism brought new evidence of how deeply worried newspeople are. Steps being taken by employers may be vitally necessary if we are to protect the seekers after truth from the blandishers of gifts.*

Professors Sanders and Chang conducted a survey, sending a questionnaire to a stratified sample of 200 newspapers selected at random from the *Editor & Publisher Yearbook.* Most mailings went to managing editors along with a request to give an additional enclosed copy to another staff person. The questionnaire had three sections. The first sought demographic data ("sex, job title, educational level, total years in the journalistic profession"). The second asked journalists whether acceptance of freebies altered their objectivity. In section three, respondents were asked their views on twenty-one opinion statements.

The response was quite adequate, encompassing 52 percent of the newspapers solicited. On the average, the respondents were seventeen-year-veterans in journalism. Fourteen respondents were women; 89.4 percent had college degrees, and 26.8 percent had graduate degrees; 77 percent had been journalism majors as undergraduates.

In response to questioning about whether particular types of freebies would "affect most journalists' objectivity in reporting related stories," the percentages of the respondents affirming influences on objectivity ranged according to the gift from 77.1 percent to a low of 32.7 percent.

The respondents rated certain freebies as more damaging to objectivity than others. Most powerful influences were offers of a foreign trip (77.1 percent); "membership in local country club" (70.9 percent); gifts (61.1 percent); a U.S. trip (58.9 percent). At the bottom of the influence range were free meals or drinks (38.9 percent); "samples of foods, toiletries, perfumes, etc., etc., that routinely came into the office" (33.6 percent); movie or theater tickets (32.7 percent).

Sanders and Chang concluded, "If journalists have such a low regard for the ability of their colleagues to maintain their integrity by the

---

*The National Labor Relations Board (NLRB) in at least two cases has ruled on whether a publishing company can mandate an ethical code without negotiating with the employees. In the Peerless Publishing, Inc. (publisher of the Pottstown, Pa., *Mercury*) case, an NLRB judge on September 25, 1978 ordered cancellation of a code of ethics and general office rules affecting editorial staff on the grounds that regulations on working conditions have to be subjected to a bargaining process with the employees' union. In the *Capital Times* (of Madison, Wisconsin) case, the NLRB held on January 16, 1975 that the company had committed an unfair labor practice in establishing a code without prior bargaining with employees. Later, in 1976, the NLRB reversed itself and declared by a three to one vote that newspapers have the right to adopt codes unilaterally. For NLRB rulings in Pottstown *Mercury* and *Capital Times* cases, see Keith P. Sanders and Won H. Chang, "Codes—the Ethical *Free*-For-All," Freedom of Information Foundation, Columbia, Missouri, Freedom of Information Series no. 7, March 1977. For reversal in *Capital Times* see *The Capital Times Company,* 223 NLRB, no. 87 (1976).

temptation of even the least valuable of freebies, it is obvious that the public hardly can be expected to have much confidence. The house must be put in order."[13] Perhaps we can take cold comfort from the fact that only 15 percent of the respondents admitted personal susceptibility to freebies.[14] This research was supported by a grant from the American Newspaper Publishers Assocation Foundation. Assuming the validity of the data, the reactions from all media managers will be most interesting.

A brighter picture does not emerge from a survey conducted by the Public Relations Society of America and reported in 1975. Looking back over the previous year, "Forty percent . . . said they had been offered a combination deal on advertising and editorial space." An equal percentage related that reporters and editors had asked for special favors, including all sorts of freebies.

There is some hope in 1974 evidence suggesting that new employer strictness and new employee attitudes have reduced ethical malpractice.[15] We need more than hope to justify the obviously high regard that Sanders and Chang's respondents had for their own integrity, as compared with the low ratings they gave to associates.

MEDIA ETHICS AND PUBLIC OPINION

Standardized codes of ethics for the mass media are hopeful signs, but their usefulness is limited. Other ethical resources are needed.

I conclude that only a high ethical level of individual professional work by each of us in the media is the answer to the problem. The ethical standards of the media will be determined by the number of people who care. To the extent that we constitute a responsible public, public opinion is a powerful influence.

However, I have doubts about more sweeping comprehensions of public opinion containing assumptions about the whole populace. A dedicated democrat and staunch upholder of the First Amendment is not required to have illusions. Each profession must be based on the highest ethics; each professional must, by his contributions, act as the guardian of those ethics. My reasons for reaching these conclusions about mass public opinion follow.

Why the General Public Waits

Some overly idealistic observers of the media argue that public opinion is a reliable checking influence that ensures that the general welfare will ultimately be served. Like all such generalizations about democratic society, this view has just enough validity to hide the specious logic.

Actually, *public opinion* is the label given to rallied attitudes directed for a brief time in the shape of a coherent idea or concept. Often it has no direct target, no apparent concrete goal. In between moments of group consensus that can be detected by astute recorders of social or political change, it is almost always residual, virtually formless, and composed of leftover attitudes, views, and concerns formed from momentary enthusiasm or anger. The melange that builds into public opinion on an issue or a cause has some basic ingredients at all times, such as self-interest and emotional needs that create views and attitudes. We often have views and attitudes that are not properly called opinions.

Some opinions are shared or handed down from generation to generation. Such opinions are frequently invisible mental clothing that is not changed or checked or cleaned. They include both bitter thoughts and hatreds and good feelings and loving ideas.

Too few members of the public examine ideas intellectually, reaching conclusions in an objective way. Although intellectual arguments based on careful inspections can galvanize an individual or a group, emotions triggered by self-interest usually are basic to the formation of public attitudes.

The theory that public opinion normally forms in timely reaction to the needs for advice from the citizenry is dubious. Frequently, publics are swayed by savants or demagogues with wrong ideas or unethical motives. It is extremely difficult for people to resist clever publicists who lead by cloaking their true intentions. Public opinion, sadly enough, is often manipulated by phrasemakers and entertainers.

In the mass media, there is increasing managerial emphasis upon entertainment for publics with a great deal of leisure time. Managers are too busy diverting minds from serious subjects to expend much effort on ethical problems, except for the very serious, legally motivated concerns for accuracy, fairness, rights of privacy, libel and defamation law, objectivity. For too long the prevailing attitude has been, if the public buys it, it's good.

Thus the violence, the downplaying of minorities, the pandering to the lowest common denominator of taste, the ignoring of the aged, the infirm, the poor are characteristic of television today. And the press fails to assume more responsibility to push for social reforms. Too many reporters and editors are devoted to stories about people in power rather than attentive to those over whom power is exercised.

For this reason, information and analyses provided must be as accurate and objective as high professional efforts can ensure. Moreover, the ethical necessity of truthfully outlining the altruistic goals of our society should never give way to desires to match sensationalist competitors who profit by deliberately, and out of all proportion, concentrating on displays of the worst evidence of human nature. Third, all aspects of self-interest should be shown, as they are to be found in the stories of humankind. If that is accomplished, the truths about what are called *the real* and *the ideal* will be more frequently in evidence. Fourth, emotion should be considered in all of its forms. It should not be forgotten that in addition to the emotional outbursts so typically considered newsworthy, a spectrum of emotions exists behind all our hopes and fears and is part of too many uninvestigated stories.

When a professional media person wonders why, at a vital time, a public hesitates to support some constructive step, or lauditory goal or necessary risk, personal anxiety about level of attainments is in order. A prime question to be inner-directed is, have I the feeling that my work is at a high enough ethical level? Public opinion in an age of mass communications is increasingly influenced or misshapen by the media. Behind every public crisis and achievement there is a contribution of practical media ethics.

Critical Advice

Tom Wicker of the New York *Times* has earned the right to criticize colleagues by virtue of his works on politics and government, from the presidency to prison reform. He recently told the audience at a statewide journalism conference in Tennessee, "I call on you . . . and the free American press everywhere to become the last engine of reform" and institute "vigorous disclosure" of private and governmental exploitation and self-interest. He advised them to "care passionately" about humanity and about justice. At the same meeting the renowned journalist David Halberstam, who won the Pulitzer Prize for his Vietnam War reporting and evaluations, advised his professional audience, "Your press card is really a social credit card."[16]

On a similar social theme Arthur Taylor, president of the Columbia Broadcasting System, in a 1976 address to the conferees at the annual assembly of the International Press Institute hit on a vital media obligation.

> With their expanded responsibilities, journalists also must also realize that there are other rights to be balanced with press freedom—privacy, a fair trial, simple human dignity. Human beings must not be exploited as mere objects of attention, to be drained of their public

interest and discarded ... mass communications carries with it an inherent danger of dehumanization of the individual.[17]

There are more specifically directed complaints about press ethics. John B. Connally, the former governor of Texas and secretary of the treasury, has spoken of press failure to keep in check its power to "oppress." He cites some of the "petty" ways, such as misleading or damaging headlines reflecting the bias or anger of "some deskman." Page makeup that magnifies a story out of proportion to its worth is on his list, along with "benign neglect or burial of another story." Connally is also disturbed by the "growing volume of news reporting on serious subjects by writers and broadcasters with superficial understanding of the issues."[18] This last point is substantially confirmed in the 1977 book *Big Business and the Mass Media.*[19]

At the 1977 media ethics conference of the Institute for Democratic Communication of Boston University, nationally syndicated columnist Ellen Goodman lambasted the press for including so few women in decision making about what stories to cover. In her view, newspapers are "essentially the record of the games men play: sports, politics, and business." Robert M. Crocker, the secretary-treasurer of the Newspaper Guild, told a panel on "Corporate Influences on Media Ethics" that his organization was formulating an ethics code to include a declaration against news slanting in order to please advertisers, "friends or associates of media proprietors," or institutions. He wants a definite distinction between the news and advertising activities of newspapers, as regards solicitation, preparation, and presentation. Boston *Herald-American* editor-in-chief William McIlwain, as a member of a panel discussion on "Challenges to the Canons of Journalism," urged his listeners to turn away from a trend to make a newspaper "a pop, razzmatazz blend of sports, entertainment, and hot graphics." On that same panel, Loren Ghiglione, the publisher of the Evening News (Southbridge, Massachusetts), warned that "boosterism" is an important ethical problem. "Many newspapers," said Ghiglione, "aren't willing to risk reprisals and so give a Chamber of Commerce-type version of the truth."[20]

These criticisms demonstrate the variety of ethical issues confronting journalists and the difficulties of resolving them satisfactorily. Most of the ethical questions depend for solution not on any pat formulas but on the essential morality of media professionals.

It is not out of order to seek a basis for ethical imperatives from the extraordinarily wise and practical professor of divinity, Harvey Cox of Harvard University. He told a gathering of Nieman Foundation scholars that ethical questions drive us back to the "moral issue," which takes us back to what he called the "whole issue," a "religious issue." He asked his listeners to consider

> questions of one's basic and cardinal perspective on the world—one's capacity for imaginatively entertaining and feeling the pains of other people, one's capacity to enter into some kind of empathy with people whose situations are not one's own. But I think we would be missing the point if we talk as though we were simply in need of help in making choices which are already forced.[21]

CHOICES FORCED

An editor of a daily newspaper each morning or afternoon ponders such problems as whether a headline is provocative but does not comport with the story that follows; a photograph makes a politician look ridiculous whereas he is characteristically serious; a story plays up a racial identification when such information lacks significance; a feature about old people makes them out to be mentally deficient, although a better reporter would have stressed that a substantial number of them are as intellectually alert as ever but are trapped in one of those dumping-ground institutions for the aged poor. Not to forget: the business story about a local corporation that is puffery and should even be questioned as purchased advertising material. And what about the terse reports typical of his paper's coverage of biting public arguments over issues of abortion, homosexuality, child abuse, or women's rights? Should these be replaced with background reports based on investigative work? On his list are the publisher's hints and directives about the political candidates to be supported. Is the staff being directed to create a virtual blackout on what other candidates are doing? That editor's instructions about these problems set the ethical framework of his organization and drastically influence the ethical awareness of the readers.

Sometimes the ethical questions have more long-range importance, covering the permanent ability of a news organization to do its duty. It is, for example, well known that Ultra High Frequency (UHF) television stations are often good moneymaking machines, concentrating on the running of ancient "sitcom" series and old motion pictures because they are cheap to rent or purchase. There are many contributions made by such UHF stations. For one example, the scheduling of the old "sitcoms" and movies previously referred to, often provides important segments of the public with better fare than is available on the more affluent VHF channels because the general level of current programming is so mundane. Recently, I was the sole guest on one of the early morning half-hour talk shows presented by a UHF station in the metropolitan Boston area. My host was a most intelligent young woman. In the format of that program she also delivered the news and weather reports along with introductions to frequent advertisements. During our discussion dealing with the relationships between the goals of the professional communicators and politicians, I was impressed with the sincerity and knowledge of my host—rare in one who every weekday talked to guests called upon to make comments on a great variety of subjects. At one point, the issue of local television station responsibility (in any community) for community affairs came up. I discussed the needs and possibilities for better reporting. In turn, I inquired about how much live or delayed on-the-spot coverage of that type the station provided. Somewhat apologetically, though she bore no responsibility, my host admitted that because there were no portable cameras in the station's inventory, and virtually no public affairs staff, there was no live or delayed on-the-spot work. My response was that more important matters were obviously not dealt with if a fire down the street from the station would be outside the range of the equipment. We were both distressed and unable to do much about it.

The ethics of that station's management—running a profitable venture without investing more than token amounts in public affairs staff or equipment—are not commendable. As I left the building, my thoughts turned to the moderator who obviously was capable and interested in greater community-service reporting. Noticing a large liquor store close by, I was at that moment struck by the similarity of the two businesses.

ETHICAL CASES IN POINT

The following brief summaries of recent situations involving ethic problems are intended to be representative and are not presented in any order, since, in a practical approach to ethical problems, the most important problem is the one at hand.

The Santa Clara Exclusive

"Weekend," a monthly television news-feature magazine on NBC, devoted the ninety-minute telecast of May 7, 1977 to a documentary on the work of the Santa Clara Child Sexual Abuse Center (California), specifically dealing with incest. The producers got the clinic's directors to agree verbally not to give interviews about the program to any other electronic-industry journalists. NBC people from other units were included in the ban: a reporter for the radio news service of NBC (NIS) was in April refused interviews for a radio series on incest. The ban was to be in force until the telecast. The founder of the clinic said that his organization made the decision to grant the exclusive arrangement because the "Weekend" people had worked hard on the documentary: "We think they're equipped to do the best job of informing the public about our program, and we don't want anyone upstaging them before they go on the air."

An NBC radio reporter, Tom Giusto, called it a "bad situation.... We have an organization dedicated to the rights of free speech being party to an agreement that prevents public officials from talking to the news media on a problem of major public importance."

Protection of an exclusive is well established in journalism. The ethics of any attempt to defer or deny commentary to rivals are debatable, especially when no interference with the actual television product, the documentary, was posed. Any and all responsible reporting on the subject of incest is in the public interest. The wall of silence thrown around the clinic is counter to the public interest. When dealing with any general subject, such attempts at exclusivity border on censorship contrary to the First Amendment.[22]

Post Scripts

A former editor-in-chief of *Newsweek* magazine, Osborn Elliot, was deputy mayor for economic development in 1977 during Mayor Abraham Beame's tenure in New York City. In July, he took issue with Rupert Murdoch, the publisher of the New York *Post* over the headline "24 Hours of TERROR" that appeared following a blackout. In a "Dear Rupert," letter Elliot wrote, "Perhaps you wouldn't have gotten so many people to buy your papers—for that one Friday—if you had been more responsible." Commenting on what he called the city's "first big crisis" since Murdoch, the Australian publishing magnate, had taken over the *Post,* Elliot asked, "Are you proud of what your headlines produced?"

Murdoch defended the headline and the story, saying that his newspaper took the phrase from Mayor Beame. As for a *Post* conclusion that looting during the blackout was "the worst outbreak of rioting during the city's history," Murdoch told a *Times* correspondent, "I don't know anything about that. You'd have to ask the journalist who wrote it."[23]

Murdoch was absolutely right in referring to the reporter. Publishers and editors should never try to respond to a question about any story about which they lack personal knowledge. However, Elliot was right in raising the issue about the headline if he had concluded, on the basis of a long-term career in journalism, that it was irresponsible. There is no obvious right or wrong here, only a clear ethical problem. At times of public crisis, the duty of news organs to inform places a heavy burden on them. The truth, however distasteful, is the immediate and ultimate goal. There are times, though, when the full story on the publisher's or editor's desk goes beyond the copy or photographs or films made available by staff. It is necessary to avoid sensationalism that creates further distress or disorder. The public must have the facts, warts and all, and news managers must exercise all their wisdom and manifest the common sense acquired through the years.

Still, the distinctions between what is proper and what is not are much fuzzier than we would like to admit during a crisis. The newspeople are not detached from crisis; they are perhaps more involved than many other citizens. At the actual moments when the news manager's eyes range over controversial material, only personal ethics suffice.

Rupert Murdoch has not been exactly out of the limelight since his New York *Post* acquisition. In October 1977, fifty of his reporters presented him a petition because of "disquiet over slanted news coverage" during the mayoral campaign then in progress in New York City. One of the petitioners noted concern about the placement and display of stories favorable to the candidates for mayor and president of the City Council already endorsed editorially by the newspaper. The petitioners wanted editorials and endorsements to be different from political news coverage which they wanted to be objective, *i.e.*, factual in basis, even-handed and not favorable to any candidate. Murdoch rejected the petition's allegations and, after a conference with the publisher over the petition, one long-time *Post* reporter posted a bulletin-board notice that Murdoch felt that any person who doubted his integrity should look for another job.

Should the group of petitioners have been disturbed by the *Post* centerfold of September 16, 1977, three days before a runoff election between the *Post's* candidate for City Council president and the opponent? The headline, "Cinderella Carol" (State Senator Carol Bellamy) was over what is described as "a profile . . . illustrated with 11 pictures from her family scrapbook, showing the politician from the age of 10 months, 'with Santa at 6,' 'at 9, on the way to church' and 'relaxing after a hard day's campaigning.' "[24]

To Get the Story

The barely satiable desire to *get the story* is what makes a good newsperson. Like all other qualities, this ambition if carried to extremes ceases to be a virtue. Robert Scheer has acquired some personal publicity from his success in getting interviews with people in the public spotlight. In one such interview during the 1976 presidential campaign, he managed to get candidate Jimmy Carter to speak of *lust* in the heart and other subjects not traditionally discussed by those seeking to live in the White House.

Scheer toyed with outrageousness when he spoke at the A. J. Liebling Convention sponsored by *More: The Media Magazine.* His subject was "The Art of the Interview." He told the conferees:

> Politicians try to prevent you from knowing what's going on because that's how they survive. And they have lots of people employed to help them. The journalist's job is to get the story by breaking into their offices, by bribing, by seducing people, by lying, by anything else to break through that palace guard. . . . I can't say now I wouldn't lie. I think the most important thing to a journalist is to get the story . . . maybe I would promise anything, as long as I could get out of the country on time.

Scheer says he is out of a tradition he labels "counterjournalism." He has good credentials as an activist-critic. He edited the magazine *Ramparts* for five years, and his books include *How the U.S. Got Involved in Vietnam,* a very early antiwar analysis, and *America after Nixon,* dealing with the powerful multinational corporations. Still, his comments about how far he would go to reach his goals make most newspeople cringe.

Interviewed at length after the convention by a *More* contributor, New York *Daily News* political correspondent Ken Auletta, Scheer went into more details about "guerrilla journalism," which he sees as different from "access journalism." Specifically responding to a question asking how he separates "what is permissible from what is not permissible," he offered the Watergate Deep Throat as an example of permissible tactics. "I don't know what laws he violated," said Scheer, adding, "A hell of a lot of the investigative journalism of the last five years has come from such information. Files that are lifted, people who are violating the conditions of their jobs, and so forth."[25]

Scheer some time ago was one of the *Ramparts* group that produced the exposé of secret CIA financial backing of American student organizations. Is the pot calling the kettle black? If, in the name of ethical response to illegalities and unethical behavior, the press condones conduct similar to that deserving condemnation, there is no end to the storm hurling long-fought-for and cherished democratic guarantees out of sight of civilized humanity.

In opposing those who knock on the doors in the dark of night and drag citizens away, we democrats destroy our own power by imitating those we stand against with the excuse that the means are justified by the ends. Here we may be dealing with the most vexing ethical problem of all, since by extension it does damage to all professional ambitions.

Privacy or Publicity?

The right of privacy does not derive from a specific guarantee in the U.S. Constitution. Professor Alan F. Westin, in his exhaustive analysis *Privacy and Freedom* (1967), gave the definition, "Privacy is the claim of individuals, groups, or institutions to determine for themselves when, how, and to what extent information about them is communicated to others."[26]

Privacy law as we now follow it has origins in the classic 1890 article by Louis D. Brandeis and Samuel D. Warren, "The Right of Privacy," which appeared in the *Harvard Law Review.* They noted the individual's increasing sensitivity to publicity and concluded that "solitude and privacy have become more essential to the individual; but modern enterprise and invention have, through invasions upon his privacy, subjected him to mental pain and distress far greater than could be inflicted by mere bodily injury."[27]

Invasions of privacy by government and private groups have become so commonplace that many citizens are fearful that lost liberty to maintain individual dignity through appropriate aloofness from associations cannot be regained. A significant number of novelists concentrate on plots built around evidence of the reduction of privacy and related independence.

Privacy law—as it constructively protects the individual in society against the invasions by the computer manipulators, the snoopers who use electronic devices to discover bad practice in everybody's business but their own, and the mass media, which have capitalized on personal distresses at the expense of public good—is obviously necessary. However, such legal defenses are insufficient; we must have the highest possible ethical standards observed by all in important public positions. Only through the combination of legal protections (fortunately expanding) and high ethics can we hope to, as Thomas J. Emerson says, "maintain the oneness of the individual despite the demands of the collective."[28]

The Supreme Court has protected individual right to privacy against certain types of media coverage, especially in matters of defamation and libel. Several tests are now applicable to determine whether a complaint of invasion of privacy is justified. For example, "public" persons have less claim to privacy than have citizens whose activities are predominantly of a private nature.

In *New York Times Co.* v. *Sullivan* (1964), Mr. Justice Brennan, speaking for the majority, said, "The constitutional guarantees require, we think, a federal rule that prohibits a public official from recovering damages for a defamatory falsehood relating to his official conduct unless he proves that the statement was made with 'actual malice'— that is, with knowledge that it was false or with reckless disregard of whether it was false or not."[29]

In *Gertz* v. *Robert Welch, Inc.* (1974), Mr. Justice Powell delivered the opinion for the majority. "Absent clear evidence of general fame or notoriety in the community, and pervasive involvement in the affairs of society an individual should not be deemed a public personality for all aspects of life."[30]

Time Inc. v. Firestone

The public versus private distinction arose in a most interesting way in the 1976 case *Time Inc.* v. *Firestone.* It was the culmination of a tangled divorce action brought by Mary Alice Firestone in 1964, after a then three-year-old marriage to Russell Firestone (scion of the important industrial family). She sued for divorce. He then counterclaimed, charging extreme cruelty and adultery. The circuit court of Palm Beach County, Florida, gave him a judgment granting divorce.

A week after the decree, *Time* magazine, in its "Milestones" section published a short paragraph.

> *Divorced.* By Russell A. Firestone, Jr., 41, heir to the tire fortune: Mary Alice Sullivan Firestone, 32, his third wife; a onetime Palm Beach school-teacher; on grounds of extreme cruelty and adultery; after six years of marriage, one son; in West Palm Beach, Fla. The 17-month intermittent trial produced enough testimony of extramarital adventures on both sides, said the judge, "to make Dr. Freud's hair curl."

Mary Firestone demanded a retraction from *Time,* contending that part of the published paragraph was "false, malicious and defamatory." The publication declined the demand. She consequently sued *Time* in the Florida circuit court and won a judgment of $100,000, later affirmed by the district court of appeal and the Supreme Court of Florida. *Time* appealed to the U.S. Supreme Court, charging that the First and Fourteenth Amendments limited state court powers in the area of damage awards for defamation. Moreover, *Time* claimed to be guilty of no actual malice *(New York Times* v. *Sullivan)* and said that Mary Firestone was a public figure *(Gertz* v. *Robert Welch, Inc.).*

Mr. Justice Rehnquist noted that Mary Firestone "did not assume any role of especial prominence in the affairs of society, other than perhaps Palm Beach society, and she did not thrust herself to the forefront of any particular public controversy in order to influence the resolution of the issues involved in it." Putting aside *Time's* argument that the words of the Florida Supreme Court about the divorce, a *"cause célèbre"* in its characterization, Rehnquist stated that was not justification for the claims that there was a public controversy or that she was a public figure. "Dissolution of a marriage through judicial proceedings is not the sort of 'public controversy' referred to in Gertz, even though the marital difficulties of extremely wealthy individuals may be of interest to some portion of the reading public."

Reaching the conclusion that there was technical reason to remand the case, the Supreme Court deftly left Ms. Firestone a private person in law and reaffirmed the doctrine that a case of press libel or defamation must rest on whether a public figure was involved who had been voluntarily exposed to "increased risk of injury from defamatory falsehood."[31]

These cases, especially the Firestone case, point to the element of privacy that the press must respect. Salacious material in legal transcripts suits the tastes of many readers, viewers, and listeners. Should the media fail to discriminate between what is properly public and what is not, ordinary private citizens will fear to go to court to obtain justice because of the threat of defamation through publicity. Such stories obviously tantalize publishers and editors, and the Firestone case makes us all aware that fairness requires that the law intervene where temptations are too great for media managers—temptations that, when succumbed to, can lead to ruined reputations and lives. I find it hard to go along with Mr. Justice Marshall, who in his dissenting opinion felt that active membership in the "sporting set . . . whose lives receive constant media attention" shrivels personal rights.

More palatable to opponents of censorship are comments made by Mr. Justice Brennan in his dissent. "With respect to judicial proceedings . . . the function of the press serves to guarantee the fairness of trials and to bring to bear the beneficial effects of public scrutiny upon the administration of justice."[32] That view is highly commendable, but the fairness of our system of justice requires that citizens can settle private matters in court. Dirty linen in a court of law is only evidence; in the press it is material for flagrant display. Let public officials' linen, clean and dirty, be waved before all; let a free press be mindful of the need to cover legal affairs professionally so that private lives will not be needlessly shattered.

Televising Mrs. McShane and Mrs. Mott

From Great Britain, where an unwritten constitution has evolved from centuries of case-law decisions, a situation of enormous importance to all ethics-minded communicators arose in 1977. It involved rather special police–television industry cooperation.

In August 1977, British television audiences were offered a Yorkshire TV documentary, "The Case of Yolande McShane." The documentary was a shorter version of a 3 1/2-hour recording that the Sussex police had had made secretly, using professional filmmakers. Their standing with the police was based upon an earlier production of another documentary involving a murder case.

The original videotapes, in full, were offered in evidence at the trial of Mrs. McShane, who at the time of the program was serving a two-year prison term for her efforts to get her mother to commit suicide.

Just before the documentary version was shown to the nation, the mother, Mrs. Mott, died of natural causes at eighty-seven in Saint George's Retreat, a nursing home near Brighton run by an order of nuns.

It was alleged at the trial that Mrs. McShane, motivated by debts running into more than 200,000 pounds and desiring to benefit from the will, urged her wealthy mother to take a fatal dose of nembutal. The police had been informed of what was going on.

To make the videotaping possible, the nuns' permission was obtained. There was thus no question of trespass. The requisite legal warrant to make the film avoided obstacles in English law. It is highly unlikely that the filming would have been allowed had Mrs. Mott been a "tenant," or had she or her daughter lived in their own houses. Mrs. Mott was, legally speaking, a "licensee," and only the owner's permission was required. In England, only telephone tapping requires a warrant "under the hand of a secretary of state."[33]

A small hole had been drilled through one of the walls of Mrs. Mott's room, and videotaping was carried on at the times of the daughter's visits. Unknown to either woman, picture and sound evidence was being built up by the police.

The videotape, already the key evidence behind Mrs. McShane's conviction, was offered by the chief constable of the Sussex police to YTV at no charge. The police felt that the general public should be made aware of such dangers to the aged.

Mrs. McShane's husband did not denounce the program. He said his wife had nothing to fear from it. A YTV spokesman observed, "I think they feel it has an important social message about the problems of the elderly within the family."[34]

At the time of Mrs. McShane's trial, the dialogue between her and Mrs. Mott was published in the press and reported on television newscasts. The ethical issue is whether the showing of the film should be added to the penalty of the prison sentence. Should the crime of murder and punishment of an offender be followed by sensational films depicting the actual crime? Should the hideous and the macabre be added to the instruction-entertainment offerings of the mass media, at the price of essential privacy? Should the punishment fit the crime, or should publicity garland the crime? The method of public education is sometimes independent of the acknowledged necessity to inform. The content of information need not be on the level of those who transgress human decency. Although the making of the original videotape can be justified, the YTV presentation has many dubious qualities. An editorial in the *Daily Telegraph* said aptly: " ... the use of the police film introduces a lurid immediacy bordering on the voyeuristic. ... By no canon of taste can public display of such a film be justified."[35]

This bizarre situation brings the theoretical and the real together. No outpouring of sympathy for Mrs. McShane appears logical or sensible. The tensions imposed upon the dying Mrs. Mott are so horrid that one hesitates to condemn out-of-hand police actions that led to the conviction. The plights of the elderly are dramatized by the case. For all that, ethical standards have been violated. The late Mrs. Mott deserves more respect than she received from the mass media.

THE NEWS COUNCILS

Media people, especially those who concentrate on news gathering, dislike as a rule, overseers looking into the propriety of their actions or reports. For every individual who sees such organizations as the National News Council (created in 1973) as a professional necessity, there are many who still resent alleged interference with First Amendment rights. Collectively, the press constitutes the most organized body of critics in the nation; that may explain some of its own sensitivity to criticism.

Even ombudsmen, who act as conduits for public complaints and as sensitizers of the staffs of news organizations, are scrutinized carefully when their criticism hits too directly at raw journalistic nerves. Wise holders of such positions secure long-term, virtually unbreakable contracts that guarantee their rights to publish without editorial blocks by their employers. On some metropolitan papers, ombudsman is a good last assignment for a veteran newsperson who knows that his colleagues' desires for penetrating critiques of their work are shallow.

The press council as an institution has become a rapidly developing feature of Western European nations, Canada, and New Zealand and has taken hold in the United States. One of the first calls for the establishment of a press council was made in 1947 by the Hutchins Commission. It wanted an independent agency to assess and to report yearly on press performance. Other such recommendations came in 1951 from Senator William Benton of Connecticut, who wanted Congress to create a presidentially appointed group to appraise electronic media performance. Through the 1960s and early 1970s a variety of similar proposals were sponsored by study groups dealing with press issues.[36]

Precedents have been set since 1953 when the British Press Council was created. In 1971, the Minnesota Newspaper Association created the Minnesota Press Council, comprising nine journalists and nine laypersons. By 1974 it had decided eleven cases and acted as conciliator in others.[37] There are a growing number of independent local and state press councils, which deal with such subjects as biased reporting; checkbook journalism; protection of news sources; law-media relationships; libel; access of the press; accuracy; editorial distortion and press accountability.

The National News Council was created in 1973. Its purpose is "to serve the public interest in preserving freedom of information and advancing accurate and fair reporting of news." Its members and advisers, numbering twenty in 1975, included five lawyers (two former state judges), one member of Congress, ten media representatives, one businessperson, two civil rights leaders (one from the clergy), and one educator.[38]

Some leading media critics attack press councils, viewing the First Amendment as absolute, and any guideline-creating or guidance-recommending group as an unjustified imposition. Nat Hentoff, the celebrated journalist, has written: "The grail of 'fairness' is an enticing one, but unless editors are allowed to edit on the basis of their own judgment—however quirky and infuriating that judgment may be to many citizens—newspapers and magazines will be saddled with a fairness doctrine which, as William O. Douglas says of the doctrine imposed on television, 'is agreeable to nations that have never known freedom of the press ...' "[39] Another objection comes from publishers and editors who worry about press council investigations sparking public hostility to the press.

There are those who advocate increased nonprofessional membership on the press councils to reduce public opposition and to better reflect the variety of citizen concerns as well as the special concerns of a particular community. Many leaders of the media accept the notion of public participation but feel that experienced newspeople are best able to deal with the controversies that arise. In my view, there should not be less than 50 percent public membership. Alert and responsible leaders from all professions are daily clients of the mass media. Special knowledge needed to handle press council cases can be acquired without undue intellectual strain; media and public representatives alike would need supplemental information if a complex technical question was at issue.

National News Council Cases

NNC deals with print and electronic media problems, although it has yet to resolve its internal quandary concerning how far to go on television and radio matters regulated by the Federal Communications Commission.

In the first two years of operation, NNC dealt with fifty-nine cases involving complaints raised against the media. Twenty-one complaints were dismissed because of insufficient "specifics" or because they were "beyond the Council's purview"; thirty-three were found to be unwarranted; five were upheld. Twenty-four complaints had been raised in that period against television networks; two were upheld. Two of the eleven complaints filed about national newspaper stories were upheld.

To carry out its obligations, the NNC needs data from media organizations. The New York *Times*, not a supporter of the council, has withheld requested information. NBC-TV in November 1974 stayed away from a council hearing on a complaint brought against the network by a former governor of American Samoa who criticized a "Weekend" program. NBC did provide transcripts of the program and arranged for the viewing of a taped recording. Former Governor John Haydon described the program as inaccurate and deliberately designed to "malign the Samoan people, the administration of the territory, the Department of the Interior." NNC, after investigating, concluded that "while great latitude must be accorded to television producers in the case of any given documentary," there is and ought to be "a limit to the degree of distortion and misrepresentation. . . . We believe that the NBC documentary on Samoa clearly exceeds that limit." To reach its decision, the council called in experts, including Margaret Mead, and pondered government reports, press clippings, and academic studies, in addition to its studies of the actual documentary broadcast.

In another case in 1974, the council found justified a complaint against the *Times* by a scientist, Dr. Anton Lang, regarding an analysis of a scientific study of herbicidal spraying in South Vietnam. In his view, an article by John Finney (also published by the Washington *Post**) released prior to public disclosure of a scientific study was "based on a leak, contained outright errors, was slanted, disregarded important constructive aspects of the report." The *"Times"* had a special obligation to its readers, upon official release of the report, to disclose any differences between its original article and the official version." Moreover, the newspaper did not publish Dr. Lang's letter of complaint and, in a subsequent and fuller article providing more details about the consensus of scientists who worked on the study, did not say that the "original article was incomplete."[40]

The Panax Controversy

A 1977 council decision caused much controversy within professional media circles. At the center of the debate was Norman E. Isaacs, the veteran newsman, editor, and publisher who became the second chairman of the NNC.

The Panax case arose in June 1977 when John P. McGoff, the head of the Panax publishing organization (eight daily and forty weekly newspapers and printing companies in the United States and South Africa), sent to his newspapers' editors two feature stories written by the then Panax bureau chief in New York. Both gave unflattering pictures of President Carter's administration. One suggested that Carter encouraged sexual promiscuity among male staff members; the other claimed that the president was preparing his wife for the vice-presidency. McGoff told his editors that the articles were "explosive," asked for prompt publication, and urged front page space, if possible.

Two editors, of the Marquette *Mining Journal* and the Escanaba *Daily Press*, both in Michigan, protested. The articles were characterized by one editor as ridden with "innuendo and insinuations." There was additional comment about the writer jumping to his own conclusions "unencumbered by fact." Both editors supported McGoff's right to present his own views or other views on the editorial page. One of the reluctant editors resigned; resignations in protest followed. The other editor was fired.

Community rallies in Escanaba and Marquette opposed McGoff's actions. Protests were addressed to the NNC and other news organizations. Publisher McGoff replied to critics with the "Declaration of Interdependence" carried by the Panax papers. The management denied that

---

*The *Post* was not a party in the NNC finding because the *Times* news service had moved the article.

editors had been ordered what to print. But McGoff was held to have the right, as major Panax stockholder and executive, "to distribute whatever news copy he deems appropriate and to demand, if necessary, that such copy be printed."

Norman Isaacs, at that point, appears to have pushed the NNC review of the Panax developments in an unusual manner for a careful arbiter. A vote of council members was obtained by telephone.[41] The count was twelve to one in favor of censuring the head of Panax and his organization for "gross disservice to accepted American journalistic standards." Subsequently, two changed their votes for censure after pondering further evidence. The action became highly controversial. Some outside observers began to question the NNC's ignoring of the actual contents of the stories in favor of a quick telephone vote on the issue of interference. However, the NNC termed McGoff's policy "regressive—a throwback to the crass episodes that marked the journalism of a bygone era—and brands it as a gross disservice to accepted American Journalistic standards."

William Rusher, council member and treasurer of the *National Review,* was the original lone dissenter. In his view, "If newspaper publishers are to be held responsible for the contents of their publications—and they most certainly are and ought to be—then I do not see how we can deny a publisher the right to determine, in the last analysis, what that content should be."[42]

If the stories were worthy of condemnation because of gross inaccuracy or because they distorted news, council review would be warranted. If McGoff had obviously transgressed the professional code, NNC opinion might also have been helpful in the long run.

As it turns out, the council, which must be deemed extraordinarily careful, objective, and mindful of the most subtle First Amendment issues, is itself controversial because of this case.

Editor and Publisher (December 1977) editorialized that NNC's handling of news "of its complaint against Panax Corp. has caused it to lose stature, in our opinion."[43]

NNC, the anxious overseer, may have with more zeal than wisdom taken a temporary detour from the road leading to the achievement of its professional goals.

HORIZONS

We are always in the process of discovery when dealing with media ethics. We are always obliged to make ethics personal, to involve ourselves in the search for higher standards. And in the process a personal question arises: What am I doing about what I have discovered?

What are we to do about the ethical problems raised by all the violence directed against children on television, cloaked as entertainment but really motivated by commercial desires to sell toys or cereals or candies? What are we to do about the newest revelations about how the CIA secretly spread false news abroad, which on occasion spilled back into the U.S. media as truth? What are we to do about judicially imposed gag orders?

Let us consider two recent news stories that involve difficult issues for media professionals. The first has to do with press competence in handling crisis stories. In the second, press claims that First Amendment rights transcend the rights of the general public are defended and disputed.

Crisis Reportage

The news media are becoming more sensitive to public needs and psychological dependencies. Few professional journalists accept the notion that the press merely reports what is happening in a detached manner. At times of social crisis the reportage can and often does alter the social scene, thereby helping to create attitudes material to events that will follow. A scare headline, as we have noted, shouldn't appear just to increase newsstand sales. Reports about terrorism must educate without making the situation worse. Stories about the exploits of desperadoes should not glorify their deeds, thus manufacturing antiheroes who despite infamous activities become popular models of decisive action.

Media leaders are becoming more aware of their ethical responsibilities to educate publics through responsible dissemination of scrupulously prepared reports. They are becoming more sensitive to what amounts to censorship through interpretation. If a terrorist's demands are blurted to the public without appropriate review of the situation that the police find themselves in trying to save the lives of hostages, the public welfare is also made hostage to media irresponsibility. A caustic analysis of certain types of media coverage was offered by a scholar, "a specialist on revolutionary violence," to publishers and editors attending a panel discussion on terrorism at the 1976 International Press Institute meeting. Dr. Bowyer Bell of Columbia University warned that editors can be part of the problem. "The IRA set off bombs in London to bomb the Irish elections off the front page, and they succeeded," observed Bell. Surveying the audience, he said, "I've never before been in one place and seen as many terrorists as I have here."[44] One imagines that many in the audience agreed with his first premise, but after his rude, provocative characterization wondered how he would act as an editor when faced with the typically incomplete, disordered information that first breaks about a terrorist strike or a racial riot.

CBS News President Richard S. Salant prepared guidelines (issued in April 1977) for that network's newspeople working on stories about terrorist activities. He warned the journalists to avoid "the trap of providing an unedited platform" useful to terrorists' propaganda objectives. For example, Salant suggested that terrorists' demands might better be issued as paraphrased material. The specific words of the terrorist or kidnapper, or the use of his/her voice, might not be appropriate. Salant said this was a guideline and not an order to the reporters. All factors must be studied in order to avoid news suppression or to "give free rein to sensationalized and erroneous word-of-mouth rumors."[45] Among the practices he suggested avoiding were providing a terrorist with an "excessive platform" on television for his views or complaints; giving live coverage of the terrorist except under extraordinary circumstances (approval of the CBS News president or his deputy should be secured); interfering with telephone exchanges between the authorities and the terrorist; overplaying the story.

When in 1977 the leader of a sect of Hanafi Muslims, aided by followers from his miniscule sect, seized three buildings and many hostages in Washington D.C., he shrewdly began to manipulate the press and achieved considerable success, in large part because the media were so unprepared and so irresponsible. For example, radio and television stations tried to telephone the terrorists. Those callers were so eager for scoops that they virtually ignored police efforts and made the psychological environment for the police more difficult. Sometimes their calls jeopardized the lives of the hostages. One hostage, after release, spoke of "two days of brutalization and absolute terror." When the ordeal was over, one young black journalist was murdered, eleven hostages wounded or injured, and scores of hostages would have to carry psychological scars for years to come.

What were the ethical implications of WTOP-TV's broadcasting a telephone conversation between a newsman and one of the terrorists? What were the ethical implications of the frantic competition between television stations in the D.C. area to get the biggest audiences? Was a Washington columnist's portrait of the terrorist leader (on the day that the young newsman was buried after the end of the siege) as a man "of enormous dignity" who "could not help coming off more as a sympathetic figure than as a monster" justified?[46] What are the ethical implications of many journalists' persistent ignorance of information necessary to the coverage of crisis stories?

> Lacking the proper background to cover terrorism, reporters interview anyone—including each other. They ask questions but miss the important ones.... Reporters who don't know a Belfast Syndrome (civilian combat fatigue) from a Stockholm Syndrome (the camaraderie captors and captives develop) must be handicapped when writing about continuing violence or hostages.[47]

Press Claims for Rights Disallowed the General Public: The Gilmore Case and the Texas Controversy

The situation surrounding the trial and execution of Gary Mark Gilmore by the State of Utah deserves our attention. With the last nervous words of "Let's do it," the murderer met his death by firing squad on January 19, 1977. He had been the center of public curiosity not only for his deeds but because he demanded to be executed. For ten years previously not a single legal execution had been carried out in the United States. Because of his demand (so unlike the usual attitude of those on Death Row who seek every delay possible), Gilmore attracted civil libertarians eager to take a stand against the death penalty.

Gilmore was at the center of attention for other reasons. To show his determination to die he had, after sentencing in 1976, gone on a twenty-five-day hunger strike and twice attempted suicide. His love affair with a young woman who herself attempted suicide while he argued for execution added another sensational touch.

The Gilmore case brings up two related questions of press rights. First, does the press have a right to interview prisoners that exceeds any state's regulations governing public access? Second, does the press have the right to information beyond that allowed the general public? These questions boil down to the First Amendment issue as to whether the press can be limited under certain conditions established by government to protect privacy, to avoid sensationalism, or to maintain security.

Let us agree at this point that we are anxious to extend First Amendment rights whenever possible, to protect the public's right to know about official transgressions of any sort against individuals. That is the basic stance of all democrats.

Gilmore appears to have been clever, brutal, and emotionally unstable. His mental agitation was probably heightened by all sorts of offers from wily promoters and innumerable requests from news organizations eager to secure interviews. On November 12, 1976, press interviews with Gilmore were forbidden by the Utah State Board of Corrections because of possible disruption from interviews and the tremendous publicity.

Previously, the state had permitted prisoner interviews if the prison warden agreed and took steps to avoid disruptions. The Salt Lake City *Tribune* on November 17, 1976 appealed to U.S. district court in Salt Lake City to overturn the no-interview policy. The newspaper won for itself alone a temporary restraining order from the district court judge. That same night its suburban editor interviewed Gilmore. That story was published on December 2.

ABC and CBS and two Salt Lake City television stations—KSL and KUTV—frustrated at their inability to get interviews, went to the U.S. district court to obtain similar rights. Coincidentally, the Utah State Board of Corrections appealed to the U.S. Court of Appeals for the Tenth Circuit and was granted first a temporary order lifting the district court's temporary restraint on the board, and then (on December 3) a permanent vacating of the lower court's order. A further appeal by the *Tribune* to the Supreme Court was rejected on December 17.

At that point, the *Tribune* and KUTV returned to the U.S. district court to seek to overturn the Utah law excluding the press from sending representatives to cover executions. The general public under that same law was not allowed to attend; attendance was limited to officials (the warden, a physician, the county attorney) and persons the prisoner is allowed to invite (one or two members of the clergy, five relatives, friends, or other persons).[48]

The Utah statute was upheld on January 13, 1977, six days before Gilmore's execution. The court cited its agreement with two Supreme Court decisions (*Pell* v. *Procunier,* 417 U.S. 817 [1974] and *Saxbe* v. *Washington Post Company,* 417 U.S. 843 [1974]), which held that the press did not have "a greater right of access to individual inmates than is accorded the general public. . . . The Court in Pell did . . . balance the state's interest in discipline versus the individual inmate's freedom of speech. . . ."

The district court used more *Pell* v. *Procunier* language to show why it sided with the decision of the Board of Corrections.

> Despite the fact that news gathering may be hampered, the press is regularly excluded from grand jury proceedings, our own conferences, the meetings of other official bodies gathering in executive session and the meetings of private organizations. Newsmen have no constitutional rights of access to the scenes of crime or disaster when the general public is excluded.

The district court stressed that the Utah law in question was aimed at avoiding sensationalism, with a due regard for "reasonable deference to the condemned man under these circumstances."[49]

My own conclusion is that the press ought to have a reasonable right of access to prisoners and to all proceedings of public importance. However, members of media institutions are so independent that most would probably object to any sort of a pool arrangement whereby representatives would share a big story with all colleagues. Many would argue that such a plan would freeze interpretation according to the selection. Others would argue that the interests of the press corps are so diverse that no limitation of access would permit the variety of coverage possible. Therefore, I have an ethical puzzle to solve: how can the press afford the prisoner full protection against undue invasion of privacy? Is it better to have restraints imposed upon all by a pool arrangement or free enterprise that leads to a circuslike atmosphere?

On this latter point, I am chilled to ponder a request by a public television station cameraman in Texas to film executions of prisoners. (As of January 15, 1978, 409 inmates sat on Death Row.)[50] Tony Garrett of KERA in Dallas, Texas, requested such permission. He also asked to film interviews with the condemned awaiting the ultimate punishment of the state. On January 13, 1977, the same day that Utah State Board of Corrections rules were upheld by the U.S. District Court for Utah, Garrett got redress from the U.S. District Court in Dallas, Texas, against the refusal of the Texas Department of Correction to grant his requests. Judge William M. Taylor, Jr., ordered the state to allow him to film executions and interviews. The judge observed that if the subject offended any viewers they could switch off their sets!

I am sure that the language of his opinion pleases many First Amendment advocates.

> If government officials can prevent the public from witnessing films of government proceedings solely because the government subjectively decides that it is not fit for public viewing, then news cameras might be barred from other public facilities where public officials are involved in illegal, immoral or other improper activities that might be offensive, shocking, distasteful or otherwise disturbing to viewers of television news.[51]

I agree with the principles and shudder at possible consequences deriving from the specifics involved. Hitler ordered the perpetrators of the July 1944 plot against him hung on meat hooks to die. The scenes of their agonized writhings were filmed by propaganda crews. Earlier the scenes of their mock trials were *features* that millions of Germans were subjected to.

On the other hand, I respect such groups as the Reporters Committee for Freedom of the Press, the Newspaper Guild, and the Radio-Television News Directors Association, all of which supported Garrett with a friend-of-the-court brief. Those organizations argued that the public debate on the capital punishment issue is furthered by such reportage. Television "conveys more of the content or reality of the experience than a written or spoken word can." They argued that the admission of print journalists when electronic media reporters were barred was discrimination contrary to the First Amendment. Later, on August 3, 1977, the State of Texas position—to deny television access—was upheld by the U.S. Court of Appeals for the Fifth Circuit. The circuit court quoted a 1974 conclusion of the Supreme Court regarding prisoner-interview cases. The "Constitution does not ... require government to accord the press special access to information not shared by members of the press generally."[52]

There are no easy answers or fixed solutions for ethical problems in any area of life. Honest, upright, and courageous defenders of the First Amendment are not made from one mold. Each observer wants to listen to his own drummer. On the matter of the last problem presented, how do you feel about the idea of televising executions for public television? Did I hear you say, "Yes, but—".

NOTES

1. See Dierdre Carmody, "News of Minorities In Media Is Debated," The New York Times, September 26, 1977.

2. See Roger Wilkins, "Lessons From the Black Experience in America," The New York Times, December 26, 1977.

3. See "Blacks Blast Hub News Media on Coverage," Boston Evening Globe, May 25, 1977. Also, for Hutchins Commission evaluation, see Bernard Rubin, Media, Politics and Democracy (New York: Oxford University Press, 1977), pp. 66–69.

4. Letter to the author from Frederick W. Hartmann, executive editor and vice-president, the News-Journal Company of Wilmington, Delaware, dated November 11, 1977.

5. See Frederick W. Hartmann, "Trail Blazing toward Trust," Sunday News-Journal, Wilmington, Delaware, October 30, 1977, p. 19. Also, on the same page, see "The 'Ethics Code,'" printed in full.

6. Letter to the author from Robert Manning, editor-in-chief, The Atlantic Monthly, in response to his inquiry regarding issues of priority standing to be researched by the Institute for Democratic Communication of Boston University, dated, May 5, 1976.

7. See Sheppard v. Maxwell, Supreme Court of the United States, 1966. 384 U.S. 333, 86 S. Ct. 1507, 16 L. Ed. 2d 600.

8. See Jim Frisinger, " 'Son of Sam'—David Berkowitz," The Quill 65 (November 1977): 15, 16, 30.

9. See editorial, "Freedom and Restraint," The New York Times, May 10, 1976.

10. See Code of Ethics, The Society of Professional Journalists, Sigma Delta Chi, adopted by the national convention, November 16, 1973, appendix to chapter 2 of this book.

11. See "Code of Professional Standards for the Practice of Public Relations," Public Relations Society of America, New York City, effective April 29, 1977, n.d.

12. See "Gannett Ethics Code Adopted," *Editor & Publisher*, May 21, 1977, p. 45.

13. Keith P. Sanders and Won H. Chang, "Codes—The Ethical *Free*-For-All: A Survey of Journalists' Opinions About Freebies," Freedom of Information Foundation, Columbia, Missouri. Freedom of Information Foundation Series no. 7 (March 7, 1977).

14. Ibid, p. 7.

15. See Joseph W. Shoquist, "What Newspapers Are Doing about Their Public Image," *Public Relations Journal* 31 (August 1975): 17–19.

16. Michael Gigandet, "Press Urged to Push for Social Reforms," *Editor & Publisher*, February 5, 1977, pp. 22, 24.

17. Arthur Taylor, address to the Annual Assembly of the International Press Institute of 1976, *IPI Report* 25 (June 1976): 1, 2.

18. See John B. Connally, "Advice to the Press," The New York *Times*, May 2, 1977.

19. See Bernard Rubin, *Big Business and the Mass Media* (Lexington, Massachusetts: Lexington Books Division, D.C. Heath, 1977).

20. See Bill Kirtz, "Conference Held on Media Ethics," *Editor & Publisher*, November 19, 1977.

21. See "Ethics and Journalism," *Nieman Reports*, spring 1976, pp. 25–27.

22. See Les Brown, "Clinic in an NBC Show on Incest Pledges to Bar Rival Journalists," The New York *Times*, April 18, 1977.

23. See "Post Is Scored for Its Coverage of Blackout," The New York *Times*, July 19, 1977.

24. See Carey Winfrey, "50 of 60 Post Reporters Protest 'Slanted' Coverage of Mayor's Race," The New York *Times*, October 3, 1977.

25. See Ken Auletta, "Bribe, Seduce, Lie, Steal: Anything To Get The Story?" *More: The Media Magazine* (March 1977): 14–20.

26. Alan F. Westin, *Privacy and Freedom* (New York: Atheneum, 1967) p. 7.

27. See Samuel D. Warren and Louis D. Brandeis, "The Right to Privacy," *Harvard Law Review* 4 (1890): 196.

28. Thomas I. Emerson, *The System of Freedom of Expression* (New York: Random House, 1970), p. 546.

29. See *New York Times* v. *Sullivan,* Supreme Court of the United States, 1964. 376 U.S. 254, 84 S. Ct. 710, 11 L. Ed. 2d 686.

30. See *Gertz* v. *Robert Welch, Inc.,* Supreme Court of the United States, 1974. 418 U.S. 323, 94 S. Ct. 2997, 41 L. Ed. 2d 789.

31. See *Time, Inc.* v. *Firestone,* Supreme Court of the United States, 1976. 424 U.S. 448.

32. Ibid.

33. See "Convicted by Videotape," *The Economist* (London, England) 264 (August 27, 1977): 32.

34. See "Police Tape on TV 'To Help Aged,' " *The Daily Telegraph* (London, England), August 19, 1977.

35. See "Not A Film for the Public," editorial, *The Daily Telegraph* (London, England), August 19, 1977.

36. See Jonathan Moore, James C. Thomson, Jr., Martin Linsky, and Michael J. Israels, eds., *Report of the New England Conference on Conflicts between the Media and the Law.* September 1974–September 1976. Cooperatively sponsored by the Institute of Politics, J.

F. Kennedy School of Government and the Nieman Foundation of Harvard University, 1976.

37. For background on the Minnesota Press Council, see The Twentieth Century Fund, *A Free and Responsible Press* (New York: The Twentieth Century Fund, 1973), especially pp. 37–45.

38. See the National News Council, *In The Public Interest: A Report, 1973–1975* (New York: The National News Council, 1975), pp. 1-9

39. See Nat Hentoff, *How Fair Should TV Be?* (New York: Television Information Office, 1974).

40. See News Council, *In the Public Interest* pp. 7–12, 78–81, 113–116.

41. See John L. Hulteng, "The Performance or the Power?: The Crux of Panax," *The Quill* 65 (October 1977): 23–25, 29.

42. See "National News Council Report: Statement on John P. McGoff and Panax Corporation Policy," *Columbia Journalism Review* (September/October 1977): 83.

43. See "News Council and Panax," *Editor and Publisher,* December 10, 1977, p. 4.

44. See I. William Hill, "Japanese Newsman Urges Introspection of Press," *Editor & Publisher,* May 15, 1976, p. 9.

45. See Les Brown, "CBS Curbs on Terror," The New York *Times,* April 15, 1977.

46. See Patrick Buchanan, "Newswatch: Television—Patsy and Promoter for Terrorists," *T.V. Guide,* March 20–27, 1977, p. A–5.

47. See Mark Monday, "What's Wrong With Our Aim," *The Quill* 65 (1977): 19–20.

48. See "Gilmore Execution Leads to Utah Lawsuits Over Press Access to Executions" in *The News and the Law* 1 (October 1977): 9–10.

49. See *Kearns-Tribune* v. *Utah Board of Corrections,* U.S. District of Utah, January 13, 1977, 2 Media Law Reporter 1353 (March 8, 1977).

50. See "A Year After Gilmore Execution, 409 Await Death," The New York *Times,* January 15, 1978.

51 See *The News and the Law,* p. 8.

52. Ibid., p. 9.

2 JOURNALISTIC ETHICS:
Some Probings by a Media Keeper

James C. Thomson, Jr.

As* a Curator or Keeper of journalists for five years now, I have observed a sharply increasing preoccupation, both inside and outside the media, with journalistic ethics: the values and behavior of news organizations and individuals. The issue is hardly new. But the breadth and intensity of the concern, among Americans at least, seems new. Public officials, lay citizens, and practitioners all now have strong views on what's wrong—much less often, on what's right—with the press and its practices. And in the process one indispensable protector of First Amendment press freedom, a climate of public understanding of the media's proper role, may well be in jeopardy.

The causes of this preoccupation with journalistic ethics are multiple but fairly easy to discover in the record of the past decade:

—Never before have the media attained such visible national power—notably through the evolution of a de facto national press composed of three TV networks (ABC, CBS, NBC), two weekly newsmagazines *(Time, Newsweek)*, two wire services (AP, UPI), and at least two dailies (The New York *Times*,, services (AP, UPI), and at least two dailies (The New York *Times,* The Washington *Post*). Such power is the result of vast economic and technological changes. These changes include the primacy of television as a news source, media conglomerations, concentrations of multiple media ownership, and the striking growth of newspaper chains, along with new modes of electronic reproduction and distribution.

—The reportage of these national media, together with that of some of the others, helped end the Indochina War by turning many

---

*Used by permission of The Poynter Center, Indiana University.

Americans against that conflict and forcing the virtual abdication of President Johnson.

—The efforts of one of these organizations, The Washington *Post* —with vital assitance from the courts, the Congress, and others—un-covered gross abuse of power by the executive branch and forced the preimpeachment resignation of President Nixon.

—On other matters, from presidential election campaigns to dem-onstrations by minorities, students, and women (and, increasingly, ter-rorists), the electronic media in particular have been perceived as creators of, or at least participants in, the news. In the process, politics have seemed to become media events, with media stars—especially TV newscasters—achieving supercelebrity status.

—Meanwhile, however, a major and effective counterattack was made on these national media by the White House, and especially by a vice-president, Spiro Agnew—an attack that (despite Agnew's even-tual downfall) produced within the press not merely temporary fear but also increased self-examination and widened access (the creation of ombudsmen, more "op-ed" pages, journalism reviews, etc.).

—Meanwhile, too, journalism was subjected to severe criticism by a new generation of younger and more radical reporters who assailed their elders for alleged collusion with the Establishment. Their efforts led to so-called advocacy journalism as well as a spate of "underground" or "alternative" magazines and reviews. Some underground/alterna-tive types were eventually hired by the more orthodox media.

—Finally, in these same years, the media found themselves in-volved in a spiraling series of conflicts with the courts on issues rang-ing from the confidentiality of a reporter's sources, to fair trial vs. free press considerations, the "Fairness Doctrine" in TV, "national security" matters, and the invasion of a citizen's privacy. The high costs of litiga-tion in such press-law conflicts have posed an especially heavy threat to First Amendment freedom.

No wonder, then, that the behavior of the media, the role, values, and conduct of journalists, have become of such concern to so many Americans—this in a period when the ethics of politicians have also come under intensified scrutiny, and the "public accountability" of all professions has become a widespread demand. Inevitably, journalists themselves are also increasingly preoccupied with the issue of journal-istic ethics. Newly powerful but assaulted, newly victorious but un-comfortably center-stage, nationally scrutinized as never before but uncertain of its role-definition, the press is—and should be—defensive. Because the natives, "out there," are said to be restless.

BIT OF HISTORY

The issue—to repeat—is not new. As far back as 1923 the American Society of Newspaper Editors (ASNE) adopted a professional code, the "Canons of Journalism."[1] And before that, individual newspapers and state associations had addressed the matter.[2] The ASNE code was finally taken out of the files and updated in 1975; yet it is doubtful that either old or new versions are familiar to recent generations of reporters, much less pondered by them.

Other efforts have been made to assess the collective and individual role of journalists—most notably the 1947 report of the Commission on Freedom of the Press ("Hutchins Commission"), issued in book form as *A Free and Responsible Press.*[3] Denounced or ignored by most of the media of that time, the Hutchins report had little perceptible effect. Yet its recommendations regarding the proper function of American journalism—and by extension, the ethics of journalists—have a surprising pertinence thirty years later.

Consider, for instance, the commission's five main requirements of the media—which provided, as one observer has noted, "a theory of responsibility:"[4]

1. The press must give a truthful, comprehensive, and intelligent account of the day's events in a context which gives them meaning.
2. The press must provide a forum for the exchange of comment and criticism.
3. The press must project a representative picture of the constituent groups in the society.
4. The press must present and clarify the goals and values of the society.
5. The press must provide full access to the day's intelligence.

These injunctions, reread in 1977, raise more questions than they answer. They are the same questions that hover over the media today. A free press, yes; but also a "responsible" press. But, "responsible" to whom, and for what, and how policed?

The Hutchings Commission also proposed the creation of "a new and independent agency," a nongovernmental body of private citizens, to "appraise and report annually upon the performance of the press."[5] This turned out to be the commission's most controversial recommendation, one that caused many journalists to bridle. Such an agency, it was suggested, would perform some of the following functions:

— Help the media "define workable standards of performance";

— Point out "the inadequacy" of media services in certain areas;

— Investigate areas and instances "where minority groups are excluded from reasonable access to the channels of communication";

— Examine the "picture of American life" presented abroad by the media;

— Investigate charges of "press lying," with particular reference to the persistent misrepresentation of the data required for judging public issues;

— Appraise "governmental action affecting communications";

— Appraise the "tendencies and characteristics of the various branches of the communications industry";

— Encourage the "establishment of centers of advanced study, research, and criticism in the field of communications at universities";

— Encourage projects which give hope of meeting the needs of special audiences;

— Give "the widest possible publicity and public discussion" to all its findings.

Such were the functions of this proposed private—and entirely toothless—monitoring agency in 1947. Although a very few local and state press councils eventually evolved, the recommendation of the Hutchins Commission was emphatically rejected by most news organizations. Twenty-five years later presiding giants of the media (The New York *Times,* the AP, and the three TV networks) still rejected the concept when it finally came into being in the form of a foundation-supported National News Council.* Clearly, formal external scrutiny—

---

*The National News Council, a by-product of a Twentieth Century Fund study in 1971–72, came into being in 1973. Although several major media institutions were cool to the council and even refused to cooperate with it at first, CBS relented in 1976 and agreed to permit its president for news, Richard Salant, to sit as a council member. Since January 1977 the *Columbia Journalism Review* has begun regularly to carry the council's findings.

and the suggestion of uniform standards—is still anathema to large sectors of the media.

SOME PROBLEMS OF DEFINITION

Any discussion of journalistic ethics must tangle with a number of ambiguities about journalism, news, and the U.S. Constitution.

First, the most obvious, what is a journalist—and thereby, what is journalism? By tradition, anyone with a printing press (or its functional equivalent)—or access to such—from Tom Paine through Katharine Graham and William Paley. Journalists are not licensed to practice their profession. There is no educational prerequisite, no professional certification, necessary for becoming a journalist. Some have journalism degrees; many more do not. Some have gone through college or beyond; many have not.

Indeed, it is an old, lingering question whether journalism is a profession at all. Many practitioners would instead call it a "craft," even "trade." In some ways it is one of the last of the medieval guilds, where professional access is centrally built on apprenticeship.

So at the root of the question of ethics is the question of role definition: what codes, standards, or models could—or should—encompass the extraordinarily wide varieties of practitioners in, and avenues of approach to, journalism?"*

A second and dominating ambiguity is the nature of "news." For all the endless debate about objectivity versus subjectivity, it is a truism that "news" is an infinitesimal selection out of the totality of a day's or week's reality: selection made by the observer or reporter, the editor, and sometimes management. (As one veteran has put it, the journalist's central problem is "what to leave out, rather than what to put in.")

At one end of the process of news gathering this creates what Leon Sigal has described as "the uncertainty factor":[6] since news is not definable, the reporter faces chronic uncertainty as to what is actually news;

---

*As one perceptive commentator on this paper has put it: "Implicit in the First Amendment is a judgment that ethics in journalism are less important than other values, and less important in journalism than in, say, medicine. We require that every medical practitioner adhere to certain ethics or be barred from medicine. But we think it worthwhile to put up with continual bilge from some journalists on the theory that readers will recognize and reject dross, and some day, even the worst journalist may discover the important truth, or print an important opinion. We outlaw quacks, but protect hacks, and it follows that journalistic ethics cannot have the force of medical ethics which have the law behind them."

and so, up the ladder, do his superiors. Yet the reader or viewer is dependent upon the definition daily constructed by this chain of command. As Sigal also points out, the reporter's need for peer-group reassurance in this condition of uncertainty is what gives rise to "pack" or "herd" journalism; and it gives rise to the circularity and similarity of what appears in all parts of the previously described "national press" —and *its* pack of followers in the hinterland.

So: uncertainty about the nature of news can compound uncertainties about the definition of the profession, craft, or trade.

A third ambiguity stems from the character of news organizations. Although they may appear to the public to be monoliths, newspapers, magazines, and broadcasting enterprises exist in a state of constant internal tension on at least two grounds. One is, again, a question of role definition—this time the institution's role. Each organization is both a private, profit-making business and, simultaneously, a constitutionally protected semipublic service. Such outfits are therefore operating both To Make Money (at the least, not to lose it) *and* To Do Good (or to expose iniquity, and thereby improve society). Therefore, a first and unresolvable tension is between greed and idealism. A second and closely related tension stems from the actual internal structuring of the media. Although print and electronic institutions differ in important ways, both contain two cultures, or at least outlooks, that are often at odds with each other: on the one hand, reporters and editors, who traditionally see their role as uncovering and disseminating the truth (or some approximation thereof); and on the other hand, owners, publishers, "management," who seek to stay in business and make a tidy profit. In this sense, much of the press is pluralistic, not at all monolithic.

There is also another important tension that affects both reporter-editor types and management. This might be termed the conflict between "good citizen" and "good journalist." In smaller communities it can mean the conflict within an individual journalist between the booster and the muckraker: the civic-minded affirmer, who wants to help neighbors, peers, bosses, and the town; and the civic-minded naysayer, who wants to ferret out crime, corruption, malfeasance, abuse of power—even among those one is taught to, and wants to, esteem.

This "journalist versus citizen" tension has become most acute at the national level in recent decades. Prior to the Korean War, the press usually shared the stated and unstated national consensus that politics stopped at the water's edge and—from World War II onward—"national security" began at the same spot. The patriotic tradition and journalistic convention was that the GIs and war correspondents fought the foreign enemy or enemies in concert, all adhering to what might be called a "national security ethic." Good citizen and good journalist were one and the same, accepting the nation's stated aims—and the government's information—without much question.

Korea, a limited and ultimately unsatisfactory war, began to erode that ethic among both Left and Right. But it took the next limited and very prolonged war, Vietnam, to weaken and finally destroy the unspoken alliance between journalists and the government. Here a post–World War II generation of reporters saw for themselves that the cold war rhetoric of both Washington and Saigon was riddled with distortions and even lies. Good citizen eventually gave way to good journalist, even in semiwartime; and reporters and their editors began to break with the national security ethic. The failure of The New York *Times* to print the Bay of Pigs story in 1961 prior to that fiasco turned into that newspaper's decision in 1971 to publish the Pentagon Papers and in 1975 (after some soul-searching) the Glomar Explorer exposé.

To this observer, the collapse, or at least the waning, of the national security ethic is a belated sign of health in the media and good news for the nation. To phrase the matter bluntly, the reporter is the citizen armed with a typewriter and a print or electronic outlet. The obligations of his craft are the obligations of the citizen, but writ larger: to report the truths he observes—and especially to do so when local, state, or national authorities seek to suppress those truths.

Tensions, then, both internal and external, are inherent in a journalist's craft. And the internal, structural tensions of the media *can* create a system of checks and balances that mute unethical practices on both sides. Management cannot often afford to suppress reporters or editors who know too much—and can tell the story elsewhere; and they can cloak themselves in the First Amendment when chided at their country clubs. Similarly (but more so), a reporter or editor is constrained from excessive hell-raising by a sense of what management will tolerate. More often, however, the centrally dual nature of media organizations can blur the whole question of journalistic ethics. When the overriding function of a newspaper or TV station is to make a lot of money, the "bottom-line ethics" of business usually take command (as one observer has put it, "Ethics start upstairs.") What recourse, then, for the reporter when his discoveries collide with management's interests—usually those of the biggest advertisers? What ethical code or standard might he evolve—other than "shape up or ship out"—that would permit him to survive with some sense of integrity?

A final and large ambiguity lies in that famous ultimate protection, the free-press portion of the Constitution's First Amendment: "Congress shall make no law . . . abridging the freedom of speech, or of the press." The difficult fact, for journalists, is that the Constitution, its

.dments, and its judicial interpreters have also recognized and
.anteed several other citizen rights. And although there have al-
ys existed purists who argued that First Amendment rights held
.imacy, courts and legislatures have usually agreed that when rights
.ollide, some compromise must be found. The result is that while the
press, specially protected through a strong constitutional negative
("Congress shall make no law . . . abridging . . ."), may well be a Fourth
Estate or Fourth Branch of government, its rights are not any more
absolute than those of the other three branches, let alone those of the
general public.

Even the First Amendment, then, is a source of ambiguity. And
any code or standard of ethics based on an absolutist interpretation of
that amendment—for instance, unrestricted reporting about an arrested person, or refusal to reveal one's confidential sources to a grand
jury, or the publication of classified government documents—may run
head-on into court decisions that give primacy to other constitutional
guarantees.

One interim conclusion might be that "a journalist's lot is not a
happy one." He is unsure of his job's professional definition, unsure of
the nature of "news," unsure of his organization's priorities, and unsure
of his unique but fragile constitutional protection. So along with the
craft's great freedom comes multiple ambiguity and a vast amount of
ethical uncertainty. And that uncertainty is, in my view, both ineradicable and indispensable.

SOME OBSERVED RESPONSES

For the past five years I have watched, at close hand, nearly 100
Nieman Fellows—journalists on sabbatical study at Harvard University—and, further removed, scores of their colleagues who are Nieman
alumni or seminar speakers. During this period the question of journalistic ethics has hovered over and around our discussions, whatever the
topic under consideration. Few lay visitors, for instance, can avoid the
temptation to chastise the captive audience about media misbehavior
in his or her field of expertise. Nor can Niemans resist the impulse to
question visiting journalists or others about ethical practices in all
fields.

At the risk of gross overgeneralization, I have observed two standard kinds of responses among journalists—both Fellows and visitors—
to the issue of media ethics. They are the high-road response and the
low-road response; and they are often heard from the same person.

On the one hand, there is a tendency toward heavy grandiosity. This involves invocation of the press's specialness, also some useful shibboleths: first and foremost, "First Amendment rights," or "freedom of the press"; second, and close by, "the people's right to know"; third, "the pursuit of truth" (or "The Facts"); and fourth, the "free-press/free-nation" equation, meaning that all other freedoms wither to the extent that the press is at all constrained. This high-road response is often reflected in the stereotypical reporter who embodies some traditional male virtues: toughness, terseness, speed, authority, risk-taking, freebootery. What is usually lacking is empathy or compassion for their subjects, those reported about, or even token nods toward those qualities. Fairness, accuracy, and speed are up front; compassion is almost never mentioned.

On the other hand (or perhaps on the under side of the same hand), there is a tendency toward individual self-denigration and institutional self-abasement. Journalists are the first to tell you that they don't really know a goddamn thing about anything and (maybe) don't care; that their bosses are drunkards, liars, and perhaps worse; that their papers or broadcast stations have sold out to some kind of Mammon or Mafia; and that their profession or craft is rotten and stinks.

Somewhere in the mix of these two responses—often, to repeat, found in the same person in the same hour—there seems to me to lurk a touch of what psychiatrists have called the "Madonna-prostitute complex."

At issue in the swing between low road and high there exists, I think, an age-old question: the problem of means versus ends. The ends are so patently lofty, yet the means often so tawdry. The high-road, or idealistic, content of journalism tempts practitioners to believe that the pursuit of truth takes absolute precedence, that Anything Goes (probably) in that pursuit and its waystations, the exposure of incompetence and evil; and that, therefore, the clean and beautiful ends can justify virtually any means. This perception emerges, for me, from long hours spent listening to journalists answer one fundamental question: how far would you, personlly, go to obtain a piece of information you know (or have a 90 percent hunch) exists in order to expose a person who has committed a major offense—a felony, abuse of power, treason, etc? "Would you," the question runs, "lie, cheat, steal, pay money, wiretap, commit violence (even murder) to obtain that information?"

Well, the answers vary. Violence, including murder, all—so far—would rule out, except in self-defense. As for other means that break the law—wiretapping, for instance—most wouldn't (or won't admit it), a very few would. Here the operative subquestion is: could I get away with it? In other words, lawbreaking *if* you can get away with it can be justified by some in terms of the higher ends served. These subquestions get more complicated when one deals with the issue (for editors), "Would you ask the reporter how he/she got that information (and would you want to know)?"—and (for reporters), "Would you answer that question honestly if your editor asked it?"

But behind the bravado of some responses—that anything goes in the constitutionally protected pursuit of truth—one soon detects telltale signs of uncertainty: a difficulty in laying down hard and fast rules as to how far one would really go; self-doubt, sometimes self-hate, about overstating the specialness of journalism and the journalist; a wonder as to whether he or she actually would or, after all, should break the law; a shrinking from "playing God"; and a deep-seated cynicism about the purity of the journalist's own craft or organization while seeking out that pure commodity, "truth." The means, whether for oneself or one's institution, are never quite up to those highly touted ends.

Consider a few instances:

—One of the nation's most famous investigative reporters who has broken many U.S. government secrets says he would publish any so-called national security information he uncovered, and the consequences be damned; but when asked the usual questions about a troop-ship sailing date or an Allied mission to assassinate Hitler in World War II, he responds: "I don't deal with hypothetical questions."

—A major national columnist wonders, off-the-record and with deep seriousness, whether the media's new concern with the private lives of politicians—their excesses in matters of sex, alcohol, and income sources—should not be paralleled by truth-telling by the press about similar excesses among their own journalistic colleagues, so far usually a taboo.

—A reporter-hero of the Watergate scandal warns his peers that they should all tread with new caution, prudence, and self-criticism in the wake of the ouster of Nixon; now a supercelebrity, he seems to be asking, "What hath God wrought?"

—That hero's publisher, in accepting a national award for the Watergate achievement, urges that journalists beware of the danger of becoming participants in history rather than professionally detached observers.

Such are some responses from a profession "riding high," post-Vietnam and post-Watergate: A curious drawing-in from bravado, an indication of new doubts, an implication of barriers beyond which one should not push.

Other types of responses, under the greater temporary duress of a simulated classroom, have been gathered during two years of intensive sessions on media-law conflicts in the New England region. When confronted with members of the bench and the bar, arguing hypothetical but important cases, most journalists return quickly to their high-road self-definition; and some (not all) judges and prosecutors give them good reason. A few quotes may illustrate the point.[7]

— A television journalist: "These are areas where we are right and the courts are wrong and there is no compromise."

— A judge: "Freedom of the press is not an absolute freedom, not an unlimited freedom."

— Another judge: "Make all the rules you want affecting the press but they'll go get the story and print it anyway; and that's the game, there's nothing moral or amoral about it."

— A lawyer: "Along with the press's obligation to protect us against the misbehavior of a trial judge are the obligations to protect the right to a fair trial and to preserve the liberty of its citizens."

— Another lawyer: "I don't think any public figure has a right to privacy."

— A publisher: "We are the final judge."

— A judge to a publisher: "Nobody elected you."

— A lawyer for a newspaper: "To hell with verification, print the story and we'll go for a lawsuit."

— A reporter: "Whether or not a reporter has committed a crime to get a story should be of no concern to his editor or publisher."

So, journalists—in the post-Vietnam and post-Watergate era—present a mixed picture of feistiness and wariness, chutzpah and prudence, relative certainty about ends but uncertainty about means. None of this should be surprising since visibility brings vulnerability, and power creates resentment among the less powerful. Underneath it all lie those multiple ambiguities previously cited.

SOME POSSIBLE SOLUTIONS

A "free press"—most Americans will probably still agree—should be one of the watchdogs of the nation's other institutions, both public and private. But who shall watch this watchdog, and by what standards will it be watched? Back we come, of course, to the vexing question of journalistic ethics—the standards of behavior for both people and organizations under First Amendment protection.

Despite an interval of enthusiasm within the media for the enactment of state or federal "shield laws" to keep journalists from having to divulge their confidential sources, most reporters and editors seem to have concluded that what legislatures can give, they can also take away—and that there can be no better protection than the one provided by the First Amendment, whatever its limitations. No wonder, then, that any legislative solution to the creation and policing of journalistic ethics is anathema to practitioners.

Why not, instead, that Hutchins Commission concept, now thirty years old, media participation in the creation of a private institution, a National News Council, and media cooperation with such a council? A paramount and perhaps insuperable objection lies in the heterogeneous character of American society and the mutual lack of trust on which it was founded—a system built, for that reason, on both federalism and elaborate "checks and balances." News or press councils may gain acceptance and succeed in more homogeneous societies whose citizens share relative trust in their institutions—for instance, in Great Britain, where a Press Council has apparently won substantial acceptance and good repute, and also, closer to home, in the state of Minnesota. But can they work in areas of more clashing diversity and mutual suspicion? The irony, of course, is that those are usually the areas where such councils—such new checks or balances—are most needed.

There is a further objection to the concept of press councils that some journalists cite: a fear that the standards, codes, or guidelines adopted by press councils may suddenly be expropriated by judges and transformed into court decrees. That fear has been confirmed in a few cases. Eventually even a legislature might seek to enact such guidelines into law—a development recently impending in the Republic of South Africa, where the ruling party was for a while proposing to transform a mediawide code, together with its stiff financial penalties, into the law of the land.

For the foreseeable future it seems to me that much of the U.S. press will continue to resist participation in any nationwide press council—this despite some recent new support for the New York-based National News Council.

And yet the clock is ticking away on the matter of public attitudes for the reasons given at the outset of this essay. Is there no alternative approach to the protection of the media's freedom in a climate of widespread suspicion of, and potential acute hostility toward, all national institutions? Cannot modes of *self-restraint* be fashioned without encroaching on the reality of freedom?

The questions are inherently baffling since there is no single cure that would not be far worse than the alleged disease. Yet let me offer five very general and probably unsurprising proposals:

First, the media should push further and faster in the establishment of those two largely post-Agnew innovations: first, that mechanism to deal with both in-house and external redress of grievances, the post of ombudsman; and second, that vehicle for widened public access, the op-ed page or, better, pages. Increased self-criticism and openness can help increase public trust. More broadly—and especially among smaller dailies and weeklies that can less easily afford ombudsmen or op-ed pages—editors should become more willing both to explain and to criticize the media in editorials, columns, and the like.

Second, public understanding of the role of the media—now very often lacking among educated professionals (like lawyers, doctors, professors, government officials), much less among the general citizenry—should be fostered by the press and by colleges and universities through symposia, seminars, and other special programs for professionals as well as the public. It is astonishing how widespread one finds the judgment, among highly sophisticated citizens, that freedom of the press is important to preserve, "but only for 'responsible' journalists." That the First Amendment makes no such distinction is a point lost on millions of Americans. For, despite the Hutchins report of 1947, who shall define "responsibility"? This is a question best left unanswered, as the courts have so far left it.

Third, journalistic self-education is essential. Many more journalists should be permitted a sabbatical "breather" during their high-pressure, deadline-oriented careers: opportunities to take time out—ideally at colleges or universities, but also on congressional staffs, or even in government service—not to study journalism but to study the society that is their focus. Such pauses, or changes of pace, in the journalist's racehorse routine can deepen understanding, expand horizons, and increase personal growth. Forty years ago the Nieman Fellowships were established as a pioneering experiment at Harvard University for precisely this purpose. Today many other sabbatical programs are available for the academic study, altered vantage point, and intellectual immersion that reporters, editors, and publishers desperately need in order to do their jobs better.

Fourth, despite the previously noted obstacles to a nationwide press-monitoring body, media organizations should consider taking the initiative in establishing local, state, or regional press councils on an entirely voluntary and private basis. If, for instance, in the Northeast, the entire New England region seems too large and disparate for merely one or even two press councils, the Boston metropolitan area would seem a natural base for such an experiment. The dangers of judicial intervention remain; yet careful consultation with bar and bench organizations could minimize those dangers.

Finally, journalistic ethics can be best inculcated and supervised through a system entirely appropriate to the "guild" structure of traditional newspapers: through the hiring by mature and experienced editors—people of humaneness, self-discipline, and idealism—of reporter-apprentices who can be counted on to learn and emulate the work standards of their mentors. Mentorship is at the heart of the process—and depends, of course, on management's hiring of editors worthy of emulation. The chain may seem highly fragile and accidental; nonetheless, it is the essence of education at its best in all enterprises. I have yet to meet a successful and esteemed journalist who was not deeply influenced by some wiser, older editor or supervisor early in his or her career. (And I have met, of course, a number of hacks who apparently weren't.)

And what of the ethics themselves? Shall they be set forth in some code like a Boy Scout oath or a catechism? The answer is certainly no. The ambiguities of journalism are too endemic and ineradicable, its domain too wide and infinitely varied. Indeed, that domain is life itself —the endless contours of reality. What code can be written for such a special craft other than those of the philosophers and saints who have tried to teach men how to coexist?

In the end there seems to me no possible code, no firm guideline, for the ethical conduct of a journalist other than the craft's age-old bywords, "fairness" and "accuracy"—to which I would also add emphatically "compassion," not often highly rated in the newsroom. In this mix of qualities lies the possibility of what used to be described as "situation ethics": conduct based on sensitivity to the unique elements of each decision-situation and the consequences to others as well as oneself. For the ingredient of compassion, Kant's categorical imperative —or the New Testament's Golden Rule—can offer the journalist not firm guidelines, but at least some degree of humane self-restraint.

When a reporter has found a wise mentor, and when he or she seeks to infuse judgments with fairness, accuracy, *and* compassion, the reporter and the organization will not go further wrong than most decent but fallible mortals.

But can the American public accept such an imprecise definition of standards for such a clearly powerful institution and semipublic service? One can only answer yes if the craft itself is willing to explain its role and its decision-making processes much more clearly, criticize itself much more sharply, and open its pages and time much more generously. American journalism and its guardian angel, the First

Amendment, are a unique national asset in the contemporary world. Unless both journalists and citizens learn to appreciate the rarity, fragility, and value of our Fourth Estate, it may well go the way of too many other formerly free presses in other nations.

NOTES

1. For the 1923 and 1975 versions, see Appendix I and II. See also Appendix III for the Code of Ethics adopted in 1973 by the Society of Professional Journalists, Sigma Delta Chi.

2. For materials on these earlier efforts, see Leon Nelson Flint, *The Conscience of the Newspaper* (New York: D. Appleton & Co., 1925), and Nelson Antrim Crawford, *The Ethics of Journalism* (New York: Alfred A. Knopf, 1924).

3. Commission on Freedom of the Press, *A Free and Responsible Press: A General Report on Mass Communication: Newspapers, Radio, Motion Pictures, Magazines, and Books* (Chicago: University of Chicago Press, 1947). See also extracts and comments as reprinted in *Nieman Reports* 30 (Autumn 1976): 18–25.

4. As paraphrased in W. H. Ferry, "Masscomm as Guru," in *Ethics and the Press— Readings in Mass Media Morality,* John C. Merrill and Ralph D. Barney, eds. (New York: Hastings House, 1975), p. 48.

5. Quoted in Wilbur Schramm, "Quality in Mass Communication," in Merrill and Barney, *Ethics and the Press,* pp. 43–44.

6. See Leon V. Sigal, *Reporters and Officials—The Organization and Politics of News-making* (Lexington, Mass.: D. C. Heath, 1973).

7. See Jonathan Moore, James C. Thomson, Jr., et al. *Report of the New England Conference on Conflicts Between the Media and the Law, September 1974–September 1976* (Cambridge, Mass., 1977), pp. 3–4.

APPENDIX I

Code of Ethics or Canons of Journalism

American Society of Newspaper Editors (1923)

The primary function of newspapers is to communicate to the human race what its members do, feel and think. Journalism, therefore, demands of its practitioners the widest range of intelligence, or knowledge, and of experience, as well as natural and trained powers of observation and reasoning. To its opportunities as a chronicle are indissolubly linked its obligations as teacher and interpreter.

To the end of finding some means of codifying sound practice and just aspirations of American journalism, these canons are set forth:

I. Responsibility: The right of a newspaper to attract and hold readers is restricted by nothing but considerations of public welfare. The use a newspaper makes of the share of public attention it gains serves to determine its sense of responsibility, which it shares with every member of its staff. A journalist who uses his power for any selfish or otherwise unworthy purpose is faithless to a high trust.

II. Freedom of the Press: Freedom of the press is to be guarded as a vital right of mankind. It is the unquestionable right to discuss whatever is not explicitly forbidden by law, including the wisdom of any restrictive statute.

III. Independence: Freedom from all obligations except that of fidelity to the public interest is vital.

1. Promotion of any private interest contrary to the general welfare, for whatever reason, is not compatible with honest journalism. So-called news communications from private sources should not be published without public notice of their source or else substantiation of their claims to value as news, both in form and substance.

2. Partisanship, in editorial comment which knowingly departs from the truth, does violence to the best spirit of American journalism, in the news columns it is subversive of a fundamental principle of the profession.

IV. Sincerity, Truthfulness, Accuracy: Good faith with the reader is the foundation of all journalism worthy of the name.

1. By every consideration of good faith a newspaper is constrained to be truthful. It is not to be excused for lack of thoroughness or accuracy within its control, or failure to obtain command of these essential qualities.

2. Headlines should be fully warranted by the contents of the articles which they surmount.

V. Impartiality: Sound practice makes clear distinction between news reports and expressions of opinion. News reports should be free from opinion or bias of any kind.

1. This rule does not apply to so-called special articles unmistakably devoted to advocacy or characterized by a signature authorizing the writer's own conclusions and interpretation.

VI. Fair Play: A newspaper should not publish unofficial charges affecting reputation or moral character without opportunity given to the accused to be heard; right practice demands the giving of such opportunity in all cases of serious accusation outside judicial proceedings.

1. A newspaper should not involve private rights or feeling without sure warrant of public right as distinguished from public curiosity.

2. It is the privilege, as it is the duty, of a newspaper to make prompt and complete correction of its own serious mistakes of fact or opinion, whatever their origin.

Decency: A newspaper cannot escape conviction of insincerity if while professing high moral purpose it supplies incentives to base conduct, such as are to be found in details of crime and vice, publication of which is not demonstrably for the general good. Lacking authority to enforce its canons the journalism here represented can but express the hope that deliberate pandering to vicious instincts will encounter effective public disapproval or yield to the influence of a preponderant professional condemnation.

APPENDIX II

A Statement of Principles

American Society of Newspaper Editors (1975)

Preamble: The First Amendment, protecting freedom of expression from abridgment by any law, guarantees to the people through their press a constitutional right, and thereby places on newspaper people a particular responsibility.

Thus journalism demands of its practitioners not only industry and knowledge but also the pursuit of a standard of integrity proportionate to the journalist's singular obligation.

To this end the American Society of Newspaper Editors sets forth this Statement of Principles as a standard encouraging the highest ethical and professional performance.

Article 1—Responsibility: The primary purpose of gathering and distributing news and opinion is to serve the general welfare by informing the people and enabling them to make judgments on the issues of the time. Newspapermen and women who abuse the power of their professional role for selfish motives or unworthy purposes are faithless to that public trust.

The American press was made free not just to inform or just to serve as a forum for debate but also to bring an independent scrutiny to bear on the forces of power in the society, including the conduct of official power at all levels of government.

Article II—Freedom of the Press: Freedom of the press belongs to the people. It must be defended against encroachment or assault from any quarter, public or private.

Journalists must be constantly alert to see that the public's business is conducted in public. They must be vigilant against all who would exploit the press for selfish purposes.

Article III—Independence: Journalists must avoid impropriety and the appearance of impropriety as well as any conflict of interest or the appearance of conflict. They should neither accept anything nor pursue any activity that might compromise or seem to compromise their integrity.

Article IV—Truth and Accuracy: Good faith with the reader is the foundation of good journalism. Every effort must be made to assure that the news content is accurate, free from bias and in context, and that all sides are presented fairly. Editorials, analytical articles and commentary should be held to the same standards of accuracy with respect to facts as news reports.

Significant errors of fact, as well as errors of omission, should be corrected promptly and prominently.

Article V—Impartiality: To be impartial does not require the press to be unquestioning or to refrain from editorial expression. Sound practice, however, demands a clear distinction for the reader between news reports and opinion. Articles that contain opinion or personal interpretation should be clearly identified.

Article VI—Fair Play: Journalists should respect the rights of people involved in the news, observe the common standards of decency and stand accountable to the public for the fairness and accuracy of their news reports.

Persons publicly accused should be given the earliest opportunity to respond.

Pledges of confidentiality to news sources must be honored at all costs, and therefore should not be given lightly. Unless there is clear and pressing need to maintain confidences, sources of information should be identified.

These principles are intended to preserve, protect and strengthen the bond of trust and respect between American journalists and the American people, a bond that is essential to sustain the grant of freedom entrusted to both by the nation's founders.

APPENDIX III

Code of Ethics

Sigma Delta Chi (1973)

The Society of Professional journalists, Sigma Delta Chi, believes the duty of journalists is to serve the truth.

We believe the agencies of mass communication are carriers of public discussion and information, acting on their constitutional mandate and freedom to learn and report the facts.

We believe in public enlightenment as the forerunner of justice, and in our constitutional role to seek the truth as part of the public's right to know the truth.

We believe those responsibilities carry obligations that require journalists to perform with intelligence, objectivity, accuracy, and fairness.

To these ends, we declare acceptance of the standards to practice here set forth:

1. Responsibility: The public's right to know of events of public importance and interest is the overriding mission of the mass media. The purpose of distributing news and enlightened opinion is to serve the general welfare. Journalists who use their professional status as representatives of the public for selfish or other unworthy motives violate a high trust.

II. Freedom of the Press: Freedom of the press is to be guarded as an inalienable right of people in a free society. It carries with it the freedom and the responsibility to discuss, question, and challenge actions and utterances of our government and of our public and private institutions. Journalists uphold the right to speak unpopular opinions and the privilege to agree with the majority.

III. Ethics: Journalists must be free of obligation to any interest other than the public's right to know the truth.

1. Gifts, favors, free travel, special treatment or privileges can compromise the integrity of journalists and their employers. Nothing of value should be accepted.

2. Secondary employment, political involvement, holding public office, and service in community organizations should be avoided if it compromises the integrity of journalists and their employers. Journalists and their employers should conduct their personal lives in a manner which protects them from conflict of interest, real or apparent. Their responsibilities to the public are paramount. That is the nature of their profession.

3. So-called news communications from private sources should not be published or broadcast without substantiation of their claims to news value.

4. Journalists will seek news that serves the public interest, despite the obstacles. They will make constant efforts to assure that the public's business is conducted in public and that public records are open to public inspection.

5. Journalists acknowledge the newsmen's ethic of protecting confidential sources of information.

IV. Accuracy and Objectivity: Good faith with the public is the foundation of all worthy journalism.

1. Truth is our ultimate goal.

2. Objectivity in reporting the news is another goal, which serves as the mark of an experienced professional. It is a standard of performance toward which we strive. We honor those who achieve it.

3. There is no excuse for inaccuracies or lack of thoroughness.

4. Newspaper headlines should be fully warranted by the contents of the articles they accompany. Photographs and telecasts should give an accurate picture of an event and not highlight a minor incident out of context.

5. Sound practice makes clear distinction between news reports and expressions of opinion. News reports should be free of opinion or bias and represent all sides of an issue.

6. Partisanship in editorial comment which knowingly departs from the truth violates the spirit of American journalism.

7. Journalists recognize their responsibility for offering informed analysis, comment, and editorial opinion on public events and issues. They accept the obligation to present such material by individuals whose competence, experience, and judgment qualify them for it.

8. Special articles or presentations devoted to advocacy or the writer's own conclusions and interpretations should be labeled as such.

V. Fair Play: Journalists at all times will show respect for the dignity, privacy, rights, and well-being of people encountered in the course of gathering and presenting the news.

1. The news media should not communicate unofficial charges affecting reputation or moral character without giving the accused a chance to reply.

2. The news media must guard against invading a person's right to privacy.

3. The media should not pander to morbid curiosity about details of vice and crime.

4. It is the duty of news media to make prompt and complete corrections of their errors.

5. Journalists should be accountable to the public for their reports and the public should be encouraged to voice its grievances against the media. Open dialogue with our readers, viewers, and listeners should be fostered.

VI. Pledge: Journalists should actively censure and try to prevent violations of these standards, and they should encourage their observance by all newspeople. Adherence to this code of ethics is intended to preserve the bond of mutual trust and respect between American journalists and the American people.

3 THIS ABOVE ALL

Nora Beloff

It would be hard to find a better moral precept for aspiring reporters than Polonius's recommendation to his son, Laertes in *Hamlet*: "This above all: to thine own self be true."

Thine own self, of course, may not be suitable for this particular trade. The journalist needs a very unusual assortment of talents; neither literary excellence nor natural aptitude for original thought are necessarily sufficient. The qualities include stamina, curiosity, irrepressibility, a good deal of what Manhattan calls "noive," and also a little humility. For essentially the operators in the media are parasites, living off the actions and achievements of others. Whatever they write is likely to be forgotten within twenty-four hours or, worse still, attributed to somebody else on another paper. Even those who take journalism at its most serious refer to "the Fourth Estate": there is no question of placing it on the same level as the other three.

From the journalist's point of view, freedom means the right to communicate directly to the reader with minimal outside interference. Minimal is as much as can be expected, for it would be utopian to suppose that any writer remains in control of his material from the time he composes it in his head until it appears on the page. On the contrary, the life of a journalist has to be a series of compromises in which ethics is unlikely to be the overriding consideration. Yet most members of the profession have an urge to express themselves and take a serious view of what they would like to say. After thirty years of news reporting, I feel able to identify the four major barriers intervening between the writer and the reader (or, in the case of broadcasting, viewer or listener), and to describe the kind of accommodation that has to be reached without inflicting too much damage on the Polonius precept.

THE TECHNOCRATS

A journalist entering the profession, whether reporting the activities of the local community, diplomatic events, sports, entertainment, or gossip, will meet someone else in absolute authority who can cut, rewrite, or "spike" the copy. The person in charge has to decide, often very quickly, whether the piece is worth printing, how it should be displayed, and whether the emphasis needs changing. The reporter may find himself encouraged to distort what he sees in order to excite, appall, shock, or titillate the reader. Bloodshed and scandal boost the story—as the famous and frequently revived comedy *The Front Page* reminds us. It would be unfair to the new generation of highly educated journalists to suggest that this farce is a faithful portrayal of the contemporary press, but it still contains enough truth to make the professional laugh and to explain why news reporters are often ridiculed and despised.

Pressure from the head office will also encourage journalists to intrude into people's private lives in a way which they would never do in ordinary life. Yet it is no more ethical for a journalist than for anyone else to get into a home on false pretenses, to report a personal conversation without warning the other party, or secretively to tape a telephone call.

It is true that there are special occasions when overriding public interest justifies cheating. The London *Times* used a tape recorder to expose corruption inside the London police force. Normally crime should be reported to the police: most people agreed that in this particular case, when policemen themselves were the offenders, the *Times* intrusion was justified.

The difficulty, of course, is to identify what is "public interest": the epithet in its true meaning implies that the revelation will benefit the public, either by exposing wrongdoing or by opening the way to improving local or central administration. But the epithet is often misused to cover anything that interests the public—which opens up to public exposure the most intimate details in a public person's private life. Journalists who do this should think how they themselves would feel if similar details were revealed about their own personal affairs.

Nor is it always easy for the editor himself to know whether to draw the line. The former British foreign secretary, George Brown, was known by everyone in public life to have a weak head for drink. Reporters writing about him used such euphemisms as "overtired" or "overexcited," which seemed legally safe. The libel law is so strict—and the fines often so ruinous—that every major British newspaper employs a highly trained libel lawyer who sits at the news desk and without whose initials no copy can go to the printer. Apart from the legal risks, no British journalist writing about public affairs wanted to chance being debarred from communication with the foreign secretary, a genial and gregarious man who, on the whole, had good relations with the press.

The editor of the *Observer,* David Astor, finally decided that this was truly a matter of public interest, since it affected the conduct of public affairs, and he therefore reprinted from the New York *Times* a witty and not unfriendly profile of Brown (now Lord Brown) by Anthony Lewis, which revealed the facts.

Legislation enforcing respect for privacy is a controversial subject. In the United States the law provides protection against intrusion by listening devices that involve physical trespass. But in writing about the private lives of public people, the United States is far less restrained than Britain: indeed recent Supreme Court interpretations of the First Amendment of the United States Constitution allow almost anything to be said about anyone in the public eye.

The absence of legislation throws the responsibility back to the journalist or editor. In a competitive, consumerist society, it is a license that can be easily abused. The veteran Washington *Post* columnist, Alan Barth, a former Nieman fellow, has made a strong case against any form of legal restraint, arguing that the damage is the price a democratic society has to pay for the privilege of a free press: "There is not the slightest doubt that if the press is granted full freedom, it will sometimes abuse it. It will sometimes sully its freedom by publishing lewd and lascivious matter and pandering to prurient interests.... It will sometimes publish information regarding criminal prosecution that may make the conduct of a fair trial more difficult. It will sometimes pry into the privacy of individuals and publish stories that inflict wanton injury...." Yet having made all these concessions, Barth opposes any enforceable restraint. He sees the press as a watchdog of a free society and concludes: "if you want a watchdog to warn you of intruders, you must put up with a certain amount of mistaken barking."[1]

This view would be contested in most Western democracies. The areas of restraint are hard to define, but it should not be beyond the wit of the best jurists to draw up laws protecting individual liberty and respecting the democratic principle that all men are considered innocent until they are proven guilty. The onus of proof must surely be on the communicator who is using a paper or broadcasting channel to destroy another man's reputation, family bonds, and capacity to earn a living. In most Western countries there is some form of protection of the public against blasphemy, obscenity, libel, and branches of confidentiality. This will not prevent an aspiring reporter, often egged on by his office, from pressing to the brink of the permissible—and going beyond it if this can be done in the knowledge that no one will dare to prosecute. Personally I had no compunction in suing the British magazine *Private Eye* for libel and receiving an award of 3,000 pounds from a London jury.

In the areas uncovered by the libel law, publishers and journalists in Britain have agred to submit themselves to the supervision of a press council to whom the public and journalist can appeal against abuses. The council was set up in 1953 and guarantees at least a right of reply to those who feel they have been unfairly treated. It has no legal force, but newspapers restrain themselves, knowing that they have undertaken to publish the council's verdict. Charles Wintour, former editor of the *Evening Standard,* concedes that, quite apart from its active interventions, the council is a valuable deterrent: "The Press Council by plugging away at the ethics of journalism has performed a real service to newspapers and their editors. For, most of the malpractices which did exist in the decade after the war were caused by fear that competitors might steal a march. Today, although competition remains intense, certain ground rules are more clearly defined."[2] The council has also tried to eradicate what the British call "cheque book journalism"—payments to criminals for their "exclusive" stories.

There is of course a risk with any authority that it will curtail the freedom of inquiry, but most British newspaper readers favor having a body to protect them against the press. In my own journalistic experience I have had only one encounter with the council. I had discovered that a secret Trotskyist faction, the Revolutionary Socialist Group, had successfully infiltrated the British Labour party, even getting a member on to the National Executive, by concealing its true colors under a left-wing publication *The Militant.* The Labour organizers knew what was happening but could do nothing until the matter was publicly exposed. As usual most reporters were frightened off by the libel law. Through someone who had changed sides, I discovered that a free-lance journalist, Roger Protz, who had later shifted into another faction, had been actively involved in the founding of the revolutionary group's *Militant.* When I telephoned him, he denied knowing anything about it. I later secured letters in which he described some of the secret meetings. I wrote a page one story, using extracts from his letters exposing the infiltration of the party, which later led to an investigation that is still proceeding.

Protz complained to the Press Council that I had used his private correspondence without his consent and alleged that my conduct was therefore unethical. On April 25, 1976, the council handed down its verdict:

Letters written by private individuals about private matters should in general not be published (at least during their lifetime) without their consent. But individuals may engage in activities which are legitimately of public concern and may indeed write letters about such matters which although intended to be kept private were in truth of public interest. In such a case at least an attempt to obtain the writer's consent should be made, but even in its absence publication may be justified and in certain circumstances there might even be a duty to publish whether the writer agreed to or even knew of the intention to publish or not.

In most newspapers, journalists are never forced to go beyond the bounds of what they consider decent behavior: I can think of no case where a reporter lost his job or was demoted for refusing to pester a bereaved mother or to question the family of a kidnapped child. This is not to say that an editor would find difficulty in recruiting a less "sensitive" journalist eager to leap into the breach.

Investigation into really serious lawlessness can, of course, be physically dangerous. A chapter on journalistic ethics would be incomplete without a tribute to Victor Riesel, the New York labor reporter who lost his sight after having had acid thrown into his eyes while he was investigating the Teamsters Union.

Pressures on the reporter from his news desk will depend a good deal on fashion and changing tastes. There have been periods when news had to be "hard": selected for its "news value," in other words, for its supposed intrinsic interst to the (imaginary) ordinary reader. Comment was combed out, and everybody respected the dictum of the famous C. P. Scott: "Facts are sacred. Comment is free."[3] It was probably Norman Mailer more than any other writer who set the fashion of "new journalism," in which the news became the reaction of the writer to the event. As a perceptive and—for those who are not too squeamish—lively writer, Mailer did a splendid job on a whole series of political conventions. Unfortunately, his work had a most pernicious influence on many less talented imitators. Now we have moved on to the post-Watergate era, when the fashion is for "investigative journalism," the new five-syllable epithet for the old-fashioned muckraking business.

The deserved success of the two Washington *Post* reporters, Woodward and Bernstein, and the triumph of their best-selling book *All the President's Men* in forcing a president to resign, has had an enormous influence on the American press. Returning to the United States during the 1976 election, I was amazed to find how much energy and space was being devoted to what seemed to be trivial private matters (had President Ford been given the free membership of a local golf club? How much profit had Mr. Carter made out of his peanuts?), matters that seemed irrelevant to the basic issue: which of them would make a better president? At that time every reporter was scouring the country for scandal. Not that the new generation of political writers were either more or less interested in the people and issues than when Theodore White first refined the art of reporting presidential campaigns; but fashion had changed.

It is perhaps in the area of international affairs that the most damage is done by the news desk's principle that good news is no news. The papers rightly assume that their readers are more interested in local affairs and the fate of their own politicans than what is going on in the remoter parts of the world. It takes a very persevering and lively foreign correspondent to get himself into his paper unless there is a reasonable amount of bloodshed, scandal, or disaster in the country to which he is assigned. I can claim some experience here, as I have spent most of my own professional life abroad as correspondent in Paris during the negotiations for the Marshall Plan and the creation of the European Economic Community; then in Washington for varying periods of time under every president from Harry Truman to Jimmy Carter; also having spells in Moscow, Brussels, Rome, and many other places. I look back on the waste of huge amounts of time and energy that I spent reporting events I found fascinating but that I knew would only appear if I managed to write them to appeal to "little Englanders" who, during most of my international assignments, were in charge of the *Observer's* news desk. I might spend hours on the crucial introductory sentence that could be both truthful and likely to commend itself to people who knew little and cared less about the area. And sometimes, in the case of smaller countries, what *Observer* published might well have had a considerable political impact.

Often a "subeditor," the man who prepares the copy for the printer, would slap on a more flamboyant opening paragraph, and a misleading headline would appear over my own byline. After bouts of despair, I learned to resign myself to the fact that once the piece had appeared, nothing could be done to improve it, and that the only way of retaining friendly relations with the head office (essential for the success of any assignment) was to develop a special talent for reading the whole of the paper except my own article. It was hardly an ethical solution.

It would be wrong, of course, to assume that all the technocrats who prepare materials for the presses are less capable than the writers. Sometimes quite the opposite is true. The reporter may regard the news desk as the biggest hurdle between himself and his public; but the professional newspaper man may be protecting the reader and giving an inexperienced journalist the training necessary to prepare him for bigger assignments.

In most European countries, unlike the United States, journalists rarely go through a professional training. Most people who want to write in the serious newspapers or participate in radio and television work take a university degree in the arts (history, economics, or literature) and acquire the technique on the job. It was at Reuters News Agency, in the Paris office, that I learned how to compose a news story, with maximum speed in minimum space. It was a tough training: the bureau chief in those far-off postwar days was Harold King, a loudmouthed, frequently drunk, and remarkably disagreeable man. If anyone crossed him, he would go into black rages, and working with him was a shattering experience. But he was a master of the difficult task of extracting and conveying political news, and though he once forced me to rewrite a news story seven times before he authorized me to send it, he taught me precisely what I needed to know.

THE PROPRIETORS

The most alarming phenomenon in the newspaper industry is the steady—sometimes rapid—shrinkage in the number of newspapers. For the journalist this means that jobs are hard to come by, difficult to hold on to, and improperly dependent on the goodwill of a single employer. The degree of control exercised by the owner of the only paper in town should not, of course, be exaggerated: life is far more harrowing for writers in totalitarian societies (whether of the left-wing or right-wing variety) in which once a man is out of favor the whole profession closes against him.

Generalizations about ownership are difficult. Some newspaper owners constantly interfere in the editorial process. Others, not necessarily more tolerant or more broadminded, regard their newspaper as one aspect of a financial empire and are totally respectful of the editorial prerogative, as long as the money rolls in. In Canada, for example, there are two major chains dominating the entire country. Editors from one group told me that they are under constant surveillance from the head office, and their publications are constantly monitored. Editors from the other group said that the publisher interested himself exclusively in their balance sheet.

In Britain there was a great outcry when the Canadian businessman, Lord Thomson, who already owned the London *Times,* bought the previously independent *Sunday Times.* The British cabinet anxiously discussed whether or not to submit the transaction to the Monopolies Commission and refrained from doing so only because there was a serious risk that if Lord Thomson pulled out, the *Times* might cease to appear. Events have shown there to have been no cause for anxiety. Lord Thomson and his son, who has now inherited the empire, adopted a strictly noninterventionist attitude toward their London newspapers. The editor of the *Times,* William Rees Mogg, is a Catholic Conservative who was privately educated and once tried to win a parliamentary seat. Harry Evans, of the *Sunday Times,* is a self-made and pro-Labour man.

Nor do proprietors treat all their products or all their staff the same way. The Australian newspaper magnate, Rupert Murdoch, broke into the American market by acquiring morning and evening papers in San Antonio, Texas. He moved in to launch the two papers under their new management. But while he respected local habits and left more or less unchanged a relatively staid morning paper that had a monopoly of the market, he injected far more sensationalism and violence into the evening paper. In this field he had a rival from the Hearst empire, which he evidently intended to put out of business.

At present Murdoch has relatively little time for either paper and is behaving more like the model proprietor, respecting the independence of his editors. But buying the New York *Post,* he has imposed his will both on the content and the form of New York's only surviving evening paper and has shown eagerness to make his power felt in local politics. He enjoys meeting political leaders, assessing their competence, and, if he approves, throwing the full weight of his newspapers behind them. In Australia he lost some senior journalists when he shifted from left to right in the midstream of a federal election. In Britain, he came in backing Labour, and his staff are now nervously expecting him to place his two mass-circulation newspapers, the *Sun* and the *News of the World,* firmly behind his present favorite, Tory leader Margaret Thatcher. At the *Post* a group of journalists complained of the one-sided coverage the paper was giving to the mayoralty race in favor of his chosen (and later victorious) candidate. Murdoch reportedly replied that if they did not like the way he ran his paper, they could go elsewhere. But there are very few other places for New York journalists to go. In many cases the livelihood of the reporters and their families depended on submission.

The political consequences of American newspapers' falling into the hands of a few big corporations are very different from those that the outside world might expect. It is generally assumed among intellectuals inside and outside the United States that as the press is owned by businessmen, newspapers must be biased in favor of private enterprise and big business and against social reform, public expenditure, and state control. Almost everyone declaring themselves "on the Left" assumes this is so: the Russians, for example, are convinced that the United States is run by capitalist corporations and that their principal organ, the *Wall Street Journal,* must therefore be the most important newspaper in North America. Private firms do indeed buy most of the financially vital advertising space—though the various branches of central and local government and the private pressure groups also make a substantial contribution. It is also true that major corporations can afford to buy peak TV time and, within the strict regulations applied by the Federal Communications Commission, use the programs to their advantage. But paradoxically, although the newspapers and the TV channels also belong to businessmen (or perhaps because they do), the newspapers bend backwards to appear critical and allow a good deal of antibusiness and progovernment copy into their columns.

Two American professors, William Mackling and Michael Jensen of Rochester University, have even argued that the American press is positively helping the administration to undermine private ownership and to destroy free enterprise.[4] They argue that any group of men, whether in the public or private sector, aims to extend its power and acquire greater control, and that bureaucrats and newspaper owners happen to share a common interest in fabricating—or at least exaggerating—stories of economic and financial crisis: these, they point out, both increase the need for government intervention—and therefore the power of the bureaucrats—and also boost newspaper circulation. "The creation of crises is an old political strategem: 180 years ago James Madison described it as 'the old trick of turning every contingency into a resource for accumulating force in the government.'"

"Politicians in the United States have used this ploy as a pretence for expanding their powers in one area after another in recent years. Thus, we have had crises over aid and water pollution, automobile safety, the quality and safety of consumer products, particular drugs and food, the preservation of forests and wildlife, land use, occupational health and safety, so-called 'illicit' payments to foreign officials—the list is almost endless." The one receiving most attention currently, of course, is the energy crisis. They continue:

> The scenario for all of these crises is the same, they usually involve hearings in Congress, perhaps accompanied by the appointment of semi-official citizens' commissions asked to investigate the problem. Often there is some 'public interest' group in the background—like Nader's raiders. At every opportunity the politician entrepreneurs make exaggerated statements about the seriousness of the problem. As in the case of energy, both sides (Democrat and Republican) agree

that disaster is imminent—they only disagree over what ought to be done to avert it. The press and radio are delighted. Crises sell newspapers, attract TV viewers. . . .

In the Meckling-Jensen world, private enterprise is doomed to disaster. No doubt they are exaggerating—though probably less than the Marxists, who suppose all power is in capitalist hands. In the turbulent and changing American society, the trend is at the moment antibusiness, and the newspapers reflect the mood. The pendulum could —and probably will—swing the other way—though not all the way back to the days of robber barons and soup kitchens.

The restraint on the freedom of journalists to write is less likely to be in the procapitalist or probusiness bias of their employers than in the growing trend toward monopoly. The absence of an alternative employer is the gravest of all restrictions on a writer's freedom of expression.

In Britain, readers still have a much wider choice of morning newspapers than anywhere in the United States. From the Conservative *Daily Telegraph* to the pro-Labour *Guardian* (not to mention the Communist *Morning Star,* which is not commerically financed), from the serious *Times* to the sexy and sensational *Sun,* British newspapers probably provide a bigger variety and greater contrast than the press of any other country. But in Britain too the situation is highly unstable: most of the papers are losing money and struggling for survival. A royal commission, set up to study the newspaper industry, reported in July 1977 that unless the managements introduce "root and branch reforms" in their methods of production, several papers were likely to collapse, and famous titles would disappear. The commission took a bleak view of the future after deploring the "suicidal behaviour" of the printing unions, which had rejected the introduction of the new technology.[5]

The sad conclusion was a justifiable correction after the foolish optimism displayed by the same commission in their interim report the previous year.[6] In this document they had declared themselves confident of an agreement's being reached between workers and management which, by introducing computers, would radically reduce the huge cost of newspaper production. Over the previous decades the old craft unions had won control over the labor supply and imposed massive overmanning, wages out of all proportion to those paid to men of similar skills in other industries, and a luddite attitude toward all new machines. The newspaper proprietors, producing a highly perishable commodity, had usually preferred to give in to sudden demands rather than to endure strikes or local sabotage, which might enable rival papers to grab their readership.

Under the negotiated arrangement, which the royal commission had wrongly predicted the printers would accept, the men would have been offered substantial benefits but would have had to accept negotiating procedures for settling labor disputes and so abandon their treasured right to down tools and bring managements to heel.

The American newspapers have gone very much further in using the latest inventions, drastically reducing the labor and hardware required to publish and disseminate their product. But this has almost always been done only *after* the acquisition by the newspaper involved of a virtual monopoly of the readership in its own area of distribution. Once the rivals had been knocked out, the management could take on the unions and impose redundancies without fearing that a strike might deliver their circulation to their competitors. Despite long and bitter battles, the unions found it impossible to prevent the technological revolution.

Logically, the introduction of the new computers and the cheaper methods of production and distribution should have made it possible for the readers—and the journalists—to have more newspapers from which to choose. In the United States exactly the opposite happened: it was only *after* the establishment of a monopoly that the new methods were introduced.

The application of the new technology and its implications for the British press were examined on behalf of the royal commission by Rex Winsbury. He commented: "The fundamental significance of new technology, centering on computers and photocomposition, is that it offers the opportunity and the means for cutting costs. It therefore offers to British society at least the hope of preserving and perhaps even enlarging what many other countries have either lost or never had—a varied and powerful national press...."[7] Winsbury traveled extensively in the United States and described the dramatic difference between the old system and the new. The linotype machine, on which British national newspapers are all still published, is a clumsy-looking typesetting contraption with mechanical arms, cases of molds, and a manually operated keyboard. The new "cold type" generates the print image photographically and so dispenses with the printers and the lead. Winsbury found that the American newspaper industry had not only ceased to order new linotype machines; they had sold off the existing ones for scrap.

Accepting Winbury's contention that the new technology should help to preserve a plural press, I studied his findings in some detail and wrote an article in the magazine *Encounter* suggesting that newspaper proprietors should get together and share their means of production.[8] By doing so they could stand out against the craft unions, drastically reduce their costs, and open the way to increasing instead of diminishing the number of newspapers—for the benefit of both the reader and the writer.

Not all the plant, of course, could be shared. Editorial independence would mean that the separate editorial offices would need to acquire their own minicomputers and feed only the ready-made copy into the large co-owned installations. A start has already been made in this direction without apparently impinging on the separateness of the newspaper in question. The right-wing *Mail* and the left-wing *Guardian* already share their premises in Manchester for the publication of their northern editions. The interim report of the royal commission had further confirmed private rumors that the most serious dailies—the *Times,* the *Financial Times,* the *Guardian,* and the *Daily Telegraph* —had already discussed plans to share their plant but had failed to reach agreement. Yet the problem remains unsolved, and the talks between the publishers are likely to be taken up again as costs escalate and revenues stagnate.

The threat of an American-type monopoly alarmed the two most left-wing members of the royal commission, union leader David Bassnet and journalist Geoffrey Goodman, who produced their own minority report. They proposed that the government take over existing surplus printing capacity and set up a publicly owned "printing corporation," available to print any newspaper or periodical that might apply. The facilities would be freely available to any publication. But the majority of the commission flatly opposed state control over the publication of newspapers, whatever the safeguards.

My proposal was different: the newspapers themselves, I suggested, should share the ownership of their production facilities, just as they already share Britain's two major news agencies: the Associated Press and Reuters. A government subsidy might be needed to help the publishers buy out the unions. The new employees, brought in to operate the computers, would be highly paid and receive the marginal benefits normally reserved for business executives: in return, they would relinquish the right to strike.

American lawyers who have represented the major publishing firms told me such a proposal for joint ownership would be inadmissible in the United States, as it would constitute "a restraint of trade." Paradoxically, laws devised to protect the public against monopoly now form a barrier preventing a plural press.

The kind of free-enterprise monopoloy in the United States is in no way comparable to the tight grip exercised over the media in state-controlled societies. First, U.S. law prevents a single newspaper from also controlling local radio and TV. Nobody has to take all the news from a single source. Further, the antimonopoly tradition has thrown the owners themselves on the defensive. All but a very few open their editorial pages to the nationally famous columnists from both sides of the political arena: Joseph Kraft appears alongside William Buckley, or Mary McGrory alongside William Safire. Nonetheless, the opinion page is only a small fraction of a newspaper. The public would have a wider choice and journalists greater freedom if monopoly was prohibited as effectively in the newspaper business as it is in other industries.

UNION POWER

Journalists in some Western democracies have tried to organize themselves into a countervailing force against the increasing monopoly of the newspaper owners. In the United States many newspapers have "a union shop," in which the reporters join the printers, clerks, and machinemen in a general union or else form themselves into a branch of the Newspaper Guild. The risk is that a tightly organized union might exclude outsiders from access to the press.

This is already happening in Britain, where, for historical and social reasons, the unions are more political. In June 1977 I wrote an article in the Washington *Post* citing the case of the North London Branch of the National Union of Journalists, which had sent out recommendations to its members on how to deal with the far-right National Front. Reporters were advised to refuse to write about Front activities or, failing that, "deliberately write a report that is extremely brief or highly critical." The branch also gave its members guidance for dealing with illegal immigration, an explosive issue in a country where newcomers from Pakistan, the West Indies, and other Commonwealth countries are competing with British workers for jobs and homes.

The branch told their members they could rely on union support if they ran into difficulties: "Don't shrink from confronting your management, even if it means taking industrial action" (in other words organizing a walkout).

The press in Britain is more vulnerable to this kind of pressure than most Western societies, as there is no longer any legal barrier preventing a single union from controlling the entry and membership of the newspaper profession. How the principle of press freedom came to be renounced in the country of Milton and Locke was the subject of my book *Freedom under Foot*—a title with a double meaning, as the man who sponsored the bill allowing a closed shop in the press was Michael Foot, a former journalist, who had been Labour Secretary of State for Employment when the bill was passed and later became leader of the House of Commons.[9] The threat of monopoly union power provoked widespread alarm. In January 1975 the International Press Institute (IPI), an organization of editors founded to protect press freedom, adopted the following motion:

> IPI views with dismay the moves towards a closed shop in the British press. Journalists through the world have long looked to Britain for a lead in freedom and the liberty of the individual. The campaign to restrict access to the press in Britain to members of one trade union, which has been made easier by the pending legislation, is therefore a grave threat to the freedom of the press. The Board declares its support for those journalists in Britain who have spoken out against the danger of a closed shop. A free press and free access to the press are of such exceptional importance in a democracy that IPI has no hesitation in urging the British Government to make an exception of the press and broadcasting in their legislation. . . .

But the Labour government had promised the Trade Union Congress that it would abolish all restrictions on a closed shop and rejected out of hand the IPI suggestion that the media should be excluded. The rumpus, however, was sufficient to induce the government to add a clause to its bill laying down provisions for a press charter that would not be legally binding but would aim to prevent any group from exercising undue influence on the content of the newspapers. The opposition shook the journalist's union, which had been battling for a closed shop—on and off—for several decades. The union therefore agreed to the press charter, though they insisted that the union representatives in the newspaper offices should have a share in supervising how the rules were observed—in other words, would watch over what went into the paper. The act provides that the press charter should contain "practical guidance for employers, trade unions, editors and other journalists on matters relating to the freedom of the press."[10] Issues on which guidance should be given were to include "the avoidance of improper pressure to distort or suppress news, comment or criticism." The trouble is that questions of this kind are highly subjective, and the press charter implicitly gives the right to call into question editorial decisions. In protest, William Rees Mogg, editor of the *Times,* refused to participate in the negotiations.

Under the act, publishers, editors, and journalists were required to try to negotiate a press charter for themselves. If no agreement could be reached within a year—which has long since expired—the secretary of state for employment was to draft the press charter and present it before both houses of Parliament.

As my book shows, I am strongly opposed to union monopoly. Indeed, I resigned from the National Union in protest against having to attend a "mandatory" meeting (occasions when members can be fined for nonattendance) at a time when I should have been writing my column. Further, I objected to the union's restrictive practices which, among other things, prevented bright secretaries from being promoted into journalism and laid it down that gifted young writers should be excluded from the national newspapers until they had worked for three years in the provinces. The brightest graduates, interested in politics and international affairs, which are not covered by the local reporters in the provincial newspapers, now prefer other professions.

Regimentation and collective action should be anathema to those who make writing their profession. Yet the increasing concentration of the ownership of the newspapers and the unfair advantage this gives to proprietors over journalists seriously weakens the case against union power.

CONSTRAINTS BY GOVERNMENT

In modern society the administration plays an increasing part in everyday life, and it would be absurd to suppose political leaders could maintain a detached attitude toward the media. In theory the government could get on with governing while the reporters used their talents to pry out the secrets and report what was happening. In practice, all governments try to protect their transactions from public gaze, but —particularly in the United States—this is increasingly difficult.

Washington had traditionally been less secretive than most European capitals, notably since the U.S. Information Act of 1975, passed to satisfy the public outcry after the Watergate scandal. On the other extreme, in Britain, under the 1911 Official Secrets Act, all government business has been considered secret unless the ministers themselves declare otherwise.

Yet to be effective, the business of government—like any other business—requires a great deal of confidentiality. "Entitlement to know" is a noble principle, but the public is also entitled to be properly governed and adequately defended: and not all these rights are necessarily compatible. Very few journalists are ready to accept this embarrassing reality.

Not that this justifies Britain's obsolete Official Secrets Act, which the present government has promised to revise and which is in any case no longer operative.* The best diarist of modern politics, the late Richard Crossman, used to argue that things should be left alone: a revised version of the act, pinpointing what must remain secret, would be a far more effective barrier between the public and the authorities.

Luckily for journalists, the Official Secrets Act does not restrain leaky politicians. But it does inhibit British civil servants who remain in the bureaucracy all their lives and depend for promotion on strict compliance with the rules, which only the best of them dare defy.

It is on matters of national security that secrecy causes most trouble. The military-industrial complex—against the "undue influence" of which Eisenhower warned—is still a formidable power: the public should be protected by an informed and critical press. Yet secrecy obviously has to be preserved over such matters as contingency planning in case of enemy attack or deployment of weapons. A pacifist case can be argued for rejecting war on any terms. In Britain there is a significant faction that opposes all defense expenditure and chants the slogan "better Red than dead." In the United States the proportion is far smaller. The vast majority of Americans repeatedly elect presidents committed to allocating large chunks of the national wealth to the defense budget. It would be illogical to neutralize the effort by insisting on knowing—and letting a potential adversary know—all about it.

What about the case for publishing the Pentagon Papers? The decision required not only an ethical judgment about the breach of confidence but also the expertise to enable the journalists to make their own assessment on whether the revelations could damage national security. In my view the New York *Times* made the right decision, though the arguments were not all one-way. There is no doubt that Daniel Ellsberg, who betrayed the trust of his colleagues, did so in the conviction that he was helping to end a war that he rightly predicted was unwinnable within the limits that the American public imposed on the military establishment. It is sometimes alleged that the United States could not defeat North Vietnam. As Ellsberg knew, this was nonsense. The Americans could have destroyed the country and imposed "the peace of the graveyard"—an epithet coined in 1830, when the Russians put down the first Polish insurrection. But the United States, being the kind

---

*The Official Secrets Act was tested in court when the Government prosecuted the *Daily Telegraph* and a journalist, Jonathan Aitken, for reproducing a document relating to the Biafrian struggle during the Nigerian civil war. In a historic summing up at the Old Bailey in February 1971, Mr. Justice Caulfield assailed the proposition that "once a document emanating from an official source was stamped confidential, anyone handling that document was breaking the law." He told the jury that section 2 of the Official Secrets Act, laying down this proposition, "has reached retirement age and should be pensioned off." The jury dismissed the charge, and since then the act has fallen into disuse.

of country it was, would only back the war as long as they believed local population in the South wanted American protection against Hanoi.

I had met Ellsberg two years before the publication of the secret papers, when he was working at the Rand Corporation in California. The war was the dominant issue in Washington at the time and previously, as Paris correspondent, I had followed an earlier phase of the conflict when it was the French who were trying to preserve a separate, pro-Western southern state. In Washington I could find no one who seemed to be interested in the French experience, no one had read the very learned historical and sociological studies of Vietnam done by French scholars who had lived in the area, knew the people, and strongly opposed the war. Ellsberg knew the material as well as I did. He had studied the campaigns and was desperately anxious to persuade Nixon and Kissinger that their efforts to "Vietnamize" the war could only end in disaster. Later, when I heard him accused of having given away the documents for the sake of publicity or acclaim, I knew this was wrong, as I had watched him attempt to press his case through regular channels.

It would be wrong to assume that the journalist who received the secret documents were honor-bound to make these available to their readers. (The only clinching professional argument might have been the knowledge that these might be scooped by some other paper.) The editors needed to exercise the same judgment as the men who delivered the material. The U.S. soldiers were still dying and being maimed for life, the country was diplomatically, economically, and militarily heavily involved. The president, who is also the commander-in-chief, was an elected leader and might claim to be better placed to judge the national interest.

During the war against Nazi Germany, war correspondents saw maps and documents they would not have dreamt of revealing. But the information in the forbidden Pentagon documents related to the basic question about whether the war was justified. If, as Ellsberg and the *Times* believed, the American public agreed to sustain the hostilities only because they were misinformed about what was happening in South Vietnam, there was a strong moral obligation to expose the fraud.

Breaches of national security can be motivated by the highest form of patriotism. Nobody now blames Winston Churchill for using highly classified secrets given to him by senior officials to reveal in public speeches the frightening weakness of the Royal Air Force when Hitler was preparing for war.

Though it is primarily up to the executive to defend its secrets, journalists should have no conscientious objection to fruitful discussions with officials about how much information they should print. All serious reporters receive part of their information "off the record": those who regard such practices as intrinsically evil should go into another profession.

As Watergate showed, there are occasions when the press has to supplement the security forces and expose iniquity in high places. Collaboration with officials on certain matters of common interest does not relieve reporters from the task of being Alan Barth's watchdog. Each case has to be judged within its special context.

The relation between journalists and their sources must be delicate: James Reston of the New York *Times* has said he prefers to keep some distance between himself and the White House rather than get involved in a personal relationship that might preclude extracting information and passing objective judgments. Many other reporters, on the contrary, would give their back teeth for access to the president.

Both views can be defended. One of the best definitions of the journalist's role was by J. T. Delane, who became editor of the London *Times* when he was twenty-three years old and held the job for forty years, a term of office which ended precisely a century ago.[11] Delane conducted voluminous correspondence with every leading statesman of his generation and often knew a good deal more than they did about what was going on in the outside world. Having been publicly attacked in the House of Commons for writing offensively on Louis Napoleon when Britain was trying to improve its relations with France, Delane retorted: "We do not interfere with the duties of statesmen; our vocation is, in one respect, inferior to theirs, for we are unable to wield the power or represent the collective dignity of the country; but in another point of view it is superior, for unlike them, we are able to speak the whole truth without fear or favour."

As the present editor of the *Times* would readily admit, the paper has not always lived up to these high principles; it has sometimes betrayed fear and sometimes curried favor. But the old tradition is still honored, and every year, on the anniversary of Delane's death, the *Times* carries an *in memoriam* notice.

Since Delane's day the area of government activity has hugely increased. The media have new problems of recruiting enough competent people to write about such subjects as health, environment, energy, and other vital issues that cannot be treated intelligently without wide reading and specialization.

Journalists should not think they can avoid leg work by taking their problems to the expanding staff of government press offices. These organizations, properly used, can help put a journalist in touch with the appropriate expert or provide indispensable basic documents. On the other hand, a reporter must resist the temptation to settle for what he is told, without bearing in mind that the teller is appointed by and for the authorities and is unlikely to reveal the more embarrassing or unsuccessful aspects of his masters' record. I say "unlikely," because this is not always true. There are some public relation workers in Washington and London who recognize that they will not be taken seriously if they try to conceal troubles and reverses, which a good reporter will anyway ferret out. The relationship between the sophisticated press officers and the writer tends to resemble an Oriental bazaar: deals are struck discreetly, and each side privately believes it got the best of the bargain.

CONCLUSION

While holding to the first principle that it is the duty of a journalist or broadcaster to tell the truth as he sees it, it will have become clear from this account that a journalistic career is an endless series of deals and compromises. Nobody wields absolute power, and in a pluralist, consumerist society, there is often not much space or interest for what the reporter believes the public ought to know.

There are no simple criteria on what should or should not be published. Nor is there any clear rule about how far any writer should go in allowing his copy to be tampered with, his sources to be compromised, or his employers to use his material in ways he finds objectionable and dishonest. The question of whether or not to resign will have to be judged on its own merits, and within the context of the time and circumstances.

Any student of journalism who thinks such decisions will be easy should remember the response of Bernard Shaw's Andrew Undershaft to his young son, Stephen, who had confessed that he had no particular qualifications but claimed at least to know the difference between right and wrong:

> You don't say so. What? No capacity for business, no knowledge of law, no sympathy with art, no pretension to philosophy; only a simple knowledge of the secret that has puzzled all the philosophers, baffled all the lawyers, muddled all the men of business and ruined most of the artists: the secret of right and wrong. Why, man, you're a genius, a master of masters, a god! At 24, too.[12]

In the play, Stephen replied, "You are pleased to be facetious. I pretend to nothing more than any English gentleman may claim as his birthright." In Britain, already in Shaw's own time, the happy certitudes about right and wrong were already vanishing. In the United States they survived rather longer.

Shaw himself regarded all journalists as cynics. There are of course many in the profession who regard newspaper and TV channels as nothing more than the vehicles to carry advertisements from business firms to the consumer. There are others who are in the business for the glory or the cash. But these are unlikely to be reading this chapter. For the many who care about maintaining an open society and getting as near the truth as they can, there will be occasions when they will have to exercise their ethical as well as their professional judgment. Decisions have to be made fast and often in isolation. Journalists are lonely people. They must do the best they can.

NOTES

1. Alan Barth, "A Free and Irresponsible Press," Washington *Post*, September 5, 1977.

2. Charles Wintour, *Pressures on the Press: An Editor Looks at Fleet Street* (London, 1972).

3. C. P. Scott, editor of the *Manchester Guardian* (now the *Guardian*), 1871 to 1932.

4. *The Banker,* London, October 1977.

5. The Royal Commission on the Press, *Final Report,* July 1977 (London: HMSO).

6. The Royal Commission on the Press, *Interim Report,* March 1976.

7. Rex Winsbury, *New Technology and the Press,* prepared for the Royal Commission on the Press, (London: HMSO, 1975).

8. Nora Beloff, "Last Chance for British Newspapers" *Encounter,* July 1977.

9. Nora Beloff, *Freedom under Foot: the Battle over the Closed Shop in British Journalism.*

10. *Trade Union and Labour Relations (Amendment) Act,* March 1976.

11. Philip Howard, "J. T. Delane, Prince of Editors," *The Times,* London, November 9, 1977.

12. Bernard Shaw, *Major Barbara,* act 3.

4 THE FAIRNESS DOCTRINE

Everett C. Parker

The concept of fairness is as old as the American system of broadcasting. It was first enunciated by the Federal Radio Commission and approved by the courts in the 1929 Great Lakes Broadcasting Co. case. It was established then that "public interest requires ample play for the free and fair competition of opposing views" on the air.

Soon after the commission indicated that use of a public channel to make unfounded personal attacks was not consistent with good broadcast service.

Broadcast regulation had begun in 1927, when the fledging commercial operators—venal then as now—went to Congress to beg for government oversight that would stop them from stealing each other's frequencies. Congress gave the industry what it wanted. About 160 stations were silenced—many of them operated by churches, schools, and other nonprofit organizations. Congress recognized then, however, and has held ever since, that the airwaves are the common property of all of us. It required that few who were lucky enough to get licenses to operate their stations as public trustees and to provide time to the many who were denied licenses, so they could discuss public concerns.

The rule of fairness was refined and clarified in a number of cases over the next two decades. Consistent with the concept that the channels were to provide expression for the public and not for the station owners, it was held that "the broadcaster cannot be an advocate," which was taken to mean that stations should not editorialize.

Broadcasters strongly protested this ruling, claiming that it "muzzled" them, depriving them of freedom of speech. The rule was reconsidered in the *Mayflower* hearings. It was finally revised and set forth in a comprehensive statement of commission policy, titled the "1949 Editorializing Report." This statement reversed the previous policy against editorializing by broadcast licenses but coupled the right to editorialize with the duty to present alternative views. This policy has become known as the "Fairness Doctrine."

One of the problems in discussing the Fairness Doctrine is that few people, even broadcasting executives, understand its purpose, and even fewer understand its practical operation. If one listened only to the hoopla against it from industry and some segments of Congress, one would believe that the Fairness Doctrine is a system for bureaucratic regulation of network news. Actually, it has little to do with either networks or news.

The Fairness Doctrine is simplicity itself. The Federal Communications Commission (FCC) directs stations "to afford reasonable opportunity for the discussion of conflicting views on issues of public importance." In plain English, the Fairness Doctrine requires two things: First, every radio and television station must devote a reasonable portion of its broadcast time to the discussion of controversial issues of public importance. Second, whatever issues a station raises, it must give a balanced presentation of views. Few broadcasters disagree in principle with this requirement; but they grumble about having government officials involved in interpreting and enforcing it. Like most government regulations, the Fairness Doctrine leads to many fine distinctions and much hairsplitting, particularly when the regulated industry wants to tread very close to the line. But this is a normal burden of doing business.

The biggest outcry, though, is that the Fairness Doctrine chills discussion and intimidates journalists. This is poppycock. The affirmative obligation placed upon stations to cover controversial issues is the chief reason most broadcasters *hire* journalists. If it weren't for the Fairness Doctrine, it is likely that serious journalists would have to become scriptwriters for Norman Lear if they wanted to deal with important public questions on the air.

The FCC receives about 2,000 fairness complaints a year. Less than 3 percent of these complaints are against networks, and less than 1 percent against network news. The great majority of the requests ask for time to answer station editorials, or attacks or opinions on call-in programs or paid opinion programs, such as those of Billy James Harges or Carl McIntire. The well-healed Conservative Union recently undertook a purchased-time television blitz against the Panama Canal treaties. In such instances journalism becomes irrelevant. Decisions about program balance are left to time salesmen. There is no reason to believe that broadcasters will balance such paid programming on controversial issues unless the FCC requires them to do so.

The FCC writes about 150 letters a year asking stations to respond to fairness complaints. Since there are nearly 8,000 broadcast licensees, simple arithmetic shows that the typical station would have to answer a complaint once in 73 years—less when we take into account the fact that a few stations, such as those that carry Carl McIntire, receive the vast majority of the complaints. Most broadcast stations have never had to answer a fairness complaint.

The FCC sustains only about five complaints a year. This means that the average station will be directed to provide time for opposing viewpoints about once in every 1,300 years. Not a very frightening prospect! Balance that against the timidity of broadcasters who shy away from controversy on the air under pressure from advertisers and their own salesmen who fear the effect on audience ratings and time sales.

Without the Fairness Doctrine, probably a majority of licensees would avoid controversy altogether.

Let me give you an example of such broadcaster duplicity. Recently, the FCC, in one of its rare enforcements of the Fairness Doctrine, required a station in West Virginia to broadcast a program prepared by Rep. Patsy Mink on strip mining, which it has previously refused. The station had blandly informed the FCC that it had a policy never to deal with this issue because it might be divisive.

Today many radio stations broadcast only automated programs. They insert commercial announcements into a day-long tape recording that is supplied by a program format syndicator. These licensees have come to believe that they can get away with being only sellers of time within a canned music format. A station in New York City actually petitioned the FCC to be relieved of any obligation to broadcast news, opinion, and other public affairs programs.

The networks avoid controversy even more than do the local stations, by refraining from editorializing. But television networks have audiences in the tens of millions. One might therefore expect that they would have great difficulty with the Fairness Doctrine. However, to the best of my knowledge, neither CBS nor ABC has ever been directed to provide opposing views to their viewpoints. NBC has had two brushes with fairness directives: once when Chet Huntley editorialized against a meat-inspection bill without revealing his financial interest in the matter, and the "Pensions" case, when the management of the network decided to parlay a routine news decision into a court test of an FCC ruling that they should at some future time present views counter to those in their documentary. Obviously, neither of these episodes represented a daily problem of network news departments.

Much more serious is the provision in the Public Broadcasting Act that prohibits educational stations from editorializing and requires internal balance within each program that deals with a controversial issue. Congress has thus created an invidious bridle on free speech in public television and radio. While commercial stations are expected to present a multiplicity of views on controversial issues, they need not do so in a single program or even in the same time period.

Broadcasters have another argument against the Fairness Doctrine. They claim there is no scarcity of stations; therefore, there should be no Fairness Doctrine. In 1968, the networks hired some of the most eminent lawyers in the United States to try that argument out on the Supreme Court in the famous *Red Lion* case. The court held against them by an unanimous 8–0 vote. It pointed out that there are far more people who would like to obtain broadcast licenses than there are frequencies available. Therefore, the court held: "[I]t is idle to posit an unabridgeable First Amendment right to broadcast comparable to the right of every individual to speak, write or publish ... [t]he people as a whole retain their interest in free speech by radio and their collective right to have the medium function consistently with the ends and purposes of the First Amendment. It is the right of the viewers and listeners, not the right of the broadcasters, which is paramount."

The real reason why the networks and many stations oppose the Fairness Doctrine is the urge to make money. The networks are in the entertainment business. That is where the money is. Everything else is incidental. William S. Paley, the head of CBS, who regularly claims the Fairness Doctrine is a bridle on free speech, is reported to demand a 20 percent increase in profits every year. That kind of policy does not leave much time available "to afford reasonable opportunity for the discussion of conflicting views on issues of public importance." In the 1977–78 season the networks, in their dog-eat-dog battle for the number-one spot in prime-time entertainment programming, have thrown aside all pretense of serving the public interest with a multiplicity of programs that deal with vital controversial issues. And that in the face of a profit increase in the last year of over 70 percent!

Furthermore, the networks pitch their prime-time entertainment and advertising to a minority of less than 40 percent of the population, the people from 18 to 49 years old who are affluent enough to buy "the good life" depicted in the commercials. Network policy makers feed these people a steady diet of sports, violence, and explicit sex, evidently in the belief that they are turned off by ballot and economic issues that affect them vitally and by programs that may be culturally enriching. Equally alarming is the way the networks are transforming news into entertainment on such shows as "Today" and "Good Morning America." Some local stations—including those licensed to the networks—engage in even worse prostitution of news with their corny humor and their feature formats that are mass-produced by outside manipulators such as Megid. When there is public outcry against these excesses, the broadcasters claim free-speech privileges.

It is hard to understand why ABC and NBC and many independent stations make a mockery of news when the more progressive stations are using the new, miniaturized equipment to do imaginative, exciting on-the-spot coverage and are making money at it.

Broadcast journalists sometimes complain of the "chilling" effect of working under a system where what is reported may later be challenged by opposing views. As John O'Connor of the New York *Times* has pointed out, "No one in journalism—print or electronic—likes to be challenged. And all journalists want to maintain control over their own product." But despite the best of intentions, journalists do make outright errors and wrong interpretations. On the air, there can be biased nuances. Bulletin-type reporting usually omits diversity of opinion.

Broadcast journalism has not developed the op-ed page concept that Congress meant it to have and that is available in many newspapers. Just look at the number of corrections that the New York *Times* publishes every day; or the varied—and often opposing—viewpoints that are represented in a detailed story. Broadcast journalism has not developed equally open and adequate mechanisms that give opposing viewpoints the opportunity to be aired. Nor is there any indication that network corporate policy makers have any interest in providing such mechanisms to give access to the air to a multiplicity of persons and viewpoints.

The First Amendment was devised to protect the right of the people to speak freely and to circulate their ideas widely so they might debate issues and ferret out the truth, and thus govern themselves wisely. The framers did not contemplate a monopoly on the effective means of circulating information and ideas—especially such a monopoly as exists through television networks, our chief purveyors of information, entertainment, and taste-setting standards. Nor did the framers mean to establish a self-appointed class of individuals called journalists who can take on the role of sole arbiters of what is true and worthwhile for the people to know.

Our society is increasingly dependent upon electronic media to disseminate ideas and to provide a forum for the debate of issues. Free speech requires access to the forum where speech can be heard. Therefore, a diversity of persons must have access to the electronic media. A journalist has an important role—to seek out and expose. But having done this, the journalist cannot insist that his or her exposition is the last word. It is the beginning not the end of the democratic process of debate and problem solving.

Unfortunately, there are some broadcasters who think that their decisions should be final and irreversible. They claim an immunity from review and criticism that would have embarrassed James I. Now, I do not claim that the Fairness Doctrine or any doctrine is perfect. I have pointed out that improvements need to be made in the way in which the public forum is handled by broadcasters. Similar improvements are needed in the way in which the Fairness Doctrine is regulated by the FCC. However, no progress will be made until broadcasters acknowledge that they do have the responsibility to carry the views of others, and that they, like all other public trustees, are accountable for the way in which they carry out their responsibilities.

Part II   Covering Publics

5 How the Press Treats Women

Joan Behrmann

Even a cursory acquaintance with American newspapers and magazines might give the casual reader the notion that men and women do not fare equally. Is that impression correct? A careful examination of the evidence—the printed word, tone as well as content—indicates that the treatment of women in the press through the years has been as patronizing, sexist, and downright discriminatory as the journalistic institutions' treatment of its female employees.

Women newsmakers have not fared any better than the women who have been assigned by male editors to write about them. From the beginnings of American journalism, women and women's issues have been ignored or belittled by a predominantly male press. Even today, when young women fill the nation's journalism schools, and women reporters number in the thousands, the women who have climbed to management positions in journalism are a tiny, hardy handful.

Traditionally, the press has been a man's world. It may have shed the green eyeshade, press-card-in-fedora, and bottle-in-the-desk movie myth, but the sea of white shirts in the newsroom is as real today as in the films of the 1940s. Until recently, most women have not understood their situation or have not been willing to try to change it. Working as what one reporter has called "happy darkies down on the plantation,"[1] women reporters have endured inequities in hiring, salary, assignment, and promotion, while female news subjects have been ridiculed or ignored.

Only in the past decade have women begun to try to change this unhappy picture. The last few years have seen the launching of sex-discrimination suits against major newspapers and magazines, sit-ins in editorial offices and picketing outside, and hundreds of feminist publications.

Women now protest references that they consider sexist and photographs they consider demeaning. Even the conservatively oriented wire services are changing the way they refer to women. In fact, a backlash is emerging: reporter Sally Quinn of the Washington *Post* complained to a Saint Louis conference in September 1977 that her newspaper is obsessed with "chairpersons, congresspersons and policepersons."[2] But a large metropolitan daily like the *Post,* staffed with women who patrol its pages for signs of chauvinism, is exceptional; in most newspapers it's far too early for a backlash to develop. Newspapers are still at the barricades, just beginning to deal with accusations of sexist stories and employee discrimination.

Most observers point to the women's liberation movement as the catalyst for this new consciousness. Women who felt newly liberated wanted a press that would not belittle their aims and abilities. So the feminists involved in the movement began to call attention to the national press's errant ways. Additionally, many women reporters assigned to cover the movement's early days came back newly aware of their own lowly professional status. Both from within and without, pressure was brought to bear on heavily masculine editorial offices. Many newspapers and magazines are now in the process of altering or investigating traditional procedures. But much of the press still has a long way to go to reach a semblance of equality.

FOREMOTHERS AND THE PRESS

Early news stories often contained the same patriarchal approach to women's issues that today's feminists decry, along with a systematic devaluing of women's experience. The nation's male editors first faced the problem of the emergent woman in the 1840s, at the start of the women's rights movement. Inadequate coverage of that movement, along with the media's condescending attitude, was as much of a deterrent to the promotion of women's rights in 1848 as it is today.[3] Newspapers generally deplored the first women's rights meeting at Seneca Falls, New York, in 1848; the *Mechanic's Advocate* of Albany headlined their story, "Women out of Their Latitude,"[4] and the Worcester, Massachusetts, *Telegram* called the convention an attempt at "insurrection."[5]

Editorial pages echoed the press's hostility toward women's emergence as voting citizens. James Gordon Bennett, publisher of the New York *Herald,* wrote of the dismaying possibility that women might hear indecent language, were they to be elected to Congress. He further suggested that witnesses might see Lucy Stone in the throes of childbirth while she pleaded a court case.[6] But a sense of fair play was not entirely lost. When Susan B. Anthony was arrested for voting illegally in 1872, her strong defense gained her the support of several newspapers, and when she was found guilty, the Rochester *Democrat* and *Chronicle* headlined the story, "An Outrage."[7]

Among those newspapers that sympathized with the antisuffragists was the New York *Times*. A 1909 interview with Edward W. Bok, the editor of the *Ladies Home Journal*, quoted him at length on his belief that an overwhelming percentage of women was opposed to suffrage. The "average American woman is too busy" with home and family, said Bok.[8] When the *Times* covered the appearance of Mother Jones, the human rights crusader, at a 1914 suffragist dinner, the reporter paid more attention to her wardrobe than to her politics. Readers were informed that ". . . she wore a figured bodice with the dark skirt of her gown. There were ruffles at the neck and wrists; little dangley ornaments at the latter. . . ."[9] Jones was then eighty-two. And when Charles Evans Hughes, Republican presidential candidate in 1916, endorsed the suffrage amendment, the *Times* called it "a surprise and sorrow to many of us."[10] A 1917 editorial declared, "The sight of high-bred women disturbing the peace in pursuit of their petty whim while the nation is at war is deplorable," and a later editorial referred to militant suffrage action as "terrorism."[11] Two days before the Nineteenth Amendment was adopted, the *Times* ran this editorial:

> . . . The attainment of the right of suffrage is only the beginning of a long experiment, beset by many difficulties. Some of them are appalling. There is, for example, the question of the colored woman in the South. There are foreign-born women of the great cities in the North. There are sheltered classes and the ignorant classes. Will they not feel "the weight of too much liberty?" . . .[12]

The media generally reflect society's dominant attitudes; journalistic initiative seldom serves as a catalyst for change. Additionally, a common press function is to act as a sounding-board for opinion makers of the time, echoing the ideas of any theorist who stands ready to be interviewed. Thus the *Times* interview with Bok in 1909; thus in a 1916 *Times* story, Harvard University's physical director warned women against emulating men in sports. Women should confine themselves to the "lighter and more graceful forms of gymnastics and athletics," said this expert.[13] Thus Mrs. Samuel Gompers, bride of the labor leader, told *Times* readers in 1921 that women whose husbands earn a good salary should not seek jobs in the business world.[14] And in 1970, a Utah criminologist told Boston readers that the quest for equal rights has led some women to become "vulgar and criminal."[15]

Magazines and newspapers of the 1920s generally viewed women who worked as a threat to the family; a *McCall's* editorial in 1929 predicted that only as a wife and mother could the American woman arrive at her true eminence.[16] In *The Feminine Mystique,* Betty Friedan advanced the theory that women's magazines first set out to keep women happy at home in the years after 1945, but some researchers believe that the glorification of domesticity dominated the pages of women's magazines long before that time.[17] Was the press of that time simply reflecting the prevailing societal view, or was there a deliberate journalistic conspiracy to hold women down? Friedan thinks it was the latter. In her interviews with women's magazine editors, she found that "the new image of woman as housewife-mother has been largely created by writers and editors who are men . . . back from the war, who had been dreaming about home and a cozy domestic life. Today, the deciding voice on most of these magazines is cast by men. Women often carry out the formulas, women edit the housewife and service department, but the formulas themselves, which have dictated the new housewife image, are the product of men's minds."[18]

It may have been this male cast of mind that caused reporters to remark persistently on the physical appearance of their female subjects. Was this simply good reporting, or was it part of the patronizing tone, the "ladies, God bless 'em" attitude that feminists have objected to through the years? In the nineteenth century, the Bloomer Girls came in for their share of press ridicule when stories presented bloomers as a major issue of the women's rights movement. It reinforced the male conviction that women were solely concerned about fashion and beauty.[19]

A *Times* story in 1905 told of a visit to police court by the Prison Relief Association. The lead of the story described them as ". . . well-dressed women, a few of them armed with important-looking documents, others with the ordinary packages and reticules that usually adorn the sex when on an outing. . . ."[20] Another *Times* account, of a 1903 speech by Jane Addams, described, again in the lead,

> . . . a large audience, largely of women, so that a glance over the hall revealed a bewildering scene of millinery and the art of the dressmaker. There were so many attractive bonnets and gowns that it would seem as if the wearers could have no other thought in life than to obtain suitable raiment . . . but the eagerness of the listeners to catch every word said and the spontaneity with which they caught and applauded the more telling points in the addresses showed that

the women were in earnest and had apparently devoted more time to the problems of sociology than to the latest creations of the Parisian modistes.[21]

A 1935 *Times* story on Polly Adler has some historic interest; it marked one of the rare occasions when the *Times* made an exception to its usual style of reference to women as "Miss" or "Mrs." Charged with keeping a disorderly house, she was called "the Adler woman" throughout the story. She was described: "... short, stocky, with heavily rouged lips and cheeks and brightly tinted finger nails, the Adler woman wore an expensive fur coat ..."[22]—clearly, the wages of sin.

Newspapers have documented the enormous changes in women's lives from 1848 to today with particular emphasis on the "gee-whiz" story, or "what won't they think of next?" As the women's movement gained momentum in the early 1970s, stories of woman "firsts" became so commonplace they entered the realm of cliché. One women's-page editor recalls seeing a steady stream of wire service stories on the first policewoman, rabbi, minister, FBI agent, truck driver, telephone line-person. These were followed by stories on the "first black woman to ..." and even by stories on the "first blind woman to...."

The problem with writing such stories, journalists found, was that once they had explained the immediate news—that a woman was performing work hitherto thought of as masculine—there was little left to say. And was this truly covering women's news, or was it merely paying lip service to a burgeoning movement by noting the advances of a few pioneers?

Individual women may have been deeply unhappy about their treatment from the media, but it wasn't until *The Feminine Mystique* pinpointed the problem that national attention fixed on the media. For the first time, the media image of women was condemned: "young and frivolous, almost childlike; fluffy and feminine, passive; gaily content in a world of bedroom and kitchen, sex, babies and home."[23]

In the same year that *Mystique* was published, the President's Commission on the Status of Women asked representatives of the communications industry for advice on the portrayal of women by the media. Margaret Hickey of the *Ladies' Home Journal* opened with the charge that the mass media were "projecting, intentionally or unintentionally, an image that contains old myths, misconceptions, and even distortions, of a true image."[24] Again, this was 1963, well before the days of the so-called bra-burners, headlines about "libbers," and all the other cacaphony accompanying press coverage of the women's movement as it grew.

THE WOMEN'S MOVEMENT IN THE PRESS

Examination of media coverage of the women's movement, the major "women's story" of the past fifteen years, reveals many of journalism's major weaknesses. Feminist leaders have called stories about the movement superficial and degrading, inadequate, uninformed, and biased toward the status quo. They object to such headlines as "Women's Lib Members Act Like Ladies";[25] they resist references to bra-burners, insisting that the burning of undergarments was always a figment of some male editor's imagination.

Confronted by a story for which they were unprepared, and which they did not understand, the press tended to snicker. Most of the media treated early women's liberation activities with "a mixture of humor, ridicule and disbelief."[26] Photographers snapped feminists in unattractive poses; reporters commented on their femininity, marital status, or wardrobe more than on their views. Some reporters were told by their editors to "find an authority who'll say this is all a crock of shit."[27] Often the alternative or underground press was the worst offender, illustrating stories on the women's movement with pictures of naked women and genitalia.[28]

Regarding this treatment as a complete lack of understanding by the establishment press, some leaders of the movement reacted by declining to talk to male reporters. In fact, both sides of the issue dealt in stereotypes: television producer Gwen Dillard, then a Washington, D.C., reporter, recalls covering a movement rally and hearing constant references to the "pig media."[29] When women reporters began to cover the issue, many of the early stories became stories of personal conversion; women journalists began to focus on their own second-class working conditions. But at the same time, many disillusioned feminists had decided they could not deal with the established media at all. Assuming that only their own publications would give them fair coverage, they initiated more than 150 feminist papers and journals.[30]

The feminist tabloid *Off Our Backs,* founded in 1970, published a statement of purpose explaining its founders' bafflement at dealing with the media. The media works to create leaders, they said—a phenomenon that brings out the counterrevolutionary traits in people. They viewed the Establishment press as transforming events into whatever reality it wished to project, and women's liberation did not fit into that reality. Reasoning that each time they responded to the media they further legitimized it, the women called for a stop to all dealings with the mass media.[31]

One male critic called the movement's ability to make news its most notable characteristic. William Chafe praised feminist leaders for their skill in drawing public attention to themselves.[32] But he also admitted that in most cases the movement was being exploited by the media for entertainment purposes.[33]

Feminist author Germaine Greer described media coverage of this non-Establishment entity:

> Despite the generally derisive attitude of the press, female liberation movements have so far been very much a phenomenon of the media. The gargantuan appetite of the newspapers for novelty has led to the anomaly of women's liberation stories appearing alongside the advertisements for emulsified fats to grease the skin, scented douches to render the vagina more agreeable, and all the rest of the marketing for and by the feminine stereotype. Female liberation movements are good for news stories because of their atmosphere of perversion, female depravity, sensation and solemn absurdity.[34]

Greer believed that much of the sneering in the press was lost on women readers, and in cases where it was recognized, it provoked sympathy for the persons who were being exploited. "Every time a statement by a woman seeking liberation ... reaches the newspapers, the response is enormous. ... For every woman who writes a letter to the editor there are hundreds who can't manage it, and every time a male writes in derision and fear the point is underlined a hundredfold. It is to be hoped that more and more women decide to influence the media by writing for them, not being written about."[35]

To explore the question of why the women's movement received the press it did—and often still does—is to examine the basic media issue of what news is—and who decides.

Wilma Scott Heide became a national newsmaker as the president of the National Organization for Women (NOW) in the early 1970s. Out of her long, often bitter experience with the media, Heide says that decisions about what is newsworthy have always reflected the interests of men. "If it represents conflicts and differences, it gets more attention than stories of cooperation and compromise."

Heide believes the press has cheated women as well as the nation by shutting feminist thought out of its pages. "I see feminism as applying to every human endeavor, a different way of looking at our potential. This has not been communicated through the media. People have been deprived of our insights," she says. "We have been denied access to the forum, denied our First Amendment rights. Feminism is a process—you can't define it. We're talking about oppression of women by exclusion, by devaluing, in all our institutions, and with that the devaluing and repressing of feminine traits and values."

The newsmakers, says Heide, are "the experts—who are usually men. Or if they're women, they are not feminists."

In her view, the news media constantly emphasize conflict, differences, a win-lose setup. "Competitiveness is a male thing ... many women have tried to resist it." This is exemplified, she believes, in the media's inclination to write about shortcomings and disagreements in the women's movement. She mentions magazine stories that ask if the movement is dead, a story in the June 1977 *Saturday Review,* "Women against Women: The Clamor over Equal Rights." The issue, she says, is a rejection of patriarchy, not women against women. Then she adds an aside, "I've never been able to get anything in the *Saturday Review.*"

Even as president of NOW, Heide had problems getting into print. She wrote open letters, proposals, suggested op-ed pieces, news releases "on substantive issues, that were not picked up. If my male counterpart had written them, they would have been." "So many things I and other change agents have done that have never been properly publicized that friends have suggested they be put in a volume, 'A Women's Book of Knowledge Refused.' " She recalls occasions when her testimony before congressional committees was taken out of context, when her open letters to President Nixon were not printed. She mentions a press conference in New York after a feminist art show, when a male photographer was caught taking pictures of—legs. "We separated him from his camera," she says, "and we learned that he had been instructed by his editors to take those pictures." She sighed. "If we don't take ourselves seriously, no one else will."

Heide feels the media seek the colorful and flamboyant figure—which she is not. She has asked editors, she says, to make corrections in stories, only to have editors reply that the issue was no longer timely. Timeliness as a news criteria is "faddish," she believes—"feminism is a timeless, ongoing issue." Heide thinks the media needs a crash course in feminism. "Feminist publications wouldn't exist if the regular media covered issues of importance to women."[36]

Many of Heide's complaints have been voiced by other newsmakers, male and female. Few news figures ever get all their press releases in print. Almost everyone who has ever been interviewed complains about words taken out of context and about the media's lack of understanding and expertise in their particular subject area. Has there ever been a news-story subject who felt the press truly understood what he or she was trying to explain, who didn't think their coverage was superficial or inadequate to some degree? After all, *they* didn't write it, someone else did; that's always a problem when an event or issue is translated through another person's system of beliefs and prejudices.

But Heide is talking about something more insidious: a pervasive shut-out of women and women's issues.

IWY, ERA, AND OTHER WOMEN'S ISSUES

Criticism of the coverage of two major continuing stories—the Equal Rights Amendment (ERA) and International Women's Year (IWY)—has focused on many of the issues raised by Heide—bias, superficiality, a lack of understanding.

Jill Ruckelshaus, presiding officer of the National Commission on Observance of IWY, has been a constant critic of IWY coverage. The importance of the 1975 conference in Mexico City was underestimated, she said, because the people who decide what is news were not as familiar as they should have been with the impetus and widespread support that existed for the women's movement. Many major papers didn't send reporters to the conference, Ruckelshaus said, but relied on wire service stories or on stringers. In an interview with the Washington *Star,* she noted that the *Star* "felt perfectly comfortable about writing an editorial attacking the conference even though they had no one there sending them information ... I thought the editorial was very patronizing and sexist."[37]

Many reporters at the conference were dismayed over their home editors' deletions, Ruckelshaus added. "They would write substantive articles, then get queried about some paper running a story over a fight over a microphone and wanted some information on that. . . . What was important was thousands of women working together on a major plan, not women fighting for fifteen seconds over possession of a microphone."

Ruckelshaus reasoned that these problems occurred because the IWY was a women's conference, and the media power structure is male. Not enough women in media are in decision-making positions, she said. She seized the occasion of a speech before the National Press Club to give reporters and editors some examples of the "slick locker-room stereotypes" she said they perpetuated. At the opening day of the IWY conference, she told them, some Mexican women demonstrated outside the hall. Hearing of this, the press rushed out, causing some commotion. Secretary-General Waldheim had to gavel twice to restore order among the press. But, said Ruckelshaus, next day a wire service story read, "Waldheim had to gavel twice for order because there was so much chattering among the 5,000 women." Preconceived notions, she said, prevented accurate coverage.[38]

In spring 1977 the IWY held federally funded meetings in each state to prepare for a November conference in Houston. When Dorothy Jurney, former assistant managing editor of the Philadelphia *Inquirer*, sought nationwide publicity for those meetings, she had some difficulty convincing male editors of their importance.[39] Sey Chassler, editor-in-chief of *Redbook*, served as chair of the Press and Media Committee of the National Commission on Observance of IWY. Just before the state IWY meetings, he warned women in the media, "This is the most significant thing that's happened for women, but you know better than I do how hard it is to get coverage of news about women."[40] After the meetings were held, writer Nancy Peterson criticized the lack of advance publicity. In examining coverage across the country, Peterson found that media interest in the meetings picked up only as political controversy built around the ERA and abortion issues. The focus, she said, was on conflict rather than on education of the participants.[41]

Coverage of the Equal Rights Amendment battle has been criticized by both opponents and supporters of the measure. Jill Ruckelshaus told the National Press Club in 1975 that the ERA issue has been "a prime example of poor coverage over the years." She cited a content analysis of letters and articles that appeared in twelve South Carolina dailies at the time of that state's ERA hearings, produced by the school of journalism at the University of South Carolina. Of the sixty-nine articles surveyed, thirty-six held a negative view of the ERA, thirteen were favorable, and nineteen were rated neutral. She quoted the study: "In reporting on the issues, events and personalities surrounding the ERA, the press used almost every known stereotype of women and the women's movement." Newspapers treated the issue in a joking, cavalier way, she said. Some samples headlines: "House Bubbles, Brews Over Equal Rights Amendment"; "Sex Freedom Hearing Kicks Off Week"; "Irate ERA Supporters Seek Revenge."

Ruckelshaus also decried what she saw as a lack of true investigative pieces. Newspapers have balanced opinions of the Stop-ERA organization against the Senate Judiciary Report, she said, which she believes is wrong—"the two just aren't equal, and to report them as such in the media is to give a misleading impression."[42]

Not all critics agree with Ruckelshaus's estimation. Writer James Fordham told the media journal *More* that the press has played an advocacy role for the ERA. His reasoning stemmed from treatment afforded to an article he and his wife had written for the Washington *Post* criticizing ERA coverage. His article, he said, took up thirty-five column inches, while more than fifty inches were allotted for rebuttal.[43]

Criticism of the coverage of women's issues is so readily available that only a few examples need be given for the picture to become clear. For every James Fordham who feels that the press has given good play to a women's issue, there are hundreds who say that the press has never opened its pages to women's issues and women newsmakers in anywhere near an equal portion to its coverage of male-oriented events. For example, a study of editors' news criteria showed that editors considered women to be newsmakers only if they belonged in one of these categories: an important husband, beauty, victimization, political significance, performance in the arts or athletics, ability as a homemaker, and "first" status.[44]

Boston *Globe* reporter Nina McCain made a comparison of newsspace assignments in her paper's pages in 1973. Surveying several issues at random, she found that "the total percentage of news about women was miniscule—even counting wedding stories." McCain believes the paper's real weakness is the sin of omission, the story that never gets into print. "All of the editors are male," she says, "and they care about politics and sports coverage. Day care doesn't make it."[45] When female reporters at the Washington *Post* complained about male bias in decisions on what was to be covered, they cited inadequate coverage of such issues as women's rights, health, consumer news, day care, abortion, and welfare.[46]

Selected newspapers in the United States and Great Britain from 1968–70 were analyzed by Monica Morris to judge the extent of their coverage of the women's movement. Surveying two Los Angeles dailies and nine British papers, she concluded that newspapers in both countries tended to withhold information about the newly emerging movement, which was active enough to have been covered by the press during those time spans. If the media's function is to affirm the status quo, Morris suggests, the results of her survey are not surprising. It could be said that editors simply did not regard the women's movement as important enough to warrant newspaper space. But one of the newspapers surveyed, the Sunday *Times* of London, did give the movement extensive coverage in September 1969, indicating that at least one gatekeeper considered it important enough to be brought to public attention.[47]

Women athletes and women's sports have found it difficult to break into all-male sports sections. Women's sports don't as yet draw large audiences, nor are they big money events, an argument sports editors use to shut out news of high school, college, or professional women's teams. One female sportswriter told a 1976 journalist's meeting that her paper, the Louisville *Courier-Journal* and *Times*, was one of the few in the country that gives equal space to boy and girl high school athletics. "There were all those years in the past when we didn't do anything at all with women's athletics and now they're ... on the verge of a new frontier," she said.[48]

A near-shutout of women's issues even extends to such a prestigious media journal as the *Columbia Journalism Review.* A special issue in winter 1969–70, entitled "Are the Media Ready for the Seventies?" contains no mention of women or women's issues, thereby missing one of the larger media issues of the 1970s and answering their own question in the negative.[49] Not only has the *Review* paid little attention to women in its fifteen years of existence, but it uses few women writers. One reader, an editor on her college newspaper, wrote to the *Review* in 1973: "I find the coverage of women in journalism lacking. I have never seen an article in the *Review* on women's attempts at journalistic recognition." She adds, "I could become very discouraged as to a future for myself if I were to read only the *Review.*"[50]

THE "WOMEN'S SECTION"

For years editors have used a standard rejoinder for critics who have accused them of a blackout on women's issues. Their fail-safe has been the women's pages, the traditional ghetto for the stories and the staffers that don't seem to belong in the rest of the paper. Society news, club notes, food, fashions, home furnishings—this was the women's-page diet. Designed to placate women readers, it also served the necessary function of providing editorial matter to surround the advertising directed to female pocketbooks. Lindsy Van Gelder, writing in *Ms.,* called the women's pages "a dumping ground for anything the male editors consider a women's story."[51] On the other hand, women's-page editors argue that when they develop a good story, it is often stolen for page one. Even in the 1960s, alert women's editors complained that women's sections were not recognized as news sections. Gloria Biggs, then women's editor of the Gannett News Service, complained to the Associated Press Managing Editors (APME) that AP often did not supply the women's angle on a big news story to the women's sections of the newspapers it served.[52]

Women's pages were often designed to look different from the rest of the newspaper, an outgrowth of some (male) editor's idea that these pages should somehow emit a more feminine aura than the straightforward Bodoni Bold of the news pages. The so-called feminine typefaces are certainly more graceful and ladylike; but they are also more difficult to read than the run-of-paper display type. Newspaper designer

Edmund Arnold cheered the difference when one paper, the *Albertan* of Calgary, Alberta, changed its women's-page format from clearface type, which Arnold said was "effective for many uses but not on newspaper pages." Said Arnold, "The gals were spared from further use of this face and were cut in on the regular headline schedule, Bodoni Bold, with no loss of femininity, distinction or beauty." He concluded, "Women's pages should have faces as pretty as their readers."[53]

Columnist Nicholas von Hoffman made the case that American newspapers have done their worst job on the areas that the women's page is responsible for—food, clothing, shelter, health, consumerism. Instead of blaming women's-page reporters, he put the onus on management, which, he said, sees this section as a stepchild allowed to live off handouts and freebies. Hoffman called attention to the "direct intervention of the newspaper's own advertising department in the operation of the women's pages."[54] The fashion, food, and home-furnishings writers of most American newspapers have always been vulnerable to criticism. With much space to fill, often whole advertising sections, and not enough time or staff to originate material, they have often been forced to run press releases to a greater extent than any other area of the newspaper, with the possible exception of travel and real estate sections.

Dramatic changes have taken place in most women's pages in the last few years—from changes in name to changes in format. While at first glance the changes seem to enhance women's interests, many critics have questioned whether the new liberation of women's pages has, in fact, been good for women. First, society and club news began to shrink or disappear, spurred by media criticism, the growing women's movement, and a feeling that editors were no longer willing to chronicle the life cycles in their cities in as thorough a manner as before. Led by such papers as the Detroit *Free Press* and Miami *Herald*, in the mid-1960s many sections began to put more stress on in-depth reporting of family issues such as divorce and child care. Instead of avoiding the women's section as a professional trap, some reporters and photographers sought jobs there because of the wider latitude, the greater space given to stories and pictures. But it was still difficult to be taken seriously—at the Miami *Herald*, the prize-winning women's department was known as the "Bay of Pigs."

As the women's section broadened its outlook to include stories of interest to all, the names began to change—to "Living Today," "Family Life," "Focus," "Lifestyle." Critics have argued that these new sections mean an inevitable diminishing of news about women and women's issues. A study of the women's pages of six daily newspapers found that their efforts to upgrade women's sections resulted in replacement of the traditional copy with entertainment reviews, rather than with coverage of subjects important to their women readers.[55] Mary Utting, former women's-page editor of the Charlotte *Observer,* told an APME convention that she, too, saw a tendency for the broadening of the women's section to mean more entertainment news, less news of women.[56]

Two Oregon chapters of the American Association of University Women (AAUW) conducted a content analysis of the "Day" sections of the Portland *Oregonian* over a three-month period in 1974. They found that feature articles about local women and women's concerns took up between 3 and 6 percent of the total space available each day, ranking fourth, well behind ads (62 percent), general nonfemale news (10 percent), and entertainment (7.8 percent). Straight news about women rated only 3 percent of the space available.[57]

WOMEN AS NEWS-STORY SUBJECTS

Journalists sometimes argue whether male and female reporters cover stories differently. Some newsmakers, Wilma Scott Heide for one, feel that women reporters eventually acquire the same biases as men, the same zeal for the bizarre figure and the confrontation story. A feminist press, KNOW, Inc., once distributed a list of "reporters you can trust," with forty-three names on it—four of them men.[58] Editors of women's publications were asked in a recent survey whether the sex of journalists made a difference in the way they covered women's issues. About three-quarters of those who answered said they felt female reporters were more sympathetic and helpful in covering and transmitting news about women's issues.[59]

Jill Ruckelshaus told the National Press Club in 1975, "Reporters often ask me if I think that the coverage of the women's movement would be different if women did more of the reporting. Yes, I do. . . . Women as a whole are better versed on certain issues than their male counterparts—perhaps just because of personal interest and/or involvement. Their understanding of those issues is likely to lead to better stories."[60] The other side of the argument, of course, is that a good reporter can cover anything. Ideally, a topnotch male reporter should be able to do just as good a job on women's issues as a topnotch female reporter.

Are stories covered differently when women are the subject? One has only to be a faithful newspaper reader to vouch for that; some reporters will even admit it. Free-lance writer Evelyn Kaye of Boston recalls that when she worked for the Reuters news service in the 1960s, she was given directives on how to deal with stories concerning women. "You write for editors," she says, "and most editors are men. I had to describe a Frenchwoman as an attractive 40-year-old mother of three, when these details were of no interest to me. You are expected to conform to the code, especially at news agencies."[61]

Janet Chusmir, now assistant managing editor of the Miami *Herald,* was formerly that paper's star feature writer. "We have always colored our descriptions of women," she says. "Certainly we have covered women and men differently. We've been crueler to women, describing them as the 'aging star,' for example. We would hone in on their emotions and reactions." She feels that women reporters developed better instincts for this kind of reporting, but that they were often cruelest to other women.[62]

Free-lance writer Pam Kohler agrees that women are often interviewed differently, asked questions reserved only for women, appraised as to hairdo, clothing, and figure. A woman can't receive an objective interview, said Kohler; instead "she is judged as to how she measures up to the stereotype. If she's too accomplished to be measured against the stereotype, she'll be treated as a novelty. That's how journalists handle a woman who doesn't quite fit."[63]

How deep does this stereotyping go? An interesting study of news stories written by student reporters in journalism school showed evidence of unwitting sex biases. The study explored the effects of the sex of a newsmaker on the treatment of stories by students. Packets of information about a new appointee to a prestigious position were given to two groups of students. For one group, the appointee was female; for the other group, the appointee was male. Otherwise the groups' information was identical. The students wrote a story about the appointment, devised lists of questions to ask the appointee in an interview, and listed three picture possibilities for the story. The study's results showed suggestions of "subtle bias" in the students' work. There was a greater tendency to use assertions about qualifications for the job when the newsmaker was male, perhaps indicating that the students considered the male more qualified for the job and reflected this in their stories. Students tended to ask the female newsmaker questions about sex role in the job, perhaps indicating concern about her ability to handle both professional and traditional roles.[64]

MS., MISS, MRS., OR HEY YOU?

The evidence on years of sex stereotyping in the press is clear. Dip into the files of any American newspaper and one finds an abundance of stories and headlines that belittle women, photographs that either poke fun or are blatantly sex-object representations.

One of the most bitter battles, still far from won, centers on language. Women are now on the alert for the condescending euphemism, the tongue-in-cheek coverage that pokes fun at serious issues. Male editors have never understood, for example, why feminists dislike the terms "lib" and "libber." Even an understanding of the headline writers' lifelong search for catchy short nouns—Ike, F.D.R., L.B.J.—doesn't help. Heide once complained in a letter to the editor of *Broadcasting* magazine, which had used the term: " 'Lib,' however shorthanded, is a flip way of referring to a serious and profound, universal behavioral revolution. One would never . . . refer to the black, chicano or other minority movements as black lib or chicano lib." She called it "an attempt to trivialize what we seek."[65] Just a month after her letter, a headline in a Wilmington, Delaware, paper read, "Libber Heide Fuels Revolutionary Fire."[66]

Take a simple grammatical issue—how should women be referred to in news stories on second reference? For men the solution is simple. They are generally last-named, with some few papers like the New York *Times* still using "Mr." But what about women? Should they be Miss? Mrs.? Ms.? Or last name only?

Editors, reporters, and many women readers have squabbled over this for years. Those who worked on the new AP/UPI stylebook, published in 1977, called the Mrs./Miss/Ms. controversy the toughest problem they faced concerning the state of the language. The stylists finally concluded that "since the traditional forms remain the norm in many places, AP and UPI should put the titles Miss, Mrs. and Ms. in the copy and members can take them out if that suits local fashion." On the sports pages, however, the wire services opted for dropping of courtesy titles. Lou Boccardi, AP vice-president, called this an appropriate change, and added, "Whether this will lead to the last-naming of women on news pages remains to be seen."[67]

Many women journalists sought elimination of all social titles. Christy Bulkeley, past president of Women in Communications, Inc. (WICI), and Jean Wiley Huyler, past president of the National Federation of Press Women, issued a statement that read in part: "If the sex or marital status of a car driver in a wreck, a politician or any other newsmaker is important, those facts should be stated specifically. If courtesy and respect are important they are important for all people, not just women."[68] Columnist Jane O'Reilly wrote in the Washington *Star* of her astonishment that so much energy could be spent on worrying about whether women are married or not, "but apparently the wire services still feel it is the central fact about us."[69] O'Reilly added that if news stories do not continue to be transmitted in language that suggests that only men take part in the nation's business, then the consciousness of all will be raised.

Most newspapers still use the courtesy titles "Miss" and "Mrs.," with many editors being violently opposed to "Ms." Prior to the publishing of the new stylebook, the wire services used "Ms." with the phrase "who prefers that designation." In the new stylebook that disclaimer will be dropped.

A plaintive article, "Don't Call Her Ms. It Was All a Mstake," in the August 1977 *Quill,* the magazine of the Society of Professional Journalists, gave journalism teacher Donald Williams an opportunity to call the dropping of titles before women's surnames "an aberration." Said Williams: "My wife is at the very least my equal, but she is not my double; she is not 'Williams.' She would be angry at any reporter who took it for granted that she wanted to be, and her feeling is not unique among women." He disapproved of dropping courtesy titles for sports figures. Why assume, he asked, that female athletes are less feminine than other women? He also disliked the indiscriminate Ms. used to describe both the "divorced Boston lawyer and the Iowa farm wife." Not giving a woman's title, he said, is withholding information from the readers. "If a woman's marital status does not matter, then marriage does not matter."[70]

Hardly had the ink dried on that issue of *Quill* when the September issue appeared, full of readers' indignant replies. Betsy Wade, then head of the New York *Times* foreign copy desk, outlined a flaw in Williams's logic. "Lots of unmarried women use 'Mrs.,' " she explained, "because they were once married, or because they have children. Lots of married women ... use 'Miss' because they ... have professional names." She added that news-story subjects often consider their marital status not pertinent and refuse to tell reporters if they are Miss or Mrs. Many reporters then prefer to use Ms. to avoid misleading the reader.

Another reader asked, "Why does calling a woman 'Jones' make her less feminine than a woman called "Mrs. Jones?" And still another reader, "It is totally illogical to assume that the press is powerful enough to ruin the institution of marriage simply by treating men and women equal."[71]

SISTERS UNDER THE HEADLINE

Reaching beyond issues of identification to the broader issues of coverage, one finds that well-known women fare no better in the press than the run-of-the-mill "blonde grandmother of three." One need only recall the many references to "grandmother" Golda Meir when she was prime minister of Israel, and the stories belittling Gloria Steinem's looks, intelligence, and motivations, until she went underground to escape media attention. Eleanor Roosevelt was the focus of media jokes and cartoons in the 1930s and 1940s. Since that time, any woman brave enough to speak out on public issues has had to face similar trivialization of her work in the nation's press.

At the 1973 convention of the American Newspaper Publishers Association, Steinem told publishers how unhappy she was with coverage of herself and of the women's movement.[72] In a 1975 speech to the New York chapter of WICI, Margaret Mead charged that the press is "utterly and totally irresponsible in what it says about women." She told the women present, "You belong to a profession where nobody ever makes a headline who does anything good. Any time that anything constructive is done, it is totally ignored. . . . The women who make the headlines must be conspicuous to get any recognition at all."[73]

Former Watergate prosecutor Jill Wine Volner pointed to "a pervasive masculine tilt" in news about women in a 1976 speech to WICI in Milwaukee. Never was she called "Attorney Volner" during the Watergate case, she said; instead she was always "the blonde mini-skirted attorney."

"My colleague, Jim Neal, was not described as the handsome, blue-eyed, well-dressed man, and Rick Ben-Veniste was not the dapper curly-haired man, so why should I be described by the color of my hair and the length of my skirt? That simply is not fair reporting."[74] At the 1975 APME convention, Volner told editors that almost every time her picture was in the paper, it ran full length, so readers could see her miniskirted legs.[75] She advised editors to read stories through and decide if the same things would have been said and the same tone used were the subject a man.

Even media stars don't get equal treatment when they're female; Barbara Walters is one example. Beneath all the commotion about her $5-million move to ABC ran the theme "all that for a mere woman." The *Columbia Journalism Review* headline for an article by Judith Hennessee pointed out that in the Walters case, "the nearly all-male press showed once again that boys will be boys." The story of ABC's bid and Walters's eventual acceptance made headlines for several days. *Time's* picture captions read, "Barbara and the anchormen: ABC's Reasoner; CBS's Cronkite; NBC's Chancellor." Last names were appropriate for them, first name for her—"Goldilocks and the Three Bears," said Hennessee. She listed some of the put-down headlines: from the New York *Daily News,* "Doll Barbie to learn her ABC's"; from the San Francisco *Examiner,* "Barbara Leaves Jim for Harry"; from the Detroit

News, "Is Barb Worth a Million?" Said Hennessee, "Most of the stories were written by men, expressed male reactions only, and quoted other men exclusively." Walters was called a "million-dollar baby," "queen of the newsroom," "aggressive," "pushy."[76]

The woman editor is also vulnerable. When the Los Angeles *Times* announced the new appointments of Jean Taylor as women's editor and Jody Jacobs as society editor, they mentioned that each woman was divorced. According to the *Review of Southern California Journalism,* a male *Times* executive explained that the divorces were mentioned because it was "germane to their jobs." He also told the *Review* that he had never seen such a reference for a male appointment. Ms. Taylor's reaction: "Perhaps all male executives are delightfully well balanced and don't get divorces."[77]

"Sexism: Morning, Evening and Sunday," is the title of a scrapbook of clippings compiled by women staffers at the Boston *Globe* and presented to management in 1973. Their one-month survey provides a cross-section of the kind of coverage that infuriates many women. For example, such headlines as, "Ellsberg Jury Hears Mystery Girl" (the "girl" was twenty-seven years old); "Oops, Female Upstages Males in National Veteran's Ski Meet"; "Wellesley Coed on Danger List." How can you be a coed, the *Globe* women asked, when your school isn't coeducational?

They noted a reference to a woman as an old maid; a photo caption on two women who had received promotions, "Women's Lib comes to R. M. Bradley." They found derogatory references in an editorial on bridge playing, referring to the "character, usually a woman, who forgets what trump is"; a story on women customers for vans, campers, and trucks that ended, "There is just no place left for a man to hide"; a story on a woman officeholder, quoting the police marshal, "She's really something. She takes the job seriously." A story on lottery winners identified the female winner as a "Lynn mother of three," rather than by occupation; the male winner's occupation is his identification. A story on a rabbi's wife, Mrs. Esther Jungreis, begins, "A beautiful, vivacious young Jewish woman with flashing eyes came to Boston yesterday to enlist alienated Jewish youth." The *Globe* staffers commented: "Would a gorgeous vivacious young Jewish man with a 42-inch chest and flashing eyes be applicable or relevant if the story were of a man? And would it be in the first paragraph?"[78] Nina McCain, one of the *Globe* reporters who worked on the scrapbook, comments that the newspaper has improved—"We wouldn't do this now," she says.[79]

Even a newspaper with as liberal an aura as today's New York *Times* has come in for criticism. In 1974, a group calling itself "Women for Changing the *Times*" picketed West 43rd Street, protesting the paper's "discriminatory policies and practices."[80] One might pardon the 1940s consciousness that began a story on wartime Washington, D.C., with a quote from a "pert little stenographer at the Navy Department,"[81] but what about the 1970 interview that began: "She has skin the color of molasses taffy, eyes as black as olives and a mop of black curls that give her a piquant look. She's Margaret Harris, a musical prodigy who grew up to become the first woman—let alone black woman—conductor of the hit Broadway musical 'Hair' "?[82]

A *Times* book reviewer noted in his 1971 review of Germaine Greer's *The Female Eunuch* that Greer "can't exactly be accommodated to the argument that feminists are dogs."[83] And a 1970 interview with the author of *Fascinating Womanhood* had her "crossing her shapely legs."[84]

Editors at the *Times* took note of the fact that they "have not always given women the equal status they seek and deserve," in a 1970 issue of *Winners & Sinners,* an occasional bulletin that praises and criticizes *Times* stories. First quoting a recent story that read, "Now 18 years old, tall and pretty, she has won a tuition scholarship, . . ." the editors cited guidelines issued, after staff rumblings, by Ben Bradlee of the Washington *Post.* Said Bradlee, as quoted in *W & S;* "Words like divorcée, grandmother, blonde (or brunette) or housewife should be avoided in all stories where, if a man were involved, the words divorcé, grandfather, blond or householder would be inapplicable. In other words, they should be avoided." Bradlee also disapproved of adjectives like "vivacious," "pert," "dimpled," and stories that condescendingly suggest "pretty good for a woman." *W & S* then added, "Naturally, what has been said here does not necessarily apply to the women's page but the girls can take care of themselves. Or so it is said."[85]

In the process of researching her book, *Against Our Will: Men, Women, and Rape,* Susan Brownmiller analyzed 1971 headlines in the New York *Daily News.* Looking for stories that involved women, she found only rapes, murders, and accidents on the front pages, with no news of women's achievements. She found headlines like "Probes Blonde Mystery Death," and references to "beautiful blonde victim," and "go-go girl." She concluded, "A whole generation of women have this as a testament—it takes beauty to get on page one of a tabloid."[86]

Many women have found that it is not the all-out attack (as in the Barbara Walters story) that infuriates so much as the daily put-down, the pat-on-the-head-for-the-little-dears that can still be found in newspapers. Following is a sampling, all from Boston newspapers:

"An Arlington grandmother has been chosen president of the League for [*sic*] Women Voters. . . . Husband Norman Jacobsen . . . is understanding and somewhat pleased with having the League's president in the family . . . Mrs. Jacobsen will always have time for her two grandchildren . . . she's their best baby-sitter."[87]

Headlined "Wacky Ways of Women," a column on women's clubs: "Women, you might say, are cute—the shrewd kind of cute . . . a woman chairman is like a flowering shrub. She enters office in full bloom, radiant and vigorous. Then comes the chill and she fades, like a leaf in autumn, and disappears."[88]

Headlined "Construction Gals Aren't What You Think," a story on a male reporter's visit to a meeting of Women in Construction: Expecting "amazons pouring cement," he found the women were constructed "along the usual curvy lines." Spotting first a "voluptuous blonde," then "an enchanting brunette" and "others of the same lovely ilk," he reassures readers that the women in construction are not the vanguard of a race of female titans. "They are constructed along the usual lissome lines, thank the good Lord."[89] Headline on the founding of the Massachusetts Woman's Political Caucus: "State's Women Activists Try to Cook up a Caucus."[90] Headline on a story of a woman forbidden to compete in a rowing championship because of her sex: "Banned, She Buttons Her Lib."[91]

These brief examples are all from metropolitan newspapers of fairly recent vintage. Coverage *is* improving, but as recently as June 1977, columnist Jack Thomas of the Boston *Globe* unleashed a flood of venom at the annual contest of the New England Women's Press Association. "Just when we were beginning to understand the importance of eradicating sexism everywhere," wrote Thomas, "we are told that the NEWPA . . . contest is limited to women." How, he wondered, can women write columns complaining about sexism, then accept sexist awards? Thomas further suggested that last year's contest winner might not have won had men competed.[92]

A student group at Stanford University confronted the problems of women's coverage in 1975 and came up with some guidelines. The *Columbia Journalism Review* decided that printing the guidelines would be too controversial. Instead, it printed the transcript of a discussion between proponents of the guidelines and other journalists. The guideline suggesting that prefixes indicating marital status should be dropped brought this comment from a male panelist: "The problem . . . is the notion that the press should define and should lead language. I think the power of the press to shape language is so great, and generally so misused, that the press should not be particular leaders in shaping the language and changing usage patterns. The press should essentially reflect what the current usage pattern is."

A male copy editor felt differently: "Newspapers . . . have to lead . . ." Another discussant commented on the guideline that called for elimination of gratuitous physical descriptions of women: "Casually throwing in physical description is a kind of 'good ol' boys' approach to journalism, where all the boys get together and slap each other's back over the cute broads. It assumes a male audience, because who's described physically? It usually is the women. And who are they described for? Usually the men."[93]

The lengthy discussion, one of the rare *Review* treatments of women's issues, was accompanied by a sidebar headlined, "Person the Lifeboats: The Language is Sinking." This article proclaimed that such "barbarisms" as "chairperson" and "newsperson" violated the language and undermined the cause of women's liberation.[94]

The next issue of the *Review* brought quick rejoinders from readers who objected to the headline as well as the content of the sidebar. One response called it "fairly typical of the male-dominated press that the transcript was not allowed to run without the usual smirk." This helped, the reader said, to "reduce to humor the very serious discussion represented by the transcription. It remains too bad that men are not yet able to take discussion of women seriously."[95]

SAY CHE-E-E-ESE-CAKE

Sexism in language may be too subtle for many editors to recognize, but in the world of newspaper photography sexism has been far from subtle. The cliché photos of bathing beauties still fill space in the wire services' transmission schedule. Many photo editors admit that they don't run these pictures, but they're welcomed as additions to office files or bulletin boards. The APME Photo Committee made a survey of editors in 1976 to find if they had used a partially undraped photo of Elizabeth Ray that had been transmitted by AP. Most photo editors said they hadn't run the shot but didn't want AP to stop sending such material.[96]

In answer to a similar UPI survey, one editor wrote, "We maintain what we call a 'broads' file. Some weeks, we don't go near it. Others, when we're hard up for something bright as a change of pace, we find it's a gold mine. Keep 'em coming." One photo editor, a woman, told UPI that girlie pictures are "insulting, demeaning and totally disgusting. Sexism is a real issue in America and it is interesting that while our nation's newspapers may editorially support women's struggle for equal rights and equal treatment, their reporters and photographers continue to exploit women."[97] The Copley publication *Seminar,* which printed an eight-page special supplement for this discussion, illustrated it with eleven sizable cheesecake photos, in case readers were uncertain as to the subject matter.

The *Chicago Journalism Review* took a poke at this newspaper cliché with a photo of two well-endowed *males* at the beach. The caption read: "Temperatures sizzled past the 100-degree mark in Chicago Tuesday, and a pair of local 29-year-olds, Dan Rottenberg (right) and Ken Pierce, couldn't resist the urge to skip their Loop office jobs and frolic in the sand by Lake Michigan. Who can work when it's so beautiful out? asks redheaded Dan with a wink. Our boss knows he can't keep us inside on a day like this, adds Ken, a long-stemmed brunet. Well, boys will be boys."[98]

It doesn't have to be cheesecake to be degrading. One newspaper columnist called a favorite photo category the "funny nun": "editors continued to favor pictures of nuns playing stickball over pictures of nuns riding bicycles."[99] With fewer nuns in habits, this kind of picture opportunity is fast diminishing. But photographers still like the from-the-ground-up angle shots that show lots of leg, or the shot-from-above décolletage view. When female staff members suggested to New York *Daily News* editors that the *News* give equal space to beefcake for its female audience, the male editors responded that male beefcake was for homosexuals only.[100]

Photo coverage of women in selected issues of the Washington *Post* and the Los Angeles *Times* was analyzed in a study that compared the number of pictures of women and of men, the roles portrayed, and the sections in which they appeared. In the *Post,* men outnumbered women by three to one; in the *Times,* by two to one. Men dominated page one, the news, editorial, business, sports, and entertainment sections. Only the lifestyle sections contained more photos of women than men. Half of all the pictures of women showed them as spouses, socialites, or entertainers; less than one-fourth of the male photos showed men in these roles. Some 75 percent of the male photos showed them as professionals, politicians, or sports figures; less than 25 percent of the pictures of women showed them in these roles. Photographs of brides accounted for almost 25 percent of the photos of women in the *Post.* In the forty-six issues surveyed, the Los Angeles *Times* ran twelve pictures of beauty queens. The surveyors concluded that the newsphoto portrayal did not reflect the roles women truly occupy in the Washington, D.C., and Los Angeles communities but did conform to accepted journalistic formulas and concepts of newsworthiness.[101]

EQUAL PAY? EQUAL STATUS?

In focusing on women as news subjects, and on women's issues as they have been treated in the press, one deals in large part with ephemera. Conclusions are subjective; many women feel they have been ill-treated, many editors believe they can justify coverage in terms of newsworthiness or the prevailing social ethic. But when the focus turns to women as employees of newspapers and magazines, one finds facts, statistics, and surveys to back up the contention that women journalists have not been afforded equal treatment.

The earliest writings of pioneer women reporters tell of their struggle to be hired, to be recognized as equals in the newsroom, the difficulties in snaring a beat other than "society." The first year in which the Census lists full-time journalists by sex was 1870; 35 of 5,286 were women. By 1900, the figures had climbed to 2,193 out of 30,098.[102] *The Journalist,* a trade publication, devoted an issue in 1889 to women journalists. While noting their accomplishments, an editorial by Flora McDonald stated that women reporters could not hope to be treated equally by men: "Any well-balanced woman who works among newspaper men, one thousand and one causes make hers the miserable experiences of a freak. . . ." The woman reporter covers "sassiety," she wrote—"she is in the swim, but not of it, and, recording the slops and founders of the big fish, she in time descends to a state of mental and moral petrifaction that is simply awful . . . cursing her worst enemy, she would simply implore heaven to strike him a society reporter on the spot."[103]

Ishbel Ross, once a reporter for the New York *Tribune,* wrote a history of women journalists in 1936. There were then 12,000 women journalists, except, she noted, on the front page. "Whenever possible, they are steered into the quieter by-waters of the newspaper plant, away from the main current of life, news, excitement, curses and ticker machines." Ross discussed the tightrope walked by women who did make it to the city room. "Unless aggressiveness is backed by real ability . . . it is only a boomerang. Peace at any price is the city room philosophy." Women were never thoroughly welcome in the city room, said Ross, and they are still not quite welcome. "If the front page girls were all to disappear tomorrow no searching party would go out looking for more, since it is the fixed conviction of nearly every newspaper executive that a man in the same spot would be exactly twice as good."[104]

Were Ross alive today, she would find little reason to change her view. Thousands of women now hold entry-level or slightly higher jobs in the nation's press. But management ranks have, with few exceptions, been closed to women. Inequities in salary still exist, along with inequities in promotion and job placement. It took years before women were allowed the full privileges of membership in the National Press Club; it took years for the Society of Professional Journalists, Sigma Delta Chi, to decide that women were journalists, too; it took eight years before the prestigious Nieman Foundation at Harvard University began granting fellowships to women journalists,[105] and the women selected are still very much a minority.

The most recent statistics on the status of women in journalism come from 1971 Census and U.S. Department of Labor figures. They show that while the total full-time U.S. labor force, twenty and older, breaks down to a ratio of males, 66.4 percent to females, 33.6 percent, the ratio in journalism is males, 79.7 percent; females, 20.3 percent.[106] In journalism, men outnumber women four to one, compared with a two to one ratio in the total full-time labor force. Yet the skills involved in journalism are not believed to be ones in which men particularly excel.

This imbalance is not reflected in the number of students studying journalism. Of the 27,886 bachelors degrees in journalism awarded by American colleges and universities between 1964 and 1971, 38.4 percent were awarded to women.[107] Columbia University's Graduate School of Journalism announced in fall 1977 that for the first time women outnumbered men in the entering class. At Boston University's School of Public Communication, the graduate journalism program also enrolled slightly more women than men in 1977.

Salary differentials become clear after study of the median income of journalists in 1970 by sex and age.[108]

Age	Men	Women	Difference
Under 25	$ 6,934	$5,111	$1,823
25–34	10,243	8,744	1,499
35–44	14,041	8,579	5,462
45–54	14,042	8,000	6,042
55 and older	14,321	7,710	6,611

Discussing the gap in pay between men and women, John Johnstone and his coauthors lay the blame on sex, not on differences in qualifications or professional experiences. "Evidence from both this and other studies," they say, "makes it clear that career opportunities for men and women in the news media differ markedly; men have better chances of being recruited into the media to begin with; they are more likely to be assigned 'important' news beats early in their careers, and they have much better chances of eventual promotion into positions of organizational responsibility."[109]

Another salary survey of a random sample of male and female women's-page editors, taken in 1973, also found that women's salaries were significantly lower than men's. Some 65 percent of women surveyed earned less than $9,000 a year; only 6 percent earned more than $15,000.[110]

Based on interviews with 1,300 practicing journalists, they found that women were more likely to be "stayers" rather than "shifters." Women generally hoped to remain with their current employers, perhaps a reflection of their more restricted mobility. Job satisfaction was found to be somewhat higher among women than among men, despite the discrepancy in earnings and status. This suggests that levels of satisfaction are a function of the relation between achievements and aspiration. For example, asked to define the elements of a good job in their field, 52.4 percent of male journalists, compared with 38.7 percent of women, stressed the importance of opportunities for advancement within an organization, while 28.7 percent of men and 15.3 percent of women said pay was very important.[111]

The traditional male editor's view has been that women were flighty, prone to leave their jobs for marriage or children, forcing editors to train newcomers to take their places. Many women journalists recall being asked pointblank in job interviews if they were engaged, had marriage plans, or intended to have children. Now it seems that it is the men who job-jump while women stay, hoping their competence will eventually be recognized and rewarded.

Why are there so few women managers in journalism? Many women believe it's because they've been denied the jobs that are the traditional routes to the top—the political beat, courts, business. Syndicated columnist Ellen Goodman feels that politics is clearly the management route: "The newspaper is a record of games men play—politics, sports, and business."[112]

Upward-striving women have been told, "Men don't want to work for women." Or even, "Women don't want to work for women." When the Indiana University School of Journalism surveyed more than 600 newspaper managers at more than 200 dailies in 1976, they found that all the newspapers, regardless of circulation, averaged about one woman manager per paper. Women receive substantially lower salaries than their male counterparts, they learned, and most women managers perceive a difference in the treatment of men and women, particularly in criteria for promotion.[113]

Women have been extraordinarily slow to realize their position. Even in the early 1970s, a survey of women journalists reported that nearly two-thirds "hardly" perceived sex discrimination on their newspapers. The findings were based on a Perceived Discrimination Index that indicated discrimination in salary, promotion, hiring, and assignments. But more than half the male news executives surveyed at the same time agreed that women with comparable qualifications would neither advance as quickly nor earn as many top newspaper positions as men. Women were not executives in great number, the men said, because they had not sought newspaper work in large numbers a decade ago and lacked seniority.[114]

At present, few women hold prestigious management positions. Carol Sutton, once the nation's first and only woman managing editor, is now assistant to the editor and publisher of the Louisville *Courier-Journal;* Janet Chusmir is assistant managing editor of the Miami *Herald;* Marjorie Paxson, the assistant managing editor of the Boise, Idaho, *Statesman;* Christy Bulkeley, the publisher of the Danville, Illinois, *Commercial News.* And there are a few more—lifestyle editors, editors of special sections, assistant city editors of smaller papers.

What can be done to move more women up the corporate ladder? At Boston University, workshops for Women in Communications Management, sponsored by the School of Public Communication and the Division of Continuing Education, have so far involved forty women in seminars designed to explore their own management styles. The Frank E. Gannett Newspaper Foundation funded a conference on Women in Newspaper Management at Indiana University in spring 1977, at which newspaper executives, journalists, and educators explored the problem in a series of panels. Gannett also sponsored a meeting of some of their top female executives in 1976 to discuss sexism in the newspaper business.[115] Participants were asked to suggest how the male newspaper environment might be improved to help women. They concluded that management should take responsibility at first to encourage talented women to seek leadership roles. Later, they suggested, the responsibility could be shifted to women. They also promoted the idea of joint sessions for male editors and female reporters to discuss sexism on the job.

These are basically self-help programs. Many other women employees of magazines and newspapers, despairing of these avenues, have taken to the courts. The American Newspaper Guild reported forty newspapers facing sex-discrimination complaints in 1977.

At the New York *Times,* an affirmative-action suit filed five years ago by women staffers was granted class-action status in fall 1977. The *Times* women first petitioned their publisher, then filed charges of discrimination with the U.S. Equal Employment Opportunity Commission (EEOC) and the New York Commission on Human Rights. They then sued the paper under title VII of the Civil Rights Act. Their lawsuit asks for an injunction requiring that goals be established for promotion of women into higher and better-paying jobs; equal pay and benefits for equal work; and monetary awards for salary lost owing to discrimination dating back to 1969.

By May 1977, according to a *Times* spokesman, women numbered 31 percent of the editorial staff. But imbalance is still seen in prestige reporting posts—three of twenty-two foreign correspondents are women. At the Washington bureau, five of thirty-five are women; there is one woman among the twenty-five regional correspondents.[116]

Newsweek magazine recently negotiated an affirmative-action settlement; another suit has been settled at *Time;* the *Reader's Digest* agreed in fall 1977 to pay 2,600 past and present employees more than $1.5 million to settle a suit brought by eight women four years ago. The Sacramento *Bee* agreed in 1976 to a work force that reflects the working population in the Sacramento area (36.7 percent female) by April 1979.[117]

Suits are still in litigation at *Newsday* and several other papers. Women employees at the Detroit *News* filed discrimination charges in 1976 with the EEOC; their grievances included discriminatory hiring, salaries, assignments, working conditions, and chances for promotion. Their competing paper, the Detroit *Free Press,* reported at the time that the *News* had no women reporters in the Washington bureau or on the business news staff and no women editorial writers or photographers; the city room had only one female general-assignment reporter.[118]

Perhaps the most famous confrontation between women and media management occurred in March 1970, when women writers and activists held an eleven-hour sit-in at the offices of John Mack Carter, then editor of the *Ladies' Home Journal.* The women demanded hiring of an all-female advertising staff, a female editor, and an end to sexist advertising campaigns.[119] Carter invited them to produce an eight-page supplement to the magazine in the August 1970 issue. Both Carter and Lenore Hershey, the current *Journal* editor, are now members of the IWY Commission.

The Newspaper Guild called a national conference on women's rights in fall 1970. The conference called for equality in hiring, pay, jobs; integration of press clubs; maternity leave, and day-care facilities. According to reporter Ellen Hoffman, "The Guild conference provided a beginning, a basis for organized national action, but newswomen themselves will have to continue to call attention to discrimination directed at them if they are to eliminate it."[120]

Women employees of *Time, Newsweek, Fortune, Sports Illustrated, Readers Digest,* and other media outlets contributed essays on their jobs for a book compiled in 1974 by the Media Women's Association. Almost all the writers depicted a gloomy present and future for woman journalists. One woman said of the Associated Press: "to a lot of old guard newsmen and executives, AP women are children whose careers are only temporary aberrations."[121]

Journalist Bill Moyers wrote in a June 1972 editorial for *McCall's:* "Any male editor on a newspaper who objects to 'Women's Lib' has to look no further than his own salary scale, his employment policy or his own writing style ... I can talk about journalism because I am a part of it—and have contributed to the very practices I have come to realize were so unfair to women."[122]

ON THE JOB—AND GETTING TO IT

Anne Hecker, national president of WICI, likes to recall her first day in class as a freshman journalism student many years ago. Her professor marched in, looked over the predominantly male classroom, and intoned: "I do not approve of women in journalism, in this school or in this classroom."[123] Today pressure for change is building not only from threats of legal action but from the sheer numbers of potential women journalists now filling colleges and universities. Women journalism students now constitute 43.3 percent of the 64,502 enrolled; women seeking graduate degrees are 45.3 percent of the 4,938 graduate students.[124]

Today's woman student is probably far more alert to discrimination than her mother or older sister was. Student members of the Madison, Wisconsin, chapter of NOW distributed leaflets at the Association for Education in Journalism convention in Madison in August 1977. Entitled "Where are the Women?" the leaflet called journalism a "sexist profession." It noted that the convention listed only one woman among its twelve major speakers, "and although we are happy to see her included, she is not from the field of journalism. Even the women's magazine editor invited to appear here [John Mack Carter] is male!" Sexism flourishes in the Madison media, the leafleteers said, because television, radio, and newspapers "are controlled by men, few of them feminists."[125] If the University of Wisconsin students typify a new consciousness, it won't be easy in the future to shut women out of journalism.

Given a well-functioning economy, entry-level journalism jobs are usually no more difficult for women to secure than for men. Young, tractable workers with low salary expectations are welcomed: not so with the older, more experienced, more aggressive woman who wants to move ahead in the ranks. Free-lance writer Caryl Rivers still gets angry when she remembers her rejections by newsmagazine bureaus in Washington, D.C., after she had acquired experience and awards at a medium-sized daily.[126] Almost every woman journalist has horror stories of jobs she sought and lost because she was seen as "threatening" or likely to leave. Journalist Helen Drusine endured a months-long series of put-offs and run-arounds from UPI's Paris bureau. At one point a male editor told her, "Quite honestly, I am looking for a young male reporter. Call me a male chauvinist if you want to, but that's what I am." She was later told, "Our policy is three females in Europe and one female to a bureau. The only possibility you have of getting a job with us is if one of them decides to leave."[127]

A 1977 column by Diane White of the Boston *Globe* showed that sexism pervades the newsroom. White described a so-called red alert in the *Globe* newsroom; male editors signaled each other by phone when an attractive female worker appeared in the city room. "In this instance," White informed *Globe* readers and coworkers, "a certain highly placed editor had stolen a few minutes from his presumably busy day to alert the columnist, among others, that a young copy aide had turned up for work looking most fetching." Most newsmen are so easily titillated, White commented, that the garb that caused a red alert could have been worn to serve mass.[128]

Women have had to fight for the newsroom beats they want. They have been forced to come to terms with a buddy system among male reporters that can shut them out of important stories or jobs. And they must often work far harder than men to develop channels for getting and keeping news sources. Women journalists have complained that tactics that would have been praised as aggressive reporting in men were termed "ballbreakers" when used by women. Washington AP reporter Peg Simpson had to battle for assignment to the 1972 political conventions; after a confrontation with her boss, she was named to replace a reporter who had dropped out. Women need to learn to fight for and ask for what they want, she concluded, especially from male bosses.[129]

Members of the National Press Club received this message from Jill Ruckelshaus: "It's easy to determine that the highest prestige a reporter can receive is to be a full-time national political reporter—so few women are."[130] Along with other public figures, Ruckelshaus has suggested that coverage often suffers when women's perceptions are not brought to an event. Ellen Goodman noted the paucity of women reporters at the 1972 Democratic Convention. The convention was as much a conclave for political reporters as for Democrats, she said. But while the Democrats had agreed on a 40 percent proportion of women delegates, the journalistic delegations quite accurately reflected the underrepresentation of women in the elite role of political reporter. Goodman estimated that of 7,500 persons with media identification, fewer than one in seven were female. Even fewer, she wrote, were in the working press, in contrast to errand runners or secretaries.[131]

Susan B. Anthony wrote in 1900: "As long as newspapers and magazines are controlled by men, every woman upon them must write articles which are reflections of men's ideas. As long as that continues, women's ideas and deepest convictions will never get before the public."[132] The notion is still apt today.

NOW surveyed nine Washington, D.C., and suburban newspapers in 1972–73. Their findings reflected the male dominance of "important" stories. In the Washington *Post,* NOW found that 94 percent of the section A bylines were by males; 94 percent of the front page stories were reported by males; 94 percent of the editorial page columns were written by males; 80 percent of the metro section stories were reported by males; 75 percent of the stories on page one of the "style" section (formerly the women's pages) were written by men.[133]

In spring 1977, a survey of membership in the American Society of Newspaper Editors (ASNE) found 803 members, 3 percent of them women. The ASNE study, conducted by Dorothy Jurney, also found that in 227 cities with newspapers having a daily circulation of 40,000 or more, 1,128 males are in policy-making positions; only 30, or less than 3 percent, are females.[134]

Washington's Gridiron Club, the country's most prominent group of editors and columnists and a men-only group for eighty-nine years, voted in 1974 to continue to exclude women journalists. On the same night as the annual Gridiron dinner, a group of about 500 women and men journalists (Journalists for Professional Equity), held a counter-Gridiron party in protest. Later in the year, the club changed its policy, and UPI's Helen Thomas became the first woman member.[135]

As a young Washington reporter in the early 1960s, Caryl Rivers, with other women journalists, was forbidden to sit on the floor seats at the National Press Club. When Carl Rowan was invited to speak at the club, relating tales of the days when blacks were forbidden entry to all but theater balconies, the male reporters' eyes swept up to the balcony of the Press Club—there were Rivers and her compatriots, taking notes.[136] The National Press Club has since admitted women to the floor.

The Society of Professional Journalists, Sigma Delta Chi operated as a men-only organization for more than sixty years before finally voting to admit women in the early 1970s. One debate on the issue in 1969 stated the case against women: "If women are admitted to membership, wives and husbands of members will feel free to attend and a dangerous precedent will be set. There are many outstanding, talented women journalists, but with few exceptions they are sojourners on the way to matronhood, motherhood and matriarchy. ... Is professionalism to give way to sentimentalism, dances, socials, picnics?"[137]

The society today has a minority of women members, with more entering at the student level through college chapters. Regional and national offices continue to be held by males. This journalistic organization is perhaps the only body in which, theoretically, it is possible for women to take an equal role. Membership is open to working professionals regardless of job title, unlike the ASNE and APME. The 1976 APME Red Book listed eight women among 529 members.[138] Some women attend the APME's annual meetings, but they are generally spouses, not editors.

The APME functions throughout the year with working committees that monitor AP wires and share ideas on personnel, news coverage, new technology, legal issues, and other journalistic concerns. Members are newspaper managing editors from large and small newspapers, along with AP executives. The organization does not normally make headlines; but it became extraordinarily controversial in the eyes of women journalists when in 1969 it issued two sets of guidelines in a manual for editors.

The first set, "For Men: Ten Commandments for Working With Women," included these words of advice: "Avoid impatience with a woman, she NEEDS to have confidence in you; What ego is to a man, security is to a woman. Make her feel safe and needed and she'll make you feel ten feet tall. As a man, provide the reason, the authority and the security to direct a woman in the use of her constant emotional drive. Praise a woman on every possible occasion, her appreciation is fourfold that of a man. So is her sensitivity, she requires one-fourth the criticism."[139]

The APME then listed rules "For Women: Your Dealings With Men." Since the number of women who received APME materials in 1969 was miniscule, the APME apparently thought male editors would pass these on to their women employees. The guidelines are interesting enough to relate in full:

1. The first and most important commandment for women in dealing with men and the foundation for all others is this—be pleasing in ways suitable to the time, to the place and the man. Man's ego is outrageous. He likes the company of the pleasing woman, all others he avoids.
2. Learn to understand the ways and wishes of a man. If he sees red when you wear red, don't.
3. Do your best to do everything the way a male boss wants it done.
4. Be willing to subordinate your personality—not your individuality—to make a man FEEL like the boss.
5. Use every means possible to ease your boss's natural, however prejudiced, fear of women.

6. Never make a man wonder how you'll take what he has to say. When tempted to make a scene, ask yourself these two questions: "Will this display, that I feel like making, accomplish any useful purpose?" and "How will blowing my top affect this man's opinion of me?"
7. Never betray a trust—even unintentionally. The first secret you reveal will be the last you'll get.
8. Don't try to be "one of the boys." It will get you no place with the "boy" you're trying to influence. This means avoiding off-color stories, swearing and all unfeminine conduct.
9. Don't be afraid to stand your ground in an argument with the boss, but be sure you're on solid ground. Peel off sentiment, prejudice and emotion and present only the core of fact.
10. Be proud of being a woman, even though at work you have to be better than a man to be considered as good. As a woman, you have one tool in your kit that, used properly, will compensate for all the unfairness you suffer. That tool is charm.[140]

The compliment did not compensate for what many women read as blatant sexism. Staffers at the *Daily Iowan,* student newspaper of the University of Iowa, complained to the APME that the guidelines' author never explained why a woman who is serious about her career "should have to resort to the use of sexual games to pacify men too stupid to recognize their own prejudices, and whose prejudices are so deeply ingrained, so much a part of their everyday lives, they cannot recognize them." The Iowa women called the guidelines a sad commentary on the state of American journalism and its relationship to women's rights—but an accurate reflection of the way women are treated at many newspapers.[141]

The editor of the APME guidelines, Edward M. Miller, increased the furor when he came to the defense of his document. Most women do not make good administrators, said Miller, because "they tend to look inward rather than outward. . . . Generally speaking, women are either uncomfortable or unsuccessful in the executive role because of the difficulties they encounter in divorcing their personal feelings and ambitions from the job at hand. This leads to unhappy subordinates and inefficient productions." Women are good on "people stories" and features, Miller said, but if assigned to unravel a complicated financial story a woman "is apt to fall apart. Most women do not make very good investigative reporters because they have difficulty in sorting out the essentials from the nonessentials." Women make excellent copy editors, he reassures: "They are patient, careful, cheerful, and the repetitive nature of the work does not seem to bother them." And he affirms, "The seasoned managing editor seeking a stable staff knows well the hazards of employing young women."[142]

These guidelines, never disowned by the APME, are included in the packets of materials given to participants in Boston University's seminars for women communications managers. They still make women furious.

COOPERATION FOR CHANGE

Another myth has it that the real enemies of women are other women. Some female journalists are convinced that their career boosts have come from male mentors, the kicks from women trying to protect their turf. A 1977 article in the WICI magazine, *Matrix,* recounted the experiences of several media women who felt they had been held back by other women. Most of them said they preferred to work with men.[143]

But this view seems to be held by a minority today. Increasingly, women journalists are banding together in formal and informal groups to seek parity. Their goal now is to place more women in management positions—the only way a woman's viewpoint will gain influence in the media.

Probably the best-known women's organization is Women in Communications. With approximately 8,000 members, it attracts students through college chapters and also admits professional members. Begun in 1909 as Theta Sigma Phi, with sorority trappings that included a candlelight initiation ceremony, WICI seeks to unite women in all communications fields and to recognize women's achievements. On the national level it runs a job placement bureau and publishes a magazine and newsletter. Professional chapters provide support groups for media women, run programs on media issues, and award scholarships and internships.

The National Federation of Press Women, with about 4,000 members, also runs programs through a nationwide network of chapters. Many chapters hold yearly writing competitions for area women journalists.

The NOW Media Task Force operates out of NOW's action center in Washington, D.C. This group assists NOW chapters and members working to promote the employment and image of women in the media. Many chapters run media-monitoring units; they have been particularly active in noting instances of sexism in advertising.

Dr. Donna Allen of Washington, D.C., founded the Women's Institute for Freedom of the Press in the early 1970s as an information clearing house for women. Its original newsletter became the *Media*

Report to Women. This monthly bulletin runs twelve to sixteen pages an issue and has 1,500 subscribers. Now in its fifth year, the *Report* includes information on affirmative programs, media lawsuits and court decisions, workshops, seminars, and jobs.

A new group, Media Women in Action, formed in 1976 with the announced purpose of eliminating sexism in media, especially in employment practices and in portrayal of women.

With networks of formal and informal organizations like these working on national and local levels, the woman journalist need not feel alone. Her colleagues now share information on jobs, court actions, policy changes. They monitor the media for signs of sexism; they try to alert male editors to women's issues that might otherwise be overlooked.

Women have also made recommendations that, if adopted, would alter cherished journalistic precepts. The *Media Report to Women* proposed three guidelines as a new set of standards to improve or replace current journalism. Their "principles of feminist journalism": don't attack people; include more factual information; let people speak for themselves.[144]

In its evaluation of the role of women in the media, the National Commission on the Observance of IWY compiled its own guidelines for press treatment of women. Pat Carbine, editor of *Ms.,* chaired the committee that produced these guidelines:

> 1. The media should establish as an ultimate goal the employment of women in policymaking positions in proportion to their participation in the labor force. The media should make special efforts to employ women who are knowledgeable about and sensitive to women's changing roles.
> 2. Women in media should be employed at all job levels—and in accordance with the law, should be paid equally for work of equal value and be given equal opportunity for training and promotion.
> 3. The present definition of news should be expanded to include more coverage of women's activities locally, nationally and internationally. In addition, general news stories should be reported to show their effect on women. . . .
> 4. The media should make special sustained efforts to seek out news of women. Women now figure in less than 10 percent of the stories currently defined as news.
> 5. Placement of news should be decided by subject matter, not by sex. . . . Wherever news of women is placed, it should be treated with the same dignity, scope and accuracy as is news of men. Women's activities should not be located in the last 30–60 seconds of a broadcast or used as fillers in certain sections or back pages of a newspaper or magazine.

6. Women's bodies should not be used in an exploitative way to add irrelevant sexual interest in any medium.... The public violation of women's physical privacy tends to violate the individual integrity of all women.

7. The presentation of personal details when irrelevant to a story —sex, sexual preference, religious or political orientation—should be eliminated for both women and men.

8. It is to be hoped that one day all titles will be unnecessary. But in the meantime, a person's right to determine her (or his) own title should be respected without slurs or innuendoes....

9. Gender designations are a rapidly changing area of the language, and a decision to use or not to use a specific word should be subject to periodic review. Terms incorporating gender reference should be avoided ... in addition, women, at least from age 16, should be called women, not girls....

10. Women's activities and organizations should be treated with the same respect accorded men's activities and organizations. The women's movement should be reported as seriously as any other civil rights movement; it should not be made fun of, ridiculed, or belittled...."[145]

These guidelines, written in 1975, are still far from standard policy for the media. Ten years from now, will we still need guidelines for the treatment of women in the nation's press?

NOTES

1. Nancy Borman, "Newspaper Reporting," *Rooms With No View, a Woman's Guide to the Man's World of the Media,* ed. Ethel Strainchamps, (New York, Harper & Row, 1974), p. 246.

2. Boston *Globe,* September 30, 1977.

3. Marcia Boundy, "Press Coverage of the Woman Suffrage Movement: An Historical Perspective, 1848–1920," Boston University, 1977, p. 1.

4. Ibid., p. 4.

5. William Henry Chafe, *The American Woman: Her Changing Social, Economic and Political Roles, 1920–1970* (New York, Oxford University Press, 1972), p. 4.

6. Eleanor Flexner, *Century of Struggle: The Woman's Rights Movement in the United States* (Cambridge, Mass.: Harvard University Press, 1976), p. 82.

7. Boundy, "Press Coverage," p. 9.

8. Elizabeth Janeway, advisory ed., *Women: Their Changing Roles* (New York, The New York *Times*—Arno Press, 1973), pp. 78–82.

9. Ibid., p. 89.

10. Boundy, "Press Coverage," p. 17.

11. Ibid., p. 21.

12. Ibid., p. 23.

13. Janeway, *Women,* p. 8.

14. Ibid., p. 116.

15. Boston *American,* December 3, 1970.
16. Chafe, *American Woman,* p. 105.
17. Ibid., p. 231.
18. Betty Friedan, *The Feminine Mystique* (New York: Dell, 1963), p. 48.
19. Boundy, "Press Coverage," p. 5.
20. Janeway, *Women,* p. 25.
21. Ibid., p. 41.
22. Ibid., p. 175.
23. Friedan, *Mystique,* p. 30.
24. *American Women: The Report of the President's Commission on the Status of Women and Other Publications of the Commission* (New York: Scribner's, 1965), p. 214.
25. Boston *Herald,* March 19, 1972.
26. Maurine Beasley and Sheila Silver, *Women in Media: A Documentary Source Book* (Washington, D.C.: Women's Institute for Freedom of the Press, 1977), p. 112.
27. Ibid., p. 113.
28. Ibid.
29. Remarks before the Media Ethics Conference, Institute for Democratic Communication, Boston University, November 4, 1977.
30. Beasley and Silver, *Women in Media,* p. 111.
31. Ibid., pp. 117–18.
32. Chafe, *American Woman,* p. 238.
33. Ibid., p. 318.
34. Germaine Greer, *The Female Eunuch* (New York, Bantam, 1972), p. 327.
35. Ibid., p. 329.
36. Interview with Wilma Scott Heide, Framingham, Mass., June 20, 1977.
37. Washington *Star,* July 20, 1975.
38. Remarks before the National Press Club, Washington, D.C., Sept. 12, 1975.
39. Telephone interview with Dorothy Jurney, June 2, 1977.
40. "IWY Press Chair Urges Coverage," Women In Communications, *National Newsletter,* July 1977, p. 10.
41. Nancy Peterson, "Conflict Sharpened Interest in IWY Meeting," Women in Communications, *National Newsletter,* September 1977.
42. Remarks before the National Press Club.
43. James Fordham, "Just a Matter of Simple Justice?" *More,* June 1976, p. 25.
44. Sheila J. Silver, "Covering Women: Women's Publications and the Mass Media," paper given before the Association for Education in Journalism, Madison, Wisc., August 1977, p. 3.
45. Interview with Nina McCain, October 8, 1977, Boston, Mass.
46. Silver, "Covering Women," p. 4.
47. Monica Morris, "Newspapers and the New Feminists: Black Out as Social Control?" *Journalism Quarterly,* spring 1973, pp. 37–42.
48. Maxine Mullins, "Interest Increases in Women's Sports," Women in Communications, *National Newsletter,* April 1976, p. 14.
49. *Columbia Journalism Review,* winter 1969–70.
50. Letters, *Columbia Journalism Review,* November/December 1973, p. 66.
51. Lindsy Van Gelder, "Women's Pages: You Can't Make News Out of a Silk Purse," *Ms.,* November 1974, pp. 112–16.
52. *The APME Red Book, 1968* (New York, Associated Press, 1968), pp. 148–49.
53. Edmund C. Arnold, "Restyling Ends Head Difference," *Editor & Publisher,* March 18, 1967, p. 33.

54. Nicholas Von Hoffman, "Women's Pages: An Irreverent View," *Columbia Journalism Review*, July–August 1971, pp. 52–54.

55. Zena Beth Guenin, "Women's Pages in American Newspapers: Missing Out on Contemporary Content," *Journalism Quarterly*, spring 1975, pp. 66–69.

56. *The APME Red Book, 1968*, p. 147.

57. Beasley and Silver, *Women in Media*, pp. 148–51.

58. Silver, "Covering Women," p. 7.

59. Ibid., p. 16.

60. Remarks before the National Press Club.

61. Interview with Evelyn Kaye, Boston, Mass., June 1, 1977.

62. Interview with Janet Chusmir, Boston, Mass., April 29, 1977.

63. Pam S. Kohler, "Objectivity Ends at the Hemline," *The Quill*, October 1972, pp. 25–27.

64. Dan G. Drew and Susan H. Miller, "Sex Stereotyping and Reporting," *Journalism Quarterly*, spring 1977, pp. 142–46.

65. Correspondence from Wilma Scott Heide to Sal Taisheff, ed., *Broadcasting*, October 19, 1972, unpublished.

66. *Evening Journal*, Wilmington, Del., November 14, 1972.

67. Eileen Alt Powell, "Media (Is) (Are) Getting New 'Bible,'" *The Quill*, July–August 1977, pp. 24–27.

68. "AP-UPI Criticized for Title Usage," Women in Communications, *National Newsletter*, November 1976, p. 13.

69. Washington *Star*, May 9, 1977.

70. Donald M. Williams, "Don't Call Her Ms. It Was All a Mstake," *The Quill*, July–August 1977, pp. 28–29.

71. Letters, *The Quill*, September 1977, pp. 7–8.

72. Margaret Cronin Fisk, "Steinem Knocks Newspaper Coverage of Women's Issues," *Editor & Publisher*, May 5, 1973, p. 11.

73. Catherine Hemlepp and Kay Lockridge, "Margaret Mead Lambasts the Media," Women in Communications, *National Newsletter*, December 1975, p. 3.

74. Junetta Davis, "Volner Confronts the Issues," *Matrix*, fall 1976, pp. 24–25.

75. *The APME Red Book, 1975* (New York: Associated Press, 1975), pp. 55–58.

76. Judith Hennessee, "The Press's Very Own Barbara Walters Show," *Columbia Journalism Review*, July/August 1976, pp. 22–25.

77. "LA: Sexism in Announcements," *Columbia Journalism Review*, March/April 1972, p. 36.

78. Boston *Globe* staff members, "Sexism, Morning, Evening and Sunday," 1973, unpublished.

79. Interview with Nina McCain, October 8, 1977.

80. Tracy Young, "Taking Their Case to the *Times*," *More*, April 1974, pp. 12–13.

81. Janeway, *Women*, pp. 212–14.

82. Ibid., pp. 354–55.

83. Ibid., p. 397.

84. Ibid., p. 413.

85. Winners & Sinners # 297, September 3, 1970.

86. Nancy Iran Phillips, "The Subject—Rape—Raises News Questions," *The Quill*, January 1976, p. 29.

87. Boston *Herald*, January 23, 1970.

88. Boston *Globe*, March 20, 1962.

89. Boston *Herald*, July 27, 1965.

90. Boston *Globe*, July 20, 1971.

91. Boston *Herald*, August 30, 1970.

92. Boston *Globe,* June 15, 1977.

93. "Kissing 'The Girls' Goodbye: A Panel Discussion," *Columbia Journalism Review,* May/June 1975, pp. 28–33.

94. Boyd Wright, "Person the Lifeboats! The Language is Sinking!" *Columbia Journalism Review,* May/June 1975, p. 32.

95. Letters, *Columbia Journalism Review,* July/August 1975, p. 62.

96. APME Photo Letter 1976, report of the APME Photo Committee, Joseph M. Ungaro, chairman.

97. "The Great Cheesecake Debate," *Seminar,* March 1972, supplement, pp. 1–8.

98. "A Scorcher," *Columbia Journalism Review,* March/April 1972, p. 37.

99. "The State of the Press," *Columbia Journalism Review,* summer 1966, p. 55.

100. Ann Marie Cunningham, "Shall I Compare Thee to a Summer's Day?" *More,* March 1975, pp. 14–15.

101. Susan H. Miller, "The Content of News Photos: Women's and Men's Roles," *Journalism Quarterly,* spring 1975, pp. 70–75.

102. Beasley and Silver, *Women in Media,* p. 38.

103. Ibid., pp. 45–46.

104. Ibid., pp. 68–73.

105. Louis M. Lyons, ed., *Reporting the News: Selections from Nieman Reports* (New York: Atheneum, 1968), pp. 12–13.

106. John W. C. Johnstone, Edward J. Slawski, and William W. Bowman, *The News People: A Sociological Portrait of American Journalists and Their Work* (Urbana, Ill.: University of Illinois Press, 1976), p. 197.

107. Ibid., p. 231.

108. Ibid., p. 237.

109. Ibid., p. 137.

110. Won H. Chang, "Characteristics and Self-Perceptions of Women's Page Editors," *Journalism Quarterly,* spring 1975, pp. 61–65.

111. Johnstone, Slawski, and Bowman, *News People,* p. 152.

112. Remarks before the Media Ethics Conference.

113. Celeste Huenergard, "Outnumbered, Underpaid and Overlooked," *Editor & Publisher,* June 18, 1977, p. 18.

114. Joann S. Lublin, "Discrimination against Women in Newsrooms—Fact or Fantasy?" *Journalism Quarterly,* summer 1972, pp. 357–61.

115. "Gannett Employes Cheer Bulkeley, Paxson," Women in Communications, *National Newsletter,* November 1976, p. 13.

116. Richard Pollak, "Women's Suit Nears Showdown at the 'Times,' " *More,* October 1977, pp. 34–38.

117. *Media Report to Women,* May 1, 1976, p. 1.

118. "Another Male Enclave Beseiged," *Columbia Journalism Review,* March/April 1977, pp. 56–58.

119. *Media: A Workshop Guide,* National Commission on the Observance of International Women's Year, Washington, D.C., 1977, p. 14.

120. Ellen Hoffman, "Women in the Newsroom," *Columbia Journalism Review,* winter 1970/71, pp. 53–55.

121. "Associated Press," *Rooms With No View,* p. 124.

122. *Media: A Workshop Guide,* p. 12.

123. Anne Hecker, "From the President's Desk. . . ." *Matrix,* summer 1977, p. 3.

124. Gloria S. Brundage, "Promotion and Tenure Opportunities for Women Faculty in Journalism Education," paper given before the Women's Committee, Association for Education in Journalism, Madison, Wisc., August 1977.

125. "Where are the Women?" leaflet, Women on Watch, Wisconsin Task Force, National Organization for Women, August 1977.

126. Remarks before the Media Ethics Conference.

127. Helen Drusine, "Diary of a Woman Job Hunter," *Columbia Journalism Review,* November/December 1972, pp. 58–60.

128. Boston *Globe,* June 2, 1977.

129. Peg Simpson, "A Basic Strategy for Capitol Hill," *The Quill,* February 1975, pp. 24–26.

130. Remarks before the National Press Club.

131. "Women's Caucus," *Columbia Journalism Review,* September/October 1972, p. 3.

132. *Media: A Workshop Guide,* p. 1.

133. Ibid., p. 4.

134. Ibid., p. 11.

135. Ibid., p. 15.

136. Remarks before the Media Ethics Conference.

137. George W. Wolpert, "Women in Sigma Delta Chi? The Case against," *Seminar,* September 1969, pp. 23–26.

138. *The APME Red Book, 1976* (New York: Associated Press, 1976).

139. "For Men: Ten Commandments for Working With Women," *APME Guidelines,* fall 1969, p. 68.

140. Ibid., p. 73.

141. "APME's Guidelines: A Women's Review," *Columbia Journalism Review,* May/June 1971, pp. 55–56.

142. Edward M. Miller, "APME's Guidelines a 'Sexist Document'? An Editor's Reply," *Columbia Journalism Review,* September/October 1971, pp. 62–63.

143. Jackie Hartel, "Who Is a Woman's Worst Enemy? Another Woman?" *Matrix,* winter 1976–77, p. 25.

144. Beasley and Silver, *Women in Media,* pp. 177–78.

145. Ibid., pp. 163–69.

BIBLIOGRAPHY

Books

American Women: The Report of the President's Commission on the Status of Women and Other Publications of the Commission. New York: Charles Scribner's Sons, 1965.

The APME Red Book 1968. New York: Associated Press, 1968.

The APME Red Book 1975. New York: Associated Press, 1975.

The APME Red Book 1976. New York: Associated Press, 1976.

Beasley, Maurine, and Silver, Sheila. *Women in Media: A Documentary Source Book.* Washington, D. C.: Women's Institute for Freedom of the Press, 1977.

Chafe, William Henry. *The American Woman: Her Changing Social, Economic and Political Roles,* 1920–1970. New York: Oxford University Press, 1972.

Flexner, Eleanor. *Century of Struggle: The Woman's Rights Movement in the United States.* Cambridge, Mass.: Harvard University Press, 1976.

Friedan, Betty. *The Feminine Mystique.* New York, Dell, 1963.

Greer, Germaine. *The Female Eunuch,* New York, Bantam Books, 1972.

Janeway, Elizabeth, ed. *Women: Their Changing Roles.* New York: The New York *Times*/Arno Press, 1973.

Johnstone, John W. C., Slawski, Edward J., and Bowman, William W., *The News People: A Sociological Portrait of American Journalists and Their Work.* Urbana, Ill.: University of Illinois Press, 1976.

Lyons, Louis M., ed. *Reporting the News: Selections from Nieman Reports.* New York: Atheneum, 1968.

Media: A Workshop Guide. National Commission on the Observance of International Women's Year, Washington, D.C., 1977.

Strainchamps, Ethel, ed. *Rooms With No View: A Woman's Guide to the Man's World of the Media.* New York: Harper and Row, 1974.

"Another Male Enclave Beseiged." *Columbia Journalism Review,* March/April 1977, pp. 56–58.

APME Photo Letter 1976, report of the APME Photo Committee, Joseph M. Ungaro, chairman.

APME's Guidelines: A Women's Review." *Columbia Journalism Review,* May/June 1971, pp. 55–56.

"AP-UPI Criticized for Title Usage." Women in Communications, Inc., *National Newsletter,* November 1976, p. 13.

Arnold, Edmund C. "Restyling Ends Head Difference," *Editor & Publisher,* March 18, 1967, p. 38.

"A Scorcher." *Columbia Journalism Review,* March/April 1972, p. 37.

Boundy, Marcia. "Press Coverage of the Woman Suffrage Movement: An Historical Perspective, 1848–1920." Boston, Mass.: Boston University, 1977.

Brundage, Gloria S. "Promotion and Tenure Opportunities for Women Faculty in Journalism Education." Paper read at meeting of Association for Education in Journalism, August 1977, at University of Wisconsin, Madison, Wisconsin.

Chang, Won H. "Characteristics and Self-Perceptions of Women's Page Editors." *Journalism Quarterly*, spring 1975, pp. 61–65.

Columbia Journalism Review, winter 1969–70.

Cunningham, Ann Marie. "Shall I Compare Thee to a Summer's Day?" *More*, March 1975, pp. 14–15.

Davis, Junetta. "Volner Confronts the Issues," *Matrix*, fall 1976, pp. 24–25.

Drew, Dan. G., and Miller, Susan H. "Sex Stereotyping and Reporting." *Journalism Quarterly*, spring 1977, pp. 142–46.

Drusine, Helen. "Diary of a Woman Job Hunter." *Columbia Journalism Review*, November/December 1972, pp. 58–60.

Fisk, Margaret Cronin. "Steinem Knocks Newspaper Coverage of Women's Issues." *Editor & Publisher*, May 5, 1973, p. 11.

Fordham, James. "Just a Matter of Simple Justice?" *More*, June 1976, p. 25.

"For Men: Ten Commandments for Working With Women." *APME Guidelines*, Associated Press Managing Editors Association, fall 1969, p. 68.

"Gannett Employes Cheer Bulkeley, Paxson." Women in Communications, Inc., *National Newsletter*, November 1976, p. 13.

"The Great Cheesecake Debate." *Seminar*, March 1972, supplement, pp. 1–8.

Guenin, Zena Beth. "Women's Pages in American Newspapers: Missing Out on Contemporary Content." *Journalism Quarterly*, spring 1975, pp. 66–69.

Hartel, Jackie. "Who is a Woman's Worst Enemy? Another Woman?" *Matrix*, winter 1976–77, p. 25.

Hecker, Anne. "From the President's Desk. . . ." *Matrix*, summer 1977, p. 3.

Hemlepp, Catherine, and Lockridge, Kay. "Margaret Mead Lambasts the Media." Women in Communications, Inc., *National Newsletter*, December 1975, p. 3.

Hennessee, Judith. "The Press's Very Own Barbara Walters Show." *Columbia Journalism Review*, July/August 1976, pp. 22–25.

Hoffman, Ellen. "Women in the Newsroom." *Columbia Journalism Review,* winter 1970/71, pp. 53–55.

Huenergard, Celeste. "Outnumbered, Underpaid and Overlooked." *Editor & Publisher,* June 18, 1977, p. 18.

"IWY Press Chair Urges Coverage." Women in Communications Inc., *National Newsletter,* July 1977, p. 10.

"Kissing 'The Girls' Goodbye: A Panel Discussion," *Columbia Journalism Review,* May/June 1975, pp. 28–33.

Kohler, Pam S. "Objectivity Ends at the Hemline." *The Quill,* October 1972, pp. 25–27.

"LA: Sexism in Announcements." *Columbia Journalism Review,* March/April 1972, p. 36.

Letters, *Columbia Journalism Review,* November/December 1973, p. 66.

Letters, *Columbia Journalism Review,* July/August 1975, p. 62.

Letters, *The Quill,* September 1977, pp. 7–8.

Lublin, Joann S. "Discrimination against Women in Newsrooms—Fact or Fantasy?" *Journalism Quarterly,* summer 1972, pp. 357–61.

Media Report to Women, May 1, 1976, p. 1.

Miller, Edward M. "APME's Guidelines a 'Sexist Document'? An Editor's Reply," *Columbia Journalism Review,* September/October 1971, pp. 62–63.

Miller, Susan H. "The Content of News Photos: Women's and Men's Roles." *Journalism Quarterly,* spring 1975, pp. 70–75.

Morris, Monica. "Newspapers and the New Feminists: Black Out as Social Control?" *Journalism Quarterly,* spring 1973, pp. 37–42.

Mullins, Maxine. "Interest Increases in Women's Sports." Women in Communications Inc., *National Newsletter,* April 1976, p. 14.

Peterson, Nancy. "Conflict Sharpened Interest in IWY Meeting," Women in Communications, Inc., *National Newsletter,* September 1977, p. 3.

Phillips, Nancy Iran. "The Subject—Rape—Raises New Questions." *The Quill,* January 1976, p. 29.

Pollak, Richard. "Women's Suit Nears Showdown at the 'Times.'" *More,* October 1977, pp. 34–38.

Powell, Eileen Alt. "Media (Is) (Are) Getting New 'Bible.'" *The Quill,* July-August 1977, pp. 24–27.

"Sexism: Morning, Evening and Sunday." Compiled by staff members, Boston *Globe,* 1973.

Silver, Sheila J. "Covering Women: Women's Publications and the Mass Media." Paper read at meeting of Association for Education in Journalism, August 1977, University of Wisconsin, Madison, Wisconsin.

Simpson, Peg. "A Basic Strategy for Capitol Hill." *The Quill,* February 1975, pp. 24–26.

"The State of the Press." *Columbia Journalism Review,* summer 1966, p. 55.

Van Gelder, Lindsy. "Women's Pages: You Can't Make News out of a Silk Purse." *Ms.,* November 1974, pp. 112–16.

Von Hoffman, Nicholas. "Women's Pages: An Irreverent View," *Columbia Journalism Review,* July–August 1971, pp. 52–54.

"Where are the Women?", Women on Watch, Wisconsin Task Force, National Organization for Women, August 1977.

Williams, Donald M. "Don't Call Her Ms. It Was All a Mstake." *The Quill,* July–August 1977, pp. 28–29.

Winners & Sinners #297. Bulletin of the New York *Times,* September 3, 1970.

Wolpert, George W. "Women in Sigma Delta Chi? The Case against." *Seminar,* September 1969, pp. 23–26.

"Women's Caucus," *Columbia Journalism Review,* September/October 1972, p. 3.

Wright, Boyd. "Person the Lifeboats: The Language is Sinking." *Columbia Journalism Review,* May/June 1975, p. 32.

Young, Tracy. "Taking Their Case to the *Times.*" *More,* April 1974. pp. 12–13.

6 ETHICAL PROBLEMS IN TELEVISION ADVERTISING TO CHILDREN

F. Earle Barcus

In the past several years, increasing attention has been given to the problems of television advertising directed toward children. The problem has created a full-blown controversy among consumer groups, governmental agencies, and the advertising, television, and other industries producing products for children.

Some of the principal players in the controversy are (1) Action for Children's Television (ACT), an action-oriented group based in Newton, Massachusetts, and dedicated to improving the quality of children's television; (2) the Council on Media, Merchandising and Children (CMMC), which has raised numerous issues related to the ethics of advertising of cereals and other products to children; (3) the Federal Communications Commission (FCC), which holds certain regulatory powers to ensure that the public interest is served in broadcasting; (4) the Federal Trade Commission (FTC), which has regulatory power in the area of unfair and deceptive advertising practices; (5) the National Association of Broadcasters (NAB), which through its Television Code Authority sets guidelines for television industry broadcast practices; and more recently (6) the Council of Better Business Bureaus (CBBB), whose National Advertising Division (NAD) issued a self-regulatory code, "Children's Advertising Guidelines," in 1975.

Many other parties with special interests in children have entered the fray from time to time. Thus, the Toy Manufacturers Association has been involved because of its interests in increasing the sale of toys to children; cereal manufacturers have sought to protect their own markets; advertising agencies specializing in the youth market at times have been vocal when threatened with limitations on methods of reaching children. Similarly, national professional associations such as the American Dental Association, the American Medical Association, and groups of nutritionists have all spoken out on the need to protect children from advertising considered adverse to good health care and nutrition. Many other national organizations with child-related interests have joined the battle*

The extent of concern can be seen in a number of major recent events. As early as 1961, the NAB issued self-regulatory Toy Advertising Guidelines in response to public complaints. In 1970, issues about the effect of food advertising on children were raised in the White House Conference on Food, Nutrition, and Health.[1] In 1974, three years after a 1971 ACT petition urging the prohibition of all TV advertising to children, the FCC issued a policy statement on children's television, reviewing its own legal powers to control television advertising and leaving the solution of the problem primarily to industry self-regulation.[2] Also in 1971, the FTC held a series of hearings on modern advertising practices at which spokespersons from academia, industry, and consumer organizations appeared. Another set of hearings, "Broadcast Advertising and Children," was conducted in 1975 before the House Subcommittee on Communication of the Committee on Interstate and Foreign Commerce.[3] That year the attorneys general of nineteen states requested a ban on medicine advertising between 6:00 A.M. and 9:00 P.M. in a petition before the FCC. As of this writing, the most recent research activities resulted from a series of grants from the National Science Foundation to investigate the effects of advertising on children—resulting in the review and recommendations published in *Research on the Effects of Television Advertising on Children.*[4] And the current chairman of the FTC has promised a much more active role in protecting children from unethical advertisers.[5]

THE ETHICAL ISSUES

Numerous policy issues are involved in this continuing debate. Rather than attempting to treat each issue and subproblem in detail, however, it may be better to look at them in the perspective of four basic questions. As is so often the case, the overriding issues all involve conflict of private and public interests.

---

*For example, representatives from fourteen national organizations such as the American Academy of Pediatrics and the National Congress of Parent Teachers Associations met with FTC Chairman Pertschuk in July 1977 seeking a ban on televised candy advertising directed to children. (See *RE:ACT,* Action for Children's Television News Magazine, fall 1977).

1. Should we advertise to children?
2. How much should we advertise to children?
3. What should we advertise to children?
4. How should we advertise to children?

To date, most industry concern has been directed to question 4. Government and self-regulatory bodies have issued guidelines primarily addressed to question 4 and to some extent to questions 2 and 3. Only ACT has officially raised question 1.

WHETHER TO ADVERTISE

ACT has marshaled several arguments supporting its initial petition filed in 1971 and accepted by the FCC for rule making—namely, that "there shall be no sponsorship and no commercials on children's programs."[6] The arguments supporting this position are based in law, tradition, theory, and practical problems.

There is a long tradition of laws protecting children. As stated in a petition to the FTC:

> The law has traditionally recognized that children require special protection: children are not allowed to buy alcohol or cigarettes; children may not enter into contracts without the assistance of an adult guardian; children are not allowed to drive a vehicle until the age of 16, to vote until the age of 18, or to own a credit card until the age of 21. Yet in the world of television, the child is treated as an adult from the day he begins watching television as an infant.[7]

A similar view is given by William Melody in his book *Children's Television: The Economics of Exploitation:* "The issue is whether children should be protected from being isolated as a specialized audience for the specific purpose of applying pinpoint and tailor-made advertising directed toward their particular vulnerabilities as children."[8] other support is based in child-development theory:

> Piaget's theory as a whole suggests a proposition, which, although quite general, should have important consequences for education. The proposition is that the young child is quite different from the adult in several ways: in methods of approaching reality, in the ensuing views of the world, and in the uses of language.[9]

In addition to legal tradition and theoretical statements in support of their petition, ACT has made a number of more obvious and practical points. Aside from the child's being different in mental development —in his or her ability to discriminate, discount, perceive, and choose among products—he or she lacks the purchasing power to buy the products advertised. It is the parent who buys. Thus, the child becomes an agent used by advertisers to manipulate their parents to buy. This raises ethical questions and sparks parent-child conflict.

Both industry groups and government regulatory agencies have accepted the principle that children are indeed different from adults and deserve some kind of special protection from advertisers. The preamble to the NAB's "Children's Advertising Guidelines" states: "Since children, especially when unsupervised by adults, may not in all situations be able to discern the credibility of what they watch, they pose an ethical responsibility for others to protect them from their own potential susceptibilities."[10] At the same time, the NAB does not feel that prohibition of advertising is the answer: "However, broadcasters believe that advertising of products or services normally used by children can serve to inform children not only of the attributes of products/services but also of many aspects of the society and the world in which they live."[11]

The National Advertising Division of the CBBB takes a similar view in its statement of principles: "Since younger children have a limited capability for discerning the credibility of what they watch, they place a special responsiblity upon advertisers to protect them from their own susceptibilities."[12] Again, prohibition of advertising is not considered as a solution. Rather, the division recognizes that the child "may learn practices from advertising which can affect his or her health and well-being." To guard against any possible ill effect, they urge the advertiser to be a positive force: "Advertisers are urged to capitalize on the potential of advertising to influence social behavior by developing advertising that, whenever possible, addresses itself to social standards generally regarded as positive and beneficial, such as friendship, kindness, honesty, justice, generosity and respect for others."[13]

For the time being, the question of whether to advertise to children has been at least temporarily answered by the FCC in its 1974 report and policy statement. Refusing to adopt ACT's proposal, the FCC resolved the issue "by balancing the competing interests in light of the public interest."

Banning the sponsorship of programs designed for children could have a very damaging effect on the amount and quantity of such programming. Advertising is the basis for the commercial broadcasting system and revenues from the sale of commercial time provide the financing for program production.[14]

Although the FCC did not accept the principle of prohibiting directing advertising specifically toward children, it did recognize that too much time is given to such advertising and supported self-regulatory NAB efforts to reduce the amount of time allowed.

HOW MUCH TO ADVERTISE

If the critics have not been able to eliminate TV advertising to children altogether, they have reduced the amount. During the period of the FCC investigation into children's television between 1971 and 1974, the NAB adopted guidelines reducing the permissible time devoted to TV advertising on children's programming (defined as "those hours other than prime time in which programs initially designed primarily for children under 12 years of age are scheduled").[15] Since Saturday and Sunday mornings had traditionally been considered nonprime time, and there were time standards for prime time, there was virtually no limit on the amount of advertising and promotional messages that could be presented. Indeed, my own studies in 1971 disclosed some stations carrying more than 25 percent of each hour devoted to commercial messages.[16]

By 1973, the code restricted Saturday and Sunday nonprogram time (including commercials, promotional announcements, and public service announcements) to twelve minutes per hour; by 1975 it was again reduced to ten minutes per hour; and beginning in January 1976 to 9.5 minutes per hour. Reductions in after-school hours Monday through Friday were less severe, remaining at twelve minutes per hour. At the same time, independent (non-network-affiliated) stations were given special consideration; nonprogram material is permitted up to fourteen minutes per hour currently.

Is this too little, enough, or too much? At least one industry group was sufficiently dissatisfied to set its own standards. Westinghouse Broadcasting withdrew its member stations from the NAB Code Authority membership in 1969 to protest loose time standards. Donald H. McGannon, president and chairman of the board of Westinghouse Broadcasting Co., Inc., explained in testimony before the House Subcommittee on Communications:

> Group W has ... developed special restrictions on the amount of commercial advertising which may appear within a children's program under its control. Our policy limits commercial content in a children's program to ... 6 minutes per hour, exclusive of station breaks.[17]

The effect of NAB's reductions has been more apparent than real. They have not led to predicted revenue losses. According to a study by Dr. Alan Pearce of the House Subcommittee on Communications, "gross advertising revenues for all three networks combined for both regularly scheduled and special children's programs reached an all-time high in 1975 ($90,805,400) ... representing an overall increase of 16 percent over the previous year in spite of a reduction of from 12 to 17 percent in the amount of advertising allowed on children's programs."[18]

The NAB time standards reduced permissible nonprogram time from 16 to 9.5 minutes per hour from 1973 to 1976—a 41 percent reduction. From 1971 to 1975, however, the *actual* reduction was from an average of 11.3 to 9.5 minutes of nonprogram time during the same period—only a 16 percent reduction in time.[19] In addition, the NAB guidelines pertain only to the amount of time—not to the number of commercials (or exposures to ads). During the 1971–75 period, there was a *real* reduction of only 5 percent in the number of commercial messages on weekend children's programs (from an average 21.7 commercials per hour to 20.5 per hour). This was accomplished by the airing of fewer one-minute commercials and more thirty-second commercials.[20]

The answers to how much is too much may not be forthcoming until research gathers more information in four areas—(1) long-term exposure effects, (2) effects on heavy viewers, (3) clustering effects, and (4) repetition effects.[21]

Long-term negative exposure effects relate to whether the child may develop materialistic values or become more susceptible to persuasion. On the more positive side, useful consumer socialization may be achieved by viewing advertising.

Heavy viewing effects relate primarily to certain age groups of children who spend long hours viewing. Although preliminary evidence indicates that children who watch a lot are more positively disposed toward commercial messages, there is little evidence that this leads to worse understanding or greater persuasibility.

Clustering effects refer to the clustering rather than spreading out of commercial messages. It is argued that such clustering will help children discriminate between program and advertising matter, although perhaps making individual commercials less efficacious sellers.

Finally, it is claimed that repetition may make the child susceptible to persuasion—not to mention irritated. At present, however, there seems to be no support for this contention, other than that children who are exposed more frequently to commercial messages are better able to remember the brand name mentioned.

WHAT TO ADVERTISE

Most of us are aware that legal restrictions have been placed on television advertising. The banning of cigarette advertising is the most obvious recent example. The NAB code also currently prohibits advertising hard liquor, firearms or ammunition, fortune telling and other occult practices, and tip sheets for betting purposes. It also places restrictions on advertising of beer and wines, institutions such as schools guaranteeing employment, products of a personal nature, legalized lotteries, "bait-switch" advertising, and personal endorsement advertising.

At least two classes of products neither prohibited nor severely restricted by the NAB code have been the subject of most concern when broadcast in and around children's programming. They are: (1) medicines, over-the-counter drugs, vitamins, and (2) edibles—primarily cereals and candies.

Medicine and Drugs

Although never constituting a large porportion of child-directed commercials, vitamin ads for children were appearing on national television as recently as 1971. Threatened by possible FTC action on an ACT petition to ban vitamins from children's programs, three major pharmaceutical companies voluntarily withdrew their ads that year. This did not end the practice, however, and neither the FTC nor the NAB were anxious to develop any prohibitions regarding such advertising.

In the meantime, another pharmaceutical corporation initiated a $1-million campaign to sell children "delicious and chewable" super-hero Spiderman vitamins and began airing the ads on television. This prompted another petition and formal complaint to the FTC by ACT in September 1975. In November 1976, the FTC ruled against the Hudson Pharmaceutical Corporation, stating, in part: "Children are unqualified by age or experience to decide for themselves whether or not they need or should use this product."[22]

Interestingly, but not surprisingly, Spiderman was a popular comic book figure in Marvel Comics, and the Cadence Industry Corporation owned both the Marvel Comics Group and Hudson Pharmaceutical Corporation.[23]

In 1975 the NAB prohibited such advertising "in or adjacent to programs initially designed for children under 12 years of age."[24] The key phrase in the NAB prohibition relates to programs "initially designed for children."

Robert Choate, chairman of the Council of Children, Media and Merchandising, pointed out that approximately 85 to 90 percent of children's television watching was in the late afternoon and early evenings. According to audience data from A. C. Nielsen, twelve of the top fifteen programs most viewed by children appear during the late afternoon and evening before 9:00 P.M. Choate listed twenty-two commercials for over-the-counter drugs in a sample week in the top forty programs that children watched. These included aspirins, cold remedies, cough supressants, household cleansers, and other similar products. It was estimated that children view about 1,000 such commercials each year. CCCM filed a petition before the FTC suggesting a regulation covering products advertised on any program that many children watch.[25]

The problem of child exposure to drug and medicine advertising in programs not produced for children had been raised. This situation may have prompted the petition of attorneys general from nineteen states seeking a ban on such advertising between 6:00 A.M. and 9:00 P.M. According to the petition, the officials had authority to "secure the health, safety, and general welfare" of citizens in their respective states.[26] The petition argued: (1) drug advertising creates an artificial demand for drugs; (2) children are particularly susceptible to drug advertising; and (3) over-the-counter drugs can be dangerous to children.

After a series of hearings before the FCC, the petition was denied. To date, little research evidence exists to support the charges made, according to the most recent review.[27] The problem nevertheless remains of the potential effect of children's exposure to certain advertising in nonchild-oriented programming. It is more difficult to solve than that of controlling advertising in programs specifically produced for the child audience.

Food

The topic of food advertising has been debated at many levels—by consumer advocate groups, several congressional subcommittees, at a White House conference, by food corporations and food advertisers, and members of the professional health communities of nutritionists, pediatricians, and dentists.

Food constitutes the largest single category of products advertised during children's programs. According to 1975 data, 68 percent of all commercials in Saturday and Sunday morning programs were for food products and eating places. This figure comprises 25 percent for ready-to-eat cereals, 25 percent for candies and sweets, 10 percent for eating places, 4 percent for snack foods, and 4 percent for other foods such as milk, fruits, juices, and breads.[28]

Although this advertising has come under much criticism as to methods (appeals to sweetness and fun; the use of premiums), a major question relates to the *types* of food advertised. The basic complaint is that the child may be influenced by the emphasis on non-nutritious foods, and that influence may affect his knowledge of nutrition, attitudes toward food, eating habits, and physical health. It is argued that the parent, once the gatekeeper of the child's food habits, has been replaced by the TV pitchman who entices children to pressure mom into buying sugary cereals and other nutritionally suspect products.

There have been some efforts to correct the situation through public service announcements by such organizations as the American Dairy Council. Nevertheless, commercials dubbed as "counternutritional" outnumber messages on behalf of nutrition by a large margin.

Two studies were conducted in this area. The first looked at 25½ hours of weekend programming of the three networks and two independent stations in the Boston market. The second was a sampling of ten independent stations across the United States in the "after-school hours" from 3:00 to 6:00 P.M.[29]

In April 1975, a study of 25½ hours of weekend children's programming revealed only twelve brief public service messages on behalf of good nutrition, or one nutrition message every 2.1 hours. There were 76 commercial announcements for sugared cereals, 100 commercials selling candies and other sweets, 16 for snack foods, and 20 for so-called quick-service eating establishments. The ratio of counternutritional commercials to messages on behalf of nutrition causes was 212 : 12, or about 18 to 1—one message encouraging the consumption of sugars and snack every 7.2 minutes, on the average.

At the same time advertising for all other edibles (dairy products, fruits, meats, breads, vegetables, and unsugared cereals) constituted less than one-fourth of all food advertising on weekend children's TV.

Another sample of children's television revealed an even more extreme ratio. In the after-school hours on ten independent TV stations, only *one* nutrition-related message was found in the thirty hours studied. At the same time there were 65 ads for sugared cereals, 73 for candies and sweets, 2 for snack foods, and 42 for fast-food eating places —a ratio of 182 counternutritional messages to one public service message.

In terms of frequency, children watching after-school TV programming may be exposed to one message encouraging good nutritional habits every thirty hours; whereas announcements urging the consumption of sweets, snacks, and fast foods occurred on the average of one every 9.9 minutes.

Few would complain were children urged to eat celery, apples, or bananas. The emphasis on high-profit processed foods raises serious questions, however. There is evidence that this advertising does indeed affect parents' food choices. In one study of 591 mothers of six to fourteen-year-old children, 75 percent said they were influenced in product selection by children's requests. Another study observed the behavior of 516 families in supermarkets, noting that in two-thirds, the child initiated the selection of a cereal by "demanding" or "requesting" a specific brand.[30]

In light of current evidence, it is difficult to deny that a national nutritional problem exists. Television may play an important role in nutrition education (or miseducation). A 1968–70 ten-state nutrition survey conducted by the Department of Health, Education, and Welfare reported that "a significant proportion of the population surveyed was malnourished or was at high risk of developing nutritional problems."[31] The 1969 White House conference on food, nutrition, and health recommended immediate action to increase public awareness of nutritional problems and suggested specific ways to improve Americans' understanding of good nutrition. The report recommended further that a special task force of top representative communications professions be formed to plan, devise, and execute an immediate and continuing program of mass communications on behalf of nutrition education. This task force was asked to use all the arts and techniques of advertising, promotion, and public relations in its efforts to plan, coordinate, and carry out a national nutrition campaign.[32] To date the task force is not in operation.

According to a recent report,

> Television's ability to serve as a major source of information for the American public marks it for a potentially important role in such a national program. What seems to be necessary is the assumption of responsibility by various groups, including government, industry, and educators, for determining ways to implement such a program.[33]

HOW TO ADVERTISE

In the past decade, probably the most attention has been focused on the questions of technique, style, appeals, and other practices of advertisers in marketing products to children.

Both industry self-regulatory and government regulatory groups have formally acknowledged the potential influence of production techniques on children's perceptions (or misperceptions) of products advertised on television. The NAB guidelines state:

> In order to help assure that advertising is non-exploitative in manner, style and tone, such advertising shall avoid using exhortative language. It shall also avoid employing irritating, obtrusive or strident audio techniques or video devices such as cuts of less than one second in length, a series of fast cuts, special colors, flashing lights, flashing supered copy or other effects which could overglamorize or mislead.[34]

There are also provisions relating to messages that cajole the child to ask a parent to buy a product, imply that the product will make the child better than his peers, contain violent or antisocial behavior, or violate standards of safety. Real-life authority figures and celebrities are not allowed to endorse or give testimonials for the products, and audio-visual disclosures about what is and is not included (e.g., "batteries not included") and method of operation are required.

In a similar vein, the NAD advertising guidelines for children address the problem of how such advertising may be presented:

> Particular control should be exercised to assure that:
>
> Copy, sound and visual presentations—as well as the advertisement in its totality—do not mislead on performance characteristics such as speed, method or operation, size, color, durability, nutrition, noise, etc.; on perceived benefits such as the acquisition of strength, popularity, growth, proficiency, intelligence and the like; or on the expectation of price range or cost of the product.[35]

Many other provisions are included relating to endorsements, safety, comparative claims, pressure to purchase, and premium advertising.

The most specific provisions are contained in the NAB toy advertising guidelines. These include rules relating to audio-visual disclosures, exaggerating product qualities, and using competitive claims, as well as warnings about certain camera angles, special lenses, special lighting, "dazzling visual effects," music, sound volume, and other seductive production techniques.

We may discuss the basic issue of how to advertise under three headings: (1) format and audio-visual technique, (2) source effects, and (3) the use of premiums.

Format and Techniques

Whether certain techniques are indeed unfair or misleading to children depends upon whether such techniques lead to changes in perception, recall, and interpretation of product qualities so as to lead to unreasonable expectations in the child who ultimately obtains the product.

Preliminary research indicates that special audio-visual features can cause misperceptions, especially among younger children. Disclosures may be ineffective with younger children. In a recent study, for example, three versions of toy commercials were shown to a group of 240 youngsters, six to eight years old. In one version, a commonly used disclaimer, "some assembly required," was used. In another modified version, the more common phrase "you have to put it together" was substituted. In the third version, no disclaimer was used. The standard disclaimer (version one) did no better than no disclaimer at all in making children understand that the toy needed to be assembled after purchase. The modified disclaimer, however, resulted in a much greater understanding.[36]

Although further studies are needed to resolve the questions of effects of certain production techniques, there is little doubt that camera angles, slow or accelerated motion photography, and other tricks of the trade can be abused. Many reputable advertisers hesitate to use such tricks, but we still need protection from those who do not.

Source Effects

Source effects of advertising refer to potential harmful or unfair results of the use of certain kinds of characters in commercials. Adler noted four categories of such effects.[37] (1) *Confusion Effects*—the child confuses program and advertisements when the same characters are used in both; (2) *Endorsement Effects*—the use of authority figures to lend credibility to a product; (3) *Social Stereotype Effect*—the learning of undesirable stereotypes of race, sex, occupation, age, and so on through viewing characters used to present a product, and (4) *Self-Concept Effect*—the possible harmful effects upon the child's self-concept through commercial appeals to social status or personal enhancement. The more common name for practices illustrating the above effects are "host selling," "program tie-ins," "host lead-ins" to commercials, and endorsements/testimonials by program characters or celebrities.

Although the NAB and NAD advertising guidelines have provisions relating to these effects, there is still considerable confusion as to the interpretations of the guidelines as well as the extent of demonstrated harmful effects on children.

Considerable attention given to the problem of source effects over the past few years has resulted in some improvements. In 1971, ACT was critical of the syndicated format program "Romper Room" for some questionable practices in product promotion. A line of Romper Room toys was being sold. Not long before the Romper Room complaint, Romper Room had merged with Hasbro Toy Company. During March 1971, ACT videotape-recorded five days of forty-five-minute Romper Room programs in Bangor, Maine. Close study of this program revealed that if one were to consider only the "formal" advertising messages (those that would appear on the station's program log), only 9 percent of the total time was devoted to commercial content. When various, more subtle commercial practices were analyzed, however, almost one-half of the total week's programs was devoted to promoting brand-name products. The following are illustrative of the practices used:[38]

1. The hostess for the program introduced commercial announcements: "Listen everybody, I hear a big "Moo." That's right, it's our friend Daisy. Let's listen right now." (A commercial for a local dairy followed.)
2. The hostess gives the commercials (five of twenty commercials on the program).
3. The hostess plugged and mentioned product names (forty-eight such instances during the week).
4. The hostess engaged the children in games and toy play with Romper Room/Hasbro toys during the program. No other brands of toys were used (36 percent of the time during the week was devoted to playing with these toys).

When these plugs are added to the formal commercial messages, 47 percent of the week's time was devoted to promoting products—the bulk of which were for Romper Room/Hasbro toys.

Reacting to unfavorable publicity, the "Romper Room" executives immediately issued new rules (which they called "voluntary changes") that directed its member stations nationwide to discontinue host selling, host lead-ins and lead-outs, endorsements of any commercial products, plugs for brand-name products, and playing with or otherwise promoting its own toys on "Romper Room" programs or adjacent segments.

By 1975, such practices were rare indeed. Both the NAB and NAD guidelines prohibit such practices today. Nevertheless, there are still some such instances remaining on stations that do not subscribe to the NAB code and do not choose to follow industry self-regulation guidelines.[39]

The Use of Premiums

Those who argue against using premiums (and sometimes contests) to sell products say that such gimmicks have nothing to do with the nature of the product—what the FTC has described as irrelevant product characteristics. It is argued that these only tend to confuse the child who should be taught to distinguish among products on the basis of their qualities.

Approximately 17 percent of all commercials on weekend commercial TV for children contained premium offers in 1975. Cereal products most frequently utilize such offers, although candies and some fast-food places also use them.[40] There is little doubt that such appeals are effective—especially among younger children. In addition to sometimes confusing the premium with the product being sold, the child often requests purchase of products with premium offers. Research by Atkin revealed that 75 percent of mothers yield to requests from their children in the supermarket. Denials of such requests based on premium offers was found to lead to greater mother-child conflict.[41]

Currently, the FTC has pending action that would eliminate all forms of premium offers in commercials directed to children under twelve. According to the FTC,

> The injection of a premium into a buying decision cannot help but multiply the difficulties of choice.... Merely by adding another group of factors that compete with those already demanding the child's attention, the premium must inevitably increase the likelihood of confusion and of the purchase of an inferior product.[42]

SUMMARY AND CONCLUSIONS

Consumer groups such as ACT have succeeded in many areas. The time that may be devoted to advertising has been reduced. Rules have been promulgated prohibiting some potentially hazardous products from being sold on TV. Continuing attention is being given to the techniques advertisers may use and to research to demonstrate the effects of these techniques on children.

Government agencies have moved slowly to correct any but the most flagrant abuses—and seldom act on their own initiative.

Industry self-regulation, although often effective, has resulted primarily from threats governmental action. It has also been criticized for providing standards too loose to have much effect. And not all stations are governed by the guidelines set down by industry self-regulators.

Although some progress has been made in the protection of children from unethical advertising practices, many problems remain. There will most likely continue to be conflicts until all interested parties, including companies producing products and advertising agencies responsible for promoting them, accept their ethical responsibilities to ensure that young children in the audience are protected from undue advertising influences.

To protect the future of our youth, children's television must be treated like public interest programming—private profit must be subservient to public necessity.

NOTES

1. White House Conference on Food, Nutrition and Health, *Final Report* (Washington, D.C., 1969).

2. U.S., Federal Communications Commission, "Children's Television Programs—Report and Policy Statement," *Federal Register* 39 (November 6, 1974).

3. U.S., Congress, House Committee on Interstate and Foreign Commerce, *Broadcast Advertising and Children: Hearings before the Subcommittee on Communications,* Washington, D.C., July 14-15, 16, and 17, 1975.

4. Richard P. Adler, "Research on the Effects of Television Advertising on Children: A Review of the Literature and Recommendations for Future Research," report prepared for National Science Foundation, NSF/RA 770115, 1977.

5. See Action for Children's Television, *RE:ACT,* fall 1977.

6. U.S., Federal Communications Commission. *Public Notice,* 44625, February 12, 1970.

7. Action for Children's Television, "Petition to Prohibit Advertisements for Toys on Children's Television Programs," December 15, 1971, p. 16.

8. William Melody, *Children's TV: The Economics of Exploitation* (New Haven: Yale University Press, 1973), p. 118.

9. Action for Children's Television, "Toy Petition."

10. National Association of Broadcasters, "Children's Television Advertising Guidelines," *Code News,* October 10, 1975.

11. Ibid.

12. "Children's Advertising Guidelines," Children's Review Unit, National Advertising Division, Council of Better Business Bureaus, Inc., n.d.

13. Ibid.

14. U.S., F.C.C., "Children's Television Programs."

15. National Association of Broadcasters, "The Television Code," 19th ed. (Washington, D.C.: NAB, 1976).

16. F. Earle Barcus, "Saturday Children's Television" (Newton, Mass.: Action for Children's Television, 1971).

17. U.S., Congress, House, *Broadcast Advertising,* p. 6.

18. Action for Children's Television, *RE:ACT.*

19. F. Earle Barcus, *Children's Television: An Analysis of Programming and Advertising* (New York: Praeger, 1977).

20. Ibid.

21. Adler, "Effects of Television Advertising," p. 109.

22. Boston *Globe,* September 10, 1976.

23. *Broadcasting Magazine,* August 18, 1975.

24. NAB, *Code News.*

25. Council on Children, Media, and Merchandising, "Petition to Issue a Trade Regulation Rule Governing the Private Regulation of Children's Television Advertising," before the Federal Trade Commission, March 1975.

26. "Petition of the Attorneys General of Massachusetts, Alaska, Colorado, Delaware, Hawaii, Illinois, Maryland, Nebraska, New Hampshire, North Carolina, Maine, Pennsylvania, Rhode Island, and Wyoming to Promulgate a Rule Restricting the Advertising of Over-the-Counter Drugs," before the Federal Communications Commission, July 1975.

27. Adler, "Effects of Television Advertising."

28. Barcus, *Children's Television,* pp. 25–26.

29. See F. Earle Barcus, "Weekend Commercial Children's Television," and "Television in the After-School Hours," (Newton, Mass.: Action for Children's Television, 1975).

30. Adler, "Effects of Television Advertising," p. 104.

31. U.S., Department of Agriculture, Agriculture Research Service, "Homemakers' Food and Nutrition Knowledge, Practices, and Opinions," Home Economics Research Report no. 39 (Washington, D.C.: November 1975).

32. White House Conference.

33. Adler, "Effects of Television Advertising," p. 108.

34. NAB, *Code News.*

35. "Children's Advertising Guidelines."

36. Liebert et al., "Effects of Television Commercial Disclaimers on the Product Expectations of Children," *Journal of Communication* 27 (winter 1977): 118–24.

37. Adler, "Effects of Television Advertising," p. 43.

38. E. Earle Barcus, "Romper Room: An Analysis," report prepared for Action for Children's Television (Newton, Mass.: ACT, 1971).

39. See Barcus, "Television in the After-School Hours." In two of the ten independent station markets studied, the host during the children's shows gave commercials for products during the program. These are non-TV code stations.

40. Barcus, *Children's Television,* p. 38.

41. Charles Atkin, "Effects of Television Advertising on Children—Survey of Children's and Mother's Responses to Television Commercials" (East Lansing, Mich.: Michigan State University, Report #8, 1975).

42. U.S., Federal Trade Commission, "Food Advertising: Proposed Trade Regulations, Rule and Staff Statement," *Federal Register* 39 (1974): 218.

7 FOR A "BLUNDERING INQUISITOR": The Pressures and Hazards of Third World Coverage

William Worthy

From Miami airport in September 1962, five weeks prior to the Cuba missile crisis, before heading for sentencing in United States District Court, I telephoned Garth Reeves, publisher of the weekly Miami *Times* and member of the Negro Newspaper Publishers Association.

"You've nothing to worry about in court today," he volunteered. Months earlier, in Washington, his politically active brother, Frank, had warned Attorney General Robert F. Kennedy of the protests—in the streets of Harlem and in the press of Africa—building up in the novel case of *The United States of America* v. *William Worthy Jr.*[1]

"The judge is not going to throw the book at you," Reeves continued. "Bobby Kennedy himself has intervened with him behind the scenes."

Six months later, while the conviction and the token sentence were on appeal, President Kennedy was asked at a White House press conference about the U.S. ban on travel to Cuba. Within a few minutes the phone began to ring. For in his reply to the general question the president became specific and volunteered: "There has been some criticism, as a matter of fact, about an action we took against a newspaperman."[2]

In April 1962, a few days after the Justice Department's unprecedented indictment of me for "illegal re-entry" from Cuba into my native land, the late Elijah Muhammad, leader of the Black Muslims, was talking over coffee with his then first minister, Malcolm X.

"Before this case is over," Muhammad remarked, "Worthy will lose all his illusions about these two-legged rattlesnakes [in those days a favorite Muslim term for whites]. He will come to realize that he is up against the Devil himself."*

Long before then, I held no illusions about the police-state types that permanently staff the Passport Office and the Justice Department's Internal Security Division. Following an "unauthorized" trip to China in 1957, my passport had been revoked (not to be returned for 11½ years). In that five-year interval before my indictment in the Cuba case, I had locked horns repeatedly with those officials while fighting—successfully politically, unsuccessfully legalistically—to have the passport renewed in a three-year civil suit against the secretary of state (*Worthy* v. *Dulles*).[3]

A memorable little incident comes to mind from a recess in one of several State Department passport hearings. In the men's room with my two American Civil Liberties Union attorneys, I started to discuss the case. But William Kunstler and Rowland Watts hushed me. They both cautioned that even that place was likely to be bugged.

But Elijah Muhammad did correctly assess my illusions about many presumed friends and sympathizers in the liberal-intellectual-journalistic community. Even though large numbers of them were fairly timid in criticizing Secretary Dulles for taking the role of the nation's foreign assignment editor, nevertheless they had for the most part upheld my right as a citizen and as a journalist to travel to China. The three years that had elapsed between the bitter end of the Korean War and my arrival in Peking had allowed passions on China to subside.

The response to my trip to Cuba without a passport—half a year after the break in diplomatic relations—was another story. For many North Americans, Cuba was not a country inhabited by human beings but rather a highly charged emotion. From the Alien and Sedition Act of 1798 up to the Smith (1940) and McCarran (1950) Acts, it has been altogether traditional in this country to withhold libertarian safeguards from anyone caught in the vortex of one of our periodic national obsessions.

The federal indictment, handed up by a grand jury sitting in the superheated, exile-filled city of Miami, spelled this out in 1962 terms: It was from "the Republic of Cuba" that I "did unlawfully, willfully,

---

*The conversation was related to the writer shortly afterward by Malcolm X. It is only fair to note that, in the year before his death in 1965, Malcolm's racial philosophy had undergone drastic change—a result, he said, of 1964 conversations in Africa with Presidents Nasser, Nkrumah, and Ben Bella, as well as with Che Guevara (on visit there at that time). On his return home, Malcolm publicly repudiated an antiwhite stance as such. By the 1970s, Elijah Muhammad also had considerably softened his earlier views.

and knowingly enter the United States without bearing a valid pass-port."[4]

Twenty-two months after the indictment, three federal judges of the Fifth Circuit Court of Appeals in New Orleans did what most of the professional liberals, the scholars, and nearly all white journalists had revealed themselves morally and intellectually incapable of doing. The jurists cut through the irrelevancy of my support of the Cuban right to revolution by unanimously declaring unconstitutional the section of the 1952 McCarran Immigration and Naturalization Act that stated a citizen cannot come home from a proscribed country without a pass-port.

On February 20, 1964, the circuit court stunned my State and Jus-tice Department adversaries, whose original goal was a five-year prison sentence, by ruling: "The government cannot say to its citizen, standing beyond its border, that his reentry into the land of his allegiance is a criminal offense; and this we conclude is a sound principle whether or not the citizen has a passport."[5]

The editorial support that followed within a few days from the New York *Times*—when I no longer needed support—left a bad taste. Looking back, I could see that the general editorial silence that greeted my prosecution in the Cuba affair was foreshadowed by numerous little episodes during the time I was involved in pressing my earlier China passport case. In February 1957, while I was broadcasting from Buda-pest (then out of bounds) on my way home from Peking, a CBS News staffer in New York asked me on a two-way radio circuit if, on my return to New York, I would speak on a right-to-travel, right-to-know panel at the Overseas Press Club (OPC).

On the night of the panel (February 25, 1957),* I was informed that the club's Freedom of Information Committee was planning a party to honor me and a *Look* magazine reporter-photographer team who had also defied the State Department's China travel ban.

But the party, without explanation or further word to me, never came off. It was not until a year or so later that, quite by accident, I learned why: Secretary Dulles had passed the word that a testimonial would "embarrass" the Department of State.

Several hours after the panel discussion, which itself went off without incident, I appeared as Bob Considine's guest on the NBC "To-night Show." By long-distance telephone, the show's producer had en-

---

*Second OPC Forum, "Responsibility in Communications." Subject: "Reporting on China." Panel members: William Arthur, managing editor of *Look;* James Wechsler, editor of the New York *Post;* Peggy Durdin of the *New York Times Sunday Magazine;* Morris Ernst, New York civil liberties attorney; myself.

thusiastically informed me that Considine wished to talk about both China and passport restrictions. To assure my acceptance amid the flood of invitations from across the country, a fee of $250 plus expenses was offered.

Six hours before air time the telephone rang again. An apologetic NBC staff member explained that only China would be discussed on the program. "I'm sorry," he said. "Newsmen don't run networks. Salesmen do."

A year earlier, at the time of the Montgomery bus boycott, I'd learned a similar business fact of journalistic life. Although I had been praised in the annual report to CBS stockholders for having made the first live voicecast from Moscow in seven cold war years—after a direct face-to-face appeal to Khrushchev—the network's station relations department had vetoed my broadcasting from the Montgomery affiliate's all-white studio out of fear of offending southern sensibilities.

Ironically, in that same year, I made a lengthy voicecast from even more segregated Pretoria, South Africa, with full technical cooperation from the South African Broadcasting Corporation engineers—prior to being deported.

As I reviewed the period preceding the surprise indictment and the wearying, financially difficult, one-track life it immediately imposed upon me, it was possible to identify some of the milestone events when the interlocking apparatus of the Central Intelligence Agency, the Federal Bureau of Investigation, and the State Department was silently closing in.

From the fall of 1960, for example, I remember having filed from the Western Union office in Havana an exclusive dispatch to my newspaper, the Baltimore *Afro-American.* Through their technically excellent intelligence services, the amazingly calm and self-confident Cubans knew—as they told me over an unforgettable lunch at the Hotel Vedado—that the CIA was readying an invasion of their land from Florida and from elsewhere in the Caribbean.

The publication of my dispatch in the October 15, 1960 New Jersey edition of the *Afro-American* told the American people for the first time of what was to become the Bay of Pigs fiasco.

During that summer and fall, on assignment from producer Robert Drew of the ABC-Time, Inc., "Close-Up" series, I had been working in Cuba with cameramen Albert and David Maysles on a documentary entitled *Yanki, No!* By then, distrust of North American journalists was so strong that we were twice detained by provincial police and, once in Havana, held overnight under armed G2 (intelligence) guard in our Hotel Riviera rooms—in each case with eventual profuse apologies and the return of all confiscated materials.

On my return to New York, I was able to spend an hour in *Time's* "morgue"—a permission withdrawn the very next day. Already there was a large file of as-yet unpublished dispatches of *Time* correspondents—from Miami, Guatemala, Spain, and other points—on the CIA's invasion plans.

A year later, on October 5, 1961, from a now off-limits Havana, I filed a copyrighted story reporting the sensational escape to Cuba of Robert Williams, who had been the NAACP president in Monroe, N.C. Several months earlier, he had been indicted on a kidnapping charge after some of his militant supporters held a white couple who had been driving through the Monroe ghetto at the height of racial tension over the Freedom Rides for several hours.

Fearing that a fair trial was impossible, Williams fled rather than face an almost certain long prison sentence. In this country and in Canada, in conjunction with the Royal Canadian Mounted Police, J. Edgar Hoover—long a target of Williams's criticism for failure to protect civil rights in the South—threw more than 200 FBI agents into the hunt.

The Baltimore *Afro-American* editorialized that my recital of Williams's odyssey via a new underground railway mocked Hoover's invincible image. For that sin, some means had to be found to punish and retaliate. To the FBI chief, it was intolerable that a patchwork network of amateurish civil rights activists in this country and skilled Cuban operatives in Canada could outwit his own overrated agents.

During this period I was naïvely unconcerned about official reprisals. Weeks after I had flown from Havana to Miami on October 10, 1961, a sophisticated civil liberties attorney in Cleveland assured me that as long as my influential editor and publisher backed me, as they did, and as long as I maintained broad support across the country, an indictment under the passport laws was unlikely. After all, despite the considerable bluster of Secretary Dulles, the Eisenhower administration had not indicted any of the three of us newsmen who went to China.

Then, in February 1962 I addressed the Massachusetts Board of Rabbis. As usual, I attacked the FBI for its perennial game of footsie with southern cops and sheriffs. Afterward, one of the rabbis, a man who had fled from Germany in the 1930s, took me to lunch.

"Bill," the rabbi advised. "I think you've gone as far as you can go without getting into trouble." He correctly sensed that the mixture of open defiance of travel bans, unorthodox reporting on the Cuban revolution, and outspoken racial positions taken at home was more than our police/penal/intelligence/diplomatic apparatus was willing to tolerate.

Two months later, with no advance warning, the ax from Washington fell. Had it not been for a fast-thinking Miami newspaperman, I would have been forced to go through a routine familiar to many persons charged with political crimes: a deliberate late-night knock on the door; a husky cry of "FBI" or "U.S. marshals"; neighbors peering from doors and windows as a handcuffed prisoner is led away. (In 1951, there was a loud outcry after federal marshals handcuffed the 82-year-old scholar W. E. B. DuBois upon his later-dismissed indictment under the Foreign Agents Registration Act.)

Fortunately, in my own case, as soon as the special Justice Department attorney from the Internal Security Division in Washington obtained the indictment from the grand jury in Miami, an alert reporter from the Miami *News* telephoned Cliff Mackay editor of the *Afro-American,* who in turn reached me in New York City before the marshals arrived with the warrant. After a few quick calls to attorneys and arrangements with a bonding company for a voluntary surrender the following day, I disappeared and stayed overnight in the suburbs with friends.

Before that mild spring day, I'd passed the U.S. Court House in New York's Foley Square a hundred times, and it was just another building. But after one is fingerprinted there and held for an hour in a cell, it never looks the same again. Nor does the United States government. Nor does this society, reflected as it is in both the incongruous political indictment and the hard faces that congregate in every courthouse—rural South or urban North, state or federal, juvenile or adult.

In that same building where impartial justice is to be served, I saw a bondsman slip cash to a functionary who had considerable authority over the setting of bail. (Later, I wrote about that incident but was never visited by the FBI and asked for the details.) At that moment of preoccupation, I was in neither the mood nor the position to expose or protest the act. Some bondsmen, I learned, have close ties to the underworld. As an object lesson to defendants who might be inclined to flee from prosecution—a thought that uncontrollably crossed my mind upon contemplating the lynch-law atmosphere among Cuban exiles in Miami—there are bondsmen who dispatch hoods to hunt, beat up, and bring back defendants who jump bail. Knowing this, some judges prefer the use of bondsmen to cash or property bail.

Before going to bed on that memorable and lonely night—after paying an exorbitant fee for a $5,000 bond—I had become acutely aware of how unfree I had really been during the 6½ months that the federal government was stalking me. In twenty-four hours, I had learned the hard way the limits of dissent on domestic and foreign policies. The deadly serious criminal indictment was the price I paid for ignorance.

With notable individual exceptions—such as Richard Starnes, syndicated Scripps Howard columnist, and Harrison Salisbury and Peter Kihss of the New York *Times*—institutional, white-press support in my Cuba passport case was as absent as it had been prominent, five years earlier, in *Worthy* v. *Dulles*. During that half-decade, because my reporting on Cuba did not follow the press party line about Fidel Castro's "imminent collapse," I had lost respectability. Friends on the CBS desk from the time of my China trip couldn't understand, I learned, why I'd gone off the deep end and why I was confident that a U.S. invasion of Cuba would flop.

When both the president of the United States and the attorney general reacted to criticism of my prosecution—Bobby Kennedy, for example, by slipping into side doors to avoid demonstrations in different cities—they were not responding to a chorus of an outraged, liberty-defending, white press. There was no such chorus. Rather, they were reacting to protests, at home and at embassies abroad, mostly generated by a defense committee organized to fill the journalistic vacuum. For strategic political reasons, whites were excluded from actually joining the committee but not from other forms of support.

As soon as the committee was organized in August 1962 at a meeting in the Harlem office of A. Philip Randolph, president of the Brotherhood of Sleeping Car Porters, a delegation was appointed to call at the Justice Department to demand that the prosecution be dropped. The four committee representatives—Methodist Bishop D. Ward Nichols, *Afro-American* editor Clifford Mackay, Baptist minister E. Luther Cunningham, and national vice-president of the American Federation of Teachers, Richard Parrish—spent two angry hours with an assistant attorney general. Obviously under rigid instructions, the Justice Department official, Burke Marshall, did not budge. But he was deeply shaken when, finally, the delegation warned him it would take the case to all our Harlems and to the newly independent African nations.

That and other incidents made me aware of the overwhelming momentum of a judicial-penal bureaucracy once its wheels are set in motion. Burke Marshall and the equally sophisticated Kennedys knew that right-wing Justice Department underlings had plunged the administration into an untenable pursuit that could win only ridicule and contempt. The prosecution of a native-born citizen for coming home was absurd; everyone knew I was really under attack for my views.

But to reverse course and to drop the indictment would have required the courage to take on the formidable Mr. Hoover and the FBI, plus their reactionary stalwarts in both houses of Congress.

The defense committee's threat was not an idle one. A well-attended, committee-sponsored street rally in Harlem two days before

I was sentenced came close to exploding into a riot and may have been a factor in Bobby Kennedy's wholly improper, *ex parte,* go-easy-on-the-sentencing approach to my trial judge. When the unsympathetic police tried to prevent the committee from taking up a collection of money after an impressive array of important speakers, the crowd surged toward the soliciting clergyman on the platform, holding up bills and shouting indignantly.

A serious clash would have erupted if any of the white policemen had put their hands on the young ladies with the collection plates. The startled police backed down, sanctioning what two minutes earlier they had termed "illegal."

"I've lived in Harlem all my life," one of the twenty speakers remarked in happy dismay. "I've never before seen Harlemites *demand* the right to give their money away."

In 1957, with even *Editor & Publisher* and the American Newspaper Publishers Association in my corner on the right to travel to China, it came as no surprise when the Departments of State and Justice opted for the civil rather than the criminal route and refused to renew my passport.

But that by no means meant that they ruled out criminal prosecution on some unrelated matter if a skeleton in my closet could be uncovered. Even before my six-week trip to China had concluded, federal agents were busily digging into my past—as far back as Dwight Grammar School in Boston, I subsequently learned.

Late one afternoon around March 1957, shortly after returning from Peking, I went downstairs to answer a loud, demanding doorbell ring in our family home in Roxbury. Huddling on the front porch were three grim-faced and heavy-set men. In bulk and demeanor, each met all the prerequisites of a Mafia enforcer. Long before the current obsession with crime and public safety, I would have been greatly distressed to encounter any of them, let alone the whole trio, on a dark and lonely street. Through the glass in the door, they signaled that they wanted in. And I countersignaled that I wasn't about to admit them until I knew their business. At that point they produced impressive-looking badges: U.S. Treasury Department—Internal Revenue Service—Intelligence Unit.

Once inside the house, they had no time for amenities. Hats stayed on. They weren't interested in sitting down. Everything was direct and brusque. I was not asked *if,* but rather was told *that* I had committed a felony by failing to file income tax returns for three consecutive years. It would not have surprised me if, in their supreme, lip-smacking confidence that they had me, they had arrested and handcuffed me on the spot.

Were it not for the thuggish looks of the three humorless gents, I would have been tempted to laugh in their faces. Never in a thousand years would I have journeyed to China or otherwise stepped out of line politically had I been vulnerable on a tax matter. Possibly because my mother had worked for the Internal Revenue Service for a dozen years, I had long perceived how easily a political figure in the government could order tax records destroyed and could instruct IRS to deny ever having received them. Therefore, every year I have always sent mine via certified or registered mail and kept all records in our safe deposit box for at least ten years. Several days after the visit by the tax intelligence agents, I sent them photocopies of the registered mail receipts. That was the last I ever heard of the three "unfiled" tax returns.

From behind imaginary prison bars I still shudder in retrospect. In 1957, there was no acknowledged credibility gap and no popular mood of disenchantment. It would have been next to impossible to convince a gullible, middle-class federal jury that their government would deliberately conspire to frame innocent persons for political reasons. Such are the perils of living in a society that "kings [and cold wars] can corrupt" and con. Folksinger Phil Ochs sang in his "Ballad of William Worthy"—composed after my Cuba passport case indictment—that if you live in the Free World, then by God you must stay there.

When rebuffed on one front, ideological right-wingers pop up on another. A month after my return home from China, the Senate Judiciary Subcommittee on Constitutional Rights, whose members upheld the right of citizens to a passport, invited me to testify on administration pressures on me and on top CBS management officials. In the hearing room,[7] a State Department representative was seen slipping a note to Senator Sam J. Ervin, Jr., later of Watergate fame. Immediately afterward the senator queried me about an arrest as "a draft dodger." Before the matter quieted down several days later after headline stories across the country, I found myself being ardently defended, and the State Department roundly denounced, by members of the subcommittee, by editorial writers, and by others who maintained that a past record of conscientious objection to war—and even an arrest and prosecution—had no relevance whatsoever to the constitutional right to travel and to the public's right to know.

Clearly, the State Department wasn't just going through the motions of enforcing its travel bans. Travel control is thought control. Sustained and reasonably sophisticated reporting out of China would have soon demolished the Washington myth (later transferred intact, word for word to Fidel Castro) of Mao's "imminent collapse." With Calvinistic passion, John Foster Dulles argued: (1) newsmen and others must be kept out of China because Washington could not protect them;

(2) the presence there of U.S. newsmen would bestow respectability on Mao's communism, which, as late as August 1958, Dulles was publicly depicting as a passing phase; (3) freedom of the press involves only the right to publish the news and not the right to gather it.

To elderly author and radical Scott Nearing and his wife, a security official at the U.S. Consulate General in Hong Kong complained: "That guy William Worthy almost caused me to lose my job. Dulles almost fired me for letting him slip through to China." To Britishers accustomed to thinking of Hong Kong as "their" crown colony, it must have been news to learn that a U.S. functionary controlled border crossings into the People's Republic.

On Christmas Eve 1956, when I dodged Mr. Dulles's vigilant borderwatching subalterns and made it across that famous small bridge into China, I was wholly unaware that an obscure and bedraggled band of Latin American revolutionaries, including Fidel Castro and Che Guevara, had just landed on the coast of Cuba from a leaky boat and had, after overwhelming casualties, fought their way into the hills for two years of history-making guerrilla warfare.

Little did I dream that, just 3½ years later, Havana would be recognizing China and that I would be spending seven weeks in Cuba with the famous camera team of Albert and David Maysles. On assignment from Time, Inc., for the ABC Close-Up series, we filmed the hour-long documentary "Yanki, No!".

ABC-TV showed *Yanki, No!* to 25 million North Americans on December 7, 1960, the State Department made known its grave displeasure and virtually demanded a print. A scheduled second screening was, under pressure, cancelled. While still in Cuba, our crew had already been investigated back home by the FBI after we spent a day at and around Guantanamo naval base. Guantanamo was well into secret preparations for the impending Bay of Pigs invasion, and the instant FBI investigation reflected official sensitivity, as well as a desire to intimidate us and the network. Up to the evening of December 7, we were never sure from one day to the next if the documentary—accurately depicting the Cuban revolution as very much a going concern—would ever be televised. When it was finally aired, the network switchboards in New York and Miami were flooded with protests from Cuban exiles whose versions of events inside Cuba were in no way borne out by the camera.

It was partly because of my screen credit in the well-reviewed *Yanki, No!* that all kinds of groups invited me to lecture on Cuba. Many of them were not necessarily in sympathy with the Cuban revolution. But the film created a healthy skepticism toward the official U.S. fantasies about "chaos" in Cuba and a Hitler-type tyranny under Castro.

One such group that wanted a firsthand report was the Junior Management Association at the General Electric plant in Lynn, Massachusetts. My talk was arranged by the Boston lecture bureau that, through good and bad political times, has represented me since 1958.

A week before the specified date, military intelligence officials from New York intervened to block my appearance, using the plant's huge government contracts as leverage for heavy pressure. Fortunately, old-fashioned New England rectitude surfaced; a gut commitment to free speech came to the fore. The president of the Management Association told the lecture bureau that military intelligence operatives might have him fired, and that he might find himself working in a toy factory, but that if he had anything to say about it, I was going to speak as scheduled. And speak I did—to a surprisingly receptive audience not interested in swallowing popular notions of reality.

In April 1962, after my "illegal re-entry" indictment, a postal worker friend at the Manhattan branch post office on East 23rd Street remembered that the American Civil Liberties Union had defended me five years earlier in *Worthy* v. *Dulles*. Giving me what he intended as friendly advice, he suggested that this time I steer clear of the ACLU.

The reason: That postal branch delivered mail to the ACLU national office on nearby Fifth Avenue. All incoming letters (by the hundreds of thousands, from across the political spectrum) were under a "mail cover"—that is, the Post Office was under FBI instruction to keep a record of the name and address of everyone who wrote to the ACLU. It was a prelude to the Watergate spirit ten years before the famous break-in.

By 1966, the State Department was still not ready to issue me a new passport unless I promised to obey all travel bans. But at least to all outward appearances, efforts to prosecute me for a forbidden late 1964 trip to North Vietnam just before the massive U.S. intervention in the war were shelved. In 1966, when defense counsel Leonard Boudin argued a similar Cuba passport case *(U.S.* v. *Helen Travis)*[8] before the Supreme Court, I made a point of being present. The issues in her case were practically the same as in mine, and almost certainly she had been hastily indicted to counter worldwide charges that I had been singled out for prosecution because of race.

At that time, Thurgood Marshall had not yet been appointed to the Supreme Court by President Johnson. A Solicitor General in the Department of Justice, he and one of his assistants were in the courtroom that morning to present the government's position to the nine judges.

At lunch, in the Court's basement cafeteria, I ran into Thurgood, whom I have known for a long time, but never well. To my complete surprise, he told me of a recent visit from a CIA agent who had asked him intimate personal questions about me—as if I were undergoing a security check for a federal job.

I could not understand why the CIA had gone to a top Justice Department official with whom I had had no contact since his days as staff counsel of the NAACP. Even now I haven't figured out why Marshall was queried about me—unless the CIA got from J. Edgar Hoover's files a hoary *1928* notation that when Thurgood Marshall was a Lincoln University undergraduate, my parents had him and the Harvard University debating team to dinner at our home prior to a well-publicized intercollegiate debate on the then "far out" subject of racial intermarriage.

Quite possibly, the CIA investigation related to my "sensitive" visits, without a passport, to North Vietnam, Cambodia, and Indonesia. The taint from Cuba had faded, but again I was a journalistic heretic during still another binge of press nationalism and press party-lining. For my dispatches to the Baltimore *Afro-American,* the Milwaukee *Journal,* the *Guardian,* and other papers reported Hanoi's unblinking confidence—even then—in ultimate victory over the United States—as well as Prince Sihanouk's strong denunciations of U. S. imperialism in Indochina, and President Sukarno's explanations for Indonesia's confrontation posture vis-à-vis Washington. The views of both leaders, forcefully expressed in interviews and specially directed to Afro-American readers, were undoubtedly upsetting to the funtionaries serving on the State Department's "Harlem" and Afro-Asian desks.

At the time of my trial in Miami, the Justice Department's Internal Security Division attorney who was especially sent down from Washington to prosecute the case argued vehemently and successfully against our motion for a change of venue, as if only in that city of Byzantine exile intrigue and miasma would there be any chance whatever of a conviction. To the limited extent possible, I had been publicizing in the early 1960s the violent events in Miami that were the prelude to that city's current reputation as the political murder capital of the country. There—and to a lesser extent in Tampa and New York—in ways reminiscent of Nazi-instigated violence in pre-Hitler Germany, right-wing Cuban exiles whose CIA ties have in recent years been fully documented were beating up pro-Castro Cubans without police interference.

Although I wrote articles (not, needless to say, in the mass media) and lectured, I found it almost impossible to convince North Americans that such hoodlumism was taking place with the connivance of the CIA and the local police. That was the period when the U.S. press was prostituting itself by glamorizing all Cuban exiles as devotees of freedom, and by painting even well-known Batistiano torturers and murderers in heroic anticommunist colors.

The atmosphere generated by an irresponsible press and government was so intense that today's college generation would find it hard to believe the extremes of public reactions—short of original, penetrating research into that mad segment of our national history. Without a visceral, "fundamentalist" commitment to the First Amendment (recently referred to as "just another amendment" by a CIA witness before a congressional committee), any journalism department or school is cheating the students. Fresh back from my "unauthorized" Cuba trip in the fall of 1961, on an extended lecture tour, I was interviewed on tape by a journalism professor at Carbondale, Illinois.

Quite some time later, and far from that campus, in one of those coincidences that I'm convinced are really not coincidences, I learned that the good professor, not liking my first-hand account of life in Cuba, had completely censored the interview. It was never aired on the campus radio station.

The content of my remarks aside, their accuracy and objectivity aside, the university was the poorer for this rape of the Bill of Rights. Cuba was certainly not the loser. Fidel Castro did not fall from power as a result of my dissenting views being silenced in that Middle America community. But an apparently very insecure U.S. academic had violated every tenet of freedom of the mind—all for some transient expediency that didn't work.

I often wonder how U.S. journalists who violated fidelity to professional principle feel, in 1978, about what they did when they allowed themselves to be caught up in passions of U.S. nationalism. Take a not untypical incident told to me in the summer of 1961 by a Ministry of Telecommunications official in Havana. Through mercenaries and through thoroughly discredited Batistianos, the CIA was masterminding extensive sabotage inside Cuba. It was a wildly insane policy doomed to failure, not only because anti-Castro endeavors lacked a popular base but also because there were strong suspicions that schools, department stores during shopping hours, and similar public places were among the targets being bombed. In no country does a foreign power mobilize mass support by killing women and children.

On one such occasion a bomb went off at 9:08 P.M. Five minutes earlier, a well-known U.S. wire service correspondent filed an "urgent press" dispatch from the Western Union teleprinter in his bureau office in the center of Havana, reporting the explosion, which awkwardly for him, came five minutes after the CIA's scheduled time. When that patriotic correspondent and most of his U.S. colleagues were locked up for a week or two during the CIA-directed Bay of Pigs invasion and were then expelled, many U.S. editorial writers were predictably indignant. But the basis and the rationale for that security precaution by the Cuban government were not communicated to the North American public.

With its dossiers, computers, and surveillance practices, the CIA presumably psyches out newspersons before deciding whom to approach for help with its dirty work. I like to think that a "prickly rebel" family reputation stretching over three generations in rebel Boston explains why I've never been solicited and never been asked to agree to a debriefing on any of the forty-eight countries I have visited, including the four (China, Hungary, Cuba, and North Vietnam) that were verboten.

The secret agency has nevertheless shown intense interest in my travels. Years after my visit to Budapest in early 1957 en route home from China, I learned that the U.S. "vice-consul" there who twice came to my hotel to demand (unsuccessfully) that I hand over my passport was in fact a CIA agent operating under a Foreign Service cover. During a subsequent lecture tour, I met socially in Kansas City a man who had served his army tour of duty in mufti, in detached service in North Africa and elsewhere, with the National Security Agency. Out of curiosity, I asked him what would be the "premium" price for a newsman's debriefing on out-of-bounds China. He thought for a moment and then replied: "Oh, about ten thousand dollars." 1957 dollars. Out of the CIA's petty cash drawer.

A year or two after returning from China, while I was lecturing for a day at Texas Southern University, a dark-complexioned faculty member came up at the end of a seminar and identified himself to me as an economics professor. In a voice audible to everyone in the room and with a broad "I know all about you" grin on his face, he said:

"You know, Mr. Worthy, when you were in China, I was working in Washington on the CIA's China desk. Every morning, we used to receive a top-secret report of your movements in China the day before."

Such designed-to-scare surveillance tactics are effective with those who choose to be easily scared and chilled—like billion-dollar networks. Twice from Peking and once from Shanghai I was able to broadcast for CBS News. The first voicecast was of course a scoop, and the cablegram from the New York news desk several hours later expressed professional delight. The signal to Oakland had been satisfactory, the content fine. But there was one political problem. Not being at all attuned to the State Department's "nonrecognition" nonsense, I had used "Peking" in the broadcast, instead of the old Kuomintang name for China's capital. Thus the punch-line suggestion in the cablegram. In future voicecasts, the CBS news desk would prefer "Peiping—pronounced B-A-Y-P-I-N-G."

If acted upon in the then very hostile U.S.-China climate, the suggestion would have been totally self-defeating, and I had not the slightest intention of heeding it. Justifiably, the Chinese would have been offended and probably would have made no more studios and transmitters available for future broadcasts. Knowing that David Chipp, the British correspondent for Reuters in China, would be both amused and scornful of this typical American childishness and journalistic kowtowing to power, I let him read the cablegram.

"I'll tell you what you should do, Bill," he said. "On your next broadcast, when you reach the return cue, just say: 'This is Bill Worthy in Peiping. Now back to CBS News in New Amsterdam.' "

Throughout my China passport case—but not during my Cuba case, by which time he had become director of the U.S. Information Agency—Edward R. Murrow supported my position. Sitting at the bar in the CBS building at 485 Madison Avenue, New York, shortly after my return from China, Murrow told me that he had been "ashamed" of the company's quaking and quivering in the face of improper official pressures. After I had lost the ACLU-supported *Worthy* v. *Dulles* suit for passport renewal in both U.S. district court and the Court of Appeals for the District of Columbia, he devoted his evening network radio commentary (June 11, 1959) to the issue:*

A three-judge U.S. Court of Appeals has upheld the State Department's action—has in effect said that the Secretary of State, acting on behalf of the President, can at his discretion deny American citizens the right to travel to specific areas. The court said: "In foreign affairs, especially in the intimate posture of today's world of jets, radio and atomic power, an individual's yen to go and to enquire may be circumscribed." And it went on to say: "A blustering inquisitor, avowing his own freedom to go and do as he pleases, can throw the whole international neighborhood into turmoil."

This curious doctrine may come as a surprise to foreign correspondents who have worked for many years under dictatorships without either blustering or creating turmoil. . . .

The State Department has revised its policy about American reporters going to Communist China. The Department has agreed to give passports for Red China to representatives of a number of periodicals and agencies normally dealing with foreign news. The num-

---

*"Edward R. Murrow with the News," CBS Radio Network, Thursday, June 11, 1959, 7:45–8:00 p.m. EDT. Placed in the *Congressional Record* by Rep. James Roosevelt on July 29, 1959—pages A6557–8, appendix.

ber has now risen to forty-four. But the Chinese are insisting on reciprocity—that an equal number of Chinese correspondents be permitted to enter this country. The presence of these reporters in China would be no more a peril to peace, nor more a cause of turmoil than the presence of Mr. Worthy. And the President would be just as incapable of guaranteeing their safety. So what Mr. Worthy strove for has been going on even if he goes on losing. But the principles involved in this case have not been satisfied by the revised rules for newsmen in Communist China. The State Department is still saying "No" to everybody else who wants a passport to go to the forbidden areas. . . .

It seems to this reporter that more is involved in this case than just Mr. Worthy's right to go where he pleases. His ability as a reporter is not in question. Whether he is a "blustering inquisitor" or a mild, scholarly man, has no bearing. What is most at stake is the public's right to know, not only in China but everywhere, any place at any time. A close reading of the Court's ruling does not reveal any mention or recognition of this right. It is perhaps fantasy to suggest that at some future time some future Secretary of State could lock us all up in this country, could deny the right of exit, but under this ruling it could happen.

Through his personal attorney, Murrow had sought to file an *amicus curiae* brief in my behalf in the Court of Appeals. But the government lawyers had objected, and the motion for the necessary court permission was consequently not granted. If the Justice Department attorneys had approved, as did my ACLU lawyers, the court almost routinely would have affirmed the motion. Only recently have I learned that in that period Murrow made what was apparently a very substantial contribution to the ACLU.

At the hearing of the Senate Constitutional Rights Subcommittee, I testified that the State Department had put strong pressure on Baltimore Afro-American editor Cliff Mackay to order me home from China immediately, and—after my first voicecast from Peking—on CBS News to keep me off the air.[10] The objection had been to my presence in the forbidden land, not to the content of the broadcast. On my return, John Day, then CBS News director, had told me the details of the arm-twisting, details with which Murrow was also wholly familiar.

I named Robert Murphy, deputy undersecretary of state for political affairs, as the official who had telephoned CBS President William Paley very shortly after the first shortwave transmission from the Chinese capital. Naturally, in my testimony, I did not betray my source at the network.

On arrival at the CBS newsroom in New York from the Washington hearing, I happened to see an internal memorandum that had been circulated as soon as my charges against Murphy had moved on the national wires: "There will be no—repeat, no—comment on Bill Worthy's testimony today at the Senate hearing."

Four days later, Murphy testified at a Senate Foreign Relations Committee hearing on State Department passport policies. The following exchange took place between him and Senator Hubert H. Humphrey:

> *Mr. Humphrey.* On that point, Mr. Secretary, is it true that Mr. Worthy, having gotten into Red China, did take some motion pictures, and had made those available to the Columbia Broadcasting System, and that pressure was brought from the State Department not to show those pictures to the American television viewers?
>
> *Mr. Murphy.* I don't believe any pressure was exercised by the Department of State, as far as I know, on the Columbia Broadcasting System or on any other news medium, to prevent the telling of the story, the publication of the facts as the correspondent saw them. I know of none.
>
> *Mr. Humphrey.* Do you know whether or not Mr. Worthy did take such movies?
>
> *Mr. Murphy.* I understood he took pictures. I did not know whether they were movies or not.
>
> *Mr. Humphrey.* Or film? Do you know whether or not they were sent to the Columbia Broadcasting System?
>
> *Mr. Murphy.* No, sir, I don't.
>
> *Mr. Humphrey.* Do you know whether or not any official of the government contacted any radio or television station, system, or network, suggesting that it might be better, that it would be appreciated, if such film, pictures, or movies were not run?
>
> *Mr. Murphy.* I would like to answer that question, Mr. Senator, by saying that I noted the testimony of Mr. Worthy before another committee of the Senate in which he referred to pressure by the Department, and mentioned my name, on the Columbia Broadcasting System.

There was no pressure brought to bear on the Columbia Broadcasting System or any effort to bring pressure to bear on it. We did make an inquiry. Mr. Paley, who is president of the Columbia System, is an old friend of mine, and we had never heard of Mr. Worthy prior to that incident. We were told he had some arrangement with the Columbia Broadcasting System.

We made an inquiry, I think on January 4, of Mr. Paley, as to what the relationship was. It went no further than that—a simple inquiry, no pressure.[11]

Any number of persons who heard Murrow report Murphy's testimony on his April 2, 1957 evening radio newscast told me that Murrow had made it unmistakably clear that he knew the answers to Senator

Humphrey's questions to be false. Later, Murrow said to me in a private conversation that he had deliberately violated the network's policy against editorializing with one's voice in order to ridicule Murphy's version of that telephone call to Paley.

Besides wishing to let the public know about this specific (and unsuccessful) instance of high-level pressure, I also wanted to alert any and all government officials to the full and embarrassing public disclosure they would face if such tactics were to be attempted again.

That was also my approach after an incident in Budapest. On the way home from China, during a stop of several days in Hungary, I went to the U.S. legation to pick up a registered letter, with a check, from New York *Post* editor James Wechsler. Apparently I was expected to swallow hard and say nothing about the handwritten notation on the *Post* envelope: "Opened in error by E. T. Wailes."

There wasn't the slightest possibility of an error. All registered mail, worldwide, has to be signed for upon delivery. To me, the only saving feature was that the U.S. minister was a big enough person not to palm off the blame onto some low-level mailroom clerk. He took personal responsibility for this Washington-directed invasion of privacy. One can imagine his British counterpart, under a similar order, exercising the honorable English tradition of resigning in protest.

The vice-consul in Budapest who actually handed me the opened envelope later confided that Wailes was chagrined and ashamed of the whole sordid episode, to which I had immediately given worldwide publicity. Never again, in all my travels, did I have mail sent to me in care of a U.S. diplomatic mission. Five years later, at the time of my indictment for coming home from Cuba without a valid passport, many persons perceived in that serious though laughable prosecution a clear case of revenge and retaliation for all the embarrassment that the perennial right-wing elements in the State and Justice Departments had brought on themselves. They would have resented my disclosures if they had come from a white, Anglo-Saxon, Republican correspondent who supported all U.S. wars. They found altogether unacceptable and intolerable those same awkward disclosures when coming from me.

To the Court of Appeals judges in Washington I was a blustering upstart. To their social equals and their counterparts across town at State and Justice, my travel-ban defiance put in political jeopardy their weird and fragile nonrecognition policy. In an earlier and harsher era, both branches of government—judicial and executive—wouldn't have hesitated to use that good old plantation adjective "uppity."

Newsman Carl Rowan and I last met and talked in 1955 at the first Afro-Asian summit conference called by President Sukarno in Bandung, Indonesia (labeled by one Dutch newspaper a conference of children without their elders). So I don't know precisely what Rowan had in mind in 1969 when, preceding me as a speaker at Central State University in Ohio, he told an administration official, "Bill Worthy could have gone far if he had played the game."

NOTES

1. *U.S.A.* v. *William Worthy, Jr.* United States District Court, Southern District of Florida Miami Division Cr. No. 214–62-M-Cr. Filed 4/24/62.
2. New York *Times,* March 22, 1963.
3. *Worthy* v. *Dulles* (redesignated *Worthy* v. *Herter* after John Foster Dulles resigned as Secretary of State) 106 U.S. APP DC 153; 270 F.2d 905.
4. Edward F. Boardman, United States Attorney (Miami); Alta M. Beatty, Special Attorney, U.S. Department of Justice, Internal Security Division, Washington, D.C.
5. *U.S.A.* v. *William Worthy, Jr.* U.S. Court of Appeals for the Fifth Circuit 328 F.2d 386 Docket No. 20062 February 20, 1964 Chief Judge Tuttle Circuit Judge Jones (author of the decision) Circuit Judge Bell.
6. Phil Ochs "The Ballad of William Worthy," in the album "All The News That's Fit To Sing," Electra Records no. 7269.
7. U.S., Congress, Senate, Committee on the Judiciary, *The Right to Travel, Hearings on S. 49,* March 29, 1957.
8. *United States of America* v. *Helen Maxine Levi Travis* U.S. Court of Appeals CaCal 353 F2d 506 Docket no. 19628.
9. New York *Times,* March 30, 1957.
10. U.S., Congress, Senate, Foreign Relations Committee, 85th Congress *Hearings: Department of State Passport Policies,* 85th Cong., April 2, 1957, p. 23.

EDITOR'S NOTE

During World War II and in the growing cold war tensions of the years that followed, the State Department restricted travel by controlling passports in order to protect "the best interests of the United States." The criteria of fitness to travel were political beliefs and associations. The traveler had to take an oath regarding past or present membership in the Communist party. As of 1952, such refusals to take that oath constituted grounds for the revocation or denial of a passport. Under these rules Paul Robeson, the singer, and Corliss Lamont, the writer, were denied passports.

The internationally known artist Rockwell Kent applied for a passport in order to attend a meeting of the World Council of Peace in Finland and was refused. In *Kent* v. *Dulles* (357 U.S. 116 [1958]) the majority opinion affirmed that the right to travel was a part of that "liberty" that could not be denied a citizen without due process of law under the Fifth Amendment. For a time this decision prevented the State Department from withholding a passport on these grounds.

There were, however, alternative means; the State Department could ban travel to a particular country or area on the grounds of national security and national interest. In the early days of the Eisenhower administration, John Foster Dulles, in his capacity as secretary of state, imposed a travel ban on Communist China. American journalists condemned the restriction and argued against it vigorously. Whatever the "evils" of the Peking government might be, they considered the American people's right to know a preeminent principle. The issue became sensitive on both sides.

When William Worthy, as a reporter for the Baltimore *Afro-American,* crossed the Hong Kong border late in 1956, his passport was not validated for entry into China. He was the first journalist to enter China in seven years. The subsequent experiences he reports indicate an intense interest on the part of both his fellow journalists and the State Department.

Dulles appeared to modify his position somewhat on August 22, 1957, when he offered permission to twenty-four hand-picked news organizations to send correspondents to Communist China on a kind of trial basis. Each organization would be allowed to send one representative for a seven-month period, but no photographers were to be allowed.

The Communist Chinese rejected this "unilateral" arrangement and demanded reciprocity. The State Department insisted that no reciprocal visas would be granted to Chinese reporters.

Some forty newsmen received official authorization to enter China by 1959, but only one, John Strohm of Newspaper Enterprise Association, was accepted by the Chinese.

Secretary Dulles based his arguments for travel restrictions on national security, but his position is more easily understood as a political maneuver pressing cold war objectives. Supreme Court Justice William O. Douglas, who was researching an article on China for the *National Geographic,* was denied permission to travel there in 1959. Representative Charles O. Porter was refused a passport to visit the People's Republic of China in 1960 on the grounds that he was a congressman.

Worthy's decision to enter Cuba in July 1961 came after the Eisenhower administration's severance of diplomatic relations with the Castro régime and after the State Department edict that specific approval must be requested for travel to Cuba. After being tried and convicted Worthy won the appeal in the U.S. Circuit Court of Appeals for the

Fifth Circuit. The section of the federal statute making his reentry into the country a crime was held unconstitutional.

Also in 1961, the Supreme Court upheld the order of the Subversive Activities Control Board requiring the registration of Communist party members. Once again the State Department demanded an oath of non-membership from passport applicants. Under section 6 of the Internal Security Act, any member of a Communist organization required to register under the provisions of that act was even denied the right to request a passport.

Three years later section 6 was declared invalid by the Supreme Court decision in *Aptheker* v. *Secretary of State* (378 U.S. 500, 507, 514, 511, 512 [1964]). Once again the decision was based on Fifth Amendment grounds, although Justice Goldberg, who wrote the majority decision, pointed out that First Amendment-guaranteed freedom of association was impaired if the right to travel could be denied because of membership in a given association.

After the Aptheker decision, the State Department no longer had the prerogative of refusing to grant passports on the basis of an individual's political belief, opinion, or association. The power to refuse a passport for travel to a particular country remained in use. It was challenged on First Amendment grounds in *Zemel* v. *Rusk* (381, U.S. 1, 16-17 [1965]). The Court agreed unanimously that passport restriction was a denial of "action," not "expression." The majority opinion stated that the right to speak and to publish did not carry with it an unlimited right to gather information. This decision upheld particularized restrictions of the right to travel on the basis of clear national interest.

In March 1971 the thaw in relations between the United States and the People's Republic of China was initiated by President Nixon's removal of the travel ban. The State Department predicted there would be no sudden increase in the number of Americans traveling to Communist China, pointing out that only three entry visas had been granted to Americans in the preceding eighteen months. Quickly, the Chinese granted visas to a fifteen-member table-tennis team. President Nixon responded with an announcement that visa-granting procedures for visitors from China would be expedited.

On the basis of a 1967 State Department ruling, an oath of allegiance to the Constitution was not required of passport applicants. Late in 1971, Secretary Rogers ordered that passports be denied to Americans who refused to take such an oath. Today it is requested but not required.

For two decades, the only direct American links with Communist China were established by the extraordinary efforts of individuals such as William Worthy and Edgar Snow. Suddenly, in January 1972, President Nixon entered China accompanied by an elite horde of eager newspaper and television journalists. Three hundred American tourists applied for visas to visit China at the same time as President Nixon. By 1973, thousands of American visa applications overwhelmed the tourist accommodations of the People's Republic of China and confounded State Department predictions.

The State Department ban on the use of passports by Americans who traveled without permission to Cuba, North Korea, and North Vietnam was renewed in September 1975. At the same time the ban was extended to Cambodia and South Vietnam. The Cuban government was eager to earn foreign currency credits by attracting tourists. The travel ban was circumvented by routing tours through Mexico and Canada. Stanley Sommerfield, foreign assets control director of the United States Treasury Department, responded by ordering the investigation of any American who wrote a check to a private travel agency of Toronto, Canada. That tour wholesaler, which had invited Americans to join tours to Canada, discontinued the program.

On March 18, 1977, all territorial travel bans were ended. President Carter, citing his desire to improve human relations, announced the removal of all remaining restrictions on travel to Cuba, North Korea, Vietnam, and Cambodia.

8 SMALL-TOWN JOURNALISM HAS SOME BIG ETHICAL HEADACHES

Loren Ghiglione

The newspaper movies on the Late, Late Show have it all wrong. The small-town paper is not a miniature Washington *Post.* The editor does not—*à la* Dan Duryea in *The Underworld Story* and James Cagney in *Johnny Comes Lately*—crusade unrelentingly for truth, beauty, and justice.

The typical small daily, like the typical large daily, behaves more like other businesses in the real world—paying as much attention to improving the bottom line as to improving the lot of those at the bottom of society's barrel.

But aren't the ethical problems that face the small-town paper different from those that confront the Washington *Post,* the New York *Times,* and other metropolitan dailies?

Probably not. The problems everywhere, as William Allen White explained, come down to attempting to tell the truth about the world the newspaper chooses to cover: "The only excuse an editor has for being is that his paper shall print the news. The question that comes to every man running a newspaper is: 'What is news?' That he must settle for himself, and having found a rule, must stick as closely to it as possible. When an editor begins monkeying with his conscience, stretching his rule to shield his friends or to punish his enemies he is lost."

And yet the small-town paper is more susceptible to certain kinds of ethical problems. Some of the strengths of the typical small-town paper—the closeness of the owner to the community and to the paper, the enthusiasm and idealism of a young news staff, the citizens' sense of the paper as, almost literally, belonging to them—also are the bases for major weaknesses.

First, boosterism abounds. It is expected by community leaders that the small-town paper will support locating the new county courthouse on Main Street, even if it really should be located elsewhere. It is expected that bad news about local businesses—layoffs, building-code violations, ethically questionable practices—will be played down. It is expected that businesses—which, after all, are private concerns, not public officials, and pay for the advertisements that represent 75 percent of a paper's revenue—will be treated with respect.

To operate a small-town paper in defiance of those expectations is to risk retaliation. Recently our 6,200-circulation paper published a front page article about building-code violations, precipitating a letter to the editor from one named landlord who also happens to be a restaurant owner. The letter concluded with great subtlety: "The article is very unprofessional!! If I ran my restaurant so unprofessionally, I'd be shut down. Who shuts down the local newspaper? Nobody, I guess . . . unless it's your advertisers!" A week later, when news and editorial-page coverage of the building-code violations continued, the restauranteur pulled his ads.

Sometimes advertiser pressure results from something as innocuous as reporting news of town government. A used-car dealer demanded that our paper cease publishing articles about several Southbridge gas stations that wanted town permission to sell second-hand cars. The paper refused, and the dealer canceled his advertising for six months.

Editorials or opinion-page columns that actually question businesses' conduct virtually guarantee retaliation. Steve West, the owner of Bentley's, a department store chain with a branch in Southbridge, twice ran full-page ads in our paper proclaiming, "I can show you how to live like a millionaire in 30 days. I did it!" The ads plugged one of his four books. In *Mental Calisthenics,* West described himself as "a respected applied psychologist" and as president of the American Association of Applied Psychology. West readily admits he formed the group himself and named himself president.

Next to West's photo in the live-like-a-millionaire advertisement was a small block of type inviting the public to meet him when he came to town to promote his books. One of our editors—a skeptical sort with a touch of sportswriter in his blood—was part of the welcoming committee.

The editor wrote an opinion-page piece that noted in passing:

The full-page newspaper advertisements are misleading in that Steve West is not a svelte, stylish millionaire about town with eight layers of lacquer holding down the thinning strands of blonde hair atop his head, the gold watch chain glistening from the folds of a 45-piece custom suit.

This night in Southbridge he wore yellow slacks that must have doubled as a napkin at chow stops between appearances and the silk shirt was open at the neck and covered by a leather jacket, though the shirt collar was twisted behind the neck. He could have been stopping at Bentley's on the way to his third-shift job at American Optical.

Needless to say, West did not take kindly to our editor's column. He had someone call me to ask for a retraction. I also had watched West perform that evening and didn't feel a retraction was appropriate.

Bentley's did not advertise in our paper following the appearance of the column, and checks to us for approximately $2,000 bounced. Perhaps it was a coincidence, and, then again, perhaps not.

Some editors and publishers say that advertisers seldom attempt to dictate news policy and virtually never succeed. I disagree. But it is also true that many newspapers do such a good job of self-censoring—keeping from print news articles and opinion pieces that might offend advertisers—that businesses feel little need to exert pressure, subtle or otherwise. Such papers give their readers a kind of Chamber of Commerce version of the truth.

On well-staffed metros, pressure on reporters to publish hard-nosed exclusives, to avoid Chamber of Commerce journalism, is more likely. Charles Seib, the ombudsman of the Washington *Post,* once referred to his paper's "urge to expose gone wild." And British playwright Tom Stoppard has a character in *Dirty Linen* say, "It's like a competition, you see. They're not writing it for the people, they're writing it for the writers, writing it on the other papers. 'Look what I've got that you haven't got.' There don't have to be any *people* reading it at all so long as there's a few journalists around to say, 'Old Bill got a good one there!' "

Although there is peer-group pressure, as the academics like to say, on even small papers, the real danger with us is not using the freedom we have to investigate the wrongs around us. It's more likely that we'll be irresponsible by not using our First Amendment freedom than by abusing it.

Advertiser pressure, the high cost of conducting investigations, a new generation of less aggressive college graduates-turned-reporters— a number of excuses are available for the smaller paper that doesn't want to undertake the kind of investigative work it should. K. Scott Christianson, an investigative reporter from Albany, New York, profiled in John Behrens's *The Typewriter Guerrillas,* predicts, "There will be less boat rocking, and because of the shortage of jobs, young reporters will do what management wants them to do, which is to increase profits. And to hell with social improvements, righting wrongs, and so on."

A second big problem for those of us on smaller papers is establishing the proper degree of independence from the community. The small-town newspaper should not be so independent as to be arrogant about its readers—in a town of older, deeply religious people, it should not, for example, totally ignore religion news just because the news staff, average age twenty-five, defines religion as essentially unimportant.

I was reminded how isolated even small-town journalists can be from the values of readers when I recently asked for public reaction to four controversial photos. Three of them had been published in our paper.

The first photo showed three dead dogs at the local pound during a period when the dog officer was being charged with negligence. The second was of a very pregnant woman being comforted by a police officer the moment after she had learned that her husband had been killed in a logging accident. The third showed a small girl sitting in front of the rundown tenement where she lived—a building cited for safety-code violations. The fourth was of a rabbit, his head severed from the rest of his body; the rabbit was the victim of a dog that allegedly had killed several animals in the neighborhood.

Of the thirty people polled, only five would have published even one or two of the photos. The public was concerned about the newspaper's invading the privacy of the subjects and violating standards of good taste. Only the photo of the rabbit with the severed head had been rejected for publication by the paper; the paper had reached a different conclusion than the public about the newsworthiness and appropriateness of the other three photos.

However one feels about the publication of the three photos, in certain areas the reporter, editor, and publisher should clearly isolate themselves from the values of the community. I confess I don't always know where to draw the line.

Codes of ethics encourage an editor and publisher to be monogamous—married only to the newspaper. But an editor also feels obligated to contribute to the community that provides him with a livelihood. And he knows from experience that participating in the life of the community, he will know far more about what's really happening. (I believe that most journalists know only 20 to 25 percent of what there is to be understood about most topics they cover.) Finally, the community feels cheated if an editor observes, writes, but never participates.

How independent should a small-town newspaper person be? When we interviewed editors and publishers for the New England

Daily Newspaper Survey, we found widely varying answers. Campbell Niven of the *Times Record,* Bath-Brunswick, Maine, involved himself in practically everything—as director of a savings and loan association, director of a bank, president of the Chamber of Commerce, member (and past president) of Rotary, selectman, and chairman of the Democratic town committee. Niven said his activities did not undermine the credibility or independence of the *Times Record.* "It's a thin line and one walks it precariously, but it can be done."

Others were less certain, prohibiting involvement of their staff in business, politics, and even service clubs. Gordon Smith, publisher of the *Caledonian-Record,* St. Johnsbury, Vermont, joined all the town's service clubs when he returned from World War II. "But then I found I was being used by every organization. So I resigned from them all. Now we treat them all alike."

My own experience has been that even participating in something as safe as a YMCA board of managers creates split loyalties. In my innocence, I accepted a request to join the local Y board. I soon discovered it was faced with the apparent misappropriation of funds by an employee. That was news. Did my presence on the board discourage staffers from uncovering and reporting the news? Should I tell the newsroom about the apparent misappropriation? Was I obligated to the Y to keep quiet? In an untenable position, I resigned from the board. Our paper reported the $58,500 insurance settlement that went to the Y because of the apparent misappropriation.

I learned a lesson: any involvement with community organizations, however harmless on the surface, compromises the integrity of the paper. But perhaps this lesson is being learned very slowly—if at all—at many smaller papers.

Third, smaller newspapers emphasize local, names-make-news journalism, and that emphasis can often distort the public agenda. What is published (or not published) in a paper shapes a community's priorities.

The local, names-make-news focus is understandable. The sense of community that big-city folks always praise in small towns comes partly from a common knowledge provided by the local paper of who is ill, whose son scored the winning touchdown at the high school game last weekend, and whose daughter married whom. But too often this kind of journalism is all that the community paper offers.

Reporting about housing, medical services, welfare, and the schools—issues that relate directly to the poor, children, and the elderly—is infrequent. There are simple explanations. On the very rare occasions when the *Evening News* assigns two reporters to an investigation, the paper loses one-third of its staff for day-to-day news; some important coverage of government meetings inevitably has to be sacrificed for the period of the investigation.

The daily deadline also encourages the small-town editor to delay until tomorrow any assignment that requires background work—a time-consuming examination of out-of-town public records, a lengthy series of interviews to understand the history of a problem, or a reading of books and professional journals.

I put off for years a story that involved the local schools. Did they fail to encourage—or actively discourage—free expression by students? Was it a coincidence that none of the high schools in Southbridge had a school newspaper? Were students learning how to deal responsibly with freedom of the press, or were they simply being gagged?

I finally attempted to find the answers. After four months of interviewing teachers, students, and administrators from as far back as 1959, I wrote a two-part series that documented a pattern of censorship in the public school system. The series was personally satisfying and may have helped lead to the reinstitution of student papers at the town's two high schools. But don't ask me whether the people of Southbridge were best served by my spending one-third of a year on that single story.

That said, it still seems to me that the primary obligation of an editor is to remain true to his values, both on the news pages and the editorial page, and to aspire to put out more of a paper than the publisher thinks his pocketbook can bear.

When my wife and I acquired the *Evening News* in 1969, its editorials—all nonlocal, of course—were purchased from an editorial-writing service in Arizona that deserved a Pulitzer Prize for blandness. Needless to say, it's difficult for a paper to convey the image of an aggressive, local conscience to the community when its soul is being bought for $4.50 a week. Yet, the New England Daily Newspaper Survey discovered as late as 1974 that 20 percent of the dailies in the region—mainly small papers—were occasionally publishing editorials provided by outside services.

As to the news pages, I still suffer from the quaint notion that they should contain real news. Press mogul Rupert Murdoch wants something more, or should I say less. "The average American paper fails to communicate with the mass market.... There is a lack of urgency in writing, a tendency to be dull, to write for the upper ten percent of the market in educational and money terms." And so we have titillating headlines (over articles that are so short that they tell little more than the headlines) and "Ear," "Eye," and other gossip columns.

And we have small-town editors who are beginning to sound like miniature Murdochs. Carl A. Veno, editor of the 9,000-circulation *Free Press* in Quakertown, Pennsylvania, says, "Young people, our number-one target, are interested in what a newspaper can do for him or her. Can it entertain them? Can it tell them where to buy wisely? Can it give them health, consumer and entertainment news? Blend this with a little sex and crime and you have a marketable product."

Newspaper researchers package the Murdoch philosophy in slightly more dignified dress. Joe Belden talks about using research "to make it possible for more news people, and managements, to do things that get more readers." Some of those things involve deemphasizing what readers see as "negative" news and emphasizing soft rather than hard news. In a nice bit of doublespeak, Belden explains, "We are not suggesting omission; we are calling attention to the habits of positioning, intensity, and repetition in editing such news."

Bah, humbug, Belden. If the press is to continue being a community conscience and, in Mr. Dooley's words, "comfort the afflicted and afflict the comfortable," then it should set the right agenda. It should not forget to give ample coverage on its news pages to those issues and subjects of critical importance to its community.

Newspapers need to continue reporting on the challenges to the civil rights of all people—women, Puerto Ricans, and blacks. (We were amazed to discover in interviews of Southbridge students who had a day off from school on the holiday honoring Martin Luther King's birthday that most did not know anything about him. Paula Aponte, twelve, said, "I guess he was a king. I don't know."

The press should pay particular attention to segments of the society that are, if not invisible, less likely to be represented by spokesmen. Are we reporting about unwanted children being shuttled from state facilities to foster homes and back? Are we covering the mental patients who are kept locked up even though there is no legitimate reason for institutionalization? Are we adequately reporting the plight of isolated elderly people on fixed incomes?

Newspapers need to be guardians of human respect, civility, and literacy—matters rarely seen as newsworthy "issues." Not only, for example, do we need to attack editorially those who degrade the English language, a national disaster "up with which we will not put," to quote Winston Churchill, but we need to hire reporters and editors who really care about language. Humorist S. J. Perelman wrote about Harold Ross, his editor at *The New Yorker,* "Ross loved to nitpick. He once wrote an inquiry raising 96 points about a piece. . . . Where, nowadays is there an editor who takes that much time?" Not, I'm afraid, on most newspapers.

The press needs to report regularly on the environment—manmade as well as natural. Are our factories safe places to work? Is the local hospital as sanitary as it should be? What is the condition of the air and water? Is the developer of the housing tract bulldozing crucial wetlands out of existence?

Newspapers should continue to be the fourth branch of government. "Publicity is the strong bond which unites the people and their government," wrote President James A. Garfield. "Authority should do no act that will not bear the light." Regardless of open meeting laws and the post-Watergate mentality that is supposed to be present among public officials, government needs the attention of the press now more than ever.

This nation is undergoing a dangerous change in attitude. It is not simply a political movement with everyone shifting to the right of Ronald Reagan; nor is it merely a new mood on our campuses, rebellion being replaced by grade-grubbing. " 'We-ness' and 'me-ness' are the two key words," writes Malcom Cowley. "During an expansive period, the general attention is turned outward to broad issues affecting 'us,' the nation or the world."

But now, in Cowley's language, we're in a contracting period with attention focused on " 'my' success in a stable society." Maybe that helps explain the current rush to worship the deity of privacy.

Judges close trials to the press and public now, for the first time, because of, to quote a Massachusetts superior court case involving armed robbery, "the extremely emotional nature of the testimony being given now." Boards of university trustees and school committees avoid the requirements of open-meetings laws by simply arguing that their secret meetings are special and don't fall within the bounds of the laws. In the process, freedom of the press is being eroded. With no access, the press cannot report to the public. And without the press's reports, the public is ignorant and, therefore, no longer free. "If a nation expects to be both ignorant and free," Thomas Jefferson wrote, "it expects what never was and never will be."

So finally, newspapers—yes, even the smallest weeklies—need to go beyond their historical role of reporting and editorializing about the news. They should be activists—fighters in every forum for the First Amendment. They should bark at their legislators about privacy bills that are really secrecy bills. They should take school committees and town managers to court when necessary to achieve open meetings.

The press has failed miserably to educate the public about the necessity of press freedom in a democratic society. So now newspapers must pay the price, literally. Litigation, for example, is expensive. A simple lawsuit against the Southbridge school committee under the Massachusetts open-meeting law—now on appeal to the Massachusetts Supreme Judicial Court—cost us thousands of dollars.

But the press, representing the public, has an obligation to fight for the First Amendment, even in those cases where the fight doesn't appear to be to the short-run advantage of newspapers. As this is written, the Federal Trade Commission is attempting to ban certain television commercials aimed at children, giving short shrift to the First Amendment protection provided for "commercial speech." And the U.S. House of Representatives argues for creating its own television system to report its sessions, rather than permitting network coverage.

Television is the press's worst enemy in many respects—just ask the advertising director of any paper. But print journalists should battle for the First Amendment rights of their television brethren as ferociously as for their own. If the press doesn't fight, and the public comes to accept half-freedom for television, the First Amendment rights of even the smallest hometown daily are threatened.

Alas, the small paper should not expect the applause of most of its readers for fighting the good First Amendment fight.

Why does a reader pick up his community paper? I'm reminded of John Greenleaf Whittier's words from *Snow-Bound,* published more than 110 years ago:

> At last the floundering carrier bore the village paper to our door. Lo! broadening outward as we read, to warmer zones the horizon spread in panoramic length unrolled we saw the marvels that it told. Welcome to us its week-old news, its corner for the rustic Muse, its monthly gauge of snow and rain, its record, mingling in a breath the wedding bells and dirge of death: just, anecdote, and love-lorn tale, the late culprit sent to jail; its hue and cry of stolen and lost, its vendue sales and goods at cost.

A paper that goes beyond this kind of bulletin board journalism to engage in First Amendment fistcuffs will not necessarily be rewarded with the kind of fan mail that inundates Farrah Fawcett-Majors. But the paper still has the responsibility.

Oh, yes, if you feel uncomfortable with what I've said, let me remind you that I am a publisher as well as an editor. And you remember what Mark Twain had to say about publishers: "Take an idiot man from a lunatic asylum and marry him to an idiot woman, and the fourth generation of this connection should be a publisher."

9   LEGAL-ETHICAL INTERACTIONS IN JOURNALISM

Richard P. Nielsen

Most of us believe that the goal, admittedly vague, of free and responsible journalism is desirable, but we have trouble agreeing on the roads that lead to this goal.

Some believe in structural reform—First Amendment and antimonopoly action, for example. Others think that individual ethical reform among the people composing the journalism profession will make journalism what it should be.

Sometimes the two approaches approaches conflict. In this chapter, examples of controversial journalism actions that have been restricted by law are described. Sometimes the two approaches appear independent: examples of controversial journalism actions that have been ignored by law are also described. While recognizing that we should not oversimplify; that different reforms may be attempted simultaneously; that a certain amount of irrationality is unavoidable; and that the basic question of the interaction of law and ethics in journalism is vast and complex, we must try to find a synthesis nonetheless in order to achieve the goal of free and responsible journalism. This essay attempts a fragmentary outline of such a synthesis, which is better than no synthesis at all.

ACTIONS RESTRICTED BY LAW

The Protection of Confidential Sources

Branzburg v. *Hayes* (40 LW 5025, 1972)*

Paul Branzburg, a reporter for the Louisville *Courier-Journal*, observed two people synthesizing hashish from marijuana and wrote about it. He subsequently refused to answer a grand jury's questions.

---

*All the court decisions cited are referenced from *United States Law Week*, published by the Bureau of National Affairs, 1231 25th St. N.W., Washington, D.C. 20037.

Branzburg's case was decided with two others in a combined decision. Paul Pappas, a television journalist from New Bedford, Massachusetts, visited Black Panther headquarters during civil turmoil in July 1970. He refused to testify to a grand jury about what he had seen. Earl Caldwell, a black reporter for the New York *Times* in San Francisco who regularly covered Black Panther activities, was called by a grand jury and refused to appear or testify.

The Supreme Court decided that none of the three men should be protected by the First Amendment. The court said that the First Amendment protects a journalist if grand jury investigations were not conducted in good faith, or if the press was harassed by government officials seeking to disrupt a journalist's relationship with his news sources. In the absence of these conditions, the journalist's obligation is to respond to grand jury subpoenas and answer questions relevant to commission of crime, the Court decided.

Morgan v. *Florida* (46 LW 2124, 1976)

In this case a reporter refused to tell officials about the source of official information. The information was sought not to further a criminal investigation but so that authorities could silence the source. The Court stated, "These contempt proceedings were not brought to punish the violation of a criminal statute and were not part of an effort to obtain information needed in a criminal investigation.... Thus, the case falls squarely within this language in the Branzburg plurality opinion: 'Official harassment of the press undertaken not for purposes of law enforcement but to disrupt a reporter's relationship with his news sources will have no justification.'" Presumably, according to this court, if the purpose had been law enforcement, "official harassment" would have been acceptable.

Herbert v. *Lando* (46 LW 2251, 1977)

In this case Herbert charged that the television program "60 Minutes" together with a subsequent *Atlantic Monthly* article written by the producer of the program, maliciously portrayed him as a liar seeking to use the issue of Vietnam war crimes to cover his own alleged failures in the army. Herbert sought information about the sources of information Lando used and about Lando's editorial conclusions during the investigation and preparation of the program. Lando supplied the requested transcripts of interviews, reporters' notes, and videotapes of interviews but refused to answer questions concerning his conclusions during the investigation of persons or leads pursued, on the veracity of sources interviewed, and on conversations with CBS reporter Mike Wallace as to material to be included in the program. The Court of

Appeals stated that the answers to such questions "strike to the heart of the vital human component of the editorial process. . . . Faced with the possibility of such an inquisition, reporters and journalists would be reluctant to express their doubts. Indeed, they would be chilled in the very process of thoughts." To require answers would raise "grave implications" for the vitality of the editorial process, "which the Supreme Court and this court have recognized must be guarded zealously."

Reporting of Trials

Sheppard v. Maxwell (34 LW 2031, 1966)

In this murder case the Court held that prejudicial publicity deprived the defendant of a fair trial. The Court recommended steps to protect fair trial from prejudicial publicity. These recommended steps were implemented in guidelines adopted by the American Bar Association (ABA) in 1968 and the Judicial Conference of the United States in 1969. Included in the list of prohibited extrajudicial communications are statements concerning the prior criminal record or reputation of the accused; the existence or contents of any confession, statement, or admission; the performance of tests on the accused or his refusal to submit to such examination; the identity or testimony of prospective witnesses; the possibility of a plea of guilty to the offense charged or a lesser included offense; and any opinion as to the merits of the case or as to the guilt or innocence of the accused. These standards, aimed primarily at lawyers, obviously affect the ability of the press to gather information and report about trials. One ABA guideline also provided that pretrial proceedings may, at the request of the defendant, be held in chambers closed to the public and press.

Nebraska Press Association v. Stuart (44 LW 5149, 1976)

A Nebraska state trial judge restrained newspapers, broadcasters, journalists, news media associations, and national wire services from publishing or broadcasting accounts of confession or admission made by the accused concerning his murdering a family and other facts "strongly implicative" of the accused. The Supreme Court reversed the decision but stated,

> While the guarantees of freedom of expression are not an absolute prohibition under all circumstances . . . the heavy burden imposed as a condition to securing a prior restraint was not met in this case. . . . There is no finding that measures short of prior restraint on the press

and speech would not have protected the accused's rights. . . . It is not clear that prior restraint on publication would have effectively protected the accused's rights, in view of such practical problems as the limited territorial jurisdiction of the trial court issuing the restraining order.

The way was left open for prior restraint if a court found that other specific measures short of prior restraint would not have worked or if a higher court with greater jurisdiction had issued the restraining order.

Chicago Council of Lawyers v. *Bauer* (44 LW 2073, 1975)

In the Sheppard case, the Court decided that the right of free speech must give way to the right to a fair trial when there is an irreconcilable conflict. The issue in the Chicago Council of Lawyers case relates to how far courts can restrict lawyers without violating their First Amendment rights.

The rule of the local court was, "If there is a reasonable likelihood that such dissemination will interfere with a fair trial or otherwise prejudice the due administration of justice," lawyers could not comment to the press.

The federal district court ruled that such a rule was "overbroad and therefore does not meet constitutional standards. . . . Only those comments that pose a serious and imminent threat of interference with the fair administration of justice can be constitutionally proscribed. Given the objectives of clearness, precision, and narrowness we are of the view that this formulation is more in keeping with the precepts announced by the Supreme Court . . . than the one used by the local rules of the district court." As types of communications between lawyers and journalists are defined more narrowly, precisely, and clearly, journalism may be further restricted.

Libel

New York Times Co. v. *Sullivan* (39 LW 4879, 1964)

An editorial advertisement was written and paid for by a group concerned with civil rights. L. B. Sullivan, commissioner of public affairs for the city of Montgomery, Alabama, brought suit against the New York *Times* and four black ministers who were among the sixty-four persons whose names were attached to the advertisement.

The advertisement, "Heed Their Rising Voices," told of a "wave of terror" that met black students at a state university. Sullivan was not named in the advertisement, but he stated that because he was in charge of the police department, people would blame him for police action at the local college. Sullivan's charge that there were errors in the advertisement was not disputed. The manager of the *Times* Advertising Acceptability Department said that he did not check the ad for accuracy because he had no reason to believe there were errors.

The Supreme Court ruled that where public officials and public issues are involved, "a profound national commitment to the principle that debate on public issues should be uninhibited, robust, and wide-open" prevents recovery for libel about the public acts of public officials unless actual malice is present.

Gertz v. Robert Welch, Inc. (42 LW 5123)

Elmer Gertz, a civil rights lawyer, was accused in *American Opinion,* the monthly magazine of the John Birch Society, of being a "Communist-fronter" and of leading a national campaign to discredit police. The Supreme Court ruled that Gertz, as a private citizen, should be awarded damages more easily than a public official or public figure.

In this case the Supreme Court further defined the meaning of "public figure" that was made an issue in *New York Times* v. *Sullivan:* "For the most part those who attain this status have assumed roles of special prominence in the affairs of society. Some occupy positions of such persuasive power and influence that they are deemed public figures for all purposes. More commonly, those classed as public figures have thrust themselves to the forefront of particular public controversies." The Court also rejected the contention that journalists should be protected concerning falsehoods about private persons whenever the statements concern matters of general or public interest.

Time, Inc. v. Mary Alice Firestone (44 LW 4262, 1976)

In this case a woman who married into a very wealthy industrial family became party to a divorce trial lasting seventeen months. The matter received a great deal of media coverage—in fact Firestone called several press conferences during the trial.

The Court found that *Time* magazine exceeded the bounds of its First Amendment privilege when it erroneously reported that the Firestone tire heir and his third wife had been divorced on the grounds of extreme cruelty and adultery. Despite Mrs. Firestone's public activities, she was not considered by the Court to be a public figure and therefore did not have to prove actual malice as defined in *New York Times* v. *Sullivan* in order to recover damages. The Court made a distinction between a legitimate "public controversy" and "controversies of interest to the public." The latter, the Court concluded, are not protected.

Access to Government Information

Freedom of Information Act (FOIA) (Administrative Procedure Act, 5 U.S.C.)

This act's stated purpose was "a general philosophy of full agency disclosure unless information is exempted under clearly delineated statutory language." The act further states that it does not "authorize withholding of information or limit the availability of records to the public, except as specifically stated. . . ." The problem for journalists involves the specific exceptions: if Congress adds to the list of exemptions, journalists cannot have access to that type of information (S 1002 [1964] [Public Disclosure section, section 3]).

Presidential Recording and Materials Preservation Act (Presidential Recordings and Materials Preservation Act, 44 U.S.C., section 2107)

This act requires the General Services Administration to seize and impound an estimated 900 tape recordings and 42 million pages of documents from the Nixon presidency but restricts access to any of the tapes and documents unless special legislation is passed specifically stating which tapes and documents journalists may inspect.

Reporting on Inquiry of Judges (New York Times, May 1, 1977, p. 22)

Richmond Newspapers, Inc., was convicted and given the maximum fine of $2,000 for violating a state law that prohibits the news media from reporting that judges are under investigation. In 1977 the Virginia State Supreme Court upheld a lower court's conviction of a Norfolk newspaper on a similar violation of the 1971 law establishing the State Judicial Inquiry and Review Commission.

Access to Corporate Information

Reliance Insurance Co. v. Barron's (45 LW 2454, 1977)

In this case, the Court refused to issue a protective order that would prevent the magazine from using, in any manner unrelated to the suit itself, the nonpublic information produced by the corporation in the court case. The Court concluded that such a court order would constitute "prior restraint" unless the corporation could demonstrate the likelihood that trade secrets would be exposed, or that the material was indeed confidential information and its publication would cause it to suffer serious and irreparable injury.

FAA v. Robertson (43 LW 4833, 1975)

The Supreme Court decided that the Freedom of Information Act, 5 U.S.C. S 552 that stated that it "does not apply" to matters that are "(3) specifically exempted from disclosure by statute; (4) trade secrets and commercial or financial information obtained from a person and privileged or confidential" applies to any statutes on the books that direct government agencies to withhold corporate information, not just those statutes included in the Freedom of Information Act.

Westinghouse Electric Corp. v. Schlesinger (45 LW 2210, 1976)

This case involves the disclosure of certain data contained in the affirmative-action plans and compliance reports submitted to the government by three contractors. The Court concluded, "The FOIA itself, it would seem, confers on a supplier of private information, an implied right to invoke the equity jurisdiction to enjoin the disclosure of information. . . ." The legislative history of the FOIA indicated that Congress "had balanced the right of the private party to protection and had opted for the right to privacy in favor of the private interest."

Reporting Classified Information

New York Times Company v. United States (39 LW 4879, 1971)

The New York *Times* won its case against prior government restraint preventing its publication of the Pentagon Papers. However, something was also lost for journalism. As Alexander Bickel, the chief counsel for the *Times* in the case, has written:

> Law can never make us as secure as we are when we do not need it. Those freedoms which are neither challenged nor defined are the most secure. In this sense, for example, it is true that the American press was freer before it won its battle with the government in New York *Times* Company v. United States in 1971 than after its victory. Before June 15, 1971, through the troubles of 1798, through one civil and two world wars and other wars, there had never been an effort by the federal government to censor a newspaper by attempting to impose a restraint prior to publication, directly or in litigation. The New York Times won its case, over the Pentagon Papers, but that spell was broken, and in a sense freedom was thus diminished. . . . We

are, or at least we feel, freer when we feel no need to extend our freedom. The conflict and contention by which we extend freedom seem to mark, or at least to threaten, a contraction; and in truth they do, for they endanger an assumed freedom which appeared limitless because its limits were untried. Appearance and reality are nearly one. We extend the legal reality of freedom at some cost in its limitless appearance. And the cost is real. [Alexander M. Bickel, *The Morality of Consent* [New Haven: Yale University Press, 1975], pp. 60–62)

In its 1974–75 term the Supreme Court declined twice to review an appeal by Victor Marchetti and John Marks, the coauthors of a book about the Central Intelligence Agency, against a ruling by the Fourth Circuit Court of Appeals in March 1974 that had upheld the CIA's fight to enforce its secrecy agreement with Marchetti, a former employee, and required him to submit material before publication. The book was published with spaces showing where the passages were deleted by the CIA.

A Secrets Act for the United States

The 1976 Criminal Justice Reform Act (S.1), which in various forms is still being considered in Congress, contains provisions to restrict journalism that in effect amount to a "Secrets Act." According to section 1121, "A person is guilty of an offense, if, knowing that national defense information may be used to the prejudice of the safety or interest of the United States, or to the advantage of a foreign power, he communicates such information to a person who he knows is not authorized to receive it." In section 1123 it states, "A person is guilty of an offense if . . . being in unauthorized possession or control of national defense information, he: (a) engages in conduct that causes its loss, destruction, or theft, or its communication to another person who is not authorized to receive it; or (b) fails to deliver it promptly to a federal public servant who is entitled to receive it. . . ." According to section 1733, "A person is guilty of an offense if he buys, receives, possesses, or obtains control of property of another that has been stolen." All these sections apply to journalists who might publish or broadcast classified government information.

Restrictions in Government Areas and Institutions

Spock v. Greer (44 LW 4380, 1976)

The Supreme Court upheld an army base commander's regulation to ban the distribution of certain publications on the base and to exclude civilians from the base. The Court stated, "The business of a military installation like Ft. Dix is to train soldiers, not to provide a public forum." The commander has "the historically unquestioned power" to exclude civilians from the base in furtherance of the military's unique function. Accordingly, there is no "generalized constitutional right" to make political speeches or distribute literature within the base's boundaries. Under this interpretation fundamental rights of journalists and citizens could be denied when the military thinks its functions would be enhanced by doing so.

Garrett v. Estelle (45 LW 2334, 1977)

Previously, Texas allowed press interviews with condemned prisoners during certain hours each week and allowed two pool representatives of the print media to witness any execution. The director of the State Department of Corrections ordered that representatives of the news media, both print and electronic, be excluded not only from the executions but also from any access whatever to prisoners on death row. The Court recognized that "prison officials have broad authority to regulate and limit press access" but concluded that the director had gone too far and ordered the state to restore the limited access it previously allowed, and, in addition, to permit one television reporter with camera to witness any execution.

Pell v. Procunier and Saxbe v. Washington Post Co. (42 LW 4998, 1973; 422W5006)

In these cases the Supreme Court decided that prison officials could exclude the news media when the media were reporting the day-to-day operation of the prisons, or when there were problems relating to security, discipline, and rehabilitation. The Court also expressed concern that the granting of press interviews might diminish the deterrent value of imprisonment.

Extra Restrictions for Broadcasters

The Fairness Doctrine

"In fairness to various complaints alleging that a station had been 'one-sided' in its presentations on controversial issues of public importance, the licensee concerned rested upon its policy of making time available, upon request, for 'the other side.' Ruling. The licensee's obligations to serve the public interest cannot be met merely through the adoption of a general policy of not refusing to broadcast opposing views where a demand is made of the station for broadcast time. As the commission pointed out:

> If, as we believe to be the case, the public interest is best served in a democracy through the ability of the people to hear expositions of the various positions taken by responsible groups and individuals on particular topics and to choose between them, it is evident that broadcast lincensees have an affirmative duty generally to encourage and implement the broadcast of all sides of controversial public issues over their facilities, over and beyond their obligation to make available on demand opportunities for the expression of opposing views. It is clear that any approximation of fairness in the presentation of any controversy will be difficult if not impossible of achievement unless the licensee plays a conscious and positive role in bringing about balanced presentations of the opposing viewpoints." (Federal Communications Commission, *The Fairness Doctrine*, part II, B9).

Red Lion Broadcasting Co., Inc. et al. v. *Federal Communications Commission* (37 LW 2014, 1969)

The station, Red Lion Broadcasting Co., refused Fred J. Cook free time to answer attacks made on him by the Rev. Billy James Hargis, who associated Cook with left-wing activities. Cook took the case to the FCC. The FCC told the station to provide free time for Cook to reply. The station appealed the case to the courts.

The Supreme Court stated with respect to FCC regulations concerning personal attacks and political editorials:

> As they now stand amended, the regulations read as follows:
> "Personal attacks; political editorials. (a) When, during the presentation of views on a controversial issue of public importance, an attack is made upon the honesty, character, integrity or like personal qualities of an identified person or group, the licensee shall, within a reasonable time and in no event later than 1 week after the attack, transmit to the person or group attacked (1) notification of the date, time and identification of the broadcast; (2) a script or tape (or an accurate summary if a script or tape is not available) of the attack; and (3) an offer of a reasonable opportunity to respond over the licensee's facilities. . . . (c) Where a licensee, in an editorial, (i) endorses or (ii) opposes a legally qualified candidate or candidates; the licensee shall, within 24 hours after the editorial, transmit to respectively (i) the other qualified candidate or candidates for the same office or (ii) the candidate opposed in the editorial (1) notification of the date and the time of the editorial; (2) a script or tape of the editorial; and

(3) an offer of a reasonable opportunity for a candidate or a spokesman of the candidate to respond over the licensee's facilities ..."

Believing that the ... promulgation of the regulations ... are both authorized by Congress and enhance rather than abridge the freedoms of speech and press protected by the First Amendment, we hold them valid and constitutional. ...

The amended Communications Act of 1934 states in section 399, "No noncommercial educational broadcasting station may engage in editorializing or may support or oppose any candidate for political office."

In section (g) (1) (a) of the larger section 396, it states that public broadcasters must maintain "objectivity and balance in all programs or series of programs of a controversial nature." Commercial stations may editorialize and must maintain balance across all programming not within specific programs. The print media are subject to none of the restrictions listed in this section.

Monopoly

Associated Press v. *National Labor Relations Board* (13 LW 1472, 1945)

In this case the Supreme Court decided, "The business of the Associated Press is not immune from regulation because it is an agency of the press. The publisher of a newspaper has no special privileges to invade the rights and liberties of others. ... He may be punished for contempt of court. He is subject to the anti-trust laws. Like others he must pay equitable and non-discriminatory taxes on his own business."

Newspaper Concentration

In the United States, no or few competing newspapers within a city is the rule rather than the exception. The trend toward fewer competing newspapers within cities has been increasing. Christopher Sterling found that within areas the number of newspapers declined and the ownership concentration increased steadily between 1922 and 1970. Ben Bagdikian found,

Today 71% of daily newspaper circulation in the U.S. is controlled by 168 multiple ownerships. Concentration of control over daily newspapers is accelerating. In 1930, chains controlled 43 percent of circulation; in 1960, 46 percent. In terms of control of individual newspapers, the share held by chains has grown even more sharply: 16 percent in

1930, 30 percent in 1960, 60 percent today. The approaching disappear-
ance of even small independent newspapers is not only economically
but politically important, because almost all dailies are local monopolies, exerting substantial influence in their congressional or state
legislative districts. . . . Too many consolidations have already taken
place, and the giants in the business are too influential in policy to
make likely corrective action by any forseeable government.

There is some support for this assertion in addition to the obvious
increasing concentration and lack of antitrust enforcement. The internal revenue laws permit newspapers to set aside profits at special tax
advantages when they use the money to buy other newspapers. Donald
Dixon, a former head of the Federal Trade Commission, when asked
why more attention was not paid to the newspaper industry as required
by law replied, "I kind of suspect that nobody wanted the newspapers
mad at them." (Sterling, "Trends in Daily Newspaper and Broadcast
Ownership: 1922–1970," *Journalism Quarterly,* summer 1975, pp. 247–
56; Bagdikian, "The Myth of Newspaper Poverty," *The Columbia
Journalism Review,** March/April 1973, pp. 16–25; Bagdikian, "Newspaper Mergers—The Final Phase," *The Columbia Journalism Review,*
March/April 1977, pp. 17–22.)

Broadcast Competition Regulation

In *Home Box Office* v. *FCC* (45 LW 2446, 1977), the Court decided,
"In determining the commission's authority to promulgate these rules,
we recognize that the Communications Act must be construed at least
in some circumstances to allow the commission to regulate cable television. The commission does not have carte blanche authority, however;
the Supreme Court recognized in *U.S.* v. *Midwest video,* 406 U.S. 649
(1972), that the commission can act only for ends for which it could also
regulate broadcast television. It is clear that the thrust of the commission's rules is to prevent . . . competition by pay cable entrepreneurs. . . .
How such an effect furthers any legitimate goal of the act is not
clear. . . . An essential precondition of the Red Lion theory—physical
interference and scarcity requiring an umpiring role for Government
—is not present in cable regulation. In this area, there is nothing in the
record to suggest a constitutional distinction between the treatment of
cable television and of newspapers."

In *CBS Television Network Affiliates Assn.* v. *FCC* (45 LW 2467,
1977), the Court decided,

---

*Hereafter *CJR.*

The affiliates assert that the commission has either abandoned or disregarded one of the primary supports for the 1965 rules. This argument misconceives the role unfair competition has played in the development of nonduplication policy. In 1965 the commission decided not to ban distant signal importation entirely and concluded that such importation could serve the public interest so long as it did not threaten the viability of local stations. In other words, the commission's concern was not so much with the "pirating" of signals per se; rather, it was the broadcasting of those signals in competition with local affiliates. The commission's goal was to establish zones that would protect local affiliates from debilitating economic competition.

The commission has done well in protecting network affiliates' profits by restricting market entry and competition. R. H. Coase has estimated that the profits of network-affiliated television stations in the top fifty U.S. television markets was, on the average, 36 percent of gross revenues, and the rates of return on capital frequently were in the 200 to 300 percent range per year, after taxes. In the top twenty-five markets the profits are even higher. (Coase, "The Economics of Broadcasting and Government Policy," *American Economic Review,* May 1966, pp. 440–47.) The January 1976 report of the U.S. House Subcommittee on Communications estimates that the average Very High Frequency station earned a 100 percent annual return on investment. (U.S., Congress, House, Subcommittee on Communications of the Committee on Interstate and Foreign Commerce, *Cable Television: Promise Versus Regulatory Performance,* January 1976.)

ACTIONS IGNORED BY LAW

Conflict of Interest—Ownership

The Denver Post

The profits and assets of the Denver *Post* are partly owned by the Denver Center for the Performing Arts, a foundation founded by the owners of the *Post.* The city of Denver also contributes funds to the arts center. If the city decided to cancel its support of the center, the foundation might sell the stock it owned in the *Post* to outsiders, and the present management of the paper might lost control. According to one *Post* executive, the paper has been "playing footsies with the city administration" editorially to protect control of the paper with the present management. This executive thinks that such a financial arrangement has the paper "in a horrible ethical bind. Here we are, the most important paper in the Rocky Mountains, and to stay that way we've got to take it easy on [Denver Mayor William] McNichols. . . . There's not an editor or reporter here who doesn't know the score. We could lose our jobs, too. That's why I say nobody needs any written guidelines to know how to report on the administration." (Bill Sonn, "The High Cost of Owning the Denver *Post*," *CJR*, September-October 1976, pp. 35–38.)

Milwaukee Journal

Stephen L. Cashner, Milwaukee *Journal* investigative reporter, wrote a series of articles about the American Bankshares Corporation's huge unreported losses. When the price of the stock fell from twenty dollars to twenty-two cents, Cashner bought the stock. He was fired for violating the Journal's code of ethics, which prohibits reporters from engaging in "outside activities that would create a conflict of interest or give the impression of one." (*CJR*, January–February 1976, pp. 35–36.)

The Westport News

B. V. Brooks, publisher of the Westport *News*, used the paper to air, almost exclusively, his side of a disagreement with the local planning and zoning commission. In a series of unsigned articles, the paper criticized the commission's delay on zoning changes. The publisher owned much of the property in question and did not acknowledge such ownership in the articles. (Peter Nichols, "Brooks Brooks Rebuttal, at Last," *CJR*, November–December 1975, p. 47.)

Conflict of Interest—Moonlighting

Anchorman, WISN Milwaukee

Carl Holland is a morning newscaster for WISN. He is also the director of press relations for the suburban Greenvale Police Department.

Reporter, Nashville Banner

From 1964 to 1968 Jacque von Stubbel worked as a reporter for the *Banner* and as an informant for the FBI with the approval of her publisher, James G. Stahlman. In 1976, while working for *The Tennes-*

sean, her contacts with the FBI continued. On May 5 she was fired by the editor of the *Tennessean,* John Seigenthaler, for maintaining her relationship with the FBI and possibly supplying the FBI with information about other reporters at the paper. (Sanford J. Ungar, "Among the Piranhas: A Journalist and the FBI," *CJR,* September–October 1976, pp. 19–26.)

Senate Report on the CIA, FBI, and the Media

> In pursuing its foreign intelligence mission the Central Intelligence Agency has used the U.S. media for both the collection of intelligence and for cover. Until February 1976, when it announced a new policy toward U.S. media personnel, the C.I.A. maintained covert relationships with about fifty American journalists or employees of U.S. media organizations. They are part of a network of several hundred foreign individuals around the world who provide intelligence for the C.I.A. with direct access to a large number of foreign newspapers and periodicals, scores of press services and news agencies, radio and television stations, commercial book publishers, and other foreign media outlets.... The F.B.I. has attempted covertly to influence the public's perception of persons and organizations by disseminating derogatory information to the press, either anonymously or through "friendly" news contacts.... The F.B.I. attempted to influence public opinion by supplying information or articles to "confidential sources" in the news media. ("The C.I.A., the F.B.I., and the Media: Excerpts from the Senate Report on Intelligence Activities," *CJR,* July-August 1976, pp. 37–42.)

Conflict of Interest—Gifts

"Evaluation Kits"

Three hundred reporters and photographers attended the April 20, 1976 press conference held by Eastman Kodak to introduce a new product. They also accepted "evaluation kits" of gift cameras and equipment. (*CJR,* July-August 1976, p. 5.)

South Texas Press Association

The association accepted and thanked several corporations for providing gifts for its annual convention. In the 1975 program it stated: "Your thanks should go to the General Telephone Company which is your host.... Beer, boiled shrimp and hot tamales on the high seas sponsored by Group VII, Texas Electric Cooperatives, Inc." (*CJR*, July-August 1975, p. 5.)

Rosslyn Review, Editor

John Jacobs, editor, Arlington, Virginia, *Rosslyn Review*, accepted a free trip by an Arizona land developer. He then published several articles and thirty-one photographs of the trip. (*CJR*, January-February 1976, p. 6.)

Self-Censorship—Political

New York Times Editorials

The New York *Times* endorsed Daniel P. Moynihan in his primary election campaign against Bella Abzug. John B. Oakes, editorial-page editor, wrote a letter to the editor, and Roger Wilkins wrote an op-ed article criticizing the endorsement. The letter to the editor was not printed, and the op-ed article was not published until the day after the election. (*CJR*, November-December 1976, p. 9.)

Associated Press

The Associated Press did not publish for five months these remarks, made by the governor of Rhode Island, Philip W. Noel: "Take a kid from a black ghetto, bus him across town to a white school. He is there for four hours of classroom instruction. Then he is back in the ghetto for the other nineteen hours with an hour for transportation back and forth, five hours in the building, six hours' experience. The other eighteen hours he is back in that sweathole, wherever he comes from, with a drunken father and a mother that's out peddling her ass or whatever, you know, all the problems you have in the ghetto." Noel had been running for head of the Democratic party platform committee. Jack Anderson obtained a tape of Noel's remarks and published them. The AP's response was first that "the APs Boston bureau chief, Joe McGowan, Jr., said Saturday that a decision was made last fall to pursue the quote in a later interview. Inadvertently, this was not done." Later a spokesman for the AP said, "The quote should have been used; whether anyone was told to go back for clarification is beside the point. . . . The quote is in context in the interview and reflects the tone and substance of what the governor was saying." Later, Governor Noel withdrew his candidacy for permanent chairman of the platform committee.

The Chicago Tribune

Although the Chicago *Tribune* subscribes to the *Times* News Service, it chose to condense the first and not publish subsequent installments of a story by Seymour Hersh about a Chicago lawyer's mob and political connections in Chicago and Illinois. One reporter for a local paper said, "You couldn't get a story about him in the paper." In the series Hersh wrote that the lawyer boasted that he was able to influence the *Tribune* to tone down or soften stories about him. (*CJR*, September-October 1976, p. 49.)

Distortion—Political

Television News, Inc. (TVN)

TVN is the largest non-network source of national and international news film for the nation's commercial TV stations. Jack Wilson is the president of TVN. In his memos Wilson has written:

[*Agnew speech:*] Very good. Clip showing Agnew in a relaxed and human fashion. This was one of the stories we could be proud to show our friends.... [*Critique of daily news feed:*] Martin Luther King was an avowed communist revolutionary. It is not necessary for us to cover him or any of his subordinates (Abernathy) just because the other networks do so. We are going to be different—if we are going to be the same then we are going to continue to cover all of the communist stories and carry all of their lines.... [*Summit meetings:*] In the story he says, "the leaders are working for peace." So now Nixon is a leader and Brezhnev is a leader and the two are the same in the minds of the viewers. This subtly obscures the fact that there is a real difference in our systems.... [*Cambodia bombing veto:*] We all know that the one who speaks last has the impression with the viewer. Here Jerry Ford was put on the very beginning with three liberals allowed to stomp on him so that you forgot he was even on the same story.... [*David Rockefeller:*] Nothing like this should ever be allowed on our air. Rockefeller took a communist public relations tour, the same as Ramsey Clark did in Hanoi when he reported our prisoners were all well fed, healthy, happy men. Rockefeller said the same thing here. In addition to that, the statement implies that freedom means nothing and that we as a nation are abandoning freedom for others as our goal. We are not providing this service to give voice to that kind of propaganda.... [*Elderly:*] This matter of the elderly is obviously a problem, but why was only Hubert Humphrey given a chance to voice his socialist viewpoints on food stamps, housing, medical care and the provision of federal funds. This was a chance to damn those who made it the welfare state that it is today.... (Stanhope Gould, "Coors Brews the News," *CJR*, March-April 1975, pp. 17–29.)

The Wilmington, Delaware, Morning News and Evening Journal

The du Point family owns these papers. In 1964 an independent executive editor was forced to resign because a Du Pont Co. public relations specialist was installed as his boss to give the owners better control of the news. (Philip M. Boffey, "The Second Battle of Wilmington," *CJR*, March-April 1975, pp. 31–33.)

Panax Corporation Newspapers

In June 1977 the editors of two Panax papers in Michigan lost their jobs after refusing a corporate order that they publish two stories about the Carter administration. In one story it said that Carter "condones promiscuity—affairs with other women—for male staffers who work for him." The other story suggested that Rosalynn Carter was being prepared for the vice-presidency. Panax Corporation owns forty-nine newspapers. (*CJR*, September-October 1977, p. 6.)

In a public statement the corporation's policy was stated as follows: "John P. McGoff not only has the privilege but the right as principal stockholder, president and chief executive officer of Panax, to distribute whatever news copy he deems appropriate and to demand, if necessary, that such copy be printed." (*CJR*, September-October 1977, p. 83.)

Self-Censorship and Distortion—Economic

The Tennessee Valley Case

In March 1975 the most serious fire in the history of the civilian nuclear industry occurred. According to Deborah Shapley, editorials and news stories in the area "overlooked a number of acts that made the TVA's foresight seem less than commendable.... There one might have expected alarm, one found reassurance. And where one might have expected strong arguments to be made for delaying the opening of the Browns Ferry plant until safety could be assured, one found repeated appeals for haste.... Within the Tennessee Valley region, where boosting the TVA has become a habit, information on both sides of the nuclear power story has been, and remains, exceedingly hard to come by." (Deborah Shapley, "Reporting on Nuclear Power: The Tennessee Valley Case," *CJR*, March-April 1977, pp. 23–27.)

WCBS

"Consumer Alert," a daily radio spot series on WCBS by New York Consumer Affairs Commissioner Elinor Guggenheimer, fictionalized and embellished reports to consumers "to make them more interesting." (*CJR*, March-April 1977, p. 6.)

Press room health hazards

Several major newspapers failed to report on their refusal to admit to their press rooms a team of medical researchers employed by the government to investigate health hazards. The American Newspaper Publishers Association tried to discredit Dr. Irving J. Selikoff, the medical researcher in charge of the federal press-room study. (Wade Roberts, "Phosvel: A Tale of Missed Cues, An Occupational-Health Story That, Finally, Made the Front Page," *CJR*, July-August 1977, pp. 23–29.)

Self-Censorship and Distortion—Military/Police

New York Times and Cuban Invasion

There has been a good deal said and written about the *Times* coverage of that invasion and, most importantly, of the period just before the invasion, when rumors and reports of it were spreading through the hemisphere. Most of the attention centered, correctly, on an article by Tad Szulc that appeared on our front page on April 7, ten days before the invasion. Arthur Schlesinger, Jr., the historian later said, quite incorrectly, that the Times had "suppressed" Szulc's story of the coming invasion. Schlesinger was correct in that we had not printed all we knew or thought we knew. . . . In early April, rumors of an impending invasion were spreading. According to Arthur Schlesinger, the editor of The New Republic sent him the galleys of "a careful, accurate and devastating account of CIA activities among the refugees and asked if there was any reason why it shouldn't be published. President Kennedy asked that the editor not print the story, and he agreed. . . . Would we be responsible if hundreds, even thousands, of Cuban exiles died on the beaches of their homeland? (I suspected that Castro already knew about the pending invasion, and the real question was not whether we would be responsible for deaths during the invasion, but whether, however unfairly, we might be blamed for them . . . Reston warned against printing anything that would suggest an invasion was in the works or might otherwise upset the government's plans. . . . In the case of the Bay of Pigs story, I think Scotty allowed his news judgment to be influenced by his patriotism. My own interest was less elevated—I wanted to print the story, as fully as possible. . . . Later Kennedy said to me in an aside, "Maybe if you had printed more about the operation you would have saved us from a colossal mistake." He told the same thing to Dryfoos. But his logic seemed to me faulty. On the one hand, he condemned us for printing too much and in the next breath he condemned us for printing too little. He wanted it both ways, and he did not change my view that the newspapers, not the government, must decide what news is fit to print. (Turner Catledge, *My Life and The Times* [New York: Harper and Row, 1971], pp. 257–67.)

Orlando Sentinel-Star

An Orlando *Sentinel-Star* sportswriter was fired by his editor for defending Rommie Loudd, who was tried, convicted, and sentenced to fourteen years in jail for possession of four ounces of drugs. Subsequently, the new editor, Jim Squires, stated that by publishing unsubstantiated charges, the paper had indeed "systematically created a climate in which there was no way Rommie Loudd could get a fair shake from the law." Squires's statement was the result of a three-month investigation. (*CJR,* September-October 1977, p. 7.)

Wounded Knee

A June 27, 1975 UPI story: "Two FBI agents were ambushed and killed with repeated blasts of gunfire Thursday in an outbreak of bloodshed appearing to stem from the 1973 occupation of Wounded Knee." This report was based on official FBI reports at the scene. However, there was not necessarily an ambush. For example, the killings could have been panicky and unpremeditated. It is not clear how the UPI could have determined only hours after the deaths that the violence had stemmed from the 1973 Wounded Knee incidents. UPI took and published the FBI reports without questioning them. Later it was determined that an ambush was unlikely and that much of the rest of the UPI reporting was inaccurate, based solely on FBI agent opinions but published as fact. (Joel D. Weisman, "About that 'Ambush' at Wounded Knee," *CJR,* September-October 1975, pp. 28–31.)

Checkbook Journalism

Nixon

David Frost paid Richard Nixon over $1 million for 28¾ hours of interviews which were in turn sold to television stations across the country. With respect to the checkbook journalism aspect of his deal with Nixon, Frost said that the precedent had been established already when former President Johnson sold his memoirs, in the form of a series of television interviews, to CBS, and in the form of a book to CBS's subsidiary Holt, Rinehart, and Winston. Frost argued that Nixon would get "four times as much" for the published memoirs as for the television interviews. He also said that it required at least as much "nervous energy" to sit through interviews as to write a book. (*Broadcasting,* May 30, 1977, p. 22.)

Daniel Schorr

Daniel Schorr "sold" a government document, the Pike report on secret intelligence activities, to Clay Felker, editor of *New York* magazine and the *Village Voice* for publication in the *Voice.* The money was to go to the Reporters Committee for Freedom of the Press. The 358-page report contained few conclusions that had not already been leaked to the press. (Lawrence Stern, "The Daniel Schorr Affair," *CJR,* May-June 1976, pp. 20–23.)

Xerox's "sponsored" articles

Xerox paid $55,000 to Harrison Salisbury for a twenty-three page article, "Travels through America," and $115,000 in advertising to *Esquire,* which published the article in their February 1976 issue. Through an extraordinary exchange of letters between E. B. White and W. B. Jones, then Xerox's director of communications, Xerox decided to abandon future plans for "sponsored" print articles. ("What E. B. White Told Xerox," *CJR,* September-October 1976, pp. 52–54.)

Advertising as News

Fortune magazine

In its July 1976 issue *Fortune* published a ten-page article called "The Philippines: A New Role in Southeast Asia." The article was not labeled an advertisement by the Philippine government, despite the fact that the government paid *Fortune* $183,000 to print it. The only identification of the article as an advertisement came in the index to advertisers, where "The Philippines" was listed as an advertiser on the pages of the article. (*CJR,* November-December 1976, p. 12.)

Nassau County Newspapers

"Many of Nassau County's small weekly newspapers were found to have a 'business interest' in the campaign for County Executive.

These weeklies were believed to solicit political advertising on the unspoken understanding that if the candidate bought advertising in the paper, the paper would reciprocate by running the candidate's picture and a story. Therefore, weekly newspapers were employed as part of Wachtler's [a candidate] visibility campaign." (Stephen Creyser, *Cases in Advertising and Communications Management* [Englewood Cliffs, New Jersey: Prentice-Hall, 1972], p. 621.)

Newspaper supplements that are advertisements

More than 200 daily newspapers distributed as a genuine supplement "Garden Time '76," which was in fact a sixteen-page handout from Ortho, a manufacturer of garden supplies. (*CJR,* January-February 1977, p. 10.)

Secret Sources

Woodward and Bernstein

"Nothing in this book has been reconstructed without accounts from at least two people." However, in certain cases their anonymous informants were not speaking from personal knowledge. In the Kissinger-Nixon prayer scene: "Nixon got down on his knees. Kissinger felt he had no alternative but to kneel down, too. The President prayed out loud, asking for help, rest, peace and love. How could a President and a country be torn apart by such small things?" Woodward and Bernstein say that they did not speak to at least one of the participants. What happened to their claim that they talked to at least two people? Did they talk to two people who talked to one of the participants? Could a reporter say he had two personal sources who had personal knowledge of an event, but when challenged claim source protection and print the story?

Alexander Butterfield

L. Fletcher Prouty was interviewed on television by Daniel Schorr on CBS and by Ford Rowan on NBC. Schorr: "Can I ask you of someone in the immediate office of the White House whose CIA background was not generally known?" Prouty: "I think the description would fit Alexander Butterfield, Colonel Butterfield as I knew him in the Air Force." Schorr: "What was his CIA connection?" Prouty: "Assignments to the agency as a contact officer for the agency—as I was with the CIA operations. And he was contact officer in the White House." Rowan: "Is there any doubt in your mind that Alexander Butterfield was a man with CIA connections, who went to the White House staff and whose CIA connections persisted at the time he was in the White House?" Prouty: "No, I've never had any doubts about that." Mike Wallace later interviewed Butterfield on CBS, and the story was denied. Schorr didn't bother to check the story with other sources before airing it. Rowan checked the story with his sources, and they confirmed the charges. However, Rowan still said on the air, "We have no evidence that Butterfield was involved in any such relaying of information to the CIA." Mike Wallace checked with his sources, who denied the charges against Butterfield. Two different sets of secret sources came to different conclusions. Unsubstantiated charges were broadcast and printed in many newspapers nonetheless.

Thomas Eagleton

Jack Anderson printed a story that claimed that Thomas Eagleton several times drove while drunk. His source was secret. No evidence was ever producted to support the charge. Despite the lack of evidence, the story was carried by hundreds of newspapers and broadcast stations on the basis of a secret source that never materialized. (Robert Morris, "Taking Aim at Jack Anderson," *CJR,* May-June 1975, p. 20.)

CONCLUSION

Examples have been presented where law restricts controversial actions and ignores commercial jouralism actions in favor of ethical control. Bickel is correct when he says, "Law can never make us as secure as we are when we do not need it. Those freedoms which are neither challenged nor defined are the most secure." As illustrated in the preceding pages, law challenges, defines, and restricts journalistic actions. It does so when through the courts or the legislatures it considers journalistic rights to be in conflict with other rights it considers more important. But is there another way of protecting such rights in conflict?

The First Amendment is based on the principle of a free market of ideas. Implicit in this principle is the necessity for a nonconcentrated media market. For some of the rights in conflict, a freer, nonconcentrated media market could alleviate the pressure of journalistic rights upon other rights. Among the controversial journalistic actions restricted by law, several would not need to be as restricted if there were less media concentration. For example, were media less concentrated, reporting of trials would not need to be limited so much, since there would be more opportunity for different interpretations of trials and therefore less danger of opinion being prejudicially influenced. With less concentrated media, there would be more opportunity for accurate reporting of events, thus reducing the damages done by libel. Since concentration is given as the main reason why it is necessary to have extra restrictions for broadcasters, less media concentration would be a direct remedy for the need to have such extra restrictions.

Less concentration in the media would also directly aid in alleviating the damages done by many of the controversial journalistic actions ignored by law in favor of ethical control. The negative effects resulting from conflicts of interest, regarding ownership, moonlighting, and gifts, political self-censorship, political distortion, economic self-censorship and distortion, censorship and distortion in favor of the military/police, checkbook journalism, unverified sources, and advertising as news could all be reduced with less concentrated media. Less concentration in the media would provide opportunities for journalism to correct its own ethical abuses in a freer marketplace of information and ideas. But can we have a nonconcentrated media market?

In principle, the answer is of course yes. But we must be realistic. As illustrated in the preceding pages, both the newspaper and television media are concentrated. There has not been sufficient antimonopolistic enforcement to date. Conservative capitalists such as Milton Friedman and William Buckley continue to call for such antimonopolistic enforcement, but are there any indications that action is forthcoming? Liberal economist John Kenneth Galbraith says that it might be nice, but given the foreseeable political environment, it is not likely to happen; therefore we should have more goverment regulation in the public interest. However, this is just what we are trying to avoid— direct legal regulation of journalistic actions. Ben Bagdikian has suggested an alternative would be for "professional staffs of American newspapers and broadcasting stations to choose their own top editor, to have a delegate on the company board of directors, and to have access to the committee that allocates the annual news budget. This is done on a number of quality European papers, including *Le Monde* (*CJR*, March-April 1977, pp. 17–22).

I agree with Galbraith and Bagdikian that the political environment precludes effective antimonopolistic enforcement. But I would go much further than Bagdikian suggests. Access to budget committees is only access, not real power. Journalists already have access to budget committees. Journalists can also do all the electing they want, but if the publisher-owner or broadcaster-owner does not like what they elect, he or she can ignore the election. There is a more powerful path through responsible unionization. Local newspapers and broadcast stations could have union contracts that either permit journalists in the union to elect their own editors or ensure that local editorial managers perform these functions. Interference from the corporate level in violation of the decentralized union contracts would be prevented by enforcement of the contracts by the National Labor Relations Board. Precedents do exist. The Screen Actors Guild and the Writers Guild have contracts with the television networks that limit the networks as to choice of actors and writers and prevent interfering with actors and writers' work with independent producers. A strong emphasis on such union contract provision would certainly be a significant departure from the present situation. But such a solution should not be dismissed without further in-depth investigation and consideration.

However, sometimes even such a radical attempt for a synthesis solution will not work. Protection of confidential sources, protection of notes and outtakes, can conflict with rights in trial defense and prosecution. Access to government information can conflict with national security. Access to corporate information can conflict with personal privacy and property rights. Perhaps the best we can hope for is that our judicial and journalistic traditions continue to compete vigorously in defending their rights, and in the process, find working solutions as they evolve.

I suggest, then, a legal-ethical synthesis encompassing (1) vigorous antimonopolistic enforcement and/or decentralized unionized protection of journalistic functions; and, (2) vigorous adversary competition between the journalistic and legal traditions.

Because the issue is important, this fragmentary synthesis is offered. When enough other syntheses are offered, perhaps we shall through the working of a free marketplace of ideas arrive at a solution.

BIBLIOGRAPHY

Aron, Raymond. *An Essay On Freedom.* New York: World Publishing, 1970.

Barnouw, Erik. *Tube of Plenty: The Evolution of American Television.* New York: Oxford University Press, 1975.

Bickel, Alexander M. *The Morality of Consent.* New Haven: Yale University Press, 1975.

Cahn, Edmond. *The Moral Decision.* Bloomington: Indiana University Press, 1955.

Camus, Albert. *Resistance, Rebellion, and Death.* New York: The Medern Library, 1960.

Cardozo, Benjamin N. *The Nature of the Judicial Process.* New Haven: Yale University Press, 1921.

Cox, Archibald. *The Role of the Supreme Court in American Government.* New York: Oxford University Press, 1976.

Emerson, Thomas I. *The System of Freedom of Expression.* New York: Random House, 1970.

——. *Toward A General Theory of the First Amendment.* New York: Random House, 1963.

Frankfurter, Felix. *The Public And Its Government.* New Haven: Yale University Press, 1930.

Georgetown Law Journal. Media and the First Amendment In A Free Society. Amherst: University of Massachusetts Press, 1973.

Harrington, Michael. *Socialism.* New York: Bantam, 1970.

Holmes, Oliver Wendell. *Collected Legal Papers.* New York: Harcourt, Brace and Howe, 1920.

Hume, David. *Moral and Political Philosophy.* New York: Hafner Publishing Co., 1948.

Huxley, Aldous. *Ends and Means.* London: Chatto & Windus, 1951.

Kahn, Frank J., ed. *Documents of American Broadcasting.* New York: Appleton-Century-Crofts, 1973.

Merrill, John C. *The Imperative of Freedom.* New York: Hastings, 1974.

Mill, John Stuart. *Autobiography.* New York: Columbia University Press, 1924.

Milton, John. *Areopagitica.* New York: E. P. Dutton, 1927.

Mott, Frank Luther. *American Journalism.* New York: Macmillan, 1941.

Nelson, Harold L., and Teeter, Dwight L. *Law of Mass Communications.* New York: The Foundation Press, 1973.

Pound, Roscoe. *The Spirit of the Common Law.* Boston: Marshall Jones, 1921.

Scheingold, Stuart A. *The Politics of Rights.* New Haven: Yale University Press, 1974.

Schwartz, Bernard. *The Law in America.* New York: McGraw-Hill, 1974.

Part IV Manufacturing Media Images—Motion Pictures and Television

10 MEDIA ETHICS HOW MOVIES PORTRAY THE PRESS AND BROADCASTERS

Roger Manvell

THE DELICATE BALANCE

In advanced societies where the great media of public expression (the press, broadcasting, and film) are what is termed "free," the recognition, practice, and maintenance of this freedom are always precarious —as much dependent on lively, alert public opinion as on the standards observed by editors, journalists, broadcasting executives and performers, and filmmakers. There are no absolutes in this field; everything is relative, a delicate balance of forces of expression and repression reflecting constantly the current shifts in values operating in the different media. In this sense we really get the press, the broadcasting, and the films that we deserve, whatever the public respond to with their patronage. Newspapers operate individually on very differing levels, providing the various genres of readers with the subjects and level of coverage they (the editors and the public alike) feel have come to suit their needs and tastes.

If we actually believe that the maintenance of democracy depends substantially on freedom of expression, we would do well never to relax our vigilance so that the values we believe essential to our well-being are observed in every local, regional, and national publication and broadcast in our various countries. Any noticeable infringement should be followed by exposure and protest in editorials, in letters to the press, in articles, and in broadcast comment. Journalists are watchdogs on behalf of the public, as J. T. Delane, the all-powerful editor of the London *Times* a century and a quarter ago, said in 1852:

> The first duty of the press is to obtain the earliest and most correct intelligence of the events of the time, and instantly, by disclosing them, to make them the common property of the nation. . . . The press lives by disclosure; . . . it is daily and for ever appealing to the enlight-

ened force of public opinion—anticipating, if possible, the march of events—standing upon the breach between the present and the future, and extending its survey to the horizon of the world.*

Behind this statement lay a tradition born of the great battles for the freedom to publish daily news and comment in what the writers felt to be the public interest. Earlier John Wilkes, a journalist who was also a member of the British House of Commons, fought in the courts for the right—finally achieved in 1771—to publish reports on the proceedings in Parliament. However, reporters were not given official seats in the public gallery of the House until 1803, when William Cobbett began to publish the verbatim parliamentary reports subsequently taken over in 1812 by Hansard. In earlier times Dr. Johnson had scratched together a living editing into reasonable prose the surreptitious and illegal reports memorized or written down secretly in shorthand by men slipped into the House for this purpose.

It was not therefore for nothing that in the United States the celebrated First Amendment had been passed, guaranteeing the general principle of absolute freedom of expression: "Congress shall make no law . . . abridging the freedom of speech or of the press." However, the majority public has played little part in achieving and maintaining this right, and in consequence they have remained to this day in general satisfied with what we might call a merely popular manifestation of free expression. The popular press in Britain, as in America, has always aimed more to entertain than to offer a balanced presentation of the day's news. The London *Times* inveighed against this tendency in an editorial on July 31, 1955, on the centenary of the abolition in Britain of the notorious Stamp Duties. These duties had kept the cost of newspa-

---

*See Roger Manvell, *This Age of Communication,* p. 29. Compare, too, the statements quoted by Professor Bernard Rubin in his book, *Media, Politics, and Democracy,* notably Henry Fairlie on the essential tasks of the mass media: "First, to try to reconcile the multiplicity of conflicting interests and wills which exist in any free society and to produce from their conflict a policy. . . . [Second,] to maintain public interest in political issues, for without such interest free government is meaningless. [Third,] to act as a catalyst on public opinion. [Fourth,] to be a link between informed and public opinion. The two are very different" (p. 14). Professor Rubin also quotes Alfred E. Smith, who spoke of the "fundamental right of the people to enjoy full liberty in the domain of idea and speech. To this fundamental right there is and can be under our system of government but one limitation, namely, that the law of the land shall not be transgressed, and there is abundant statute law prohibiting the abuse of free speech. It is unthinkable that in a representative democracy there should be delegated to any body of men the absolute power to prohibit the teaching of any subject of which it may disapprove" (p. 112). Smith, as governor of New York, vetoed bills that sought to license what was to be taught in schools.

pers artificially high in order to restrict their circulation and so keep them (in theory) in the hands of the moneyed (and, therefore, technically speaking, the educated and so "responsible") classes:

> The race for mammoth circulations has led in some cases to a disgraceful lowering of values. The baser instincts are being pandered to, not only in lasciviousness—the influence of this can be overrated —but in social attitudes and conduct as well. Envy, jealousy, intolerance, suspicion are all too often being indirectly fostered. Irresponsibility is rife. The tone of voice is a perpetual shriek. So-called brightness is all. By no means all popular papers are thus (it is in fact deplorable that some of the worst examples should be classed as newspapers at all), by no means all the journalists on even the worst newspapers wish them to be thus. But the turning of the press into predominantly a business enterprise, the fact that in the present state of newspaper economics readers have to be fought for by the million to make popular journalism viable, have engendered forces greater than the journalists. (Manvell, *This Age,* p. 28)

The tenets of Harry Guy Bartholomew, the ruthless editor of the London *Daily Mirror,* appointed in 1934, depended entirely on giving the public what he instinctively knew they liked. I have described his principles elsewhere:

> His one idea was to produce a paper which matched his own tastes and those of the men and women to be found everywhere in bars, back streets, factory canteens and, when war came, in the services. No news was to appear which they would not want to read; no holds were barred in exploiting the readers' interests in sex, violence and sensationalism. Given the objectives, the *Mirror* of that time succeeded resoundingly. The great black headlines screamed blue murder, and stories of lurid "human interest" pushed all but the most sensational current news out of pages that used "cheesecake" pictures of girls and banks of strip cartoons to jack up the circulation. The *Mirror* was a daily affront to bishops, magistrates, schoolmasters, the retired élite and the combined forces of officialdom and respectable society—the greater British public revelled in it, and still do. (Manvell, *This Age,* p. 25)

JOURNALISM AS ENTERTAINMENT: THE NEWS "STORY" AND ITS PURVEYORS

The greater public uses the press largely for its daily entertainment —not all the news that's fit to print, but all that's fit to entertain. This gives the cue to the majority of films that have portrayed the press. The characterization of the journalist is far more often than not that of the ephemeral writer who uses his or her talents solely to entertain. Truth may or may not be their additional concern—their job is to secure a "story," the very term giving a fictional slant to the appeal that must be built into the choice and the retailing of news. Newsmen and news-women become standard protagonists in fiction—whether in print or on the screens. The more cynical and unscrupulous they are, the more they entertain the viewer. Like criminals, gangsters, police officers, spies and special agents, sailors, soldiers, show people, newsmen and newswomen become adventurers on land and sea, prone to danger, pursuing careers that differentiate them sharply and amusingly from the "normal" citizen—the dull deskworker, the flagging factory worker, the assiduous salesman, all leading lives of deadening routine.

It goes without saying that most journalist-protagonists on the screen are cynics, especially in American films. Countless Hollywood pictures have shown the journalist as an amusing but more or less unscrupulous news purveyor, a go-getter for the popular press. He is given all the sharp lines, all the wisecracks, and his feverish figure flits from situation to situation, wherever he thinks he can ferret out the redder meat for his voracious readers. This has been the case in movies from *The Front Page* to *Ace in the Hole (The Big Carnival)* and *The Sweet Smell of Success.* The parallel in Europe would be Fellini's *La Dolce Vita.* Far more rarely has the journalist been shown in a light that reflects the kind of aspirations recognized by Delane 125 years ago. *All the President's Men* is a recent exception.

Yet it is undesirable that the public carry a partly conscious, partly subconscious image of the journalist as yet another cynical exploiter, the con man of the printed word. The fictional journalist should, like the real journalist, often be a fighter for the public good—as the film priest or doctor often is. Even the lawyer seems to receive juster treatment than the journalist.

Let us examine how the press and the other media have been represented in certain notable films. Although a few of the films involved are European, the great majority are American.

FRONT PAGE CYNICISM

With the coming of sound in 1928, one of the earliest of the Hollywood films featuring the press was Lewis Milestone's *The Front Page* (1931) with Pat O'Brien, Adolphe Menjou, Clarence Wilson, and Edward

Everett Horton.* Emphasizing the complete cynicism accepted as normal in the American journalist, *The Front Page* was to become a classic of the early sound-film period on the strength of the sharpness of tongue and quick-spoken dialogue created for the newsmen by Ben Hecht and Charles MacArthur. Milestone's sharp cutting from scene to scene added visual pace to the slickness of the speech—which is, however, sometimes difficult to catch because of the limitations of early sound recording. *The Front Page* became the leading presentation in a whole genre of yellow-press films in 1931, including *Five-Star Final, Big News,* and *The Power of the Press;* it had first appeared in the theater in 1928 and had been a resounding success. Allardyce Nicoll comments on the play and the genre it represented in his book, *World Drama:*

> Another style of American realistic comedy displays its interest in the social scene in a diverse manner. From the time when Ben Hecht and Charles MacArthur won their resounding success for their noisy, quick-tempo *The Front Page* (1928) to the appearance of *The Women* (1936) by Clare Boothe, the American theatre has developed one peculiar kind of drama of its own—a kind wherein sensational scenes are scrambled up with scenes of raucous laughter, wherein the actions and characters are given a spurious air of naturalistic authenticity, and wherein vituperative rudeness of phrase is substituted for wit. Although we may readily conceive that journalists testify to the exactitude with which *The Front Page* reproduces American newspaper life and that Clare Boothe has faithfully recorded the conversation of the ladies' retiring-room in *The Women,* both of these thoroughly typical plays are to be seen, on examination, as conceived in terms of modern melodrama . . . while they may contain matter fit for satire, [they] are not created in the true satiric mood. (p. 847)

The Hecht-MacArthur comedy-melodrama concerns an unscrupulous editor and his star reporter, who takes possession of the escaping murderer of a black police officer in order to secure an exclusive story. Hecht and MacArthur set out, of course, more to entertain than to satirize the unethical behavior characteristic (they imply) of the American popular press. Milestone introduces a direct note of moralizing and social comment into the screenplay (the film was adapted, with

---

*Lee Tracy had played Johnson on the stage, and Louis Wolheim the editor. The director was George S. Kaufman, who was to insist on the characteristic speedy dialogue, carried forward into the film.

additional dialogue, by Bartlett Cormack and Charles Lederer). They even add a new political touch with mention of the "Red scare."

There is, of course, a world of difference between using dark comedy for deliberate, satiric attack and exploiting the spurious entertainment value of cynicism for its own sake, leaving viewers to draw any moral they may wish, or none at all. With considerable changes, *The Front Page* was remade by Howard Hawks in 1940 with the new title of *His Girl Friday,* again adapted by Charles Lederer, and starring this time Cary Grant as Walter Burns (the unscrupulous editor played in the previous film by Adolphe Menjou) and Rosalind Russell as Hildy Johnson, made a woman this time around, who is also the editor's divorced wife. Cary Grant, as might be expected, removed the sinister element from the character of the editor, giving him the smooth charm and elegance associated with Grant on screen, while exploiting his unscrupulousness for sophisticated comic effect. Through his contriving charm Burns keeps the highly professional journalist, Hildy, under his spell; however hard she tries, she cannot finally escape being reunited with him. Perhaps personal rather than press ethics are involved here, or both combined—the wife who escapes temporarily with another man only to be lured back to remarry her former husband; however, it is clear that her drive for a scoop pushes her back into her profession against all rational judgment. After this, Walter easily entices her to develop the story of the city's political corruption in a series of articles that will (no doubt) crown her journalistic career. The more positive role of the journalist as social watchdog is slipped in at the close.*

This was not to be the end of *The Front Page* on the screen. With the reporter a man once again, Billy Wilder made a third screen version in 1974. He kept the period of the action back in Chicago of 1929 but considerably updated the dialogue, written by Wilder himself with his long-time partner, I. A. L. Diamond. The well-established comedy team of Walter Matthau and Jack Lemmon took over the parts of Burns and

---

*One of the unfortunate effects of *His Girl Friday* was that distribution of *The Front Page* was withheld until the early 1970s, since Howard Hawks acquired the exclusive rights for a prolonged period. Women journalists were also featured characters in *Front Page Woman* (1935), directed by Michael Curtiz with Bette Davis and George Brent, in *Dance, Fools, Dance* (1931), with Joan Crawford, and in *A Woman Rebels* (1936), with Katharine Hepburn. In *Front Page Woman,* for example, the comedy consists in the professional rivalry between male and female reporters covering a murder case. The British Film Institute's review written at the time of release is revealing "The tone of the film is light-hearted cynicism, which, together with quick wits and complete readiness to disregard all laws, written or unwritten, is convincingly portrayed as the make-up of the successful, sensational reporter" 2 [1935]: 124).

Johnson, with Lemmon trying to escape from his profession and marry a girl from Philadelphia. Williams, the escaping murderer, is shown as a crazy anarchist, and the victim remains a black police officer; the anarchist shoots his way out to momentary freedom while in the charge of a psychiatrist. The story then follows the same path to the payoff—when Burns prevents his star reporter from slipping through his fingers by having him arrested for stealing the watch he has just been given as a parting gift for his services.

Wilder had himself been a newsman, working at one time for *B.Z.am Mittag* in Berlin and *Die Stunde* in Vienna, and he had previously attacked the press in *Ace in the Hole,* discussed below. Myron Meisel, in a perceptive review of these films written in 1975, calls *The Front Page* "the archetypal newspaper film," but as a piece of filmmaking he seems to prefer *His Girl Friday*—"a Hawks film first, and a newspaper film second." He comments:

> *The Front Page* revels in the lean speed of the wisecracking patois of the hep urban denizen; its dialogue is as close to an indigenous ersatz poetry as has ever been concocted in America. The audience is let in on the straight dope: everyone, protagonists included, is gloriously corrupt and the fun takes off from there. The fact that Earl Williams is due to be executed for the murder of a Negro policeman, a crime of minimal concern in the context of the '20s social priorities, is quite beside the point of beating the other sheet to the street with the day's exclusive; an exclusive that lasts one day only, when the scramble for primacy begins yet again. Newspaper work becomes a heightened ritual of Social Darwinism played out against a souped-up Myth of Sisyphus, and *The Front Page* brings us along for the ride. After all, we're the public it's all supposed to be going on for, right? ... Of course, the whole conception if a romanticized one, but within that context, Milestone and his adapter, Charles Lederer, respect the serious implications of the story. *(Dateline ... Hollywood)*

In 1931, the same year as *The Front Page* was released, Mervyn LeRoy's *Five Star Final* appeared,* with Edward G. Robinson, Aline MacMahon, Frances Starr, and H. B. Warner; it was released six months after LeRoy's celebrated film *Little Caesar. Five Star Final* was an out-and-out attack on yellow journalism; yet again, it was an adaptation from a play by Louis Weitzenkorn, who had been managing editor of the New York *Evening Graphic* until disillusioned by its unethical exploitation of sensational stories, he left. The paper in the film is the

---

*Later also remade as *Two Against the World (One Fatal Hour),* directed by William McGann, with Humphrey Bogart.

New York *Gazette,* and its managing editor, Randall (Robinson), is pressured by the owner to give the journal a powerful circulation boost. It is decided to revive the story of a twenty-year-old *crime passionel,* in which a woman called Nancy Voorhees (Starr) had killed an unfaithful lover. She is now a married woman, living quietly, the scandal long forgotten; the reexposure ruins the lives of her whole family, though the *Gazette* achieves its circulation goal. The managing editor, however, denounces his employer and quits his job, like the author of the original play.

In 1937 Ben Hecht, whose bitterness over his collapsed career as a playwright was revealed in the cynicism of his Hollywood scripts, wrote a second classic exposure of the yellow press, *Nothing Sacred* (1937), directed by William Wellman and starring Carole Lombard and Fredric March. (S. J. Perelman, another brilliant writer caught up in scriptwriting, described the experience as "no worse than playing piano in a call house.") Hecht espoused many causes, one of them the need to attack unethical practices among newsmen and press proprietors. *Nothing Sacred* is about a woman living in a small town who is diagnosed by her local doctor, an alcoholic, as suffering from radium poisoning and therefore having only a short time to live. The case is taken up as a stunt by a paper in New York, where she is fêted at the newspaper's expense in order to make a sensational story. She falls in love with the reporter involved, and when she finds she is perfectly healthy, the pretense of her illness is maintained so that neither she nor the public will lose out. The film, kept as near light comedy as possible, exposes the sheer gullibility of the readers, with their crocodile tears for the unfortunate.*

A potentially tragic situation is also exploited by a cynical and ambitious reporter in *Inherit the Wind* (1960), Stanley Kramer's reconstruction of the "Monkey Trial" in Dayton, Tennessee, in 1925, in which a schoolteacher was indicted for teaching Darwin's theory of evolution. Again it is a matter of a newspaper's taking up a case not out of altruism but for a good story. In the film (adapted from a play by Jerome Lawrence and Robert E. Lee), a celebrated advocate, Matthew Harrison Brady (Fredric March), prosecutes for the Fundamentalists; the paper retains another giant, Henry Drummond (Spencer Tracy) for the defense. The reporter is played (most unexpectedly and rather indiffer-

---

*Nothing Sacred was later remade by Norman Taurog in 1954 as *Living It Up,* with Dean Martin, Jerry Lewis, and Janet Leigh. It was derived from a Broadway musical, *Hazel Flagg,* bereft of the satiric sharpness of Hecht's script. The comedy turns on the fact that the doctor (Martin), though realizing his mistake, does not want to pass up the trip to New York promised him and his patient by the newspaper taking up the story.

ently) by Gene Kelly, and the film concludes with Drummond's blistering attack on the journalist for his cynicism.

In these films as in many others, the press is portrayed in varying degrees as a profession without either ethics or humanity. In film after film newspaper people were given a bad name. However entertaining and pseudosophisticated the wisecracking dialogue proved to be, such films undermined the prestige of all journalists and their editors in the minds of the unthinking public. The profession became perpetually equated with cynicism and in consequence degraded Hecht, whose observation was derived from personal experience, allowed his bitterness to lapse into a form of cynicism that expressed itself in black humor. He wrote perhaps the bitterest expression of this absence of confidence in *Nothing Sacred:* "You know what I think, young feller? I think yer a newspaper man. I can smell 'em. Excuse me while I open the windows. I'll tell you briefly what I think of newspaper men. The hand of God reaching down into the mire couldn't elevate one of them to the depths of degradation. Not by a million miles."

DANGEROUS ESTATE*

So far, the films concerned with press ethics that we have been considering have deliberately adopted a light tone; however serious the stories the reporters and editors have been handling (and they have involved murder, suicide, gross misrepresentation of the truth, and sacrificing all principles and even humanity for the sake of creating and maintaining sensational copy), the treatment has been cynical and lighthearted, rarely serious enough to provoke real audience qualms.

The films—all of distinction—we now consider do take the matter of press ethics seriously. They are without exception entertaining, but their makers had a message to convey. The first is *Citizen Kane,* made by Orson Welles at twenty-five after he had established his reputation in the Federal Theatre project and with his Mercury Players both in live theater and in radio drama. This is not the place to consider the striking innovations in technique that he brought to the screen with this first film; they only served to enhance considerably the impact of the subject, which was to attack (with great daring) the irresponsible exploitation of the press by such "jingo journalists" (Pauline Kael's phrase) as Randolph Hearst, who is thinly disguised in the character of Charles Foster Kane, Welles's protagonist. Kane inherits when still

---

*The title of Lord Francis Williams's history of the press.

a very young man a near-defunct newspaper in New York and un-scrupulously uses it to further his own egocentric ambitions. He uses every evil device to increase the paper's circulation and to buy up the consciences of the best newsmen he can persuade to join him without questioning his methods. All this he disguises (from himself and his readers alike) in expressions of noble platitudes the very day he takes over: "I'll provide the people of this city with a daily paper that will tell all the news honestly. I will also provide them with a fighting and tireless champion of their rights as citizens and human beings."

However, his real attitude is revealed in his exchanges with the old-fashioned (and unsuccessful) editor he throws out on the street after their first encounter:

> *Carter:* . . . we're running a newspaper, Mr. Kane, not a scandal sheet.
> *Kane* [pointing to a rival's coverage of the story of a missing woman]:
> The *Chronicle* has a two-column headline, Mr. Carter. Why haven't we?
> *Carter:* The news wasn't big enough.
> *Kane:* If the headline is big enough, it *makes* the news big enough. . . .
> *Carter:* It's not our function to report the gossip of housewives. If we were interested in that kind of thing, Mr. Kane, we could fill the paper twice over daily—
> *Kane:* That's the kind of thing we *are* going to be interested in from now on, Mr. Carter.

The noted screenwriter Herman J. Mankiewicz wrote the film, but it is infused by Welles's overriding personality.* Mankiewicz, a former ace journalist of the 1920s and a friend of Hecht, had also been a member of the Hearst-Marion Davies circle and a frequent guest at San Simeon. But this did not prevent his taking a full part in making the most virulent attack on an American press tycoon the cinema has known. As Pauline Kael put it: "Mankiewicz betrayed their hospitality, even though he liked them both. They must have presented an irresistible target. And so Hearst, the yellow-press lord who had trained Mankiewicz's generation of reporters to betray *anyone* for a story, became at last the victim of his own style of journalism."

Like Hecht, Mankiewicz had become completely cynical by the time he had left the newspaper world of New York to become a scriptwriter in Hollywood; and he had become an alcoholic and a gambler to boot.

---

*The celebrated controversy about the "only begetter" of *Citizen Kane* was aired by Pauline Kael in *The Citizen Kane Book.*

Citizen Kane is full of references to Hearst's form of power journalism: in the parody on the *March of Time* film magazine, with its
special issue covering Kane after his death, the narrator declares:

> Kane's empire, in its glory, held dominion over thirty-seven newspa-
> pers, thirteen magazines, a radio network. An empire upon an em-
> pire. The first of grocery stores, papermills, apartment buildings,
> factories, forests, ocean liners—an empire through which for fifty
> years, in an unending stream, the wealth of the earth's third richest
> gold-mine flowed.

Kane is the kind of press lord who decides which wars are to be fought.
His lifelong associate, Bernstein, tells a reporter interviewing him
about his former employer:

> Mr. Kane was a man that lost—almost everything he had. You ought
> to talk to Mr. Leland. Of course, he and Mr. Kane didn't exactly see
> eye to eye. You take the Spanish-American war. I guess Mr. Leland
> was right. That was Mr. Kane's war. We didn't really have anything
> to fight about. But do you think if it hadn't been for that war of Mr.
> Kane's, we'd have the Panama Canal?

Kane himself is seen being interviewed on his return from Europe:

> *Reporter*: What do you think of the chances for a war in Europe?
> *Kane*: Young man, there'll be no war. I have talked with all the
> responsible leaders of the Great Powers, and I can assure you that
> England, France, Germany and Italy are too intelligent to embark
> upon a project that must mean the end of civilization as we now know
> it. There will be no war!

He lures the best talent he can buy to write for the *Inquirer*,
stealing them from his rivals' employ:

> Gentlemen of the *Inquirer!* Eight years ago—eight long, very busy
> years ago—I stood in front of the *Chronicle* window and looked at a
> picture of the nine greatest newspapermen in the world. I felt like a
> kid in front of a candy shop. Tonight I got my candy. Welcome,
> gentlemen, to the *Inquirer*. It will make you happy to learn that our
> circulation this morning was the greatest in New York.... All of you
> —new and old—you're all getting the best salaries in town. Not one
> of you has been hired because of his loyalty. It's your talent I'm
> interested in—I like talent....
> *Leland*: Bernstein, these men who are now with the *Inquirer*—who
> were with the *Chronicle* until yesterday—weren't they just as de-
> voted to the *Chronicle* kind of newspaper as they are now to—our
> kind of paper?

Bernstein: Sure. They're like anybody else. They got work to do. They do it. Only they happen to be the best men in the business.
Leland: Do we stand for the same things the *Chronicle* stands for, Bernstein?
Bernstein: Certainly not. What of it? Mr. Kane he'll have them changed to his kind of newspapermen in a week.

Welles was never to enjoy the same freedom again as he had when promoting and making *Citizen Kane* for RKO. It has caused the industry far too much trouble. In one way or another his subsequent films made in America were circumscribed, and no film he was to promote contained this level of social comment.

But films by other filmmakers were to incorporate a similar bitterness in their exposure of the worst press practices. Second only to *Citizen Kane* was Billy Wilder's *Ace in the Hole (The Big Carnival, 1961)*, which Wilder himself principally scripted, and on which he had journalistic advice from no fewer than five named journalists—Agnes Underwood, Harold Hubbard, Wayne Scott, Dan Burroughs, and Will Harrison. *Ace in the Hole* was made from an original script, and its outlook was utterly bleak and destructive.* The protagonist is a once-successful journalist who is quite without conscience, Chuck Tatum (Kirk Douglas), exiled in Albuquerque, New Mexico, for his lack of ethics. His ambition is to work his way back into national journalism. It is Tatum's good fortune that a man, played by Leo Minosa, is trapped alive in a cave while seeking Indian relics. Tatum sees his opportunity in prolonging the man's agony: he persuades the local sheriff to use a prolonged and spectacular rescue operation to gain useful publicity for a forthcoming election. At the same time he secures from the sheriff exclusive rights to exploit the story. The man's wife (Jan Sterling) is persuaded to set up a business selling refreshments to the sensation seekers and, though a nonbeliever to be filmed praying for her husband's relief; the presence of a brass band and the exploitation of souvenir seekers completes a macabre picture of human sensation-mongering. While all this is going on, the trapped man dies. Although in the end Tatum tries to rescue the man himself and regains his sense of human values, only to die when the dead man's wife attacks him, the picture was so bitter it turned sour on the promoters, Paramount, the press, rather naturally, were dead against it. For example, Bosley Crowther wrote in the New York *Times* that no reporter could ever get away with such a situation: "The responsible element would not permit

---

*The story appears to have originated in a real-life case—that of Floyd Collins in 1925, which created a nationwide sensation.

such a thing, and thus Wilder has given us not only a grim and harrowing film, but he has also given us a distortion almost as vicious as the journalistic trickery." And Myron Meisel, writing almost twenty-five years later, is scarcely kinder; he calls the film "nastier than all the others combined":

> A merciless depiction of mob behavior and a savage indictment of irresponsible media huckstering, the film's unrelenting viciousness made it box-office poison at the time of its release. Today it remains a perceptive if grotesque distillation of Wilder's most bitter themes, and despite an overly contrived denouement, an extraordinary example of commercial film-making at its least compromising. (*Dateline Hollywood*, p. 31)

Paramount had to send out a corps of public relations representatives in an endeavor to persuade the press that it was not, after all, being indicated by this story of an extremist in its midst. *Ace in the Hole* is nevertheless a brilliant film with something of Swift's acerbic observation of human behavior. Had it been released in the present period, which has produced after all films such as Pasolini's *Salo*, it might have proved more easily acceptable. Wilder might even have gotten away with a less sentimental conclusion; he might have shown the death of the trapped man coinciding with the success of his exploiter, who as a result re-creates his career in big-time journalism. This is in fact the more logical outcome.

The Sweet Smell of Success (1957), the first American picture to be made by the British director Alexander MacKendrick, has something of the same atmosphere—the devastating influence of Hunsecker (Burt Lancaster), a highly placed New York gossip columnist, on the lives of his sister, Susan, and her lover. The film spares us nothing in its exposure of corruption; and although it is essentially a film of protest, it relishes the dirt it uncovers with such brilliance. *Ace in the Hole* and *The Sweet Smell of Success* are both studies in unrelieved evil in the world of degenerate journalism; in the latter film there is little final penitence to alleviate the impression of human degradation.

The only outstanding European production in this field is Federico Fellini's *La Dolce Vita* (*The Sweet Life*, 1959), which exposes a world Fellini himself knows well, the yellow press of Rome, and in particular the unethical activities of the *paparazzi*—the press photographers who hound their chosen victims among the social elite in order to catch them in compromising situations. The protagonist is Marcello (Marcello Mastroianni), a third-rate newsman in Rome whose living depends on hunting out scandals and, with his surreptitious photographers, securing what compromising pictures he can. The film concentrates in turn on the women with whom he manages to associate —including a bored young heiress in search of new pleasures and Sylvia, a capricious Hollywood sex star—all in contrast to Paola, an innocent and seemingly incorruptible young waitress from the provincial countryside whose natural purity becomes for Marcello the final sign of the corruption to which he has given over his life. For three hours the film conducts us through this empty and pleasure-loving Roman society, with its sinister obsessions.

La Dolce Vita presents a brilliant picture of a bored and decadent pseudoaristocracy, rich eccentrics mingling with meretricious though successful show-business personalities, all living lives of purposeless self-indulgence. Fellini has claimed (in the book of interviews, *Fellini on Fellini,* and elsewhere) that this life has no attractions for him personally; he merely looks on with a half-amused, half-tolerant fascination. He appears to make no ethical judgment in the film, as the more moralistic American films take pains to do. He equates the corruption of the Roman press with the corruption in Roman society and leaves his audience to make what judgment they will. The picture is perhaps more uncompromising for its lack of a message.

The press emerges without honor from all these films, though society is guilty too for enjoying its victimization. After seeing such films, it is a relief to turn to responsible newspapers to regain balance. They still exist—for a minority readership. Beside them on the newsstands blare the headlines and the cover pictures that show the films have scarcely overstated their case, and that we must constantly strive to maintain ethical standards in journalism, lest the bad coin eventually drive out the good.

THE NEWSPERSON AS HUMANE CITIZEN

Drama and fiction thrive on trouble, and writers have always found the villain more fascinating than the hero, when the latter is merely the representative of virtue in action. Therefore, as we have seen, most newspeople in drama and films tend to be at least cynical, if not downright exploiters of human suffering. It is a welcome change when now and then we see the newsperson practicing his profession for the public good. Few of the films that present the case for the humane journalist equal cinematically those that aim to show him up. One of the first to portray the good journalist was William Wellman's *The Story of G.I. Joe* (1945), a fictionalized biography of one of America's most celebrated war correspondents, Ernie Pyle (Burgess Meredith).

The film, released during the last year of the war, reconstructed certain of Pyle's real-life experiences on the fighting front which he turned into remarkable descriptive dispatches about the American soldier at war. Pyle had been attached to C Company of the Eighteenth American Infantry and had seen service alongside them from North Africa to Sicily and southern Italy. He was able to personalize representative individuals in his stories, showing how different kinds of men developed from raw, inexperienced recruits into members of a tough and highly disciplined combat unit. Incident follows incident in the film, making up a mosaic of the company of which Pyle himself became a trusted associate. Everywhere he introduces the individual, detailed touch. For example, a sergeant becomes obsessed by the need to get hold of a gramophone to play a recording he has been sent of his infant son's voice. When at last he succeeds, the child's voice is heard amid the sounds of warfare, and the man becomes demented. The film, dramatized as it is for reasons of entertainment, is nevertheless one of the best, most authentic of the American war films. It shows the significance of the war correspondent who identifies himself with his subject instead of exploiting it for copy; he links the newspaper-reading public at home with their men fighting thousands of miles away. The film shows Pyle eating, sleeping, marching with the infantrymen, becoming their comrade: it stresses that the reporter should be part of the scene being covered. When the reporter divorces himself, becoming merely the inquisitive intruder, his worth as a human being and writer lessens. His professionalism is in doubt.

In British films, although journalists often appear, they are rarely protagonists. The British press, contending with tougher laws of libel, cannot afford to go to the lengths of certain elements of the American press and is on the whole a quieter and less exciting institution. The journalist appears for the most part as a peripheral, perhaps even a comic character in British plays and films, possibly asking awkward questions but seldom emerging as the out-and-out exploiter of trouble.

Press ethics arise fleetingly in an interesting British science-fiction film, *The Day the Earth Caught Fire* (1961, director Val Guest)—interesting in part because Arthur Christiansen, a celebrated editor of the London *Daily Express,* was invited when in retirement to reenact himself in the part of the *Express*'s editor at a time of acute (fictional) crisis. The orbit of the earth has been jolted and its climatic structure violently changed after simultaneous American and Russian nuclear test explosions. A simple matter of press ethics becomes an important element in the film—a reporter working for the *Express* obtains a vital piece of secret information from his girlfriend, a switchboard operator at the Meteorological Office, namely, that the earth is now moving gradually nearer to the sun and will eventually burn out. The reporter prints the news in spite of having promised his girlfriend he would not, feeling that the public good comes before his purely private need to keep his word. Stenning, the journalist, is represented as having done the right thing professionally in the circumstances—but otherwise he and his close colleague, a hard-drinking older man, exemplify the usual film journalists with their slick wisecracks and alcoholic indulgence.

Arguably the best press film the British have made is an unpretentious production, *Front Page Story* (1953, director Gordon Parry), on which several writers with a journalistic background collaborated. The film is presented from the point of view of a busy news editor called Grant (Jack Hawkins) who works on a London national daily. He has a deteriorating relationship with his wife, Susan, who feels neglected because of her husband's devotion to his job. (She is in consequence indulging herself in a love affair with one of her husband's colleagues.) The film presents a succession of situations, most of which involve press ethics, and the audience witnesses the decisions Grant must make. One concerns an atomic scientist visiting London and passing secrets to a foreign power; he is actually arrested at the newspaper's office after he has dictated an article declaring his beliefs. But in this particular case the film scarcely enters properly upon the issues involved. The paper "adopts" a family of homeless children when their mother dies. Kennedy, an idealistic young reporter on Grant's staff (and spokesman in the film against the stock philosophy of the cynical journalist, as indeed Grant speaks from the more balanced standpoint of age and experience) is covering a case of suspected euthanasia—though the woman concerned is found innocent, she is in such a state of distraction on leaving the court and finding herself hounded by a group of journalists that she is run over by a bus in Trafalgar Square. This gives a drunken and guilty Kennedy the opportunity to air his views on press ethics to his editor. For all its basic integrity, *Front Page Story* is always edging toward melodrama. Nevertheless, the audience is taken inside a newspaper office and sees the kind of judgments editors have to make in selecting and presenting news about matters of human concern.

THE NEWSPERSON AS FIGHTER FOR JUSTICE

Call Northside 777 (1947, director Henry Hathaway) is one of the first films to show a reporter fighting for justice. During 1932, police officers were in the forefront of the disturbances resulting from Prohibition, and this film dramatized (like *Boomerang* and *The House on 92nd Street*) in fictional form an actual case. A Pole called Majczek was wrongly sentenced in 1932 for killing a police officer but was released from jail eleven years later on a free pardon. In this documentary-styled film, this true story is fictionalized: a reporter, McNeal (James Stewart) answers an advertisement in the Chicago *Times* to call Northside 777. A reward of $5,000 is being offered for information concerning the killing of a police officer many years before. McNeal discovers the mother of a man serving time for this murder scrubbing floors in order to earn dollars to help get her son out of jail. Initially, McNeal is just out to obtain a good story, but when he visits the condemned man in his cell, he begins against his will to believe in his innocence, which he eventually becomes the principal agent in proving. In this film, the newspaper office is a center for the promotion of justice, and James Stewart exemplifies the good journalist who awakens the public conscience in his determination to see justice is not only done, but known to be done through the medium of print.

In 1948 Elia Kazan (at this time still a relative newcomer to films, after having established himself in the theater) directed *Gentleman's Agreement*, with Gregory Peck, Dorothy McGuire, and John Garfield. In this film a writer called Philip Green (Peck) is commissioned to undertake a series of articles on anti-Semitism for a progressive magazine. He decides to pose as a Jew in order to gain direct experience of bigotry. His action alienates for a while his girlfriend, Kathy, and even his schoolboy son suffers. Kazan, himself Jewish, used the film (scripted by Moss Hart, and based on a novel by Laura Z. Hobson) to expose hotels practicing restriction, and indeed every branch of American social and business life that had its "gentleman's agreement" to exclude Jews. *Gentleman's Agreement* received an Oscar as the best film of 1947, and Kazan won the director's award as well. According to Kazan (as recorded in *Kazan on Kazan*) Darryl Zanuck took a personal interest in the film as producer and shepherded it through the considerable opposition put up to its being made—largely, it would seem, by rich Jews in Hollywood. Yet, as Kazan puts it, "For the first time someone said that America is full of anti-Semitism, both conscious and unconscious, and among the best and most liberal people. In that sense the picture broke some new ground, and Zanuck, Hart and I can take some credit. It was saying to the audience: You are an average American and you are anti-Semitic.'" (At one stage even Green discovers that he's anti-Semitic.) Nevertheless, the film was to some extent tailored in outward appearance to please an audience; as Kazan writes, "Everybody had to look good." From our point of view, however, it is important that audiences for this popular, award-winning film were shown that writers could sacrifice themselves for such a cause and face its implications with honesty; Gregory Peck gave the part of Green his own fundamental decency and screen image of integrity. Kazan was at too early a stage in his screen career to assert himself; subsequently, he claims, he would have been able to make the film much more abrasive.

Later, in 1956, Humphrey Bogart took on the role of Eddie Willis, an unemployed sportswriter, in *The Harder They Fall,* directed by Mark Robson. Willis consents initially to work as press agent for an unscrupulous promoter (Rod Steiger) who stages fixed fights in order to bring an unskillful but muscular Argentinian, Tono Moreno, to the top of the fight racket. Moreno loses the key fight of his career. Bogart, sickened by his part in the affair, gives Moreno his own share in the spoils and retires to write his denunciation of the racket. Bogart plays the stereotypical cynical journalist who develops a conscience; the film itself is harsh and violent. However, he gives in the end a favorable impression of the reporter who can no longer tolerate the betrayal of the sport for which he was once an established commentator.

These Hollywood films attempted to rehabilitate the screen reputation of the American journalist. However, we had to wait until the present for the outstanding film in which journalists were the sole protagonists. This was, of course, *All the President's Men* (1976), directed by Alan J. Pakula, scripted by William Goldman, and based directly on the book by Carl Bernstein and Bob Woodward, played in the film by Dustin Hoffman and Robert Redford. Jack Warden plays Harry Rosenfeld, the Washington *Post's* metropolitan editor who encourages the junior reporters in their relentless pursuit of the clues that gradually piece together the network of Watergate corruption, and Jason Robards portrays the *Post's* editor, Ben Bradlee, who had strong initial reservations about his youthful reporters. The film presents its story as a remarkable feat in sheer detection, as exciting as it is sometimes baffling to follow, and conducted for the most part at high speed. It shifts rapidly from episode to episode, much of the action conducted in close shot. I had the advantage of viewing the film with a former member of the *Post's* staff, who vouched for the authenticity of its interoffice procedure and the portrayal of its senior editors, particularly Bradlee. No film could better reveal the importance of the reporter as guardian of the public welfare, performing his duty at whatever cost in time, energy, and personal comfort, working round the clock, and even placing himself in physical danger. The film has all the qualities of an intense political thriller; the pressures to encourage or prohibit publication added to the documentary realism with which this, perhaps the finest film on the press and press ethics yet made, was presented.* Pakula contrasts with great skill the reporters' enclosed and detailed investigation with the big-scale appearances of the political figures (seen for the most part in actuality through television recordings) around whom the slender thongs of the "woodstein" web are gradually tightening. The clatter of typewriters is the musical leitmotif to the film, beating out the fateful words, letter by letter.

THE CINEMA AND THE OTHER MEDIA

Hollywood has not been slow to satirize or at least laugh at itself —though the satire is usually softened with some degree of comforting sentiment. Even Wilder gives a somewhat rhetoretical, sentimental close to *Sunset Boulevard* (1950). But Hollywood seems to take delight in its own absurdity; indeed, as early as the silent period it enjoyed a certain pride in its own extravagances. This can be seen in such old films as *The Last Command, Merton of the Movies, What Price Hollywood,* and *A Star is Born.* But *Sullivan's Travels* (1941), *Sunset Boulevard, The Star* (1953), *The Bad and the Beautiful* (1952), and *The Big Knife* (1955) all took Hollywood pretensions apart and offset such wholly sentimental self-portraits as *Singin' in the Rain* (otherwise an excellent film) or *The Perils of Pauline.* Later films showing the less favorable side of Hollywood have included *The Goddess, Harlow, Inside Daisy Clover, The Loved One,* and *The Oscar.* Most of the more satiric films have been concerned in one way or another with the ethics of the film industry—for example, *Sunset Boulevard* shows the kind of sexual trap that exists for the screenwriter, who in this film falls under the spell of a long-retired star. Preston Sturges's *Sullivan's Travels* concerns a wealthy director of comedies obsessed by a sentimental desire to make a serious film about the poor who insists on disguising himself as a tramp in order to discover what it is like to be underprivileged. The director, who ends up in jail, emerges from his experiment convinced that laughter rather than serious drama is what the poor most need in order to enable them to forget their troubles.

Hollywood has also satirized, initially with some bitterness, its closest rival, television. The key films, Kazan's *A Face in the Crowd* (1957), Haskell Wexler's *Medium Cool* (1969), and most recent of all,

---

*In the effort to contrive realism, the studio reconstruction of the *Post's* pressroom was littered with authentic wastepaper sent by the newspaper from the East Coast to the West. Production of the film involved continual and painstaking consultation with *Post* representatives.

Sidney Lumet's *Network* (1976), have all directly involved ethical considerations.

A Face in the Crowd was adapted by Budd Schulberg from his own story, *Your Arkansas Traveller;* Schulberg had written the script of Kazan's previous success in sociopolitical cinema, *On the Waterfront.* It starred Andy Griffith as Lonesome Rhodes, a down-and-out with a glib, folksy line of patter and a guitar, who is salvaged from jail by a woman (Patricia Neal) working on the staff of a small Arkansas radio studio which experiments by giving him his own show. His instant success with the housewife audience means that he soon outgrows local radio and becomes a network television personality with an alarming capacity to sway his nationwide public on any issue his slick tongue prompts him to air—including politics, when he is adopted by an extreme right-wing group grooming an isolationist senator for the presidential nomination. The film exposed the terrifying effect an meglomaniac ignoramus could have on a gullible public, as well as the degree to which rich corporations might be prepared to exploit such spurious fame in order to promote their product or their policies. In the end, the woman who initially promoted Lonesome Rhodes is forced to destroy him; she leaves the sound channel open after the conclusion of one of his shows so that the public can hear his real opinion of them and discover the kind of man he is behind the scenes.

Kazan and Schulberg took their assignment seriously; they even attended Madison Avenue product discussions. Kazan said:

> Everything that's in that picture, we have an example for. We watched many sessions on the selling of Lipton's tea, the discussions of the word "brisk" and how to picturize it. . . . The discussions were really ludicrous; you could hardly keep a straight face at them. But . . . you could feel the intense, neurotic pressure they all worked under. (*Kazan on Kazan,* p. 113)

Kazan and Schulberg even discussed politics and television with Lyndon Johnson. Andy Griffith came himself from television—"He was the real native American country boy and that comes over in the picture," said Kazan. The significance of this film is summed up in Kazan's own words:

> We were talking about the danger of power in the television medium. . . . We weren't dealing with power abstractly, with the fact that power corrupts people, but with the fact that power is attainable in a new way that makes it specially dangerous. . . . I don't think [Lonesome Rhodes] was scheming. He always enjoyed playing with people and seducing them. . . . He lived by his wits. He was scheming in that sense. But he was also fired with a truthfulness which was the

ambiguity of his character and which perhaps we didn't get enough of in the production.... The real source of his power was not his trickiness but his knack of seeing something that everybody feels but doesn't dare say.... We thought of a man who had great attraction, great potential, and great danger.... Our basic interest in this picture was ... to warn the public: look out for television.... The film *was* in advance of its time. It fortells Nixon.... I think it would have been better if we had had a political figure in the Senator who could conceivably have won an election.... What I like in the picture is the energy and invention and bounce which are very American ... this constantly flashing, changing rhythm. In many ways. it's more American than any picture I ever did. It represents the business life, and the urban life, and the ways things are on television, the rhythm of the way this country moves. (p. 00)

Needless to add, *A Face in the Crowd* proved no box-office bonanza.

Medium Cool was the first film to be directed by the distinguished Hollywood cameraman Haskell Wexler. Set in Chicago, it deals with the ethics of a TV cameraman and his degree of involvement (or noninvolvement) in what he photographs. John (Robert Foster) is solely concerned at first with the technical quality of his coverage but finally becomes deeply involved in the study through his camera of social conditions in the city and loses his job as a consequence. The climax involves his free-lance assignment to cover the 1968 Democratic Convention. *Medium Cool,* a very committed film, excited this comment from one of the British Film Institute's reviewers:

The film is unarguably a fine one, a deeply moving questioning of America's violence and voyeurism (the title is presumably a reference to McLuhan's distinction between hot and cool media).... A central point in John's development is his discovery that his footage of protest demonstrations is being handed over to the FBI and CIA, and Wexler clearly shares his indignation about this. In making *Medium Cool,* he shot over twenty hours of demonstration footage; this has since been requisitioned by the Justice Department. (*Monthly Film Bulletin* 37 [1970]: 49)

Network, scripted by Paddy Chayefsky, contains a further warning about involvement with the "cool medium" and was apparently based on a true incident when, a few years ago, a woman threatened to kill herself before the television cameras and subsequently did so. *Network* deals, then, with exhibitionism excited by television's vast viewing potential; Howard Beale (Peter Finch, in a last screen appearance before his death) is a veteran news commentator who threatens to kill himself on TV when faced with dismissal because his ratings have fallen. We see Beale's final demented television appearances once he decides to throw discretion to the winds and become a gesticulating messiah, denouncing everything Chayefsky feels is wrong with American society from ruthless big business to sponsored television itself. Anarchic racial terrorism is equally satirized here in the "Mao Tse-Tung Hour," launched on the network by an obsessive woman executive who is prepared to show anything (however extreme) to secure ratings. Beale is finally shot down by terrorists while on camera and in the presence of an invited audience; his assassination is contrived with the active support of the television executives. In this remarkable but undisciplined film, accusations fly out in all directions at once. The film, half-actuality, half-fantasy, leaves an aftertaste of confused disillusion with American television, and most of all with the sponsorship and ratings systems, which (it claims) play havoc with what conscience is left in those controlling the medium. What survives as solid and human is William Holden's fine performance as the director of the network's news division—a man who stands for the realities of emotion and the values discarded by everyone else involved.

For the uninvolved member of the public, the journalist may well appear to be just another entertainer, whose "stories" casually wile away the journey to and from work, or fill in the odd moment between activities at home. Small wonder, therefore, that the journalist on the screen has been portrayed as a cynical observer of the human scene who seeks to fill his column at some victim's expense, usually in ruthless competition with his professional rivals. Only in rare instances has the screen shown the good journalist in his proper light, as an enlightened citizen seeking the truth and giving it considered expression. *All the President's Men* did achieve precisely this, though the casual viewer might regard this film as a thriller concerning two ambitious young journalists in pursuit of a break. The media themselves, press and screen alike, are responsible for developing the popular press into a medium dedicated to casual entertainment and representing the journalist negatively in films. The only solution to this public relations impasse lies, in my view, with the press itself, since only professional journalists know the exciting stories of persistent vigilance that lie behind a byline. These background stories should be publicized far more often than they are.* And the best of them should surely offer

---

*It is perhaps notable that in *On the Waterfront*, adapted by Budd Schulberg from a series of articles by Malcolm Johnson exposing the dockside union rackets in New York, missed the opportunity to show it was a journalist, not a dock worker or a priest, who took the risk of exposing the criminal activities of the union racketeer.

further subjects for the filmmaker or the television series producer, a welcome antidote to ceaseless portrayals of law enforcement officers striving to solve or prevent crimes. The success of *All the President's Men* has surely shown that the good journalist is good box office.

BIBLIOGRAPHY

British Film Institute. *Monthly Film Bulletin.* 2 (1935), 37 (1970).

Ciment, Michel. *Kazan on Kazan.* London: Secker and Warburg, 1973.

Citizen Kane Book. With an introduction by Pauline Kael. London: Secker and Warburg, 1971.

Dateline . . . Hollywood. Boston: Museum of Fine Arts, 1975.

Manvell, Roger. *This Age of Communication.* Glasgow and London: Blackie, 1966.

Nicoll, Allardyce. *World Drama.* London: George G. Harrap, 1949.

Rubin, Bernard. *Media, Politics and Democracy.* New York: Oxford University Press, 1977.

Seldes, George. *The Freedom of the Press.* Indianapolis: Bobbs-Merrill, 1935.

Wright, Basil. *The Long View.* London: Secker and Warburg, 1974.

11 THE FOURTH ESTATE AND THE SEVENTH ART

Deac Rossell

In our century, American newspapers and American movies have been the two great mass media. Until the rise of television in the past two decades, the newspapers and movies provided the American public with its daily and weekly diet of facts and fictions. Both served a largely urban public, one which had formed through immigration and internal migration in the first decades of the twentieth century, and their mutual jealousies and passions led to a symbiotic relationship. The popular conception of each medium was substantially the result of exposure in the other, and both pragmatically celebrated the present and disavowed the past, working on the old reporter's dictum, "What is hot stuff today is shelf paper tomorrow."

As might be expected, the earliest reporting on the new motion pictures siezed on the invention's novelty and endorsed early claims of educational utility. The Canastota *Bee* in small-town upstate New York, for example, wrote enthusiastically of the Biograph Company's new Mutoscope on August 5, 1895: "It will be of incalculable value to agents who wish to show customers the actual workings of intricate machinery and will amplify the scope of instruction in technical schools." Enthusiasm for the new inventions also ran high in New York City, where the debut of Thomas Alva Edison's motion picture device at Koster & Biall's Music Hall in Herald Square received such comments as "intensely interesting and pleasing" (New York *Herald*) and "a decided hit" (New York *Tribune*).*

---

*Both May 3, 1896. An earlier press report of Edison's work illustrates the first example of commercial influence over press reporting on motion pictures: on May 30, 1891, both newspapers in Orange, New Jersey, where Edison's laboratory was located, reported that Edison as at work on a device to reproduce motion photographically. The Orange *Chronicle,* which got Edison's printing business, gave the story half a column, while the Orange *Journal,* which didn't get Edison business, buried the story on a back page.

This early fascination was not long-lived, for the novelty of the new scientific marvel soon wore off, and movies disappeared from press reports, as the ever-more imaginative claims of inventors for talking pictures, color pictures, and a televisionlike home dissemination of movies failed to materialize. Without much public notice, the new film medium stagnated until 1902–3, when it began to develop as a storytelling entertainment medium. For the next four years, movies developed rapidly in technique and in popularity, but their popularity was mainly confined to working-class neighborhoods and immigrant audiences, well off the beat of middle-class newspapers. In this era, English literacy was still the great watershed dividing these two mass communicators. It is toward the end of the decade, when the middle classes discovered movies, and when the movies felt the power of a reform-minded press, that the real story of the press and the pictures begins.

In March 1907, less than two years after the emergence of the nickelodeon, the five-cent theater that was to provide entertainment for millions of working-class families, the Chicago *Tribune* suddenly editorialized against the popular new theaters in the strongest terms: ". . . without a redeeming feature to warrant their existence . . . ministering to the lowest passions of childhood . . . proper to suppress them at once . . . should be a law absolutely forbidding entrance of boy or girl under eighteen . . . influence is wholly vicious . . . there is no voice raised to defend the majority of five cent theaters because they can not be defended. They are hopelessly bad." At the time, Chicago had 116 nickelodeons, 18 ten-cent vaudeville houses and 19 penny arcades, all showing motion pictures. The editorial caused a flurry of debate in Chicago throughout March, April, and May of 1907, with reformer Jane Addams of Hull House presenting a resolution to the City Club on May 2 asking for regulation rather than suppression of movie theaters. Although it would take until November for Chicago's City Council to pass the nation's first censorship ordinance, the excitement of lambasting the new medium reached New York on June 8, when Major George B. McClellan accepted a report from his police commissioner advocating the total suppression of all nickel theaters and arcades. All such licenses were abruptly revoked by the mayor after a crowded aldermanic meeting on December 24, 1907. This time, news services carried the story of the shame of the motion picture across the country as if a new sport had been invented by some blustering Abner Doubleday. This sequence of events was perhaps the first notice to the fledgling motion picture industry of the real power of the press, and of the real need they had to find some accommodation with this powerful voice in the community.

The accommodation was not long in coming, and by ironic chance, the leader in establishing the first direct promotion with a movie company was again the Chicago *Tribune.* Circulation rivalries between the seven Chicago newspapers had led, as one commentator delicately put it, "to the organization of armed camps. A complex conflict raged. The wagon bosses who delivered papers to the stands and the newsboys became remarkably persuasive."[1] The *Tribune* until 1912 was an orthodox newspaper appealing to the upper classes and to literate readers under the capable leadership of the respected James Keeley. But Keeley's star declined under two flamboyant young men who inherited the family fortunes controlling the *Tribune,* James Medill Patterson and Robert R. McCormick. At great expense, two staffers of the less prestigious *Evening American* came to the *Tribune*—Max Annenberg as circulation manager and the legendary Walter Howie as city editor.

Howie was the model Ben Hecht and Charles MacArthur used for the character of Walter Burns in their play *The Front Page.** He and Annenberg believed that Chicago's newspaper-reading public demanded the most sensational and lurid treatment of the news. For their reporters, no tragedy was too private, no police-sealed room too secure, no testimony too secret to forestall a page one splash. Along with a Chicago movie producer, the Selig Polyscope Company, these two astute charlatans cooked up a scheme where the newspaper would run a serial story that would be seen simultaneously in the movie theaters. Loosely derived from the success of an Edison Company series called "What Happened to Mary?" which had been used to promote circulation of the *Ladies World* magazine in early 1912, the result was the first genuine movie serial, *The Adventures of Kathlyn,* starring Kathlyn Williams and written for the newspaper by Harold MacGrath, an author of popular romantic fiction. The *Tribune* now sought an audience among the patrons of the lowly nickelodeons—and they got one. The *Tribune* syndicated the story, the film was a popular success, and the paper's circulation rose by 50,000 readers, about 35,000 of whom became permanent readers. Annenberg and Howie's coup represented a boost of more than 10 percent in the newspaper's readership.[†] This was perhaps the first notice to the newspaper industry of the real popularity of motion pictures, and the measurable gains accruing to those papers

---

*Contradictory to many published reports, Hecht never worked for Howie, "being incapable of such treachery as he proposed."

†In Chicago, the war continued. On January 31, 1914, Edison released the first chapter of *Dolly of the Dailies,* syndicated in many newspapers. On April 4, the Universal Film Manufacturing Company released the first installment of *Lucile Love,* syndicated in the Chicago *Herald.* April 11 saw the announcement of the Eclectic Film Company's *The Perils of Pauline,* syndicated in the Hearst newspapers, including the Chicago *Examiner,* directly competitive with the *Tribune.*

who found an accommodation with this powerful new medium of entertainment.

Motion pictures and general circulation newspapers had discovered each other and had begun an intricate tango accompanied by a watchful sidelong glance. Newspapers could mobilize the populace. Movies could garner readership. Each had a product that was standardized yet ever-changing. Each had the habitual attention of millions of Americans. Each was in the process of extending the distribution of their product (stories/movies) to every city and town on a nationwide basis. Although Vachel Lindsay published *The Art of the Moving Picture* in 1915, and Harvard's distinguished chairman of the Philosophical Department, Professor Hugo Münsterberg, issued "The Photoplay: a Psychological Study" in 1916, motion pictures and the bustling new urban newspapers both appealed to an unintellectual mass population. The motto of Patterson's New York *Daily News* (founded 1919) could serve as a slogan for both partners in the dance: "Tell it to Sweeney—The Stuyvesants will take care of themselves."

By the 1920s, leadership of the motion pictures had passed into the hands of the great moguls who would organize the industry into a vertical monopoly of production, distribution, and exhibition. Zukor, Lasky, Schulberg, Mayer, Goldwyn, Fox, Loew, and the brothers Warner lavishly embellished and extended the myths of Horatio Alger with their rise to fame and fortune. The end of the pioneering period of inventor-owned companies, short-lived and haphazardly distributed, prone to patent litigation and sudden bankruptcy, meant that a steady, dependable flow of films reached every city and town. And a new staple of American newspapers arose: news of the stars, news of forthcoming productions, "reviews" of pictures in the theaters, feature stories, picture stories, interviews, fillers, announcements, contests, stunts, recipes, celebrity advice on grooming, movie-star gossip—all became an ongoing part of the daily newspaper's new film section. "It is under the heading of 'publicity' that the motion picture has probably reached its most individual development," Robert H. Cochrane, vice-president of Universal Pictures, told an audience at the Harvard Business School in 1927. "While publicity work can be defined as 'the dissemination of news' and the greater part of motion picture publicity is that and nothing more, it is nearer to the truth to define publicity work as '*the dissemination of interesting reading matter.*' "[2] This daily repetition of "interesting reading matter" institutionalized the star system and laid the foundation for America's moviegoing habit. In 1928 alone, 65 million people went to the movies each week to see one of 834 feature-length pictures released to a general minimum of 2,000 and general maximum of 15,000 of the more than 23,000 film theaters across the country.* A relationship built on mutual need had begun and would remain unchanged for almost forty years. During the next four decades, many things would change in the movies themselves: their stars, their content, their genres, their directors and styles, but the business and information/publicity practice of the industry fundamentally stayed the same. The press agent who came to a newspaper in 1971 in black jeans, black open-necked shirt, and black moustache with shoulder-length black hair was the same man who had been clean-shaven in a black suit, white shirt, and necktie only a few years before. Only the packaging had changed; the press and the pictures remained immutable like the iron rails of a roadbed, separate, parallel, firmly tied together.

Yet underneath the smoothly pulsing machinery that each day filled entertainment pages of the newspapers and plush seats in the theaters, there remained a basic difference in the place of each medium in American culture. In a decision that was to relegate motion pictures for decades to a position as an outcast where the dissemination of ideas was concerned, the United States Supreme Court in its first encounter with motion pictures and freedom of speech declared in the 1915 case *Mutual Film Corporation* v. *Industrial Commission of Ohio,*[3] "It cannot be put out of view that the exhibition of moving pictures is a business pure and simple, originated and conducted for profit like other spectacles, not to be regarded, nor intended to be regarded by the Ohio Constitution, we think, as part of the press of the country or as organs of public opinion. They are mere representations of events...."[4] This decision, on a case involving prior-restraint mechanisms in one of the first state film censorship statutes, effectively separated films from such other businesses "pure and simple" as book and newspaper publishing. Both conducted a business for profit, and the former, whether issuing works of greater or lesser merit, certainly engaged in the production of entertainment. Few decisions of the Supreme Court in the area of civil liberties have been more adversely criticized in recent years.[5] The traditional judicial suspicion of the arts in general is revealed in Mr. Justice McKenna's decision, with movies in particular called "more insidious in corruption" since they were commonly shown to mixed audiences of adults and children of both sexes. The decision itself never expressly referred to Mutual's claim that the Ohio statute violated the First Amendment of the federal Constitution, but the wording and weight of the decision had a profound effect on the film industry, with

---

*1928 figures. The weekly audience increased dramatically by 1930, reaching 90 million (for a population of 123 million), an attendance equaled in 1946–48. By 1960 this figure was 41 million (for a population of 179 million).

many states and lower federal courts interpreting the will of the Court to be that motion pictures were excluded from any protections of state or federal free-speech guarantees.[6] Ever after, the immigrant moguls and their colleagues in motion pictures right down to the local theater managers lusted after respectability as intensely as they did after the mountains of cash piling up in their box offices. Although it is clear that motion pictures can be a powerful tool for the dissemination of ideas and the persuasion of the public, and for the carrying of information to a wide mass society, this early decision relegated them to the weakest of positions in any potential defense of their content or business conduct. Although President Franklin Roosevelt would urge the widest possible circulation of William Wyler's film *Mrs. Miniver* to increase public support for an embattled England at the outset of World War II, and therefore for his Lend-Lease programs, and although many shifts in American foreign policy could be charted in the changes in motion picture story content, from the appearance of *North Star* to *The Russians are Coming, The Russians are Coming,* the film industry early formed a habit of defensiveness and cowardice in the face of pressure groups and censor boards of all persuasions. They had no recourse in the courts, and no respectability. Will Hays was brought to the film industry to establish the self-regulating Motion Picture Code, thereby heading off for the moment the serious possibility of national outside censorship; the prelude to the code read like a desultory and defensive replay of the *Mutual* case: "Motion picture producers ... though regarding motion pictures primarily as an entertainment without any explicit purpose of teaching or propaganda, know that the motion picture within its own field of entertainment may be directly responsible for spiritual or moral progress, for higher types of social life, and for much correct thinking."[7]

The movies lacked respectability, and in their partnership with newspapers they remained abidingly jealous of the freedom of expression and legal protections given to newspaper reporters. Yet the nature of movies was such that they provided in excess something that reporters saw infrequently, if at all: very large sums of money. The telegram that one former reporter for a Chicago paper sent to a broke and congenial colleague on a spring day in 1925 tells the whole story: "Will you accept three hundred per week to work for Paramount Pictures? All expenses paid. The three hundred is peanuts. Millions are to be grabbed out here and your only competition is idiots. Don't let this get around." A newspaper photograph (naturally enough) shows Herman Mankiewicz greeting his friend the "noted author, dramatist, and former newspaperman" Ben Hecht on the latter's quickly organized arrival in Hollywood. As if it were not enough to have a job at a pay scale only a few reporters attain fifty years later, Hecht records that it took him a whole week to produce the screenplay for *Underworld*, Josef von Sternberg's first hit and Hecht's first Oscar-winning film. "I was given a ten-thousand dollar check as a bonus for the week's work," he recalled in his autobiography.[8]

Newspaper people were fascinated by Hollywood and the Hollywood style. (They still are.) They were bought by it, tantalized by it, caught by it. No single profession provided a larger or steadier stream of workers for the film community. Hundreds of journalists wrote, directed, or produced thousands of films. In the pioneering days of movies, Bannister Merwin and Charles Henri France at Edison's studio had newspaper experience, as did J. Stuart Blackton and George D. Baker of Vitagraph, or Lubin directors Arthur Hotaling and George Terwilliger; Travers Vale was at Biograph and later World, Lois Weber at Universal, George Brackett Seitz at Pathe Exchange, Henry McRae at Essanay, and Richard F. Jones at Keystone. They were only the advance guard of a constantly changing cast of reporters and editors who tried their hand at movie life, drawn by glamour, money, fame, or the plain certainty that the skills that produced page one were fully compatible to producing reel one. Those on smaller papers who did not go west to join the production teams were still affected by this fascination with Hollywood style; reporters on the motion picture and entertainment beats took a cue from the stars and adapted their own mellifluous pseudonyms: where Lucille Vasconellos Langhanke became Mary Astor, Mrs. G. A. Flaskick of *The Enterprise* in Beaumont, Texas, became Betty Browne; where Samuel Jones Grundy became Wallace Ford, Earl L. Borg of the *Desert News* in Salt Lake City became Scott Boutywell.

By whatever name, Hollywood was happy. In order to help newspapers "learn" about pictures and people, movie distributors and producers created an elaborate system for hand feeding information to the eager press. In was not a difficult job in the main, for most of the people doing the feeding had come from behind the same desks, telephones, and typewriters they were now trying to shill. "In fact," noted Robert Cochrane, "the motion picture publicity man is a reporter working for the newspapers and magazines of the country. In operation, the publicity chief of a large company is a managing editor, with a staff of news gatherers, special writers, and photographers sufficiently large to get out a good-sized paper."[9] In the recollection of veteran film publicist and executive Arthur Mayer, Cochrane's analogy between publicity men and reporters was almost too true for some New York critics in the early 1920s. Press agent for the old Rialto Theater when it was operated by the preeminent showman Samuel Lionel Rothafel, known as Roxy, was none other than Terry Ramsaye, the pioneer film historian and trade publisher. Ramsaye found a new way to use the leverage of the press in the never-ending battle between exhibitors who wanted low rental rates for films and distributors who wanted high rates. According to Mayer, Ramsaye "wrote reviews of forthcoming pictures and gave them to the newspapers, whose representatives in those days greatly appreciated having their work done for them. Most of Ramsaye's reviews were favorable, even on occasions when the pictures were only passable, but when the film rental was still in dispute, he would pan them mercilessly. Several distributors were guided in this manner to see the light."[10]

Movie companies, with their huge publicity budgets and national and regional offices, have always been the primary source of information about movies, players, and trends for the working press. Whether the press took reviews or columns complete, or rewrote the material as if it had come from a wire service, there was rarely the will or the opportunity to check facts independently and verify accounts. With the exception of a very few reporters in Los Angeles, access to film stars and filmmakers, to executives, and to the pictures themselves is closely controlled by studio or independent publicity personnel. Extremely rare is the newspaper that keeps an independent reference library of film materials; in most cases there are no independently produced reference materials about current films. Comfortably wrapped in a seeming intimacy with the stars, supplied with voluminous "interesting reading matter," and periodically flown from city to city for staged events and round-robin "interviews," the press never achieved, and never really sought, independence from their symbiotic colleagues in the movies.

After all, it seemed that nothing much was at stake; newspapers too saw motion pictures as a "business pure and simple" that had a habitual readership and paid on a daily basis the top-dollar advertising rate in the paper.* The pressures on the film writer to remain docile could be either internal or external. When I printed a "wrong" but eye-catching picture of Charlton Heston after an interview in 1969, United Artists Pictures Corp. denied my paper access to materials for three months, while supplying four competing newspapers. Or take the case of a major Boston critic at a failing newspaper whose publisher was frantically

---

*Habitually, entertainment (theater, movies, music) advertising is the highest per line cost in the newspaper, with general merchandise department stores the lowest. This curious tradition might have developed from nineteenth-century traveling theater groups, notorious for nonpayment and at the same time nonresident in the community. The high rates were extra money to the papers and were paid in cash with no credit extended. The tradition of a high rate continues.

seeking youthful readers. Each time, about twice a year, the critic wrote about a new foreign film opening for the college trade in Cambridge, the paper's advertising manager would come to the office raging that "they did not advertise" and extracted a promise, always broken in another six months, that the critic would never again "publicize" a theater without a steady account. That newspaper is now dead.

Still, an uneasy power relationship, based on information, joins these two media. As much as the film industry can try to control access, slant facts, and purvey "interesting reading matter," Hollywood professionals know they cannot continue without widespread and constant access to the news media. The constant drive for publicity and editorial space in newspapers leaves Hollywood pictures and personalities exceedingly vulnerable to the whims of writers and editors. When actress Karen Black *(Day of the Locust, Family Plot)* married writer Kit Carson, newspapers across the country had been gibbering about the sudden marriage and breakup of two other celebrities, Gregg Allman and Cher Bono. Picking up on that gossip story, one newspaper had a headline story, with "quotes" from both Black and Carson about how a film commitment separated the couple on their wedding night, with Black flying off to New York on the afternoon of the wedding to sign a contract. Purportedly, her eagerness to go on with her career would keep the newly married couple separate for several days, and the "quotes" from each partner spoke not only of their undying love but also of the difficulties of a celebrity marriage. The story was patently untrue. The couple had dinner that night with this writer and his own wife in a small Beverly Hills restaurant, and there was no separation over the next several weeks—as there were no true "quotes." But the personalities involved had no defense to this invasion of privacy, no recourse to the public. The studios and the personalities who so ardently seek and so need the printed media to continue their business and their careers are fully at the mercy of the press and of its standards of professionalism and conduct. When the film *Close Encounters of the Third Kind* was negatively reviewed by *Time* magazine from a Texas screening arranged so that the precise timing and cutting sequences of the picture could be tuned up, Columbia Pictures had no recourse, and there is no definable way to judge the impact of this national break on the subsequent financial history of the picture, which on its release to the theaters was changed in several respects.

All of these examples suggest that a cynical pragmatism suffuses the operations of the American newspaper. As Max Lerner commented, the American press is "not oriented toward inner life, but toward an outward one in which almost anything can happen to give a decisive turn to life."[11] The elegent essays that grace the pages of *Le Figaro* in

Paris would seem out of place in American reporting, as would the formal prose and didactic construction of any major German newspaper. The same emphasis on event without context, fact separated from philosophy, is central to the American film. With theater programs changing weekly, American movies were geared to a production pace that made last month's film as passé as last week's newspaper. The star system, with its pressure for a leading player to portray repetitively a minimally differentiated character in a multitude of films, is analogous to the journalistic habit of repetitively covering a limited number of beats within a well-defined range of subjects. American films reflect a penchant for doing basic to our civilization. Films are about active people, makers, movers, shakers, accomplishers. Ben Hur. Charles Foster Kane. Virgil Tibbs. The films of Carl Theodore Dreyer are unimaginable in America, just as it is unimaginable that the metaphysical cinema of an Eric Rohmer or an Ingmar Bergman could flower here. The genres of accomplishment where the individual triumphs or the group succeeds became the uniquely American genres: crime pictures, westerns, spy stories. Typically, the musical film, that other uniquely American film genre, also deals with accomplishment—a chorus girl becomes a star.

Small wonder, then, that motion pictures early seized on newspapers as a primary conduit for expressing the values of accomplishment in American society. The tradition of the crusading newspaper, perhaps best exemplified by Joseph Pulitzer's Saint Louis *Post-Dispatch,* became a natural expression of the pragmatism inherent in the American film. Before World War I, movie reporters were seen as they struggled for the scoop on a train wreck story (*Tapped Wires,* 1913), foiled graft in city street work (*The Grafters,* 1913), vindicated an innocent man by capturing a counterfeiter (*The Power of the Press,* 1914). In the same era female reporters exposed collusion between politicians and a big utility (*The Reform Candidate,* 1911) and exposed corruption in a city administration (*Her Big Story,* 1913).

The movies quickly found that any kind of story could be built around a reporter as the central character. While it is true, as Pauline Kael has pointed out, that American films rarely show a character at work, the work of the newspaper reporter was so mobile and his working office so intriguing that the newspaper film genre is the one glaring exception to the rule. The reporter has mobility through society, has an activist motivation to solve problems and find out the truth, has friends of all social classes and in all places. The reporter is on the inside and knows what the public does not know about power structures and the private lives of public figures. The reporter has an excellent memory, and often uses his or her impeccable recall to further justice. And yet the reporter is human and can have the same loves, hates, prejudices, romances, ego, accomplishments as common folk. The reporter has free time, and we rarely see him or her writing. According to legend, the reporter works twenty-four hours a day, finding information in unlikely places from unlikely people at unlikely times. The reporter is a center of power, backed by his publication and sought out by persons of all types because he can give them publicity or information or fix something up among his regular contacts at city hall and the station house.

Throughout the 1920s the movies treated the press with a combination of naïveté and enthusiasm. There are films about reporters catching crooks (*Dangerous Traffic,* 1926), reporters defeating political machines (*What a Night,* 1928), reporters volunteering to help good works of a mission (*The Day of Faith,* 1923), reporters protecting a woman's reputation (*Her Reputation,* 1923), reporters exposing the decadence of high society (*Salome of the Tenements,* 1925). The purifying vocation of journalism is so remarkable that there is even a film where a crook reforms by buying a newspaper and turning it against his former colleagues (*The Man under Cover,* 1922). One reviewer wrote a not untypical comment on *The Last Edition,* a 1925 film that used the interior of the San Francisco *Chronicle* plant for much of its setting of the story of a composing room foreman who breaks a political scandal: "The picture gives an unusually clear idea of the thought and action involved in bringing out a newspaper. The work in different departments, such as the city room, the composing room, and the pressroom, are exceptionally well filmed, and the scenes for 'making over' for an extra edition are decidedly impressive."[12] Among the newspaper films of this decade there is little recognition of the potential for reportorial abuse. Few issues are raised; the reporter remains essentially a neutral, problem-solving figure working for the good of society. The moral virtue of the newsman remains unquestioned.

By the 1930s, Hollywood was taking a more jaundiced view of the press. A new generation of reporters went to the movie colony to write dialogue for the new talking pictures, and they often based their newspaper films on their own experiences or those of their colleagues. These experiences often had a more questionable moral tone, and an ideology of the press began to be discussed in public for the first time on a broad populist scale. Three 1932 films were only the beginning of a cycle based loosely on the career of Walter Winchell (*Okay, America, Is My Face Red,* and *Love is a Racket*). These films helped introduce unredeeming cynicism, staccato dialogue, the snap-brim hat and the quick wisecrack to the genre. This new cycle introduced "the types of reporters who sit on the edge of the publisher's desk" (*Sued for Libel,* 1940);

editors who are "a cross between a Ferris wheel and a werewolf" (*Nothing Sacred*, 1937); reporters described by their editors as "a cynical crazy, drunken bum" (*Murder Man*, 1935)—but who still can catch a crook before the cops. One of Lee Tracy's many portrayals of the nervy, finger-popping reporter had him nicknamed "Ego," while Ricardo Cortez in *Is My Face Red* boasted "I'm the guy that made Broadway famous!" Mervyn LeRoy's bitter portrait of scandalmongering, *Five Star Final* (1931), pulled no punches in its attack on yellow journalism and the excesses of the press. Thus came the realization that a reporter would do anything to get a story—denigrate the institution of marriage and hide an escaped convict (*The Front Page*, 1931 and 1940), coolly break the law (*Libelled Lady*, 1936), wink at suicide that builds circulation (*Five Star Final*, 1931).

The reaction to these films back at the city desk was curious. The perpetual momentum of the Hollywood publicity machine seems to have smothered any real outcry at the portrayals, and critical comments incorporate an underlying unease that smacks of a suppressed longing to join the parade west. There is an almost wistful quality to many of the printed indictments: "It is one of this department's favorite themes," wrote André Sennwald in the New York *Times,* "that films which distort the newspaper profession in their efforts to convey the glamour of that fascinating craft are always written by former newspapermen. Somehow, when the boys clear out their desks and sell out to the Mecca of the Pacific, they quickly forget the realities of the city room and proceed to simonize their fiction with the dreams that never came true when they were taking orders from the city desk."[13] Theodore Strauss commented five years later on "Behind the News": "A heartening, if left-handed, tribute to newspaper men is the fact that they have been able to survive the tributes perpetrated by ex-colleagues who have gone to Hollywood and who wax sentimental whenever they remember the boys on the city desk."[14] John T. McManus, also of the *Times* staff, had his shot in 1936: "From a newspaperman's viewpoint, there is less to carp about in Roger Pryor's screen reporter characterization than there has been in similar representations by better known players. He doesn't, for example, dictate headlines over the telephone. We did hear him set a social engagement for 8 o'clock in the evening once, however, and that is something we've never been able to do."[15]

Not all the 1930s films took a decided stance toward the role of the press and the methods of reporters. The newspaper remained in most cases an extraordinarily flexible setting for comedy, romance, and action melodrama. From *It Happened One Night* (1934) to Bette Davis in *Front Page Woman* (1935) or Clark Gable caught in the triangle of *Wife versus Secretary* (1936), dozens of films used the public's familiar expectations of the reporter and the cliché of social mobility as the basis for a wide range of film productions. From the point of view of the movies, the most unusual aspect of these films was the opportunities accorded to women. Beginning in 1911, continuing throughout the 1920s and coming to full flower in the 1930s, the newspaper film genre was the only place where an actress could portray a role that stood on an equal footing with men. Reduced to a symbol of power in the gangster film cycle, and to a symbol of civilization in the schoolteachers and reformers of the western genre, in the newspaper films a woman could take the lead, be an accomplisher, catch the crooks, save the day, scheme for power, find success. Joan Crawford saves her brother and earns the respect of their colleagues by catching gangsters in *Dance, Fools, Dance* (1931). Constance Bennett resolves a scandal in a prominent family in *After Office Hours* (1935). Joan Bennett as a manicurist-turned-reporter-editor cleans up a town in *Big Brown Eyes* (1936). Katharine Hepburn fights Victorian conventions and seeks independence in *A Woman Rebels* (1936).

After World War II, the glamour went out of newspaper films, and simultaneously the relationship between the press and the pictures began to dissolve slowly into a state of dull acrimony. Many of the best newspaper films had been created as fond reminiscences of lost youth by men graduated from the world of newswriting to screenwriting. As these talents began to move to the fringe of the film industry, their genre slowly began to dissipate. A few remarkable productions appeared: Samuel Fuller's idealistic paen to free journalism, *Park Row* (1952); Billy Wilder's bitter indictment of inhuman reportorial excess, *The Big Carnival* (1951); Phil Karlson's tough and gritty crusading true-story, *The Phoenix City Story* (1955); Jack Webb's intriguing failure at showing a day in the life of a small paper *=30=* (1959); Billy Wilder's ugly attempt to pump cynicism and morality into a third version of *The Front Page* (1975). Slowly, the reporter became a sidebar figure. Instead of a central, gangling, iridescent Lee Tracy, an elegant Adolphe Menjou or a debonair Cary Grant, the reporter became a confused, weak, shirking, falsely liberal David Janssen, a propped-up cardboard figure waiting to be set straight in a series of films like *Shoes of the Fisherman* (1968), *The Green Berets* (1968), and *Marooned* (1969).

Through the 1960s both films and newsapers slowly declined. Their unusual and special relationship began to break apart, a process perhaps hurried by previously unrecognized fissures and a barely repressed sense of guilt for past sins. With fewer papers printing fewer editions in smaller sizes, the stunts and gossip and recipes and casting announcements were crowded out of the paper. Yet film companies still paid the top advertising rate and resented it. Making fewer pictures for a shrinking audience, producers attached to each review and each mention in print a previously unexpected importance, and the newpapers felt pressured. Cutting back on publicity staffs, junkets, and habitually supplied information for the press, distributors lost touch with film writers, and the writers themselves had to work at digging up stories, which they weren't certain they liked. Under the influence of foreign films and the pressures of finding a new, younger audience, films became more esoteric, searching out the boundaries in society, and editors didn't know how to handle it. With both media under increasing pressure from a tightening economy, separate sets of difficult unions, and a public turning to television and professional sports, the energy had gone out of the marriage. Both media turned inward to their own special problems and provinces, defensive and desultory. The party was over, with some promises still unfulfilled, with some guilts unassuaged, with some potentials barely realized. The *Moving Picture World* had editorialized back at the beginning of the film/newspaper era, on March 20, 1909, with advice that was instructive then and useful now: "Criticize if you will, but criticize justly, impartially, and above all with knowledge. Then you will have the consolation of feeling that you are encouraging and not retarding the progress of a form of entertainment, the possibilities of which are only just being revealed. For the moving picture will last just as long as the newspaper. . . ."

NOTES

1. Terry Ramsaye, *A Million and One Nights* (New York: Simon and Schuster, 1926), p. 657.

2. Joseph P. Kennedy, ed., *The Story of the Films* (Chicago: A. W. Shaw, 1927), p. 238. Emphasis in original.

3. 236 U.S. 230 (1915).

4. Ibid., p. 244.

5. See especially "Motion Pictures and the First Amendment," *Yale Law Journal,* 60 (1951): 696–719.

6. The *Mutual* case was not overturned until 1952 in 343 U.S. 495, *Burstyn* v. *Williams,* over the film *The Miracle* by Roberto Rossellini. Here the Court specifically rejected the 1915 judgment: "We no longer adhere to it." See especially C. Herman Pritchett, *Civil Liberties and the Vinson Court,* (Chicago: University of Chicago Press, 1954) pp. 41 ff.

7. Raymond Moley, *The Hayes Office* (Indianapolis: Bobbs-Merrill, 1945), p. 241.

8. Ben Hecht, *A Child of the Century* (New York: Simon and Schuster, 1954), p. 448.

9. Kennedy, *Story of Films,* p. 240.

10. Arthur Mayer, *Merely Colossal* (New York: Simon and Schuster, 1953), p. 185.

11. Max Lerner, *America as a Civilization* (New York: Simon and Schuster, 1957), 2:749.

12. The New York *Times,* November 11, 1925.

13. The New York *Times,* November 13, 1935.
14. The New York *Times,* January 16, 1941.
15. The New York *Times,* October 5, 1936.

BIBLIOGRAPHY

Barris, Alex. *Stop the Presses!* New York: A. S. Barnes & Co., 1976.

Davidson, Bill. *The Real and the Unreal.* New York: Harper and Brothers, 1961.

Hecht, Ben. *A Child of the Century.* New York: Simon and Schuster, 1954.

Hendricks, Gordon. *The Edison Motion Picture Myth.* Berkeley: University of California Press, 1961.

Jarvie, I. C. *Movies and Society.* New York: Basic Books, 1970.

Kauffmann, S., and Henstell, B., eds. *American Film Criticism.* New York: Liveright, 1972.

Kennedy, Joseph P., ed. *The Story of the Films.* Chicago: A. W. Shaw & Co., 1927.

Lerner, Max. *America as a Civilization.* New York: Simon and Schuster, 1957.

Mayer, Arthur. *Merely Colossal.* New York: Simon and Schuster, 1953.

Meisel, Myron. *Dateline ... Hollywood.* Boston: Museum of Fine Arts, 1975.

Moley, Raymond. *The Hays Office.* Indianapolis: Bobbs-Merrill Co., 1945.

Munden, Kenneth W., ed. *The American Film Institute Catalogue.* Vol. 1, *Feature Films 1921–1930.* Vol. 2, *Feature Films 1961–1970.* New York: R. R. Bowker, 1976.

Ramsaye, Terry. *A Million and One Nights.* New York: Simon and Schuster, 1926.

Rossell, Deac. "Hollywood and the Newsroom." *American Film,* 1 (October 1975).

Warshaw, Robert. *The Immediate Experience.* Garden City: Doubleday, 1962.

NOTES TO THE FILMOGRAPHY

Over the past decade, as studies in popular culture and in popular film have multiplied, the notion of genre studies has gained a firm foothold in the study of film. Particularly in the genres of musicals, gangster films, and westerns, serious attempts have been made to explore uniquely American elements and patterns in groups of films. Surprisingly, the genre of the newspaper film seems to have been overlooked in its entirety. This is again a uniquely American film genre, for it is most rare for a foreign-made film to take up any issues or elements of journalism or newspaper work. The one possible exception here is in the British film. Yet the most significant proportion of British films relating to the press refers to players as "an American reporter" or even as a "woman American reporter," indicating that in this case a British genre exists mainly in imitation of the American.

As this filmography reveals, the longevity of the newspaper film in America is surprising. While there is clearly a golden age from the mid-1920s through the outbreak of World War II, the idea of the reporter as crimebuster or public conscience is clearly present in films by 1911 and throughout the following decade (where there is exceedingly sparse information on the American film available in print; it is likely there was considerably more newspaper films in this period). And the female reporter appears this early, far in advance of her advent in city rooms across the country.

The vast majority of films in this list are purely genre pictures, defined by the snap-brim hat, brash confidence, popping flashbulbs, open whiskey bottles, and wisecracking dialogue of their protagonists. Yet a number of films beginning in the early 1930s and continuing until the present day attempted to provide a public forum to debate reportorial procedures and tactics. This forum involved only a few of the issues that are debated in and by the press today, however—in the main issues of media power and of glib invasion of privacy. Almost never was the public's right to know explored, and it is rare for the press to come into direct conflict with the Establishment in the form of the legal system, legislative process, or law-enforcement agencies. Crooked cops, mayors, and financiers are fair game, but in the main the press is seen as a part of established society and not clearly separate from it or in conflict with it. One unique exception to this essentially cozy lineup is found in the films written by Martin Mooney, almost the only pictures where a reporter seriously goes to jail to protect news sources. While a reporter at the New York *American,* Mooney was imprisoned and fined for refusing to give his sources on a series of gambling stories to a grand jury, and he used these experiences in three films: *Missing Girls* (1936), *Crime, Inc.* (1945), and *Exclusive Story* (1936).

Another rarity is any exploration of the relationship between a reporter and his or her ongoing news sources, especially the moral interplay of give and take that makes a steady source of information a significant influence on reportorial conduct. A cynical and most interesting exploration of this part of a reporter's working habits is found in the relationship between the columnist and the press agent in *Sweet Smell of Success* (1957). Though a reporter often works independently to a complete a story, in contravention of orders from police, politicians, editors, and colleagues, it is also rare to find long-term investigative journalism in these films, rarer to find a story resulting from long-term structural analyses of, say, embedded power structures in a small town. Phil Karlson's *The Phoenix City Story* (1955), based on a true incident, is one exception (when the town was cleaned up in late 1954, a grand jury returned 749 indictments). Jack Webb tried to show the daily life of a small newspaper in *=30=* (1959), but the film lacked energy. Perhaps so few films deal with the plodding work of developing a complex story because films need, for dramatic purposes, to personalize conflicts and center them on a few people over a limited period of time. A successful film that illustrated the agonies of developing a long-researched story was *All the President's Men* (1976), a well-crafted work that had the advantage of widespread public knowledge of the details of the developing Watergate story.

An unusually large number of former journalists was involved with these pictures. In one period between 1928 and 1935, for which almost adequate research information is available, 70.8 percent of the films (56 out of 79 titles) had at least one identifiable former journalist involved in the production. In the same period, 32.6 percent of all credited writers (63 out of 193 writers) had identifiable newspaper experience. Clearly this is unusual, as one would not expect to see westerns written by cowboys or gangster films written by crooks. The newspapermen and women who went to Hollywoood did not turn to newspaper films exclusively: even those writers most closely identified with the genre—Sam Fuller, Ben Hecht, Allen Rivkin, Roy Chanslor—wrote many fewer newspaper films during their careers than other film stories.

FILMOGRAPHY—
AMERICAN FILMS FEATURING THE PRESS AND JOURNAL-
ISTS—1903–1969
(*indicates present or former journalist involved in production)

1903

Delivering Newspapers. American Mutual & Biograph Co. 27 feet. A large group of young boys scurries to receive copies of the New York *World* from a delivery truck in Madison Square, New York.

1910

Gallegher: A Newspaper Story. Edison Company. From the short story by Richard Harding Davis.*

The Big Scoop. Edison Company. Discharged reporter regains job with scoop on bank closing.

1911

The Reform Candidate. Edison Company. Woman reporter exposes collusion between politicians and big utility.

1913

Tapped Wires. Essanay Company. Directed by Theodore Wharton. With E. H. Calvert, Helen Dunbar. Rival news agencies try for scoops on train wreck story.

The Grafters. Reliance Company. Directed by Frederick Sullivan. With Edna Cunningham, Henry Francis Koster. Reporter foils graft in city street work.

Her Big Story. American Company. With J. Warren Kerrigan, Charlotte Burton. Woman reporter exposes corrupt city administration.

1914

Power of the Press. Biograph-Klaw & Erlanger. With Lionel Barrymore, Alan Hale. Cub reporter vindicates innocent man and captures counterfeiters.

1916

His Picture in the Papers. Triangle. Directed by John Emerson. Scenario by Anita Loos. With Douglas Fairbanks. Doug hungers for success and publicity.

1920

Deadline at Eleven. Vitagraph. Directed by George Fawcett. With Corinne Griffith.

1921

The Passionate Pilgrim. Cosmopolitan Pictures. Directed by Robert G. Vignola. Scenario by Donald Darrell and George Dubois Proctor, from a novel by Samuel Merwin. With Matt Moore, Mary Newcome, Marjory Daw. Reporter exposes crooks to win sob sister.

A Certain Rich Man. Great Authors Pictures. Directed by Howard Hickman. From the novel by William Allen White.* With Carl Gantvoort, Claire Adams. Young banker saved from shortage by new newspaper in small town; years later he is power, and publisher is drunk, but at end banker repents and distributes fortune.

Don't Neglect Your Wife. Goldwyn. Directed by Wallace Worsley. Scenario by Louis Sherwin from a story by Gertrude Franklin Atherton. With Mabel Julienne Scott, Lewis S. Stone, Charles Clary. 1876: Reporter turns to alcoholism after falling in love with married socialite; then is redeemed.

The Magic Cup. Realart Pictures. Directed by John S. Robertson. Scenario and story by E. Lloyd Sheldon.* With Constance Binney, Vincent Coleman, Blanche Craig. Cub reporter foils crooks by showing hotel maid is lost aristocrat.

The Secret of the Hills. Vitagraph. Directed by Chester Bennett. Scenario by E. Magnus Ingleton from a novel by William Garrett. With Antonio Moreno, Lillian Hall, Kingsley Benedict. American reporter in London on trail of royal treasure and a girl.

The Family Closet. Playgoers Pictures. Directed by John B. O'Brien. From a story by Will J. Payne. With Holmes Herbert, Alice Mann, Kempton Greene. Editor uses newspaper to flush out crook, then blackmails him.

Red Courage. Universal. Directed by Reeves Eason. Scenario by Harvey Gates * from a book by Peter Bernard Kyne. With Hoot Gibson, Joel Day, Molly McCormick. Newspaper in western small town starts reform campaign.

The Star Reporter. Arrow Film Corp. Directed by Duke Worne. From a novel by Wyndham Martin. With Billie Rhodes, Truman Van Dyke, William Horne. Reporter hides identity, then gets promotion to editor with scoop on kidnapping.

1922

The Man under Cover. Universal. Directed by Tod Browning. Scenario by Harvey Gates* from a story by Louis Victor Eytinge. With Herbert Rawlinson, George Hernandex, William Courtwright. Swindler reforms by buying newspaper and conning former partners.

Smudge. First National Exhibitor's Circuit. Directed by Charles Ray. Story and scenario by Rob Wagner. Titles by Edward Withers. Produced by Arthur S. Kane. With Charles Ray, Charles K. French, Florence Oberle. Publisher's son uses newspaper to fight smudge pots in orange groves; when rivals, politicians, and father fight him, he unveils new invention and wins.

The Unfoldment. Producer's Pictures. Directed by George Kern and Murdock MacQuarrie. Story and scenario by James Couldwell and Reed Heustis. With Florence Lawrence, Barbara Bedford, Charles French. Love and political scandal complicate life for guy and gal reporters when editor's attention turns from paper to playmates.

The Woman's Side. Associated First National. Directed by J. A. Barry. Written by J. A. Barry. Scenario by Elliott Clawson.* Produced by B. P. Schulberg.* With Katherine MacDonald, Edward Burns, Henry Barrows. Daughter of candidate for governor unmasks smear to rival candidate when she falls in love with newspaper publisher's son.

The Cub Reporter. Goldstone Pictures. Directed by Jack Dillon. Scenario by George Elwood Jenks. With Richard Talmadge, Jean Calhoun, Edwin B. Tilton. Reporter braves perils of Chinese underworld to recover sacred jewel.

Extra! Extra! Fox. Directed by William K. Howard. Scenario by Arthur J. Zellner, from a story by Julien Josephson. With Edna Murphy, Johnnie Walker, Herschel Mayall. Reporter uses disguises and acting abilities to get stories and solve crime.

Living Lies. Mayflower Pictures. Directed by Emile Chautard. From story and novel by Arthur Somers Roche.* With Edmund Lowe, Mona Kingsley, Kenneth Hill. Reporter uncovers and breaks traction scandal.

The Lying Truth. American Reliance. Direction, story, and scenario by Marion Fairfax. With Noah Beery, Marjorie Daw, Tully Marshall. Murder hoax leads to inheritance in newspaper family.

Front Page Story. Vitagraph. Directed by Jesse Robbins. Scenario by F. W. Beebe. Story by Arthur Frederick Goodrich. With Edward Everett Horton, Lloyd Ingraham, James Corrigan. Reporter gets job through bluff, then reconciles editor and mayor.

1923

The Day of Faith. Goldwyn. Directed by Tod Browning. Adaptation by June Mathis and Katharine Kavanaugh, from a book by Arthur Somers Roche.* With Eleanor Boardman, Tyrone Power, Raymond Griffith. Reporter hired to expose mission instead volunteers and supports its good works.

The Town Scandal. Universal. Directed by King Baggot. Scenario by Hugh Hoffman from a novel by Frederic Arnold Kummer. With Gladys Walton, Edward Hearne, Edward McWade. Small-town purity league gives up blue laws after Broadway chorine and reporter publish her story of "friends" in New York.

The Wild Party. Universal. Directed by Herbert Blache. Screenplay by Hugh Hoffman, from a story by Marion Orth. With Gladys Walton, Robert Ellis, Freeman Wood. Editor's secretary's society story causes libel suit, but her efforts to prove facts lead to marriage with plaintiff.

Legally Dead. Universal. Directed by William Parke. Scenario by Harvey Gates* from a story by Charles Furthman. With Milton Sills, Margaret Campbell, Claire Adams. Reporter on death row to prove theory that most condemned men are innocent; on parole he thwarts robbery but is thought a crook and convicted of policeman's murder; innocence discovered too late, he is executed and declared legally dead. But doctor revives him with adrenalin.

Sinner or Saint. Selznick Distributing Corp. Directed by Lawrence Windom. Scenario by Dorothy Farnum from a story by Dorothy Farnum. With Betty Blythe, William P. Carleton, Gypsy O'Brien. Fortune-teller exposed in newspaper stories.

Her Reputation. First National. Directed by John Griffith Wray. Supervised by Thomas Ince. Scenario by Bradley King. With May McAvoy, Lloyd Hughed, James Corrigan. Reporter vindicates girl, marries her, and kills competitor's story.

The Steadfast Heart. Goldwyn-Cosmopolitan Corp. Directed by Sheridan Hall. Adaptation by Philip Lonergan from a novel by Clarence Buddington Kelland.* With Marguerite Courtot, Miriam Battista, Joseph Striker. Crook turns newspaperman and saves town.

The Printer's Devil. Warner Brothers. Directed by William Beaudine. Story and scenario by Julien Josephson. With Wesley Barry, Harry Myers, Kathryn McGuire. Small-town newspaperman solves crime and gets girl.

Playing It Wild. Vitagraph. Directed by William Duncan. Story and scenario by C. Graham Baker. With William Duncan, Edith Johnson, Francis Powers. Robbery ruse of western newspaper elects honest new sheriff.

1924

The Humming Bird. Paramount. Directed by Sidney Olcott. Adaptation by Forrest Halsey* from a play by Maude Fulton. With Gloria Swanson, Edward Burns, William Ricciardi. Woman Apache loves American reporter in Paris who enlists and is wounded. They are reunited when she escapes jail to be with him.

The Fatal Mistake. Perfection. Directed by Scott Dunlap. With William Fairbanks, Eva Novak, Wilfred Lucas. Cub reporter's featured story and photo on socialite are fake, so he loses job until he gets real story and solves her jewel robbery.

The Whispered Name. Universal. Directed by King Baggot. Scenario by Lois Zellner, from a play by Rita Weiman and Alice Leal Pollock. With Ruth Clifford, Charles Clary, William E. Lawrence. Woman reporter on social beat discovers plot to sue her so socialite can get divorce, but news editor saves the day.

The Average Woman. C. C. Burr Pictures. Directed by William Christy Cabanne. Scenario by Raymond S. Harris, from a story by Dorothy de Jagers. With Pauline Garon, David Powell, Harrison Ford. Reporter's story on average woman leads to marriage.

Dynamite Smith. Pathe. Directed by Ralph Ince. Story and scenario by C. Gardner Sullivan. With Charles Ray, Jacqueline Logan, Bessie Love, Wallace

Beer. Timid S.F. reporter assigned to murder case runs off with killer's wife; followed to Alaska, finally captures crook in a bear trap.

The Flaming Crisis. Merco Productions. Produced by Lawrence Goldman. With Calvin Nicholson, Dorothy Dunbar. Young Negro reporter convicted of murder on circumstantial evidence; escapes and goes west where he falls for cowgirl, captures bandits, and reveals identity to find real murderer has confessed.

Hold Your Breath. Christie. Directed by Scott Sidney. Story by Frank Roland Conklin. With Dorothy Devore, Walter Hiers, Tully Marshall. Comedy. When brother loses reporter job, sister takes it and muffs stories, finally chasing monkey with jewelry up a skyscraper.

Hutch of the U.S.A. New California Film Corp. Directed by James Chapin. Story and scenario by J. F. Natteford.* With Charles Hutchinson, Edith Thornton, Frank Leigh. American reporter on assignment in banana republic aids revolutionaries, who are defeated by government.

The Pell Street Mystery. Rayart Pictures. Directed by Joseph Franz. With George Larkin, Carl Silvera. Reporter solves murder in Chinatown.

Midnight Secrets. Rayart Pictures. Directed by Jack Nelson. With George Larkin, Ollie Kirby, Pauline Curley. Crooks kidnap reporter's girl in hopes of stopping exposé but are captured by paper.

1925

The Devil's Cargo. Paramount. Directed by Victor Fleming. Screenplay by A. P. Younger. Story by Charles E. Whittaker. With Wallace Beery, Pauline Starke, Claire Adams. Action pic set around 1849 Gold Rush newspaper.

Salome of the Tenements. Paramount. Directed by Sidney Olcott. Scenario by Sonya Levien,* from a novel by Angia Yezierska. Jewish woman reporter marries millionaire, is blackmailed by moneylender, wins. (Setting is Jewish community on Hester Street.)

Contraband. Paramount. Directed by Alan Crosland. Screenplay by Jack Cunningham from a novel by Clarence Buddington Kelland.* With Lois Wilson, Noah Beery, Raymond Hatton. Woman publisher in small town leads campaign against bootleggers, cleans up town.

How Baxter Butted In. Warner Brothers. Directed by William Beaudine. Scenario by Owen Davis. Adaptation by Julien Josephson, from story by Harold Titus. With Dorothy Devore, Matt Moore, Ward Crane. Shy circulation clerk finds happiness.

The Last Edition. FBO. Directed by Emory Johnson. Story and scenario by Emilie Johnson. With Ralph Lewis, Lita Leslie, Ray Hallor. Composing room foreman, reporter, and girl break political scandal. Interiors used S.F. *Chronicle* plant.

Headlines. Directed by E. H. Griffith. Screenplay by Peter Milne. With Alice Joyce, Malcolm McGregor, Virginia Lee Corbin. Feature writer protects secret daughter, who marries editor after scandal breaks.

The Fighting Cub. Truart Film Corp. Directed by Paul Hurst. Story by Adele Buffington. With Wesley Barry, Mildred Harris, Pat O'Malley. Cub becomes reporter by reforming philanthropist from crime.

Youth and Adventure. FBO. Directed by James W. Horne. Story and continuity by Frank Howard Clark. With Richard Talmadge, Peter Gordon, Joseph Girard. Comedy of wastrel installed as city editor by gangster to keep him silent, but editor uses crook's own paper to expose his racket.

A Man Must Live. Paramount. Directed by Paul Sloane. Scenario by James Ashmore Creelman, from a story by Ida Alexa Ross Wylie. With Richard Dix, Jacqueline Logan, George Nash. Reporter with principles on New York scandal sheet in conflict with editor over stories that ruin lives; assaults editor and loses job but wins lawsuit against steel company.

My Lady's Lips. B. P. Schulberg Productions. Directed by James P. Hogan. Story and continuity by John Goodrich. With Alyce Mills, William Powell, Clara Bow. Star reporter poses as crook to expose gambler and save editor's daughter.

The Part Time Wife. Lumas. Directed by Henry McCarty.* Scenario by Victoria Moore and Henry McCarty. Adaptation by James J. Tyman from a story by Peggy Gaddis. Produced by Sam Sax. With Alice Calhoun, Robert Ellis, Freeman Wood. Film star marries poor reporter, and difficulties ensue until his play is a success.

1926

Oh, What a Nurse. Warner Brothers. Directed by Charles Reisner. Adaptation by Darryl Francis Zanuck from a play by Robert Emmett Sherwood* and Bertram Bloch. With Sydney Chaplin, Patsy Ruth Miller, Gayne Whitman. Reporter subs lovelorn columnist and gets involved in society marriage, crooks.

The Social Highwayman. Warner Brothers. Directed by William Beaudine. Adaptation by Edward T. Lowe, Jr., and Philip Klein, from a story by Darryl Francis Zanuck. With John Patrick, Dorothy Devore, Montagu Love. Cub reporter sent to investigate bandit is held up, then ridiculed by colleagues and rival papers who send him out to capture crook.

Stick to Your Story. Rayart. Directed by Harry J. Brown. Scenario by Henry Roberts Symonds. Titles by Arthur Q. Hagerman. Story by Ralph O. Murphy. With Billy Sullivan, Estelle Bradley, Melbourne MacDowell. Cub reporter has weakness for passing up assignments for stories he thinks are better.

Out of the Storm. Tiffany. Directed by Louis Gasnier. Scenario by Lois Hutchinson, Leete Renick Brown, from a story by Arthur Stringer. With Jacqueline Logan, Tyrone Power, Edmund Burns. Publisher's son kept from murder charge by indomitable editor.

Stepping Along. Directed by Charles Hines. From a story by Matt Taylor. With Mary Brian, Johnny Hines, William Gaxton. City hall newsboy dreams of actress and politics; achieves both after defeating crooks.

Atta Boy. Pathe. Directed by Edward H. Griffith. Story and continuity by Charles Horan, Alf Goulding. Titles by Harold Christie. With Monty Banks, Virginia Bradford, Ernie Wood. As practical joke, copy boy is told he is reporter; writes story on fake kidnapping that turns out to be real; solves crime, gets scoop and reward.

Dangerous Traffic. Goodwill Pictures. Directed by Bennett Cohn. Written by Bennett Cohn. With Francis X. Bushman, Jack Perrin, Mildred Harris. Seaside reporter breaks up smuggling ring.

Lightning Reporter. Elbee Pictures. Directed by Jack Noble. Scenario by Jack Noble. Story by Tom Gibson. With Johnny Walker, Sylvia Breamer, Barry McIntosh. Cub reporter helps railroad magnate best competition in stock market, wins daughter.

Man Rustlin'. FBO. Directed by Del Andrews. Story by William Branch. Continuity by Burl R. Tuttle and Jay Chapman. With Bob Custer, Florence Lee, Jules Cowles. Western reporter on small paper catches bandits and is so successful he becomes syndicated columnist on big eastern paper.

The Man Upstairs. Warner Brothers. Directed by Roy Del Ruth.* Screenplay by Edmund T. Lowe, Jr., from a story by Earl Derr Biggers. With Monte Blue, Dorothy Devore, Helen Dunbar. Love story starts in personals column of newspaper. (minor)

Looking for Trouble. Universal. Directed by Robert North Bradbury. Scenario by George C. Hinely. Story by Stephen Chalmers. With Jack Hoxie, Marceline Day, J. Gordon Russell. Small western newspaper catches diamond smugglers.

The Hollywood Reporter. Hercules Productions. Directed by Bruce Mitchell. Story and scenario by Grover Jones. With Frank Merrill, Charles K. French, Peggy Montgomery. Reporter wins editor's daughter by exposing boss in city.

Man, Woman and Sin. MGM. Directed by Monta Bell. Scenario by Alice D. G. Miller. Titles by John Coulton. With John Gilbert, Jeanne Eagles, Gladys Brockwell. Reporter loves society editor, who dates publisher; murder, perjury, reconciliation.

Rainbow Riley. First National. Directed by Charles Hines. Titles by John W. Krafft,* from a play by Thompson Buchanan *(The Cub).* With Johnny Hines, Brenda Bond, Bradley Barker. Reporter chased by both sides of Kentucky feud.

Is That Nice? FBO. Directed by Del Andrews. Adaptation and continuity by Paul Gangelin. Story by Walter A. Sinclair. With George O'Hara, Doris Hill, Stanton Heck. Cub reporter breaks political scandal, wins girl.

1927

The Secret Studio. Fox. Directed by Victor Schertzinger. Scenario by James Kevin McGuinness* from the novel by Hazel Livingston (serialized in the San Francisco *Call*). With Olive Borden, Clifford Holland, Noreen Philips. Woman disgraced as newspapers print that she posed for artist in nude.

Grinning Guns. Universal. Directed by Albert Gogell. Story and scenario by Grover Jones. With Jack Hoxie, Ena Gragory, Robert Milasch. Western newspaper reforms town. A blue-streak western.

A Bowery Cinderella. Excellent Pictures. Directed by Burton King. Scenario by Adrian Johnson. Titles by Harry Chandlee. With Gladys Hulette, Pat O'Malley, Kate Bruce. Reporter's girl involved with rich backer until reporters play succeeds.

The Final Extra. Gotham Pictures. Directed by James P. Hogan. Story and scenario by Herbert C. Clark. With Marguerite de la Motte, Grant Withers, John Miljan. Young columnist aspires to colleague's crime story; jails bootleggers when his own theatrical inpresario is revealed as gang leader.

Not for Publication. FBO. Directed by Ralph Ince. Scenario by Ewart Adamson, from story by Robert Welles Ritchie. Produced by Joseph P. Kennedy. With Ralph Ince, Ray Laidlaw, Rex Lesse. Editor sends reporter to burglarize safe of dam construction agent; but makes own deal with contractor before dam is blown up.

1928

Let 'Er Go Gallegher. Pathe. Directed by Elmer Clifton. Adaptation and continuity by Elliott Clawson.* Titles by John Krafft.* Based on series of stories by Richard Harding Davis. Newsboy and reporter solve crimes.

The Big Noise. First National. Directed by Alan Dwan. Adaptation and scenario by Tom J. Geraghty. Titles by George Marion, Jr. Story by Ben Hecht.* With Chester Conklin, Alice White. Newspaper exaggerates man's injury to promote subway reform, elects candidate, then ignores injured man.

Telling the World. MGM. Directed by Sam Wood. Scenario by Raymond L. Schrock. Titles by Joe Farnham. Story by Dale van Avery.* With William Haines, Anita Page, Eileen Percy. Disowned son becomes reporter, catches murderer, saves chorus girl in China. Comedy-drama.

Hot News. Paramount. Directed by Clarence Badger. Story and scenario by Monte Brice and Harlan Thompson.* Newsreel camerawoman finds happiness with Scoop Morgan.

What a Night! Paramount. Directed by Edward Sutherland. Screenplay by Louise Long. Titles by Herman J. Mankiewicz.* Story by Grover Jones and Lloyd Corrigan. With Bebe Daniels, Neil Hamilton, William Austin. Industrialist's daughter works on newspaper and breaks up political gang.

Broken Barriers. Excellent Pictures. Directed by Burton King. Scenario and titles by Isadore Bernstein. Story by Caroline F. Hayward. With Helene Costello, Gaston Glass, Joseph Girard. Reporter gets story on boss killing candidate, but editor holds story when reporter and boss's daughter marry.

Crooks Can't Win. RKO. Directed by George M. Arthur. Story by Joseph Jefferson O'Neill. Adaptation by Enid Hibbard. Titles by Randolph Bartlett.* With Ralph Lewis, Thelma Hill, Sam Nelson. Reporter clears innocent cop suspected of complicity with silk thieves.

Jazzland. Quality Distributors. Directed by Dallas M. Fitzgerald. Scenario by Ada McQuillan. Titles by Tom Miranda. Story by Samuel Merwin. With Bryant Washburn, Vera Reynolds, Carroll Nye. Reporter exposes crooks behind big-city nightclub invading small New England town.

Lightning Speed. FBO. Directed by Robert North Bradbury. Story and continuity by Robert North Bradbury. Titles by Randolph Bartlett.* With Bob Steele, Mary Maybery, Perry Murdock. Reporter thwarts kidnap of governor's daughter by crook seeking pardon of his brother.

Out with the Tide. Peerless. Directed by Charles Hutchison. Scenario by Elaine Towne. Titles by Paul Perez. Story by John C. Brownell and G. Marion Burton. With Dorothy Dwan, Cullen Landis, Crawford Kent. Reporter suspected of murder finds real killer by trailing him to Shanghai.

Show Girl. First National. Directed by Alfred Santell. Scenario by James T. O'Donoghue. Titles by George Marion. From a novel by Joseph Patrick McEvoy. With Alice White, Donald Reed, Lee Moran. Cynical reporter persuades girl involved in nightclub murder to hide out so he can build kidnapping story.

A Woman against the World. Tiffany. Directed by George Archaimbaud. Continuity by Gertrude Orr. Titles by Frederic Harron and Fanny Hatton. Story by Albert Shelby Le Vine. With Harrison Ford, Georgis Hale, Lee Moran. Girl reporter loves condemned man; proves him innocent in face of editor's antagonism.

Deliverance. Stanley Advertising Co. Directed by B. K. Blake. Scenario by Duncan Underhill, from two books by Irving Fisher. No cast. Washington politics on prohibition bill involves reporters and lobbyists.

The Power of the Press. Columbia. Directed by Frank Capra. Adaptation and continuity by Frederick A. Thompson and Sonya Levien.* Story by Frederick A. Thompson. With Douglas Fairbanks, Jr., Jobyna Ralson, Mildred Harris. Cub reporter breaks political scandal and solves crime, gets girl.

Freedom of the Press. Universal. Directed by George Melford. Adaptation and continuity by J. Grubb Alexander. Titles by Walter Anthony. Story by Peter B. Kyne. With Lewis Stone, Marceline Day, Henry B. Walthall. Crusading reporter keeps crook from becoming mayor.

Riders of the Dark. MGM. Directed by Nick Grinde. Story and continuity by W. S. van Dyke. Titles by Madeline Ruthven. With Tim McCoy, Dorothy Dwan, Rex Lease. Western newspaper is destroyed after starting reform campaign.

1929

Red Hot Speed. Universal. Directed by Joseph Henabery. Scenario by Gladys Lehman and Matt Taylor. Titles by Albert de Mord. Story by Gladys Lehman. Adaptation by Faith Thomas. With Reginald Denny, Alice Day, Charles Byer. Publisher's daughter arrested in midst of newspaper antispeeding campaign.

Gentlemen of the Press. Paramount. Directed by Millard Webb. Screenplay by Bartlett Cormack, from a play by Ward Morehouse.* With Walter Huston, Katherine Francis, Charles Ruggles. Star reporter's dedication to job keeps him from reaching own daughter, who dies in childbirth when big story breaks.

Drag. First National. Directed by Frank Lloyd. Screenplay by Gene Towne. Dialogue and adaptation by Bradley King, from book by William Dudley Pelley. With Richard Barthelmess, Lucien Littlefield. Reporter on small Vermont newspaper turns playwright, then set designer for movies in Hollywood.

Big News. Pathe. Directed by Gregory La Cava. Screenplays by Walter de Leon. Dialogue by Frank Reicher. Adaptation by Jack Jungmeyer. Story by George Brooks. With Robert Armstrong, Carole Lombard. Fired reporter investigates dope ring headed by publisher's friend, gets job and wife back with scoop.

Speakeasy. Fox. Directed by Benjamin Stoloff. Scenario by Frederick Hazlitt Brennan and Edwin Burke. Dialogue by Edwin Burke. From a play by Edward Knoblock and George Rosener.* With Lola Lane, Stuart Erwin, Paul Page. Woman reporter falls for boxing champ and proves his manager is crooked.

In the Headlines. Warner Brothers. Directed by John G. Adolfi. Screenplay by Joseph Jackson. Story by James A. Starr.* With Grant Withers, Marion Nixon, Clyde Cook. Star reporter and woman cub solve double murder.

Idaho Red. FBO. Directed by Robert de Lacey. Story and continuity by Frank Howard Clark. Titles by Helen Gregg. With Tom Tyler, Patricia Caron, Frankie Darro. Orphaned newsboy helps guardian outwit western counterfeiters.

Protection. Fox. Directed by Benjamin Stoloff. Scenario by Frederick Hazlett Brennan. Story by J. Clarkson Miller. With Robert Elliott, Pal Page, Dorothy Burgess. Bootlegging story leads to politics, as reporter moves from big paper to independent to be able to print truth.

The Office Scandal. Pathe. Directed by Paul Stein. Original story and adaptation by Paul Gangelin and Jack Jungmeyer. Titles by John Krafft.* With Phyllis Haver, Leslie Fenton, Raymond Hatton. Sob sister keeps reporter boyfriend from jail by nailing crooks.

1930

Roadhouse Nights. Paramount. Directed by Hobart Henley. Scenario and dialogue by Garrett Fort. Story by Ben Hecht.* With Helen Morgan, Charles Ruggles, Fred Kohler. After boozing reporter fails, colleague exposes bootlegger control of town.

Young Man of Manhattan. Paramount. Directed by Monta Bell. Adaptation by Robert Presnell,* from book by Katharine Brush. Dialogue by Daniel Reed. With Claudette Colbert, Norman Foster, Ginger Rogers. Sportswriter marries movie columnist, then is tempted by socialite, but regains self-esteem through colleague.

The Divorce. MGM. Directed by Robert Z. Leonard. Continuity and dialogue by John Meehan. Treatment by Nick Grinde and Zelda Sears from a novel by Katharine Ursula Parrott. With Norma Shearer, Chester Morris, Conrad Nagle. Marital adventures and crises of reporter and wife.

The Czar of Broadway. Universal. Directed by William James Craft. Story, continuity, and dialogue by Gene Towne. With John Wray, Betty Compson, John Harry. Based on the life of Arthur Rothstein.

Conspiracy. RKO. Directed by Christy Cabanne. Screenplay and dialogue by Beulah Marie Dix. Produced by William Le Baron.* From a book by Robert

Melville Baker and John Emerson.* With Bessie Love, Ned Sparks, Hugh Trevor. Reporter helps solve murder and break narcotics ring.

Night Ride. Universal. Directed by John S. Robertson. Adaptation by Edward T. Lowe, Jr., from a story by Henry LaCossitt. Titles by Charles Logue.* Dialogue by Tom Reed* and Edward T. Logue, Jr. With Joseph Schildkraut, Barbara Kent, Edward G. Robinson. Star reporter follows adventurous path to solve payroll robbery and double murder.

Sisters. Columbia. Directed by James Flood. Story by Ralph Graves. Scenario and dialogue by Jo Swerling.* With Sally O'Neill, Molly O'Day, Russell Gleason. Protagonists retire to respectability through small country newspaper.

1931

Scandal Sheet. Paramount. Directed by John Cromwell. Story by Vincent Lawrence.* With George Bancroft, Clive Brook, Kay Francis. Tyrannical and relentless editor kills wife's banker beau, then dictates story to scoop opposition and land himself in jail.

The Front Page. United Artists. Directed by Lewis Milestone. Screenplay by Bartlett Cormack, with dialogue by Bartlett Cormack and Charles Lederer. Based on the play by Ben Hecht* and Charles MacArthur.* With Adolphe Menjou, Pat O'Brien, Mary Brian. The archetype. Reporter and editor battle each other, mayor, sheriff, as they seek scoop on condemned man who escapes jail.

Dance, Fools, Dance. MGM. Directed by Harry Beaumont. Scenario by Auriana Rouveral, from the play by Martin Flavin. With Joan Crawford, Lester Vail, Cliff Edwards. Socialite becomes sob sister after the crash, saves brother, and gets respect catching gangsters (echoes of Jack Lingle case and St. Valentine's case).

The Finger Points. Warner Brothers/First National. Directed by John Francis Dillon. Story by John Mark Saunders* and W. R. Burnett. With Richard Barthelmess, Fay Wray, Regis Toomey. Reporter paid $35 to write and $1,000 not to write is finally killed over story by unhappy gangsters (Jake Lingle case).

The Secret Six. MGM. Directed by George Hill. Story by Francis Marion.* With Wallace Beery, Johnny Mack Brown, Clark Gable. Reporter gathers information for secret vigilante committee which breaks bootlegging racket.

Five Star Final. Warner Brothers. Directed by Mervyn LeRoy. Adaptation by Robert Lord, from a story by Louis Weitzenkorn.* Dialogue by Byron Morgan. With Edward G. Robinson, Frances Starr, H. B. Warner. Editor pushed for scandal copy by publisher and circulation manager causes suicides and destroys innocent lives.

Sob Sister. Fox. Directed by Alfred Santell. From the book by Mildred Gilman. With Linda Watkins, James Dunn, Minna Bombell. Sob sister proves herself to colleagues at expense of her own happiness.

Platinum Blonde. Columbia. Story by Harry E. Chandlee and Douglas W. Churchill.* Dialogue by Robert Riskin.* Directed by Frank Capra. With Jean Harlow, Robert Williams, Loretta Young. Newsrooms more appealing than ballrooms to reporter who marries a socialite.

1932

The Final Edition. Columbia. Directed by Howard Higgin. From a story by Roy Chanslor.* With Mae Clark, Pat O'Brien, Mary Doran. Sob sister fights with unreasonable editor over murder story.

Scandal for Sale. Universal. Directed by Russell Mack. From a novel by Emile Henry Gauvreau *(Hot News)*. With Pat O'Brien, Charles Bickford, Rose Hobart. Editor neglects family to build circulation, even sending reporter on risky ocean flight to take him out of the way.

The Famous Ferguson Case. Warner Brothers. Directed by Lloyd Bacon. Screenplay by Courtney Terrett* and Harvey Thew,* from the story by Granville Moore ("Circulation"). With Joan Blondell, Tom Brown, Adrienne Dore. Murder is a side issue as sensational reporters are pilloried and their methods contrasted with those of decent dailies.

The Strange Love of Molly Louvain. First National. Directed by Michael Curtiz. Adaptation by Erwin Gelsey and Brown Holmes, from the play by Maurine Watkins. With Lee Tracy, Ann Dvorak, Richard Cromwell. Nice reporter helps lady with a past.

Merrily We Go to Hell. Paramount. Directed by Dorothy Arzner. From a book by Cleo Lucas. With Frederic March, Sylvia Sidney, Adrienne Allen. Reporter who writes play wins girl even though he can't stop drinking.

Love Is a Racket. First National. Directed by William Wellman. Adaptation by Courtney Terrett.* From a novel by Rian James.* With Douglas Fairbanks, Jr., Lee Tracy, Frances Dee. Stories, dames, and drinks with Broadway columnist of cynicism and heart of gold.

Is My Face Red? RKO. Directed by William Seiler. Screenplay by Allen Rivkin.* From the play by Allen Rivkin and Ben Markson.* With Ricardo Cortez, Helen Twelvetrees, Robert Armstrong. Vain, unscrupulous columnist breaks murder story and gets in trouble with both police and crooks.

Blessed Event. Warner Brothers. Directed by Roy Del Ruth.* Screenplay by Howard Green.* From the play by Manuel Senf* and Forrest Wilson. With Lee Tracy, Dick Powell, Mary Brien. Unscrupulous columnist is still strong enough to stand up to thugs.

Okay, America. Universal. Directed by Tay Garnett. Story and screenplay by William Anthony McGuire. With Lew Ayres, Maureen O'Sullivan, Louis Calhern. Reporter nicknamed Ego writes column in conflict with publisher and police.

Hollywood Speaks. Columbia. Directed by Edward Buzzell. Screenplay by Edward Buzzell and Norman Krasna.* With Pat O'Brien, Genevieve Tobin, Lucien Prival. Hollywood reporter helps girl get screen test.

The Crusader. Majestic. Directed by Frank Strayer. From a play by Wilson Collison. With Ned Sparks, H. B. Warner, Evelyn Brent. Reporter seeks to expose shady background of crusading DA's wife.

War Correspondent. Columbia. From a story by Keene Thompson. With Ralph Graves, Jack Holt. Reporter unmasks fake Chinese war lord.

1933

State Fair. Fox. Directed by Henry King. From book by Philip Duffield Strong. With Lew Ayres, Janet Gaynor, Will Rogers. On visit to fair, family's daughter is swept off her feet by dashing reporter.

Clear All Wires. MGM. Directed by George Hill. From a play by Bella and Samuel Spewack.* Braggart head of Chicago paper's foreign news service seeks fame and stories in French colony, Russia, and China.

The World Gone Mad. Majestic. Directed by William Christy Cabanne. Screen story by Edward T. Lowe, Jr. With Pat O'Brien, Evelyn Brent, Neil Hamilton. Ace reporter catches crooked banker.

Mr. Broadway (A Times Square Travelogue). Directed by Johnnie Walker. Featuring Ed Sullivan. Follows Sullivan through three nightclubs as he gathers information for his column. Celebrities include Jack Dempsey, Ruth Etting, Bert Lahr, Hal Le Roy, Joe Frisco, Josephine Dunn, Gus Edwards, Jack Haley, Lupe Velez, Maxie Rosenbloom.

I Cover the Waterfront. United Artists. Directed by James Cruze. From a book by Max Miller. With Ben Lyon, Claudette Colbert, Ernest Torrence. Reporter exposes smuggling racket run by girlfriend's father.

The Picture Snatcher. Warner Brothers. Directed by Lloyd Bacon. Screenplay by Allen Rivkin.* Story by Danny Ahearne. Ex-con working for tabloid takes sneaky pictures, including execution photo; all is well when he gets photo of murderer in action (based on New York *Daily News* scandal).

No Marriage Ties. RKO. Directed by J. Walter Ruben. From a play by Arch Gaffney and Charles W. Curran. With Richard Dix, Elizabeth Allan, Alan Dinehart. The reporter as lush; becomes advertising man.

Boss Tweed. Columbia. Featuring Charles Coburn. First of thirteen projected "March of the Years" films. Dramatized version of true 1871 incident when George Jones, first publisher of the *Times,* was offered bribe by Boss Tweed; bribe refused, the *Times* published its story and broke the power of the Tweed ring.

Headline Shooters. RKO. Directed by Otto Brower. Screenplay by Allen Rivkin.* Story by Wallace West. With William Gargan, Frances Dee, Ralph Bellamy. Newsreel reporters are rivals for the same story. Atmosphere and narrative very reminiscent of *The Front Page.*

Advice to the Lovelorn. 20th/Fox. Directed by Alfred Werker. Loosely based on *Miss Lonely Hearts* by Nathanael West. With Lee Tracy, Sterling Holloway. Drunken reporter demoted to lovelorn column post, where he solves crimes.

Hi, Nellie! Warner Brothers. Directed by Mervyn LeRoy. Screenplay by Roy Chanslor* and Abem Finkel. Produced by Robert Presnell.* With Paul Muni, Glenda Farrell, Berton Churchill. Editor who fouls up story demoted to lovelorn columnist; turns it into hit column and vindicates himself through original story.

It Happened One Night. Columbia. Directed by Frank Capra. Screenplay by Robert Riskin* from a story by Samuel Hopkins Adams. With Clark Gable, Claudette Colbert, Walter Connolly. Runaway heiress meets journalist on a bus.

Friends of Mr. Sweeney. Warner Brothers. No director. Screenplay by Warren Duff and Sidney Sutherland from the novel by Elmer Davis. Added dialogue by F. Hugh Herbert and Erwin Gelsey. With Charlie Ruggles, Ann Dvorak, Eugene Pallette. Meek reporter emboldened by booze exposes small town's crooked politician much to dismay of publisher.

Thirty Day Princess. Paramount. Directed by Marion Gering. From a story by Clarence Buddington Kelland.* With Cary Grant, Sylvia Sidney. Editor falls for actress impersonating princess.

The Hell Cat. Columbia. Produced by Sid Rogell, from a story by Adele Buffington. With Robert Armstrong, Ann Sothern. Reporter saves socialite turned sob sister from crooks.

I'll Tell the World. Universal. Produced by Dale van Every.* Original story by Lincoln Quarberg* and Frank Wead. With Lee Tracy, Roger Pryor. Globetrotting reporter finds dirigible, rescues queen, and reports on a revolution.

The Gilded Lily. Paramount. Directed by Wesley Ruggles. Screenplay by Claude Binyon,* from a story by Melville Baker and Jack Kirkland. With Fred MacMurray, Claudette Colbert, Ray Milland. Girl who rejects British peer made celebrity by reporter, whom she later marries.

After Office Hours. MGM. Directed by Robert Z. Leonard. Screenplay by Herman J. Mankiewicz* from an original story by Lawrence Stallings* and Dale van Avery.* With Clark Gable, Constance Bennett. Romance of socialite reporter and editor as she solves scandal in prominent family.

Life Begins at Forty. Fox. Directed by George Marshall. Screenplay by Lamar Trotti.* Dialogue by Robert Quillan, from a book by Walter Boughton Pitkin. With Will Rogers, Jane Darwell, Rochelle Hudson. One-man newspaper's editor dispenses homilies, advice, captures crooks.

Front Page Woman. Warner Brothers. Directed by Michael Curtiz. Screenplay by Roy Chanslor* and Lillie Hayward and Laird Doyle, from a story by Richard MacAulay. With Bette Davis, George Brent, Winifred Shaw. Competing male and female reporters doublecross each other before true love wins out.

Murder Man. MGM. Directed by Tim Whelan. Screenplay by Tim Whelan and John C. Higgins. Story by Tim Whelan and Guy Bolton. With Spencer Tracy, Virginia Bruce, Lionell Atwill. Embittered reporter commits murder and puts blame on enemy who killed his parents; at execution interview, reporter confesses own guilt.

The Daring Young Man. Fox. Directed by William S. Seiter. Story by Claude Binyon* and Sidney Skolsky.* Screenplay by William Hurlbut. Additional dialogue by Sam Hellman* and Glenn Tryon. Produced by Robert T. Kane* with James Dunn, Mae Clarke, Neil Hamilton. Rival reporters assigned to uncover prison conditions find crooks hiding out in jail.

The Pay-Off. First National. Directed by Robert Florey. Story by Samuel Shipman. Screenplay by George Brisker and Joel Sayre.* With James Dunn, Claire Dodd, Patricia Ellis. Sports columnist is in debt to gamblers.

$1,000 a Minute. Republic. Directed by Audrey Scotto. Story by Everett Freeman.* Screenplay by Joseph Fields. Adaptation by Jack Nattefore* and Claire Church. With Roger Pryor, Leila Hyams, Edgar Kennedy. Comedy of reporter trying to spend $1,000 a minute for twelve hours to settle bet between millionaires.

The Bride Comes Home. Paramount. Directed by Wesley Ruggles. Screenplay by Claude Binyon,* from a story by Elisabeth Saxany Holding. With Fred MacMurray, Claudette Colbert, Robert Young. Penniless socialite in triangle with two guys starting magazine.

Behind the Evidence. Columbia. Story and screenplay by Harold Shumate.* With Norman Foster. Society reporter solves crimes.

The Headline Woman. Mascot. Presented by Nat Levine. Story and screenplay by Jack Natteford* and Claire Church. With Roger Pryor.

1936

We're Only Human. RKO. Directed by James Flood. Screenplay by Rian James,* from a story by Thomas Walsh. Produced by Edgar Kaufman.* With Jane Wyatt, Preston Foster, James Gleason. Girl reporter meets tough but honest cop.

Exclusive Story. MGM. Directed by George B. Seitz. Screenplay by Michael Fessier,* from a story by Martin Mooney.* With Franchot Tone, Madge Evans, Stuart Erwin. Reporter helps special prosecutor break rackets. Based on Mooney's experience in New York; suggests Morro Castle fire caused by policy racketeers. Very topical at the time.

Next Time We Love. Universal. Directed by Edward H. Griffith.* Screenplay by Melville Baker, from a book by Ursula Parrott. With Margaret Sullivan, James Stewart, Ray Milland. Stage loses an actress as foreign correspondent persuades his wife to globe trot with him after stories.

Road Gang. Warner Brothers. Directed by Louis King. Screenplay by Dalton Trumbo. Story by Abem Finkel and Harold Buckley. With Donald Woods, Kay Linaker. Reporter who starts exposé falsely sent to chain gang by crooked politicians; prisoners riot and take him to DA.

Wife versus Secretary. MGM. Directed by Clarence Brown. Screenplay by Norman Krasna,* from a book by Faith Baldwin. Additional screenplay by Alice Duer Miller and John Lee Mahin. Produced by Hunt Stromberg,* with Clark Gable, Jean Harlow, Myrna Loy. Publisher caught in triangle between wife and secretary.

Woman Trap. Paramount. Directed by Harold Young. Screenplay by Brian Marlow and Eugene Walter.* Story by Charles Brackett. With George Murphy, Gertrude Michael, Sidney Blackmer. Reporter chases jewel thieves through Mexico.

Gentle Julia. 20th/Fox. Directed by John Blystone. Screenplay by Lamar Trotti.* From a story by Booth Tarkington. With Jane Withers, Tom Brown, Marsha Hunt. In Tarkingtonesque small town, child foils saccharine suitor and links aunt up with uncertain cub reporter.

Mr. Deeds Goes to Town. Columbia. Directed by Frank Capra. Screenplay by Robert Riskin,* from a book by Clarence Buddington Kelland.* With Gary Cooper, Jean Arthur, George Bancroft. Sudden hick millionaire gets involved with big-city sob sister.

Big Brown Eyes. Paramount. Directed by Raoul Walsh. Screenplay by Raoul Walsh and Bert Hanlon from a story by James Edward Grant. With Joan Bennett, Cary Grant, Walter Pidgeon. Manicurist who instantly becomes reporter-columnist-editorial writer solves crimes with lovelorn detective's help.

The Golden Arrow. First National. Directed by Alfred E. Green. Adaptation by Charles Kenyan from a play by Michael Arlen. With Bette Davis, George Brent, Eugene Palette. Fake heiress set up for publicity campaign marries reporter sent for story.

Human Cargo. 20th/Fox. Directed by Allan Dwan.* Screenplay by Jefferson Parker and Doris Malloy, from a book by Kathleen Shepard. With Brian Donlevy, Claire Trevor, Alan Dinehart. Rival reporters seek to break smuggling ring.

Half Angel. 20th/Fox. Directed by Sydney Landfield. Screenplay by Gene Fowler* and Bess Meredyth. Story by F. Tennyson Jesse. With Brian Donlevy, Frances Dee, Charles Butterworth. Reporter singlehandedly clears girl of murder charge.

Florida Special. Paramount. Directed by Ralph Murphy. Screenplay by David Boe, Marguerite Roberts,* and Laura and S. J. Perelman. Story by Clarence Budington Kelland.* With Jack Oakie, Sally Eilers, Kent Taylor. Reporter chases jewel thieves on train.

Jailbreak. Warner Brothers. Directed by Nick Grinde. Adaptation by Robert D. Andrews and Joseph Hoffman.* Story by Jonathan Finn. With Craig Reynolds, June Travis, Barton MacLane. Reporter solves crimes while in jail.

Missing Girls. Chesterfield. Directed by Phil Rosen. Screenplay by Martin Mooney and John W. Krafft.* Story by Martin Mooney.* With Roger Pryor, Muriel Evans, Sydney Blackmer. Reporter, in jail for contempt of court, unearths plot to kill senator and scores scoop.

A Woman Rebels. RKO. Directed by Mark Sandrich. Screenplay by Anthony Veiller* and Ernest Vajda. From a book by Nitta Syrett. With Katharine Hepburn, Herbert Marshall, Elizabeth Allan. A woman fights for independence in the face of Victorian conventions.

Libelled Lady. MGM. Directed by Jack Conway. Screenplay by Maurine Watkins, Howard Emmet Rogers, and George Oppenheimer. Story by Wallace

Sullivan. With Jean Harlow, Spencer Tracy, William Powell. "Married" reporter woos heiress to stop her libel suit; editor winds up with "wife" and reporter with heiress.

The Girl on the Front Page. Universal. Directed by Harry Beaumont. Screenplay by Austin Parker,* Albert R. Perkins, and Alice D. G. Miller. Story by Marjorie and Rou Chanslor.* With Edmund Lowe, Gloria Stewart, Reginald Owen. Comedy. Managing editor runs afoul of girl who inherits newspaper.

Murder with Pictures. Paramount. Directed by Charles Barton. Screenplay by John C. Moffitt* and Sidney Salkow. From a book by George Harmon Coxe. With Lew Ayres, Gail Patrick, Joyce Compton. When cops hold press boys as suspects in series of murders, photographer hides plates revealing guilty party.

Love on the Run. MGM. Directed by W. S. Van Dyke. Screenplay by John Lee Mahin, Manuel Senff,* and Gladys Hurlbut. Story by Alan Green and Julian Brodie. Produced by Joseph Mankiewicz.* With Clark Gable, Franchot Tone, Joan Crawford. Rival European correspondents chase dame and spy ring.

Sinner Take All. MGM. Directed by Errol Taggart. Screenplay by Leonard Lee and Walter Wise. From a book by Elwyn Whitman Chambers. With Dorothy Kilgallen, Bruce Cabot, Margaret Lindsay. Newspaper crime scandal. (Made after Kilgallen achieves fame for around-the-world trip reporting for father's paper.)

Man Hunt. Warner Brothers. Directed by William Clemens. Screenplay by Roy Chanslor.* Story by Earl Felton. With William Gargan, Ricardo Cortez. Country editor chases gangsters in competition with fleet of ace city reporters and GIs.

Wedding Present. Paramount. Directed by Richard Wallace. Story by Paul Gallico. Produced by B. P. Schulberg.* With Lew Ayres, Cary Grant, Joan Bennett. City editor determined not to lose sob sister to dull suitor.

Adventure in Manhattan. Columbia. From a play by Anita B. Fairgrieve and Helena Miller. With Joel McCrea, Jean Arthur. Reporter solves crimes and falls in love with actress.

Women Are Trouble. MGM. Directed by Earl Taggart. Screenplay by Michael Fessier.* Story by George Harmon Coxe. Produced by Lucien Hubbard and Michael Fessier.* With Stuart Erwin, Paul Ketty, Florence Rice.

Two against the World. Warner Brothers. Directed by William McGann. Screenplay by Michael Jacoby, from the play *Five Star Final* by Louis Weitzenkorn.* With Humphrey Bogart, Beverly Roberts, Helen MacKellar. Remake of *Five Star Final* set in radio journalism, where rehash of old murder case causes suicides, and radio commission cleans up station programming.

1937

Love Is News. 20th/Fox. Directed by Tay Garnett. Screenplay by Harry Tugend and Jack Yellen.* Story by William R. Lipson and Frederick Stephani.

Produced by Earl Carroll* and Harold Wilson. With Loretta Young, Tyrone Power, Don Ameche. Heiress marries snooping reporter to teach him a lesson about being in public eye.

Wake up and Live. 20th/Fox. Directed by Sidney Langfield. Screenplay by Harry Tugend and Jack Yellen.* Story by Curtis Kenyon, from a book by Dorothea Brande. With Ben Bernie, Walter Winchell, Alice Faye. Exploits newspaper "feud" between Winchell and Bernie as they chitchat through musical.

Behind the Headlines. RKO. Directed by Richard Rosson. Screenplay by J. R. Bren and E. L. Hartman. Story by Thomas Ahearn. Renegade G-man devoted to gold standard captured by demon newsgetter and competing sob-sister girlfriend.

There Goes My Girl. RKO. Directed by Ben Holmes. Screenplay by Harry Segall. Original story by George Beck. With Gene Raymond, Ann Sothern, Joseph Crehan. Editor determined to prevent star woman reporter's marriage to antic reporter for rival paper. (Compared in reviews to *Front Page; His Girl Friday* yet to come!)

Exclusive. Paramount. Directed by Alexander Hall. Story by John C. Moffitt.* Screenplay by Rian James,* John C. Moffitt, and Sidney Salkow. Produced by Benjamin Glazer.* With Fred MacMurray, Frances Farmer, Charlie Ruggles. Newspapers feud after racketeer buys rival paper, causing turmoil in town.

I Cover the War. Universal. Directed by Arthur Lubin. Screenplay by George Waggner. Original story by Bernard McCornville. With John Wayne, Gwen Gaze, Don Barclay. Newsreel cameraman in Mesopotamia crushes Arab revolt.

Back in Circulation. Warner Brothers. Directed by Ray Enright.* Adaptation by Warren Duff. Story by Adela Rogers St. John. With Pat O'Brien, Joan Blondell, Margaret Lindsay. Editor makes life rough but romantic for woman reporter.

Night Club Scandal. Paramount. Directed by Ralph Murphy. Screenplay by Lillie Hayward. From play by Daniel N. Rubin. With Lynne Overman, Louise Campbell, John Barrymore. Ace reporter disproves circumstantial case against innocent man and captures true killer.

Nothing Sacred. Selznick International. Directed by William Wellman. Screenplay by Ben Hecht.* With Frederic March, Carole Lombard, Walter Connolly. Opportunist reporter and editor make celebrity of dying girl to boost circulation. When she is well, they are stuck.

The Last Gangster. MGM. Directed by Edward Ludwig. Screenplay by John Lee Mahin. Story by William A. Wellman and Robert Carson. With James Stewart, Rose Stradner, Edward G. Robinson. Gangster serves time and returns home to reclaim wife and child from protection of respectable newspaperman.

Headline Crasher. Ambassador. Directed by Peter B. Kyne. Story by Peter B. Kyne. Produced by Maurice Cohn. With Frankie Darro.

Women Men Marry. MGM. Directed by Errol Taggart. Screenplay by Donald Henderson Clarke, James Grant, Harry Ruskin. Story by Matt Taylor. Produced by Michael Fessier.* With George Murphy, Sidney Blackmer, Claire Dodd. Editor has affair with reporter's wife.

Wild Money. Paramount. From a story by Paul Gallico. With Edward Everett Horton. Small-town newspaper hits big, big story (comedy).

1938

Love and Hisses. 20th/Fox. Directed by Sidney Lanfield. Screenplay by Art Arthur* and Curtis Kenyon. With Ben Bernie, Simone Simone, Walter Winchell. Exploits newspaper "feud" between Bernie and Winchell, now over new girl singer.

A Girl with Ideas. Universal. Directed by S. Sylvan Simon. Screenplay by Bruce Manning* and Robert T. Shannon. Original story by William Rankin. With Kent Taylor, Wendy Barrie, Walter Pidgeon. Managing editor crosses wits with woman who inherits newspaper.

Making the Headlines. Columbia. Directed by Lewis D. Collins. Screenplay by Howard J. Green* and Jefferson Parker. Story by Howard J. Green. With Jack Holt, Beverly Roberts, Craig Reynolds.

King of the Newsboys. Republic. Directed by Bernard Vorhaus. Screenplay by Louis Weitzenkorn* and Peggy Thompson. Original story by Samuel Ornitz and Horace McCoy. With Lew Ayres, Helen Mack, Alison Skipworth.

Time out for Murder. 20th/Fox. Directed by H. Bruce Humberstone. Screenplay by Jerry Cady. Story by Irving Reis. Produced by Howard J. Green.* With Michael Whalen, Gloria Stuart, Chick Chandler. Reporter solves murder and saves innocent man.

There Goes My Heart. Hal Roach (UA). Directed by Norman Z. McLeod. Screenplay by Jack Jevne and Eddie Moran. Original story by Ed Sullivan.* With Frederic March, Virginia Bruce, Patsy Kelly. Runaway heiress and snoopy reporter done once again (copycat of *It Happened One Night*).

The Sisters. Warner Brothers. Directed by Anatole Litvak. Story by Myron Brinig. Adaptation, Milton Krims.* With Bette Davis, Errol Flynn, Anita Louise. Rough married life of reporter who travels and drinks.

Exposed. Universal. Directed by Harold Schuster. Screenplay by Charles Kaufman and Franklin Cohen. Original story by George R. Bilson. With Glenda Farrell, Otto Kruger, Herbert Mindin. Woman photographer uncovers disgraced lawyer and helps him capture racketeers who ruined him.

While New York Sleeps. 20th/Fox. Directed by H. Bruce Humberstone. Screenplay by Frances Hyland and Albert Ray. Original story by Frank Fenton and Lynn Root. With Michael Whalen, Chick Chandler, Jean Rogers. Reporters beat police and rivals to criminal.

Four's A Crowd. Warner Brothers. Directed by Michael Curtiz. Original story by Wallace Sullivan. Adaptation by Casey Robinson and Sig Jerzig. With Errol Flynn, Rosalind Russell, Olivia de Havilland. Editor chases sob sister and heiress, ends up with printer's ink (comedy).

Scandal Street. Paramount. Directed by James Hogan. Story by Vera Caspary.* Produced by Edward T. Lowe. With Lew Ayres, Roscoe Karns, Louise Campbell. Reporters help clear small-town girl from gossip about her relationship to murdered ladies' man.

Newsboy's Home. Universal. Directed by Harold Young. Screenplay by Gordon Kahn.* Original story by Gordon Kahn and Charles Grayson. With Jackie Cooper, Wendy Barrie, Edmund Loew. Editor beats female owner of paper to story amid streetfights among flocks of rival newsboys.

Personal Secretary. Universal. Directed by Otis Garrett. Original story by B. Laidlaw and Robert Lively. Produced by Max Gordon. With William Gargan and Andy Devine.

1939

Off the Record. Warner Brothers. Directed by James Flood. Screenplay by Lawrence Kimble,* Earl Baldwin, Niven Busch. Original story by Saul Elkins and Sally Sandlin. With Pat O'Brien, Joan Blondell, Bobby Jordan. After slot-machine exposé sends kid to reform school, woman reporter marries editor and adopts kid.

Tell No Tales. MGM. Directed by Leslie Fenton. Screenplay by Lionel Hauser. Story by Pauline London and Alfred Taylor. With Melvyn Douglas, Louise Platt, Esther Dale. Editor of dying newspaper makes own headlines by catching kidnapper.

They Asked for It. Universal. Directed by Frank MacDonald. Screenplay by Arthur T. Harman. Story by James B. Lowell. With William Lundigan, Michael Whalen, Jay Hodges. College kids take over newspaper and stir up excitement with murder hoax.

News Is Made at Night. 20th/Fox. Directed by Alfred Werker. Screenplay by John Larkin.* Story by John Larkin. Produced by Edward Kaufman.* With Lynn Bari, Preston Foster, Russell Gleason. Novice gal reporter and brusque editor save innocent man from gallows.

Each Dawn I Die. Warner Brothers. Directed by William Highley. Screenplay by Norman Reilly Raine, Warren Duff, Charles Perry. From a book by Jerome Odlum.* With James Cagney, George Raft, Jany Bryan. Crusading reporter framed and sent to prison, where he helps engineer break to clear his name.

Stanley and Livingstone. 20th/Fox. Directed by Henry King. Screenplay by Sam Hellman,* Philip Dunne, Julien Josephson.* Story by Sam Hellman and Hal Long. Produced by Kenneth MacGowan.* With Spencer Tracy, Nancy Kelly, Richard Greene. "Story of one of great journalistic achievements of last century."

Mr. Smith Goes to Washington. Columbia. Directed by Frank Capra. Story by Lewis R. Foster. Screenplay by Sidney Buchman. With James Stewart, Jean Arthur, Thomas Mitchell. Idealistic young politician is helped by reporter to learn wiles of Washington. (Personal appearance by H. V. Kaltenborn.)

Everything Happens at Night. 20th/Fox. Directed by Irving Cummings. Screenplay by Art Arthur* and Robert Harani. With Robert Cummings,

Ray Milland, Sonja Henie. Rival newshounds seek anti-Nazi intellectual by wooing daughter.

Nancy Drew, Reporter. Warner Brothers. Directed by William Clemens. Screenplay by Kenneth Gannet, from stories by Carolyn Keene. With Bonita Granville, Frankie Thomas, John Litel. Journalism's turn in the series.

Cafe Society. Paramount. Directed by Edward H. Griffith.* Story and screenplay by Virginia van Upp. With Fred MacMurray, Madeleine Carroll, Allyn Joslyn. Socialite marries ship news reporter on a bet.

Scandal Sheet. Columbia. Directed by Nick Grinde. Original story by Joseph Carole. Produced by Ralph Conn. With Otto Kruger, Ona Munson.

1940

No Time for Comedy. Warner Brothers. Directed by William Keighley. Screenplay by Julius and Philip Epstein.* From a play by Samuel N. Behrman.* With James Stewart, Rosalind Russell. Small-time reporter in New York as playwright.

His Girl Friday. Columbia. Directed by Howard Hawks. Screenplay by Charles Lederer, from the play *The Front Page* by Ben Hecht* and Charles MacArthur.* With Cary Grant, Rosalind Russell, Ralph Bellamy. The archetype redone (refs. *Wedding Present* and *There Goes My Girl*).

The Philadelphia Story. MGM. Directed by George Cukor. Screenplay by Donald Ogden Stewart, from a play by Philip Barry. Produced by Joseph Mankiewicz. With Cary Grant, Katharine Hepburn, James Stewart. Household of rich offbeats invaded by journalists.

Sued for Libel. RKO. Directed by Leslie Goodwins. Screenplay by Jerry Cady. Original story by Wolfe Jaufman. With Kent Taylor, Linda Hayes, Lillian Bond. Reporter captures killers to cancel unjust libel suit.

Double Alibi. Universal. Directed by Philip Rosen. Screenplay by Harold Buchman and Charles Grayson. Story by Frederick C. David. With Wayne Morris, Margaret Lindsay, Roscoe Karns. Accused reporter must show evidence is not pointed at him alone.

Foreign Correspondent. United Artists. Directed by Alfred Hitchcock. Original story by Charles Bennett and Joan Harrison. Dialogue by James Hilton and Robert Benchley. With Joel McCrea, Lorraine Day, Herbert Marshall. European adventures and suspense with fifth column plot.

A Dispatch from Reuters. Warner Brothers. Directed by William Dieterle. Screenplay by Milton Krims.* Story by Valentine Williams and Wolfgang Wilhelm. With Edward G. Robinson, Eddie Albert, Edna Best. Biography of Paul Julius Baron Reuter and his news agency.

Comrade X. MGM. Directed by King Vidor. Screenplay by Ben Hecht* and Charles Lederer. Story by Walter Reisch. With Clark Gable, Hedy Lamarr, Oscar Homolka. American correspondent in Moscow involved with glamorous streetcar conductress, still gets stories (follow-up to *Ninotchka*).

Behind the News. Republic. Directed by Joseph Santley. Screenplay by Isable Dawn and Boyce De Gaw. Produced by Robert North. With Lloyd Nolan,

Doris Davenport, Robert Armstrong. Young reporters indict crooked DA in face of elder colleague's cynicism.

Unholy Partners. MGM. Directed by Mervyn LeRoy. Screenplay by Earl Baldwin, Bartlett Cormack, Lesser Samuels. Produced by Samuel Marx. With Edward G. Robinson, William T. Orr, Edward Arnold. Flashback to 1920s as reporter starts own tabloid with backing from crook, who blackmails protégé and is killed by editor, who flies the Atlantic with mad pilot . . .

Confirm or Deny. 20th/Fox. Directed by Archie Mayo. Story by Henry Wales* and Sam Fuller.* Screenplay by Jo Swerling.* With Don Ameche, Joan Bennett. U.S. Reporter in London has invasion plans but can't publish. (Uncredited direction: Fritz Lang.)

Penny Serenade. Columbia. Directed by George Stevens. Screenplay by Morrie Ryskind. Story by Martha Cheevers. With Cary Grant, Irene Dunne, Beulah Bondi. Adoption tearjerker; itinerant reporter buys small-town paper and lives in fiscal and emotional crisis.

Nine Lives Are Not Enough. Warner Brothers. Directed by A. Edward Sutherland. Screenplay by Fred Niblo, Jr.,* from book by Jerome Odlum.* With Ronald Reagan, Ed Brophy, Joseph Creham. Brash, unscrupulous reporter fired for inaccuracies, stays on murder case, winds up editor when socialite girlfriend buys paper.

Meet John Doe. Warner Brothers. Directed by Frank Capra. Screenplay by Robert Riskin.* Story by Richard Connell and Robert Presnell.* With Barbara Stanwyck, Gary Cooper, Edward Arnold. Sob sister invents suicide character, only to be trapped by her own publisher who wants to manipulate story.

Citizen Kane. RKO. Directed by Orson Welles. Original screenplay by Herman J. Mankiewicz and Orson Welles. With Orson Welles, Joseph Cotton, Dorothy Comingore. Builder of publishing empire hopes to rule the world.

Wide Open Town. Paramount. Directed by Lesley Selander. From characters by Clarence E. Mulford. With William Boyd, Morris Ankrum. Hopalong Cassidy helps harassed newspaper editor rid community of outlaws.

Design for Scandal. MGM. Directed by Norman Taurog. Screenplay by Lionel Hauser.* Produced by John W. Considine, Jr. With Walter Pidgeon, Edward Arnold, Rosalind Russell. Reporter tries to smear woman judge with gossip, ends up in matrimony.

Shadow of the Thin Man. MGM. Directed by W. S. Van Dyke. Screenplay by Harvey Kuruitz* and Irving Brecher. From characters by Dashiell Hammett.* With Myrna Loy, William Powell, Barry Nelson. Sporting world of gamblers, touts, and bookies.

Washington Melodrama. MGM. Directed by S. Sylvan Simon. Screenplay by Marion Parsonnei and Roy Chanslor.* From a play by L. Durocher Macpherson. With Kent Taylor, Ann Rutherford, Frank Morgan. Congressman, reporter, and romance in Washington.

1942

The Man Who Came to Dinner. Warner Brothers. Directed by William Keighley. Screenplay by Julius J. and Philip G. Epstein. From the play by

George S. Kaufman and Moss Hart. With Monty Wooley, Ann Sheridan, Richard Travis. Convalescent tyrant meddles in romance between his secretary and reporter.

Woman of the Year. MGM. Directed by George Stevens. Screenplay by Ring Lardner, Jr.,* and Michael Kanin. Produced by Joseph Mankiewicz.* With Spencer Tracy, Katharine Hepburn, Fay Bainter. Sports columnist and world affairs reporter marry, find careers in conflict.

I Was Framed. Warner Brothers. Directed by D. Ross Lederman. Screenplay by Robert E. Kent. Story by Jerome Odlum.* With Michael Ames, Julie Bishop, Regis Toomey. Crusading reporter breaks jail to nab crooked politicians.

They All Kissed the Bride. Columbia. Directed by Alexander Hall. Original story by Gina Claus and Andrew P. Salt. Produced by Edward Kaufman. With Joan Crawford, Roland Young, Billie Burke. Formidable businesswoman terrorizes employees and family until social-minded reporter humanizes her.

Berlin Correspondent. 20th/Fox. Directed by Eugene J. Forde. Original story by Steve Fisher and Jack Andrews. With Dana Andrews, Virginia Gilmore, Mona Maris. Hindsight helps story of international intrigue.

You Can't Escape Forever. Warner Brothers. Directed by Jo Graham. Story by Roy Chanslor.* Screenplay by Fred Niblo, Jr,* and Hector Chevigny. With George Brent, Brenda Marshall, Paul Garvey. Remake of *Hi, Nellie.*

Journey for Margaret. MGM. Directed by W. S. Van Dyke. Screenplay by David Hertz and William Ludwig. From a book by William Lindsay White. With Lorraine Day, Robert Young, Margaret O'Brien. War correspondent and wife flee France, adopt war orphan in England.

Keeper of the Flame. MGM. Directed by George Cukor. Screenplay by Donald Ogden Stewart, from novel by Ida Alexa Ross Wylie. With Spencer Tracy, Katharine Hepburn, Richard Whorf. Star reporter searches for true nature of dead hero; first suppresses story of hero's fascism, then prints all.

Roxie Hart. 20th/Fox. Directed by William A. Wellman. Screenplay by Nunally Johnson.* From a play by Maurine Watkins. With Ginger Rogers, George Montgomery, Adolphe Menjou. Fake murder arrest for publicity becomes serious when politics of electorate becomes involved.

Somewhere I'll Find You. MGM. Directed by Wesley Ruggles. Adapted by Walter Reisch from a story by Charles Hoffman. With Robert Sterling, Clark Gable, Lana Turner. Asian-correspondent brothers love same woman until one is killed reporting at Bataan.

The Lady Has Plans. Paramount. Directed by Sidney Lanfield. Screenplay by Harry Tugend. Story by Leo Nirinski. With Ray Milland, Paulette Goddard, Roland Young. Female correspondent in Lisbon is taken for a spy.

Once upon a Honeymoon. RKO. Directed by Leo McCarey. Original story by Sheridan Gibney* and Leo McCarey. With Cary Grant, Ginger Rogers, Walter Slezak. American reporter in Warsaw rescues American chorus girl married to Nazi villain.

1943

They Got Me Covered. United Artists. Directed by David Butter. Screenplay by Harry Kurnitz.* Story by Leonard Q. Ross* (pseud: Leo C. Rosten) and Leonard Spiegelgass. With Bob Hope, Dorothy Lamour, Otto Preminger. Disgraced correspondent called back to Washington, gets involved with spies (comedy).

Power of the Press. Columbia. Directed by Lew Landers. Screenplay by Robert D. Andrews. Story by Samuel Fuller.* With Lee Tracy, Otto Kruger, Guy Kibbee.

Johnny Come Lately. United Artists. Directed by William K. Howard. From a book by Louis Bromfield. Screenplay by John van Druten. With James Cagney, Gladys George, Marjorie Mann. Itinerant reporter helps old lady keep small-town crooks from doing in her one-woman paper.

What a Woman. Columbia. Directed by Irving Cummings. Original story by Eric Charell. Produced by Sidney Buchman. With Rosalind Russell, Brian Aherne. Magazine writer profiles author's agent; ends in matrimony.

1944

It Happened Tomorrow. United Artists. Directed by René Clair.* Screenplay by Dudley Nichols.* Original story by Hugh Wedlock, Howard Snyder, Lord Dunsany. With Dick Powell, Linda Darnell, Jack Oakie. 1900. Young reporter gets scoops by tracing facts from tomorrow's newspaper, delivered by ghost.

Laura. 20th/Fox. Directed by Otto Preminger. Screenplay by Jay Drather, Samuel Hoffenstein, and Betty Reinhardt. From a book by Vera Caspary.* With Clifton Webb, Vincent Price, Judith Anderson. Critic becomes interpreter of dead girl's life.

Lady in the Dark. Paramount. Directed by Mitchell Leisen. Screenplay by Frances Goodrich and Albert Hackett. From a play by Moss Hart, Kurt Weill, and Ira Gershwin. With Ginger Rogers, Ray Milland, Jon Hall. Fashion editor dreams of new, more feminine lives with interesting men.

Arsenic and Old Lace. Warner Brothers. Directed by Frank Capra. Screenplay by Julius J. and Philip G. Epstein. From a play by Joseph Kesselring. With Cary Grant, Raymond Massey, Jack Carson. Theater critic finds whole family is killed.

1945

Christmas in Connecticut. Warner Brothers. Directed by Peter Godfrey. Screenplay by Lionel Houser* and Adele Commandim. Story by Aileen Hamilton. With Barbara Stanwyck, Dennis Morgan, Sydney Greenstreet. Homemaking columnist assigned to entertain returning war hero, falls in love.

State Fair. 20th/Fox. Directed by Walter Lang. Screenplay by Oscar Hammerstein II. Adaptation by Sonya Levien,* Paul Green.* Story by Phil Strong.

With Dana Andrews, Jeanne Crain, Dick Haynes. Musical remake of 1933 version.

The Story of G.I. Joe. United Artists. Directed by William Wellman. Screenplay by Leopold Atalas, Guy Endore, Philip Stevenson. Based on the wartime journalism of Ernie Pyle.

Blood on the Sun. United Artists. Directed by Frank Lloyd. Screenplay by Lester Cole. Original story by Garrett Fort. Idea by Frank Melford. With James Cagney, Sylvia Sidney, Wallace Ford. Prewar correspondent in Tokyo foresees aggression; when ignored, he takes on militarists himself.

Crime, Inc. Producer's Releasing Company. Directed by Lew Landers. Screenplay by Roy Schrock. From a book by Martin Mooney* (assoc. prod: Mooney). With Tom Neal, Lionel Atwell, Leo Carillo. Reporter faces jail for refusing to divulge information but still gets crooks.

Eve Knew Her Apples. Columbia. Directed by Will Jason. Screenplay by E. Edwin Moran. Story by Rian James.* With Ann Miller, William Wright, Robert Williams. Remake of *It Happened One Night.*

Midnight Manhunt. Paramount. Directed by William Thomas. Screenplay by David Lang. Produced by William Pine* and William Thomas. With William Gargan, Ann Savage, Leo Gorcey.

1946

Deadline for Murder. 20th/Fox. Directed by James Tinling. Story and screenplay by Irvin Cummings, Jr. With Kent Taylor, Paul Kelley, Sheila Ryan. Woman reporter solves crimes.

The Searching Wind. Paramount. Directed by William Dieterie. Screenplay and play by Lillian Hellman. With Robert Young, Sylvia Sydney, Ann Richards. Sob sister warns of fascism, is dismissed by idealist diplomat who later regrets it.

Perilous Holiday. Columbia. Directed by Edward H. Griffith.* Screenplay by Roy Chanslor.* From a magazine serial by Robert Carson. With Pat O'-Brien, Ruth Warrick, Alan Hale. Reporter and playboy team up to catch crooks.

Easy to Wed. MGM. Directed by Edward Buzzell. Screenplay by Dorothy Kingsley. With Keenan Wynn, Lucille Ball, Van Johnson. Remake of *Libelled Lady.*

The Glass Alibi. Republic. Produced and directed by W. Lee Wilder. Screenplay by Minred Lord. With Paul Kelly, Douglas Fowley, Anne Gwynne. Reporter tries to commit perfect crime but is caught.

Her Kind of Man. Warner Brothers. Directed by Frederick de Cordova. Screenplay by Gordon Kahn,* Leopole Atlas. Original story by Charles Hoffman and James V. Kern. Produced by Alex Gottlieb.* With Dane Clark, Janis Page, Zachary Scott. Sleuthing Broadway columnist solves crime.

The Walls Came Tumbling Down. Columbia. Directed by Lothar Mendes. Screenplay by Wilfred H. Pettitt. From a book by Jo Eisinger. With Lee Bowman, Marguerite Chapman, Edgar Buchanan. Columnist investigates death of a priest.

1947

Magic Town. RKO. Directed by William Wellman. Screenplay by Robert Riskin.* Story by Robert Riskin and Joseph Krumgold. With James Stewart, Jane Wyman, and Kent Smith. Media exploits the "perfect" small town.

Gentlemen's Agreement. 20th/Fox. Directed by Elia Kazan. Screenplay by Moss Hart. From a book by Laura Z. Hobson. With Gregory Peck, Celeste Holm, Nicholas Joy. Reporter poses as Jew to find out about discrimination.

The Guilt of Janet Ames. Columbia. Directed by Charles Vidor. Original story by Lenore Coffee. With Melvyn Douglas. The reporter as lush.

The Corpse Came C.O.D. Columbia. From a book by Jimmy Starr.* With George Brent, Joan Blondell, Jim Bannon.

News Hounds. Monogram. Produced by Jan Grippo. Story by Edmond Sewards,* Tim Ryan, George Cappy.

1948

Call Northside 777. 20th/Fox. Directed by Henry Hathaway. Based on article by James P. McQuire.* With James Stewart, Richard Conte, Lee J. Cobb. True story. Reporter becomes convinced of innocence of man jailed eleven years.

The Luck of the Irish. 20th/Fox. Directed by Henry Koster. From a book by Guy Pearce Jones and Constance Bridges Jones. With Tyrone Power, Jayne Meadows, Ann Baxter. Reporter torn between boss's daughter and Irish colleen.

June Bride. Warner Brothers. Directed by Bretagne Windust. Screenplay by Ronald MacDougall. From a play by Eileen Tight and Graeme Lorimer. With Bette Davis, Robert Montgomery, Fay Bainter. Lady editor and dusty foreign correspondent disrupt marriage in small town while on assignment.

On Our Merry Way. United Artists. Directed by King Vidor and Leslie Fenton. Story by Arch Oboler and John O'Hara. With Burgess Meredith, Paulette Goddard, Fred MacMurray. Classified clerk wants to become reporter; episodes.

The Big Clock. Paramount. Written and directed by John Farrow. From a book by Kenneth Fearing. With Charles Laughton, George MacReady, Henry Morgan. Murder in world of publishing.

1949

Malaya. MGM. Directed by Richard Thorpe. Screenplay by Frank Fenton. Story by Manchester Boddy. With Spencer Tracy, James Stewart. Government taps correspondent to help smuggle rubber out of Malaya and past Japanese.

The House across the Street. Warner Brothers. Directed by Richard Bare. Screenplay by Russell Hughes. Story by Roy Chanslor.* With Wayne Morris, Janis Paige, Bruce Bennett. Reporter solves murder in remake of *Hi, Nellie.*

Chicago Deadline. Paramount. Directed by Lewis Allen. Screenplay by Warren Duff. From a book by Tiffany Thayer. With Alan Ladd, June Havoc, Donna Reed. Reporter solves crimes.

Abandoned. Universal. Directed by Joseph M. Newman. Story and screenplay by Irwin Gielgud. With Dennis O'Keefe, Gale Storm, Jeff Chandler. Reporter breaks baby-adoption racket.

That Wonderful Urge. 20th/Fox. Directed by Robert B. Sinclair. Screenplay by Jay Dratler. Story by William R. Lipman, Frederick Stepham. With Tyrone Power, Gene Tierney, Reginald Gardiner. Remake of *Love Is News.*

1950

All About Eve. 20th/Fox. Written and directed by Joseph Mankiewicz.* From a story and radio play by Mary Orr. With Bette Davis, Anne Baxter, George Sanders. Manipulative star-maker shows cold-blooded will in Broadway setting.

The Underworld Story. United Artists. Also known as *The Whipped.* Directed by Cyril Endfield. Screenplay by Henry Blankfort, from a novel by Craig Rice. With Dan Duryea, Herbert Marshall, Gale Storm. When publisher directs suspicion to innocent man to shield his son, reporter prints story.

Right Cross. MGM. Directed by John Sturges. Story and screenplay by Charles Schnee. With Ricardo Montalban, Dick Powell, June Allyson. Sportswriter loses girl to boxer in melodrama.

To Please a Lady. MGM. Directed by Clarence Brown. Story and screenplay by Barre Lyndon* and Marge Decker. With Barbara Stanwyck, Clark Gable. Sob columnist hounds racing-car driver out of career and then marries him.

Born Yesterday. Columbia. Directed by George Cukor. Screenplay by Albert Mannheimer, from a play by Garson Kanin. With William Holden, Judy Holliday, Broderick Crawford. Washington journalist exposes corrupt lobbyist.

1951

Fort Worth. Warner Brothers. Directed by Edwin L. Marin. Story and screenplay by John Twist. Produced by Anthony Veiller.* With Randolph Scott, Dick Jones, David Brian. Frontier newsman has to strap on his guns to clean up town. (.44 mightier than the pen!)

Come Fill the Cup. Warner Brothers. Directed by Gordon Douglas. Screenplay by Ivan Gaff* and Ben Roberts. From a book by Harian Ware. With James Cagney, Phyllis Thaxter, Raymond Massey. Reporter is reformed alcoholic helping publisher's nephew kick the bottle.

Here Comes the Groom. Paramount. Directed by Frank Capra. Screenplay by Robert Riskin.* With Bing Crosby, Jane Wyman, Franchot Tone. Roving reporter weds in order to adopt three French orphans.

The Big Carnival. Paramount. Also known as *Ace in the Hole.* Directed by
Billy Wilder. Story and screenplay by Billy Wilder, Lesser Samuels, Walter
Newman. With Kirk Douglas, Jan Sterling, Bob Arthur. Down-and-out
small-town reporter builds up mine tragedy seeking scoop to get back to
the big time.

Bannerline. MGM. Directed by Don Weis. Screenplay by Charles Schnee. From
a story by Sampson Raphelson.* With Keefe Braselle, Sally Forest, Lionel
Barrymore. Reporter cleans up town.

The Racket. RKO. Directed by John Cromwell. Screenplay by William Wister
Haines and W. R. Burnett. From a play by Bartlett Cormack. With Robert
Hutton, Robert Mitchum, Robert Ryan.

1952

Captive City. United Artists. Directed by Robert Wise. Screenplay by Joseph
and Karl Kamb. Story by Alvin M. Sosephy, Jr. With John Forsythe, Joan
Camden, Harold J. Kennedy. Editor trying to break rackets in small city is
terrorized and finds friends won't help; runs to Kefauver Committee. Appearance by Kefauver.

Assignment Paris. Paramount. Directed by Robert Parrish. Screenplay by William Bowers.* From a book by Paul Gallico. With Dana Andrews, Marta
Toren, George Sanders.

Deadline USA. 20th/Fox. Directed and written by Richard Brooks.* Story by
Richard Brooks. With Humphrey Bogart, Ethel Barrymore, Kim Hunter.
Crusading reporter breaks racket by deadline as paper is sold and makes
last edition.

Lone Star. MGM. Directed by Vincent Sherman. Screenplay by Howard Esta-
brook. Story by Borden Chase. With Clark Gable, Ava Gardner, Broderick
Crawford. Romance of a woman editor in the west.

Park Row. United Artists. Written, directed and produced by Samuel Fuller.*
With Gene Evans, Mary Welch, Bela Kovacs. The newspaper world and
reporting at the turn of the century (Fuller, *The Story of My Heart*).

The San Francisco Story. Warner Brothers. Directed by Robert Parrish.
Screenplay by D. D. Beauchamp. From a book by Richard Aldrich Sum-
mers. With Joel McCrea, Yvonne De Carlo, Sidney Blackmer. Local tycoon
joins newspaper and vigilantes to capture crook.

Scandal Sheet. Columbia. Directed by Phil Karlson. Screenplay by Ted Sherde-
man, Eugene Ling, and James Peo. From a book by Samuel Fuller.* With
Broderick Crawford, Donna Reed, John Derek. Editor and staff outwit cops
on murder.

The Sell-Out. MGM. Directed by Gerald Mayer. Screenplay by Charles Palmer.
Story by Matthew Rapf. With Walter Pidgeon, Everett Sloane, Cameron
Mitchell. Kefauver. Editor uses newspaper to root out police corruption in
his town.

The Turning Point. Paramount. Directed by William Dieterle. Screenplay by
Warren Duff. From a story by Horace McCoy. With William Holden, Edmond O'Brien, Tom Tully. Kefauver. Crusading reporter and public investigator team up to break rackets.

Washington Story. MGM. Directed by Robert Pirosh. Screenplay by Robert Pirosh. Produced by Dore Schary.* With Van Johnson, Patricia Neal, Louis Calhern.

1953

Never Let Me Go. MGM. Directed by Delmer Daves. Screenplay by Ronald Miller and George Fraeschel.* From a book by Roger Box (pseudonym: Paul Winterton). With Clark Gable, Gene Tierney, Bernard Miles. Moscow correspondent at war's end falls for ballerina, smuggles her past Iron Curtain.

It Happens Every Thursday. Universal. Directed by Joseph Pevney. Screenplay by Dane Lussier. From the autobiography of Jane S. McIlvane.* With John Forsythe, Loretta Young, Frank McHugh. Husband-and-wife team run small-town weekly.

Roman Holiday. Paramount. Directed by William Wyler. Screenplay by Hunter and John Dighton, from a story by Ian McLellan Hunter. With Gregory Peck, Audrey Hepburn, Eddie Albert. Reporter woos runaway princess.

Little Boy Lost. Paramount. Directed by George Seaton. Screenplay by George Seaton, from a book by Margharita Laski. With Bing Crosby, Claude Dauphin, Christian Fourcade. Wartime correspondent returns to France to seek illegitimate son he has never seen.

Francis Covers the Big Town. Universal. Directed by Arthur Lubin. Screenplay by Oscar Brodney. Story by Robert Arthur, based on a character by David Stern. With Donald O'Connor and Francis the talking mule. Mule passes along overheard scoops to cub reporter.

Hot News. Allied Artists. Directed by Edward Bernds. Story and screenplay by Charles R. Marion* and Elwood Ullman.* With Stanley Clements, Gloria Henry, Ted De Corsica.

1954

Playgirl. Universal. Directed by Joseph Pevney. Screenplay by Robert Blees. Story by Roy Buffum. With Shelly Winters, Barry Sullivan, Colleen Miller. Magazine publisher found dead; newspapers dig for story.

Carnival Story. RKO. Directed by Kurt Neumann. Screenplay by Kurt Neumann and Hans Jacoby. Story by Marcel Klauber and C. B. Williams. With Anne Baxter, Steve Cochrane, George Nader. Writer solves murder in carnival.

I Cover the Underworld. Republic. Directed by R. G. Springsteen. Screenplay by John K. Butler. With Ray Middleton, Sean McClory, Joanne Jordan.

Living It Up. Paramount. Directed by Norman Taurog. Screenplay by Jack Rose and Melville Shavelson, based on a Ben Hecht* story. Loose remake of *Nothing Sacred.*

1955

The Big Knife. United Artists. Directed by Robert Aldrich. Screenplay by James Poe.* From a play by Clifford Odets. With Jack Palance, Ida Lupino,

Shelly Winters. Tired Hollywood star hounded by studio head and bitchy columnist.

The Big Tip-Off. Allied Artists. Directed by Frank McDonald. Story and screenplay by Steve Fisher. With Richard Conte, Constance Smith, Bruce Bennett. Reporter breaks charity-fund racket and solves murder.

The Phoenix City Story. Allied Artists. Directed by Phil Karlson. Screenplay by Crane Wilbur and Dan Mainwaring. With John McIntyre, Richard Kiley, Kathryn Grant. Dramatization of true-story cleanup of Phoenix City, Alabama.

Love Is a Many-Splendored Thing. 20th/Fox. Directed by Henry King. Story by Han Suyin. With William Holden, Jennifer Jones. Correspondent in Hong Kong falls in love with Eurasian doctor.

Headline Hunters. Republic. Directed by William Witney. Story and screenplay by Frederic Louis Fox and John Butler. With Rod Cameron, Julie Bishop, Ben Cooper.

Texas Lady. RKO. Directed by Tim Whelan. Story and screenplay by Horace McCoy.* With Claudette Colbert, Barry Sullivan, Greg Walcott. Lady wins at poker, pays father's debts, and takes over inherited Texas newspaper.

1956

The Harder They Fall. Columbia. Directed by Mark Robson. Screenplay by Philip Yordan. Based on a novel by Budd Schulberg. With Humphrey Bogart, Rod Steiger, Mike Lane. Sportswriter exposes hoodlums in boxing game.

You Can't Run Away from It. Columbia. Directed by Dick Powell. From a story by Samuel Hopkins Adams. With Jack Lemmon, June Allyson. Remake of *It Happened One Night.*

High Society. MGM. Directed by William Beaudine. From a play by Philip Barry. With Frank Sinatra, Grace Kelly, Bing Crosby. Musical remake of *The Philadelphia Story.*

While the City Sleeps. RKO. Directed by Fritz Lang. Screenplay by Casey Robinson, from a novel by Charles Einstein. With Dana Andrews, Rhonda Fleming, Salley Forrest. Top reporters compete for editor's job by trying to solve series of brutal sex murders.

Over-Exposed. Columbia. Produced by Lewis J. Rachmil. Story by Richard Sale and Mary Loos. With Richard Crenna, Cleo Moore. Reporter-photographer on trail of vice ring turns in photos for a gun.

1957

Designing Woman. MGM. Directed by Vincente Minnelli. Story and screenplay by George Wells. Produced by Dore Schary.* With Gregory Peck, Lauren Bacall, Mickey Shaughnessy. Crusading sportswriter marries fashion designer, hides out from mobsters.

Slander. MGM. Directed by Roy Roland. Screenplay by Jerome Weidman, from a teleplay by Harry W. Junkin. With Fan Johnson, Steve Cochrane, Ann Blythe. Scandal publisher blackmails TV star over imperfect past.

Sweet Smell of Success. United Artists. Directed by Alexander Mackendrick. Screenplay by Ernest Lehman and Clifford Odets from a book by Ernest Lehman. With Burt Lancaster, Tony Curtis, Susan Harrison. Cynical Broadway columnist and weak press agent manipulate news.

The Great Man. Universal. Directed by José Ferrer. From a book by Al Morgan. With José Ferrer and Keenan Wynn. Radio journalist finds dead hero was a heel but can't broadcast story as advertisers want reputation intact.

1958

I Want to Live. United Artists. Directed by Robert Wise. Based on letters of Barbara Graham and newspaper articles of Ed Montgomery.* With Susan Hayward, Simon Oakland. Reporter builds public hysteria against woman accused of murder, then tries to prove her innocence but must watch helplessly as she is executed. True story.

Teacher's Pet. Paramount. Directed by George Seaton. Story and screenplay by Fay and Michael Kanin. With Clark Gable, Doris Day. Uneducated editor falls for pretty journalism teacher.

1959

The Angry Hills. MGM. Directed by Robert Aldrich. From a book by Leon Uris. With Robert Mitchum, Gia Scala, Stanley Baker. American correspondent in Greece during Nazi invasion.

—30—. Warner Brothers. Directed by Jack Webb. Screenplay by William Bowers.* With Jack Webb, William Conrad, David Nelson. A day in the life of a small-city newspaper as flood story breaks.

1962

State Fair. MGM. Directed by José Ferrer. With Pat Boone, Ann-Margaret, Bobby Darin. Second remake of 1933.

The Intruder. Pathe-America. Directed by Roger Corman. Screenplay by Charles Beaumont from his novel. With William Shatner, Frank Maxwell, Beverly Linsford. Southern editor tries to calm racial tensions caused by outsider bigots.

Madison Avenue. 20th/Fox. Directed by Bruce Humberstone. Screenplay by Norman Corwin from a book by Jeremy Kird. With Dana Andrews, Eleanor Parker, Jeanne Crain. Success seems assured until manipulated journalist blows the whistle on advertising-agency intrigue.

The Man Who Shot Liberty Valance. Paramount. Directed by John Ford. Screenplay by Willis Goldbeck and James Warner Bellah from a story by Dorothy M. Johnson. With James Stewart, John Wayne, Vera Miles. Reporter finds true story of old case.

1963

A New Kind of Love. Paramount. Directed by Melville Shavelson. Story and screenplay by Melville Shavelson. With Paul Newman, Joanne Woodward. Jaded columnist on vacation in Paris pursues fashion executive.

Critic's Choice. Warner Brothers. Directed by Don Weis. Screenplay by Jack Sher, from a play by Ira Levin. With Bob Hope, Lucille Ball, Marilyn Maxwell. Comedy. Critic debates whether ethics will let him review wife's play. Based loosly on Jean and Walter Kerr.

Please Don't Eat the Daisies. MGM. Directed by Charles Walters. From a book by Jean Kerr. With Doris Day, David Niven. Home life of theater critic, complicated by family capers.

Shock Corridor. Allied Artists. Directed by Samuel Fuller.* Screenplay by Samuel Fuller. With Peter Breck, Constance Towers, Gene Evans. Reporter poses as patient in mental hospital to solve murder, begins to lose own senses.

1964

Black Like Me. Continental Distributing. Directed by Carl Lerner. Screenplay by Gerda Lerner and Carl Lerner, from a book by John Howard Griffin.* With James Whitmore, Clifton James, Lenka Peterson. Story of white southern editor who lives as a black, based on true account by Griffin.

1965

Boeing Boeing. Paramount. Directed by John Rich. Screenplay by Edward Anhalt, from a play by Marc Camoletti. With Jerry Lewis, Tony Curtis. Comedy of rival foreign correspondents and their girlfriends in Paris.

Quick, Before It Melts. MGM. Directed by Delbert Mann. Screenplay by Dale Wasserman, from a novel by Philip Benjamin. With Robert Morse, George Maharis, Anjanette Comer. Two New York newsmen study Antarctica and cause international incident.

1966

The Ghost and Mr. Chicken. Universal. Directed by Alan Rafkin. Screenplay by Jim Fritzell and Everett Greenbaum. With Don Knotts, Joan Staley, Lion Redmons. Mystery comedy of shy reporter solving twenty-year-old crime to become hero.

1968

Strategy of Terror. Universal. Directed by Jack Smight. Screenplay by Robert L. Joseph. With Barbara Rush, Harry Townes, Hugh O'Brien. Detective and girl reporter stop plot to destroy UN headquarters.

Beware the Black Widow. Nadir Films. Directed by Larry Crane. Screenplay by Walter M. Berger. With Sharon Kent, Don Caulfield, Luke St. Clair. Editor and reporter solve mafia killings.

The Odd Couple. Paramount. Directed by Gene Saks. Screenplay by Neil Simon, from his play. With Jack Lemmon, Walter Matthau, John Fiedler. Neat TV newsman and sloppy divorced sportswriter make an unlikely couple. Also successful TV series.

1969

Gaily, Gaily. United Artists. Directed by Norman Jewison. Screenplay by Abram S. Ginnes, from a book by Ben Hecht.* With Beau Bridges, Melina Mercouri, Brian Keith. Based on Hecht's memories as a young reporter in Chicago, but the snap is out of the brim.

SELECTED RECENT FILMS

1972:
> *Young Winston.* With Simon Ward, Anne Bancroft, Robert Shaw. Covers Winston Churchill's stint as a correspondent during the Boer War.

1972:
> *I. F. Stone's Weekly.* Documentary by Jerry Bruck, Jr. Examines the life and style of an independent political journalist.

1974:
> *The Front Page.* Directed by Billy Wilder, with Jack Lemmon and Walter Matthau. The third direct screen version of Hecht and MacArthur's play, this time a long and cynical attempt to draw moral themes from what is essentially a firecracker comedy.

1976:
> *All the President's Men.* Directed by Alan Pakula, with Robert Redford and Dustin Hoffman. Based on reporting in the Washington *Post* during the Watergate scandal.

A NOTE ON TELEVISION

In the 1950s some television series used newsmen as leading characters: "Big Town" (1950) had Mark Stevens and Jane Nigh as crusading editor and aide solving crimes in a series that had been popular with Edward G. Robinson and Claire Trevor on radio; "I Cover Times Square" (1950) had Harold Huber in the role of a Broadway columnist; "Front Page Detective" (1951) featured Edmund Lowe as a crimebusting columnist; "Crime Photographer" (1952) was Darren McGavin; "Wire Service" (1956) saw George Brent and Dane Clark as roving crime solvers; "Big Story" (1956) with Ben Graver dramatized actual stories and saluted the reporters who broke them; the invincible *Hi, Nellie* theme turned up in "Dear Phoebe" (1954) where Peter Lawford became the comic lovelorn columnist. Some recent TV resurrections of the newspaper genre include "No. 19 Coronado Drive," a situation comedy with Fred MacMurray as a publisher (1974) that never got beyond the pilot stage; Darren McGavin returning in "The Night Stalker" (1974) as a reporter in the world of the supernatural; Gene Barry, Robert Stack, and Tony Franciosa rotating in the series "The Name of the Game," which started with a TV movie called *Fame Is the Name of the Game;* James Sutoris in "The Andros Targets," worldwide investigative crimebusting; and an interesting attempt to bring some real newsroom sympathy and issues to the forefront with Edward Asner in "Lou Grant."

MISCELLANY

Not recorded in the filmography is the series of Torchy Blane films made by Warner Brothers beginning with *Smart Blonde* in 1937. All have Glenda Farrell as a sharp-tongued reporter. Other series include *Torchy Gets Her Man, Torchy Runs for Mayor, Torchy Blane the Adventurous Blonde, Blondes at Work, Torchy Blane in Chinatown, Torchy Blane in Panama, Torchy Plays with Dynamite.*

A subgenre of films about newsboys existed in the 1920s and early 1930s; titles include *The Cowboy Cop, For His Sake, Her Mad Bargain, Hush Money, Idaho Red, Say It with Songs, Stepping Along.* Almost all have the newsboys being hit by a car or a truck while in the course of their work, with their injuries subsequently the motivation for hush money, blackmail, or reform of the traffic laws.

In the 1960s, a subgenre exists within the sexploitation film, where a favorite plot seems to have been the expose of a nudist colony by a reporter (sometimes later convinced of the healthful benefits of nudism), or a reporter exposing a ring of deviates—mostly all an excuse for exposed flesh, with titles like *Bachelor Tom Peeping, Candy Baby, Hawaiian Thigh, Nature Camp Confidential.*

12 MAIMONIDES MEETS THE COOKIE MONSTER

Robert Rutherford Smith

A friend and I were making small talk as we rode the subway home one wintry evening last year. "Are you writing anything?" he asked.

"Yes," I replied. "I'm doing a short piece on television aesthetics."

He paused and stared at a car poster, thinking about my response. Finally, he said, "I thought aesthetics in television were like snakes in Ireland."

I looked blank.

"There aren't any!"

His words recurred in my mind as I gathered materials to write about television and ethics. What would he have responded if I had mentioned this topic? Perhaps he would have accepted it as evidence of my sense of black humor. Most of us know, or vaguely feel, that ethics in television are like snakes in Ireland.

The reasons for our suspicions are numerous. Television is a variety of show business and heir to the glamour, casting-couch pragmatism and feudal-baron management of the Hollywood studios. We are told that television is rich, and most of us harbor a populist soul that is suspicious of the rich, the powerful, and the successful. Television managers and performers have inherited the suspicions our fathers harbored toward, in George Seldes's phrase, "the lords of the press."

This paper puts forth four hypotheses that attempt to explain why television is so often attacked on ethical grounds.

1. Television is managed by greedy or power-hungry people who do not manage in the public interest.
2. A new medium makes problems formulated in an older medium irrelevant. Ethical dilemmas are print problems, no longer of importance in the television age.

3. Ethical relativism is one of the characteristic phenomena of the age. Television executives and programs are simply acting out in public what many of us confront as private problems.
4. Advancing technology has provided both new problems and solutions to older ethical problems so fast that our ethical theorists have not kept pace.

Before we begin our critical assault upon the television industry, it may be useful to look into our notions of ethics. Not schooled in philosophy, I can claim the immunity from criticism of the archetypical philistine: I may not know much about ethics, but I know what's right. Or at least I think I do. Or, to be more precise, I think I know why questions of right and wrong are not meaningful questions. And that is a very serious assertion.

When we question—or condemn—the ethics portrayed on television, or the ethical conduct of television's mandarins, we are so stunned by the glittering wrongness of it all that we seldom stop to notice that few critics have any agreed-upon criteria for making ethical judgments.

THE ETHICS OF EVERYMAN

Of course, one may say that certain kinds of program content—misleading advertising, staged news events, and appeals to children to purchase over-the-counter drugs—are so obviously wrong that only fools could quibble. Fools or philosophers, perhaps. If a television newsman makes arrangements for a news conference, is it a staged event? If consumers discount advertisers' claims and enjoy the enhancement of product qualities they see on television commercials, is it misleading? We need to probe somewhat more deeply if we are to understand the ethical dilemmas that television both reports and exemplifies.

The major obstacle to such understanding is the impatience of critics. We *know* that certain kinds of behavior are wrong, or at least undesirable. Such knowledge is usually private, however, not shared. It is based upon traditional views of what should be done in selected, recurring situations. Daily, world over, men covet another man's wife and property—and they have done so for centuries. Petty theft was a problem in Carthage, dishonesty in Elizabethan London. Agreement upon such eternal problems does not, however, indicate an agreement upon ethical principles, codes, or sanctions. It does not even imply agreement about what constitutes an ethical problem.

We often assume that the ability to negotiate everyday life without getting arrested is evidence of a competence in ethical matters. This suggests that a prudent citizen need know no more about ethics than most swimmers know about hydraulic engineering.

If one of our problems is the assumption that everyday life provides adequate knowledge of ethical problems, a second is the assumption that ethical standards (codes, practices, laws, values) change little because of time and place. Many of us who profess to be agnostics nevertheless hold, in Alasdair MacIntyre's phrase, a "belief that moral concepts can be examined and understood apart from their history." There is a simple-minded version of this belief that assumes that certain codes—honor thy father, defend thy country—are universal. There is a more sophisticated version that suggests that specific formulations may vary widely from time to time and place to place, but that there are underlying structures of moral concern that have an astonishing permanence. For the purposes of this inquiry, I suggest that we temporarily take the position that no ethical precept, principle, or practice can be rightly understood except within the society in which it was used.

MacIntyre has made this point in a more precise way:

> There certainly are concepts which are unchanging over long periods, and which must be unchanging for one of two reasons. Either they are highly specialized concepts belonging within stable and continuing disciplines, such as geometry; or else they are highly general concepts necessary to any language of any complexity. I have in mind here the family of concepts expressed by such words as *and, or,* and *if.* But moral concepts do not fall into either of these two classes.[1]

If we accept this argument and agree that ethical concepts are culture-bound, we may nevertheless attempt to escape the consequences by turning to Rousseau.[2] Concepts, we may say, are part of a Lockian social contract, instruments constructed by canny work merchants to assure a degree of uniformity in conduct. Behind the concepts, however, is the natural man who traded away some advantages in order to secure peace and a measure of tranquility. Disturb the peace, and the natural man may reassert his prior claim to those virtues that preexisted all contracts: the right of self-determination, an aggressive, self-sufficient integrity, and a sense of self not dependent upon the effete life of the city. But is natural man an observable phenomenon or merely construct? Neither, suggests MacIntyre. "The factual point is . . . that natural man is merely a man from another and earlier culture."[3]

So let us suspend, for the moment, our notions of ethical certainty and continuity.

THE EIGHTEENTH-CENTURY SOLUTION

Ethical systems may be based on any one of three major assumptions: legalism, Antinomian gnosticism, or situational factors. In the Christian tradition, the criterion used in judgment of rights or wrongs, successes or failures, is love. To know whether an act is based upon love, greed, ambition, or lust requires knowledge of the subjective state of the person whose behavior is being judged. The difficulty—until the late nineteenth century one might have said the impossibility—of attaining such knowledge led to the development of codes that were substituted for the ultimate test of love. The Ten Commandments is one example, the Hippocratic Oath another.

Thus, the very difficult criterion of love was defined legalistically. Joseph Fletcher has argued that this legalistic tradition in ethics has two dimensions: the biblical tradition which depends upon revelation for authority, and the rational tradition which has historically related to the concept of natural law.[4] If one assumes that society is essentially contractual, the development of a series of codes, regulations, tests, and sanctions may be logically developed. Americans have drawn from this tradition.

The American preference for codes concerning ethical and political matters is rooted in the birth of our nation. Historian Bernard Bailyn, in his admirable biography of colonial leader Thomas Hutchinson, has noted that the lack of a firm English constitution was a handicap to pre-Revolutionary American reformers. "The right to defy Parliament's acts is denied in terms of the nature of constitutions as such . . . in terms of the relation between law and morality; and in terms of what might be called an historicist understanding of public life as a process." He continues:

> So Hutchinson concluded perhaps the central argument of the Dialogue by pointing out that there was no organ of government capable of declaring actions of the government unconstitutional, nor could there ever be such an umpiring agency since the constitution was not fixed, written, or other-available for unequivocal and objective reference. He was right: if the opposition continued to press claims of unconstitutionality against particular actions of the [English] government they would indeed be led . . . to think of constitutions as objective, fixed, ultimately written documents; and they would be led to

conceive of organs of government specifically empowered to rule on
the constitutionality of the government's actions.[5]

In that short paragraph are the seeds of all one need know to grasp the
drift of American thought on issues of public morality. In the field of
mass communication, in the years before the Second World War, this
American preference for legalism in morality led to the formulation of
specific codes. Of primary importance to us is the development of the
Code of the National Association of Broadcasters (NAB). Developed
originally in 1929 and periodically modified since, the code was en-
forced by a committee of broadcasters. The committee on code compliance originally had the authority to drum nonconforming broadcasters
out of the organization. This was rejected by the courts as restraint of
trade, however, and the NAB code is now voluntary. It stands as exhibit
number one in the legalistic mode.

THE SHORTCOMINGS OF LEGALISM

Codes, if they are to endure, must be cast in general terms applicable to a variety of unforeseen future events. This essential ambiguity
in legalistic ethical formulations not only gives them endurance; it also
provides loopholes for those interested in conforming only to the letter
of the law.

Dissatisfaction with legalistic ethical formulations in America has
usually taken the form of a concern with effectiveness. They don't work
in specific cases, and they work best when they are needed least. A
resort to a more general test has often been urged, in much the way that
Christians are urged by charismatic evangelists to return to the test of
love.

"Love" is, of course, a rather personal term to apply to broadcasters
or publishers. The term that has been popularized in this country is
"social responsibility." Businessmen, bureaucrats, doctors, lawyers, and
broadcasters, we say, have a social responsibility to serve in the public
interest. This responsibility is an attempt to formulate love: it is a
general, all-encompassing responsibility that should inform all the decisions a manager makes.

The attempt to go beyond simple legalistic codes to the expression
of *agapé* in administrative actions occurred in the United States in the
years shortly after World War II. For businessmen it took the form of
a concern with acting responsibly within the profit framework; for
critics, it took the form of relating specific problems (violence in the
media, misleading advertising) to a general standard.

This concept of social responsibility has been increasingly legalized in the United States. Public-interest law firms bring actions for injured citizens; federal commissions attempt to regulate in the public interest; increasingly detailed regulations are developed. For instance, a broadcaster must deal with regulations relating to the number of commercial minutes he may broadcast in each hour; the number of female and minority employees in his station; the safety of devices used in his station; the time devoted to various program forms; the method by which community needs are ascertained; the time given to political candidates; efforts made to present all sides fairly when controversial issues are dealt with in programming; the adequacy and fairness of compensation; and many more.

The movement toward what Daniel Bell has termed the "sociologizing mode," which began with a general formulation of responsibility, has become a quagmire of codes and code-compliance committees in the private sector, and a labyrinth of regulations, reports, and administrative proceedings in the public sector.[6] The American genius, though informed by occasional flashes of revelation and a concern with *agapé,* remains a genius at the formulation of codes, rules, regulations, standards, directives, open letters, hearings, decisions, opinions, appeals, complaints, and executive orders. Ethical standards, for Americans, mean codes. We are a legalistic people, from seventeenth-century Puritans to eighteenth-century patriots to twentieth-century professionals. For us, ethics are manifested in *agapé* or revelation less than in the written word.

THE PHENOMENOLOGICAL REFORM

Other nations have found different ways to express their ethical concerns. The Chinese have used the spoken word and enigmatic precept; the Greeks, dialogue and oratory; American Indians, the test of skill in hunting or surviving unaided in the wilderness. Western Europeans, never as committed to the written code as Americans, responded to the events that preceded and followed World War II with a unique formulation of ethical concerns. It is, at bottom, a method rather than an ethical formulation. It is a method that has informed much of the moral discourse of Americans during the past three decades.

Prewar Germany provided a fertile garden for the analysis of ethical concerns. The German preeminence in science, the widespread interest in and distrust of the writings of Freud, the attempt to systematize subjective experience, the failure of the republic, economic problems, and the rise of fascism provided the philosopher with a library of immediate, vital, and inescapable ethical problems. This occurred against a background of an increasing distrust of formulations. "The past one hundred years," philosopher Richard Zaner has written, "but especially the past few decades, have witnessed a fundamental *relativization of perspectives.*"[7]

In Germany, Edmund Husserl attempted an exploration of consciousness much as the explorers of the sixteenth and seventeenth centuries approached the West. From the time of Descartes, philosophers had been concerned with subjectivity. Husserl attempted to develop a philosophic method for the exploration of consciousness.[8] As Carl Jung had attempted to systematize the contents of the unconscious by formulating a system of underlying symbols, myths, and significant figures, Husserl attempted to verify the subjective experience of individuals by cross-checking. Zaner provides as good a one-paragraph overview as any:

> With that began what Husserl always regarded as an urgent necessity—*the forming of a genuinely communal undertaking, a "science" in the highest, or most fundamental, sense,* with each person confirming or disconfirming the results of others' work, probing further and returning to report and share the findings with one another . . . thus building up a common, intersubjectively grounded fund of knowledge.[9] [Emphasis added]

Those who worked with Husserl—Heidegger, Marvin Farber, and a host of others—developed this "method" in quite different ways. The French philosopher Maurice Merleau-Ponty moved on from Husserl's concept of the logical *époche* (the questioning and suspension of assumptions until only fundamental experiences remained) to form an elaborate theory of perception.[10] He, Karl Jaspers, and others, working in the complex moral and political climate of postwar France, attempted to develop a theory of ethics responsive to experience rather than to codes. Perhaps the best know among them is the French journalist and novelist Albert Camus. His novel *The Stranger* is a key expression of this outlook.

A different group, exemplified if not led by Jean-Paul Sartre, moved from the concern with consciousness as a tool for analyzing ethical dilemmas to consciousness as evidence of the overwhelming, irrational, inexorable, and ultimately unsolvable character of ethical problems. Sartre is in the Antinomian tradition, a sensitive, knowing, and suffering extemporizer. This second line of development, although popularized in America as *existentialism,* had little impact on the conduct of our instruments of mass communication. The "beat generation" of the 1950s, alienated by war and a lost youth, supported for a time by GI Bill college benefits, may have been the dominant New World expression of this concern. Allen Ginsberg's poem *Howl* can be read alongside Sartre's novel *La Nausee.*

Although "existentialism" was popular on campuses, the first line of development of Husserl's thought, the use of consciousness for exploration, had a different and more fundamental impact on the ethical perceptions of code-burdened Americans.

SITUATION ETHICS: THE THIRD WORLD OF MORALITY

Earlier we noted that ethical concerns are typically expressed in one of three ways: the legalistic, as in codes, constitutions, and charters; the Antinomian, as in the gnostics, Gilbert and Sullivan operettas, and certain aspects of fascism and existentialism; and the situational.

Although the American Puritan heritage finds expression in restrictive codes, a second thread of thought in American intellectual life has traditionally been at odds with this tendency. Seventy years ago the philosopher John Dewey attempted to formulate a theory of ethics based upon his evolving philosophy of pragmatism.[11] Dewey argued that the separation of moral ends from practical means was a false dichotomy. Knowledge is related to purposes and is useful only if we relate to those purposes. Virtue or the Good, as abstract goals, have no place in Dewey's unified concept of ethics, with knowledge and action as an expression of the perhaps overemphasized American concern with immediate results. In the absence of a class that might be virtuous while removed from everyday pursuits, American intellectual life has been more directly concerned with, in the terms of pragmatism, "what works" or, in the terms of the Babbitts of the New World, "how to."

This concern with getting things done provided an appropriate setting for the imported concerns with the impact of consciousness and experience on ethical decisions. The two influences were joined in a brilliant presentation of "the New Morality" by Joseph Fletcher.[12] Fletcher admitted that his work could be called no system at all, that it could be personalistic, that it was excessively dependent upon the context of ethical problems, that the dependence upon the subjective evaluation of the person making the decision made it difficult to evaluate, and that it did not necessarily link with traditional morality.

Not all critics were unkind, however. William Robert Miller wrote that "what makes theirs [the situationists] a 'new morality' rather than a 'no morality' is that they are looking for basic criteria by which to guide conduct in the light of some ultimate purpose rather than leaving moral choice to the mercy of whim and caprice."[13]

James Gustafson noted that what made Fletcher's formulation appear radical is his "passionate . . . distress at any sign of legalism, actual or potential."[14] Despite this approval of Fletcher's attempt to invest ethical decisions with Christian love, Gustafson noted, "He wants to simplify and complicate at once, while generally professing to simplify."

Fletcher insisted that an ethical person has "the ethical maxims" of his community in mind and is thus not removed from the Christian tradition. They are, he argued, "principles, not rules," and would inform ethical decisions without predetermining them. Fletcher insisted upon his rejection of codes. "Justice," he wrote, "is love coping with situations where distribution is called for." "Love and Justice," he wrote "are the same."

Fletcher admitted, "This book is consciously inspired by American pragmatism."[15] He did not mention that it was also inspired by phenomonology. Fletcher's heroes (a cabbie who votes straight-ticket Republican except when a better Democrat is running because "there are times when a man has to push his principles aside and do the right thing"; the father in *The Rainmaker* who stops his son from shooting the rainmaker who seduced his alienated daughter, saying, "You're so full of what's right you can't see what's good") are heroes in the existential mode.

TELEVISION: TWENTY-ONE-INCH MORALITY

This new morality influenced television in two ways: in the executive suites and on the screen. The first awareness of an ethical crisis was felt among the managers; the way in which the crisis ocurred provided America with one of its best-publicized events of the late Eisenhower years.

The television industry is a difficult one for executives. Competitive pressures are intense, rewards are great, successes are widely heralded, and failures are publicly noted and instantly rewarded. In such an industry, it is not surprising that tough choices must occasionally be made. Fletcher praises those men who make them:

When T. E. Lawrence led his Arab forces against the Turks, he had to make moral choices, being a responsible decision maker. Hamed the Moor killed Salem in a personal quarrel while they were camped in the Wadi Kitan, even though Lawrence tried to stop it. He knew that Salem's people would exact "justice" by revenge, starting an endless feud and bloodletting. How should he calculate? He himself killed Hamed, to end it. Here is a real problem love faced. Bonhoeffer made the same kind of choice when he became a partner in the plot to kill Hitler. On a vast scale of "agapeic calculus" President Truman made his decision about the A-bombs on Hiroshima and Nagasaki.[16]

This is heady stuff. The rules and traditions of our culture are available as principles to guide us, but the free man, the mature man, moves in a series of situations and makes decisions as best he can.

The television executives of postwar America were faced on a daily basis with complex decisions. They heard, if they talked with intellectuals, or read, if they had the time, or felt, that the old rules (legalisms) were inadequate. It is unsurprising that not all of them had the moral clarity of Lawrence, Bonhoeffer, or Truman.

The profit-centered broadcasting business has attracted moral criticism since its beginnings. Perhaps no one expressed it more succinctly than wartime Federal Communications Commission Chairman James Lawrence Fly who said that radio was "like a mackerel in the moonlight" because "it both stinks and shines."[17]

In the late 1950s numerous game shows (the best known and most popular was "$64,000 Question") attracted large audiences. These shows came to be the battle ground on which the three networks contended for their largest audiences. With network revenues and prestige at stake, numerous executives were faced with the problem of how to ensure that the programs were attractive to large numbers of viewers. The solution, in many cases, was to rehearse the contestants, rig the questions, or otherwise manipulate what appeared to be a test of knowledge or skill.

The revelation of this breach of the unwritten rules (the NAB code did not deal with misleading entertainment programs) resulted in a prosecution in New York and congressional hearing. The persons who apparently cooperated in the numerous hoaxes in many instances were men of stature in the industry. Had greed and concerns for their jobs swayed their ethical judgment, or were they practicing a caricature of the new morality?

None of the participants in the hearings explained the ethical basis for their behavior, but sixteen years later, William Colby, former director of the Central Intelligence Agency, answered for them. Asked why he had not given full and accurate responses to a Senate committee looking into the agency's activities, he said, "I was finding my way through a very difficult situation." His use of the word *situation* can only evoke a pang of dismay from one who remembers Fletcher's attempt to create a situation-based ethical methodology.

Some four years after the quiz scandals, television entertainment programming consciously explored the moral complexity of the age. On the screen, "Run for Your Life" described a man with a year to live who ran from home, friends, commitments, and comforts in a series of weekly adventures. In each, he gave meaning to the life of someone who faced an apparently insurmountable problem; in most, he was tempted by and resisted an attractive young woman. The series came as close as any prime-time entertainment to explaining and exploring an ethical position.

A second series popular in the mid-1960s, "Route 66," also used situation ethics, although somewhat less consistently. The series, a picaresque story of two young men in a Corvette driving across the country on the famous road, romanticized the problems of the outsider called upon to exercise moral flexibility in order to sovle the problems of others.

Television programming has moved on to other concerns, but the ethical complexity of our time is reflected in soap operas (adultery, homosexuality, and perjury *in their context* are frequently forgivable), and in the medical programs in which doctors are torn between professional standards (legalisms) and ethical concerns about people (situationalism).

"The Defenders" was one of the first lawyer programs to portray the law (legalisms) as at odds with justice (situationalism), although the father-son team usually managed to reconcile the two. Somewhat heavily formated, the program was a step toward moral complexity from the pat "Perry Mason" in which seeming ethical dilemmas were resolved by simple acts of clarification. "Barney Miller" is perhaps the best current example of the situation-determined hero, although a number of detective programs have made use of alienated and ethically flexible heroes.*

Most recently, the programs designed and produced by Norman Lear—"All in the Family" and "Mary Hartman, Mary Hartman"—have demonstrated an awareness of the comic possibilities of ethical problems.

---

*Readers of Dashiell Hammett's *Continental Op,* (N.Y.: Random House, 1974) published and widely heralded in the mid-1930s, will note that television did not discover the dramatic potential of situation ethics. Many of the characteristics were anticipated by Hammett.

In short, ethical problems are as pressing for us as they have been for past civilizations. The relativization of values, however, is a distinctive characteristic of modern life. Perhaps this process causes television critics to see in the medium lost opportunities for revolution or stability, failure to serve either the masses or traditional culture, and ethical ambiguity.

FOUR POSSIBLE EXPLANATIONS

Let's examine four common assumptions concerning television to see if they are consistent with what we know about the medium.

1. *Television is managed by greedy, power-hungry people who do not work in the public interest.* If one reads, for instance, Robert Metz's *CBS: Reflections in a Bloodshot Eye,* one finds this statement plausible. Metz describes William Paley, the CBS chairman, as "bon vivant; seeker after the richest personal experiences the world has to offer; sometime lover; husband to one of the world's most-admired women; a gourmet...." He notes that Paley, "occasionally a ruthless man," has left a trail of mediocre programs behind him: "A man of exquisite personal tastes, he has nevertheless set the tone for what Newton Minow of the FCC called 'a vast wasteland.' His influence has at times been so pervasive that he has more or less dictated even what the other networks would present."[18] Throughout the book, Metz is unable to arrive at a clear judgment of Paley. Too saintly to be a devil, too flawed to be an angel, Paley bothers Metz because of his complexity.

Television has had its good guys, of course. Sylvester (Pat) Weaver, the NBC president who supervised the creation of the magazine-format "Tonight" and "Today" shows, has often been praised for his creative contributions to the early days of television. Fred Friendly, former president of CBS News, resigned to protest interference with his judgment on the importance of television coverage of a congressional hearing. Martin Mayer, in a book largely critical of the managers of the networks, noted that the first of the "new" and realistic situation comedies, "All in the Family," would not have received network exposure if CBS President Robert Wood had not taken risks to get it.

> "All in the Family" was made as a pilot for ABC, and rejected by that network. CBS research looked at the pilot and didn't think much of its chances, but when network president Robert Wood decided he *had* to have it (it was one of relatively few times in recent history at CBS that an individual put his neck on the line for a show) [others] told

him to clean up a scene in the pilot, and to recast the roles of the daughter and son-in-law.[19]

Even Wood's act of generosity is cast in a context of compromises.

Is television alone in having a management style largely dependent upon group judgments, cautious imitation of each other's products, and a concern for audiences and profits? If we look at banking, we find a similar ambiguity about what constitutes desirable behavior. After Bert Lance, President Carter's friend and budget manager, stepped down because of reports of actions that were, perhaps, unethical, the New York *Times* looked into banking practices. A. A. Milligan, president-elect of the American Bankers Association, was quoted as saying, "There are 14,000 banks and a quarter of a million bank officers in this country, and I will stack up their ethical practices against those followed by any other industry in the United States any day of the week." The *Times* investigator came to a different conclusion, however: "Mr. Lance was far less extraordinary than the public was asked to believe, and ... the United States banking industry does not in fact have a uniform national standard of banking ethics ... banking practices and regulation vary dramatically over the country."[20] The article went on to note that Lance's practices were most common in the South.

The point is that one of our most "prudent" industries lacks clear ethical standards. Television may be more commonly discussed, but the problems of its executives may not be unique.

But does it really matter? The "good guys" (Wood and Weaver) dealt with specific programs in opposition to the judgments of their peers. Is this characteristic of television's leadership? Is it characteristic of even these men in the conduct of their daily lives? Or have critics selected unique events for praise?

Joseph R. Dominick and Millard C. Pearce of the University of Georgia published a study of "Trends in Network Programming, 1953–74." They attempted to describe the direction of changes in network programming and to relate changes to a number of variables. They found that "they seem to highlight the fact that, at least as far as prime-time TV is concerned, the organizations that are leaders ... are economic creatures and respond in line with classical economic theory.... In other words, the symbolic structure has become more redundant and audiences have been presented with fewer and fewer alternatives."[21]

One of the variables they considered was the impact of key executives. After identifying the years during which certain individuals had program responsibilities, Dominick and Pearce note: "We found little relationship between programming characteristics and the tenure of these individuals. In sum, neither external pressure on the industry nor the presence of a particular executive was associated with content trends."

New York *Times* critic Les Brown has written, "The American broadcaster is one part conscience and nine parts profit motive. The better ones may be three parts conscience. Even so, it is a sorry ratio for media with such power and penetration in a society."[22] Is this a fair evaluation? The anecdotal information suggests that it is not. Broadcasters appear to be as mixed in their values as any other group. Even if Brown's evaluation were correct, the Dominick particle suggests that it makes little, if any, difference to the viewer.

2. *A new medium makes problems formulated in an older medium irrelevant.* There is a widespread feeling that television has changed our society. Writing about politics (a field containing numerous complex ethical issues because of the invisible line between private interests and the public interest), Joe McGinnis claimed:

> With the coming of television, and the knowledge of how it could be used to seduce voters, the old political values disappeared. Something new, murky, undefined started to rise from the mists. . . .
> Americans have never quite digested television. The mystique which should fade grows stronger. We make celebrities not only of the men who read reports of them aloud.[23]

The concept of the importance of the medium is relatively new. Canadian economic historian Harold Innis was the first to point out that we overemphasize content at the expense of the medium.[24] Another Canadian, Marshall McLuhan, developed and popularized concern with the importance of the medium in a number of publications, the most widely read being *Understanding Media: The Extensions of Man.*[25]

McLuhan's catch phrase, "the medium is the message," became the rallying cry of numerous "media freaks" in the late 1960s. Essentially an aesthetician of form, McLuhan had little impact on social science-oriented communication theory. He had widespread influence on the popular understanding of communication, however, and, as with existentialism, his writings benefited from their anti-Establishment character. His message that each medium favors certain content was widely discussed.

The Lincoln-Douglas debates occurred at a time when the public debate was the dominant medium for political discourse. A forensic style, however, was inappropriate for the evangelistic first three decades of this century when oratory flourished. That was the time of the inspirational, healing, transcendental style.

A forensic style, appropriate to the 1860s, would have been quite ineffective for the 1960s when "cool," "charismatic," "mystique," "image" were the buzz words used by social critics. If the telegraph made crusading frontier editors more honest by bringing outside accounts of events to their readers, if the telephone speeded up the pace of events, if the radio provided a unique opportunity to gifted orators (Huey Long, Father Coughlin, Roosevelt, Churchill, Hitler), it is obvious that television favored some kinds of communicator characteristics above others. McLuhan pointed to the cool, the uninvolved, the inarticulate, the corporate as the dominant style.

For this reason theorists have feared that television favored candidates who were not so eloquent and persuasive as those who had flourished on the rostrum, or so authoritative as those who used radio. Rhetoricians refer to the character of the speaker, and his perceived values and style, as his "ethical appeal." Television favored candidates with a style different from the earlier ethical appeals of the public speaker. If we do not do violence to the terms, television candidates were unethical because the medium did not favor those who manifested traditional ethical appeals.

We may frame these fears in the context of our earlier discussion by suggesting that the earlier styles came to seem "natural" to us. Natural man, MacIntyre suggested, was merely a man from an earlier culture. In this sense, the ethical politician was simply a man from the age of oratory.

Print, McLuhan has argued, favors privacy, the development of an individual point of view, and linear argumentation.[26] Television favors shared experience, intuitive judgments, involvement with the persona of the performer rather than with his argument. In this sense, television is likely to affect how we formulate ethical problems.

The concern with ethical behavior that manifested itself in the Watergate hearings and the popularity of the film *All the President's Men* suggest that honesty, fairness, and convincing ethical appeals are still relevant. The temporary hero status awarded Robert Woodward and Carl Bernstein, the Washington *Post* reporters who unearthed the Watergate scandal, suggests that the public has a taste for morality plays with avenging angels as the protagonists. And the popularity of Senator Sam Ervin during the congressional hearings suggests that the older ethical appeals still have a firm grip on the hearts, if not the minds, of many of us. The new medium may have changed our ethical formulations, but the widespread attention given to the slick, the cool, the electronic and the participatory also produced a backlash of nineteenth-century, Bible-based moral simplicity. The successful presidential campaign of Jimmy Carter suggests that the homily, the "good man," and the slick appeal to common decency have not lost their sway.

3. *Ethical relativism is one of the characteristic phenomena of the age.* Television executives are simply acting out in their behavior, and in the programs they produce, the ethical ambiguity of our time.

Given the historical background sketched earlier in this paper, the assertion of ethical relativism as a characteristic of the age seems a platitude.

The implications of the statement may be worth noting, however. There is a tradition in American life, perhaps we may dub it the Lincoln-Wilson-Dulles-Carter tradition, of translating problems of power, of economics, of safety into ethical terms. This tendency to moralize— that is, to make something else into a moral issue—was given added impetus by the Vietnam war. Lyndon Johnson's defense of the war in moral terms led activists in the peace movement to react with comparable rhetoric. The war was, for many, primarily an ethical issue. But the moralizing habit of mind casts other issues in moral terms.

One of the most interesting is the issue of television violence. The investigation by the surgeon general's committee produced a verdict that television may cause violence for some persons some times. This was too hesitant to justify a public policy (abrogating the First Amendment) that might curtail violent program content.[27] The finding did not end the debate, however, nor soften the virulence of critics. Why? There are two possible answers, both related to our thesis.

First, as English critic Raymond Williams has noted, we Americans are profoundly ambivalent about violence.[28] We sanction extremes of violence when it seems justified by foreign policy or the suppression of views with which we disagree. Yet we dislike, even disavow violence at other times. The problem is not that executives make ethically undesirable decisions, but rather that television is serving as an agent for the expression of our deep-seated ambivalence; "Mannix," "SWAT," and "Kojak" are a symptom, not a cause, of our violent society.

There is an alternative explanation. The concern about television violence has been expressed primarily by upper-middle-class professionals. They live in low-crime areas, for the most part, and are concerned about their children. As one expression of their concern, they and their children watch less TV than their counterparts in lower socioeconomic neighborhoods. The lower socioeconomic groups not only watch more; they live in more violent neighborhoods. Thus television is reflecting somewhat more accurately the life experience of its biggest viewers than of its upper-income critics.[29]

We hesitate to admit that social class is a problem in this country. Concerned parents frequently speak as though they speak for all parents, whereas they may be in reality a minority. To mask these differences, we translate a difference of social class into a moral issue.

We are not ambivalent about violence alone. We live in a period of experimentation in sexual behavior, in a time when our commitment to the First Amendment is at odds with the porno bookshops in the Times Squares of many cities, when reporters are challenged to rationalize their relationships to government (particularly the CIA), and corporations find themselves in a bind between traditional behavior and new public expectations. Television may not be used to clarify or express the relativization of ethics, but the medium is a prime example of our ambivalence. Ambivalence is, perhaps, one of the early way stations on the road to ethical relativity.

4. *Advancing technology has provided both new problems and new solutions to older ethical problems so fast that our ethical theorists have not kept pace.* The difficulty of "keeping up with the times" is one of the homilies of American life. We emphasize the newness of the new; we denigrate the oldness of the old. If change causes stress, we relish that stress as an indication of our ability to be "with it." In perhaps no other way are we so unlike our European ancestors.

It is plausible to argue that ethical problems increase in number and subtlety faster than our ability to solve them. We may call this principle the "weed-patch formulation" of ethical problems in the twentieth century. This terminology seems particularly apt for our age because the traditional gardeners—churches, the patriarchal family, the hierarchical society, and other institutions that used to regulate ethical behavior—have been under attack for nearly a century. Royalists may argue that one of the essential guardians of ethical conduct, the landed gentry and the royalty to whom they gave service, have been under attack for several centuries. One cannot look to churches, kings, or even local social leaders for guidance—they are having difficulties themselves.

How does this relate to mass communication? Let us look at cable television. When the "new medium" was first introduced on a large scale during the 1960s, local franchises (monopolies) were awarded by local governments. The corporations, hoping to dominate the cable industry, purchased franchises at high prices and often gave consideration to local officials. When one industry leader was convicted of bribery, the defense argued that the sophisticated corporate officers, of impeccable judgment and equipped with expensive counsel, were hopeless when dealing with avaricious local politicians. Was this the case?

Or were naive local leaders flattered, cajoled, and bribed by business-men? Where does one look for guidance in such situations? To refuse to bribe, or be bribed, may mean loss of a contract or valued office; to participate in bribery places one in a vulnerable position, subject to public prosecution and private blackmail. In cable television, the tech-nological weeds outpaced the gardeners by several years.

The engine of this change, we often say, is technology. Our least speculative citizens seem as committed to technological determinism as is Marshall McLuhan. If the medium is the message, the "new media" are themselves creatures of an inexorably advancing technol-ogy.

Technology has influenced communications. "Objectivity" as a journalistic ethic emerged only after the telegraph made it possible to cross-check sources and verify information. The emphasis on localism in broadcasting occurred only after the superheterdyne receiver was developed, making possible the occupation of the spectrum by more stations than could have been separated by the older regenerative re-ceivers. Television has emphasized the character of people as revealed in close-up camera shots. Technology does make a difference. But does it *cause* ethical problems or *create* ethical solutions?

"If we are to begin to approach any real study of effects," writes Raymond Williams, "we shall have to return to a scientific consider-ation of causes."[30] Before we blame television for our problems, we must consider why our society chose to use it as it is used.

WHO'S TO BLAME?

Professor Rose K. Goldsen has argued that television has a heavy responsibility for our rising divorce rate and our failure to promote nurturing, close-knit families.[31] Although the evidence she offers fails to support her claim, it is a comforting one to hear. We know who to blame, and we prefer to blame rather than assume that program con-tent and media effects are the result of a labyrinthine social-technologi-cal interaction that cannot be easily grasped.

The scapegoat excuses us too easily from our job as critics, how-ever. Television does appear to be becoming increasingly similar from nation to nation, culture to culture. England now has commercial tele-vision; we now have a public system. I have watched Mary Tyler Moore in an Iranian village. Why do countries with differing social systems, controls, and traditions appear to be moving toward a uni-formity of content?

Perhaps television has encouraged a habit of mind among its controllers and its viewers. Perhaps the practice of television encourages certain values. Jacob Brownowsky has written: "The values of science derive neither from the virtues of its members, nor from the finger-wagging codes of conduct by which every profession reminds itself to be good. They have grown out of the practice of science, because they are the inescapable conditions for its practice."[32]

Perhaps there is something *in the practice* of television that has created a professional staff and an audience who share an unspoken, prelegalistic understanding of the practices of the medium.

Our problem is to relate that practice to our Western tradition. Maimonides, in his *Guide to Wanderers,* attempted to reconcile Aristotelian methodology with Jewish theology. For his efforts, the Jews called him a heretic, and Christian ecclesiastical authorities were invoked against him.

Marshall McLuhan attempted to write a guide for media wanderers, but his efforts appear to have increased perplexity rather than clarity, partly because he emphasized the radical discontinuity in modes of perception resulting from the new media. Perhaps it is time to follow Maimonides' example and look for continuities rather than discontinuities, reconciliation rather than alienation. In the field of ethics, what is most surprising is the continuity of our concerns despite the changes in the media through which they are expressed. If Maimonides confronted the selfish, sentimental Cookie Monster of "Sesame Street," he might be able to reconcile the illusion of radical change with our continued interest in traditional ethical problems.

NOTES

1. Alasdair MacIntyre, *A Short History of Ethics* (New York: Macmillan, 1966), p. 1.

2. Bertrand Russell has defined ethics by purpose rather than content. The purposes, he said, were twofold: "First, to find a criterion by which to distinguish good and bad desires; second, by means of praise and blame, to promote good desires and discourage such as are bad." *A History of Western Philosophy* (New York: Simon and Schuster, 1945), p. 779. Such a definition completely omits reference to universals.

3. Ibid., p. 17.

4. Joseph Fletcher, *Situation Ethics* (Philadelphia: Westminster Press, 1966), p. 17.

5. Bernard Bailyn, *The Ordeal of Thomas Hutchinson* (Cambridge, Mass. Harvard University Press, 1974), p. 106.

6. Daniel Bell, *The Coming of Post-Industrial Society* (New York: Basic Books, 1973), pp. 268–71.

7. Richard M. Zaner, *The Way of Phenomenology* (New York: Pegasus Press, 1970), p. 19.

8. Ibid., p. 34.

9. The most accessible explication of his thought by Husserl is *Cartesian Meditations,* trans. Dorion Cairns (The Hague: Martinus Nijhoff, 1960).

10. Maurice Merleau-Ponty, *The Phenomenology of Perception,* trans. Colin Smith (New York: Humanities Press, 1962).

11. John Dewey and J. H. Tufts, *Ethics* (New York: Henry Holt, 1908).

12. Fletcher, *Situation Ethics.*

13. William Robert Miller, "Christianity's 'New Morality,' " *The New Republic,* September 3, 1966, p. 22.

14. James M. Gustafsen, "How Does Love Reign?" *Christian Century,* May 18, 1966, p. 654.

15. Fletcher, *Situation Ethics,* pp. 26, 95, 40.

16. Ibid., p. 98.

17. Erik Barnouw.

18. Robert Metz, *CBS: Reflections in a Bloodshot Eye* (New York: New American Library, 1975), pp. xvii–xviii.

19. Martin Mayer, *About Television* (New York: Harper and Row, 1972), p. 94.

20. "Banks Found to Lack a National Standard of Ethics," New York *Times,* December 20, 1977.

21. Joseph R. Dominick and Millard Pearce, "Trends in Network Prime-Time Programming, 1953–74," *Journal of Communication,* winter 1976, p. 80.

22. Les Brown, *Television: The Business Behind the Box* (New York: Harcourt Brace Jovanovich, 1971), p. 179.

23. Joe McGinnis, *The Selling of the President, 1968* (New York: Trident Press, 1969), p. 21.

24. Harold Innis, *Empire and Communication.*

25. Marshall McLuhan, *Understanding Media: The Extensions of Man* (New York: McGraw-Hill, 1968).

26. Ibid., pp. 5–7.

27. Douglas Cater and Stephen Strickland, *TV Violence and the Child* (New York: Russell Sage Foundation, 1975), pp. 65–66.

28. Raymond Williams, *Television: Technology and Cultural Forms* (New York: Schocken Books, 1976), p. 121.

29. Robert T. Bower, *Television and the Public* (New York: Holt, Rinehart and Winston, 1973), pp. 43–49.

30. Williams, *Television,* p. 122.

31. Rose K. Goldsen, *The Show and Tell Machine* (New York: Dial Press, 1977) pp. 23–30.

32. Jacob Bronowsky, *Science and Human Values* (New York: Perennial Library, 1965), p. 60.

About the Authors

BERNARD RUBIN is the director of the Institute for Democratic Communication and professor of governmental affairs at Boston University's School of Public Communication and its graduate school. He received the Ph.D. in political science from New York University. Before joining the Boston University faculty in 1959 he taught at Brooklyn College, Skidmore College, and Rutgers University.

He has been a consultant to The Agency for International Development, the United States Air Force, the Internal Revenue Service, Department of the Treasury, and other organizations. He was Chief of Research Design at the United States Information Agency from 1968 to 1969. Dr. Rubin recently served as advisor to the Malaysian government's MARA Institute of Technology and on two extended visits in 1974 and 1975 where he worked on planning for new college level, middle-management training of Malaysians in communications. In 1978 he was an American delegate to the "International News Media and World Development" conference in Cairo, Egypt.

Dr. Rubin is the author of numerous articles in the field of mass communications, administrative analysis, and politics. His books include: *Public Relations and the Empire State* (1958); *Political Television* (1967); *Propaganda and Public Opinion* (1972); *Media, Politics and Democracy* (1977); *Big Business and The Mass Media* (1977).

F. EARLE BARCUS, professor of communication research at Boston University's School of Public Communication, has spent the past several years studying the content and effects of mass communication. His teaching focuses on the social aspects of mass communication, communication theory, and research methods in broadcasting. Recent research includes several studies of children's television, supported by grants from *Action for Children's Television.* He has authored a book on alumni administration and most recently *Children's Television: An Analysis of Programming and Advertising.* Numerous articles have appeared in the *Annals of the American Academy of Political and Social Science, Journalism Quarterly,* the *Journal of Broadcasting,* and *The Progressive.*

JOAN BEHRMANN is an associate professor of journalism at Boston University. She holds an M.S. degree from the Columbia University Graduate School of Journalism and has done postgraduate work at the University of Miami and the University of California at Santa Barbara. Ms. Behrmann has written hundreds of newspaper and magazine articles in a twenty-year journalism career that includes work as reporter and editor for the Miami *Herald,* Miami *News,* Charlotte *Observer* and South Middlesex *News.* Her magazine experience includes work on the staff of *Seventeen* Magazine and *Moment* Magazine, and as a media columnist for the Village *Post,* Miami, Florida. While teaching journalism and group communications at Miami-Dade Community College–South, Miami, Florida, she also trained as a facilitator for an ongoing series of human relations laboratories. At Boston University, Ms. Behrmann teaches courses in newswriting and reporting, feature writing, production and design, and has also directed a series of workshops for women in communications management. Listed in *Who's Who Among American Women* and in *Foremost Women in Communications,* a member of Women in Communications, Inc., and the Association for Education in Journalism, she is also on the executive board of the New England chapter, Society of Professional Journalists, Sigma Delta Chi.

NORA BELOFF is an author and journalist. Her most recent book *Freedom Under Foot* was a study of the conflict about a closed shop in British journalism, which would have given one politicized trade union the right to decide who could qualify to write in the newspapers. She has published an article in the magazine *Encounter* analyzing how, in a democratic society, the new technology could and should reduce the costs of newspaper production to make the press less dependent on revenues from advertising.

Nora Beloff graduated with an Honors Degree in history from Lady Margaret College, Oxford. Most of her life has been spent on the *Observer* Sunday newspaper which she joined in 1949 and from which she resigned in the summer of 1977. During that time she served, for varying periods, as Washington correspondent under all U.S. presidents since Truman. Her last U.S. assignment was the Ford-Carter transition period. She has been chief political columnist and has also worked for the *Observer* as resident correspondent in Moscow, Paris, and Brussels, and as a roving correspondent in many other places. Miss Beloff has written and lectured widely on Britain and the EEC. She is now engaged in a study of the Communist block. Her two books are *The General Says No,* 1963, and *The Transit of Britain,* 1973.

LOREN GHIGLIONE is editor and publisher of *The Evening News,* Southbridge, Mass., and a founding officer of the National News. *Evaluating the Press,* the report of the New England Daily Newspaper Survey, won for him the national Sigma Delta Chi Award in 1974 for research about journalism. He received his B.A. degree from Haverford College in 1963 (majoring in English and history), his Master of Urban Studies degree from Yale University in 1966, his Doctor of Jurisprudence degree from the Yale Law School in 1966, and his Ph.D. in American Civilization from George Washington University in 1976.

ROGER MANVELL is visiting professor of film at Boston University. He holds a Ph.D. in English language and literature from London University, Great Britain, and a D. Litt in film studies from Sussex University—the only senior doctorate in the subject so far conferred in Britain. He is also an Hon D. Litt of Leicester University, Great Britain, and an Hon D. F. A. of New England College, New Hampshire. He was formerly head of the department of film history at the London Film School and has a Visiting Fellowship in film studies at Sussex University. He was from 1947 to 1959 Director of the British Film Academy, the British equivalent of the Hollywood Academy. In 1973 he came to the United States as Bingham Professor of Humanities at the University of Louisville, Kentucky. He is the author of numerous books on film and television, and has contributed to the *Encyclopaedia Britannica* on communications subjects. In addition to scripting many documentary and animation films, he has written many plays and documentaries for BBC radio and television. Among his more recent books are biographies of Charles Chaplin and (with Heinrich Fraenkel) of Hitler *(Adolf Hitler: the Man and the Myth)*, *The Trial of Annie Besant*, and *Films and the Second World War.* He was editor-in-chief of the *International Encyclopedia of Film* (1972) and among his works in preparation are *Theatre and Film* and a critical study of the films of Ingmar Bergman.

RICHARD P. NIELSEN does research, publishes, consults, and teaches in the area of broadcasting and mass media labor relations, management, economics, and structure. He has published articles in *Labor Law Journal, Journal of Broadcasting, The Columbia Journal of World Business, Journalism Quarterly, The American Business Law Journal, CULTURES, Journal of Consumer Affairs, Mass Communications Review, Academy of Management Review, Public Opinion Quarterly, Business and Society Review, Performing Arts Review,* and *The American Journal of Economics and Sociology.* He is currently a labor relations consultant for the WGBH Educational Foundation which is the license holder for WGBH-TV, WGBX-TV, WGBY-TV, and WGBH-FM, is on the editorial boards of several professional journals, and is an active member of the National Association of Educational Broadcasters, the American Arbitration Association, the Broadcasting Education Association, the Society of Professionals in Dispute Resolution, the Association for Education in Journalism, and the Academy of Management. Professor Nielsen is a faculty member of the School of Public Communication, Boston University.

Rev. Dr. EVERETT C. PARKER is the Director of the Office of Communication of the United Church of Christ. He has long been engaged in efforts to make broadcasting accountable to the public, and to ensure minority access to the media. Dr. Parker began fighting unfair treatment of blacks by broadcast stations in 1964 by filing a petition against license renewal for station WLBT-TV, in Jackson, Mississippi. This action resulted in the first revocation of a station's license by the U.S. Supreme Court for failure to serve "the public interest, convenience or necessity."

Among his many awards, Dr. Parker, in 1969, was the first person to receive an Alfred I. duPont–Columbia University Award, "for his long and devoted advocacy of the public interest in broadcasting." He was awarded a Citation from the Religious Heritage Foundation, "for pioneering efforts in the field of religious broadcasting." He also received the American Jewish Committee's Human Relations Mass Media Award.

Dr. Parker has written and produced numerous national radio and TV programs, and he has authored several publications including: "Religious Radio: What to Do and How" (1948); and "Religious Television" (1961). Most recently, he initiated the television documentary series, "Six American Families" which portrays family life among Americans in the '70ş.

Born in Chicago in 1913, Dr. Parker graduated from the University of Chicago in 1935. In 1943 he graduated *magna cum laude* from the Chicago Theological Seminary. Dr. Parker was awarded the degree of Doctor of Divinity by the Chicago Theological Seminary in 1964 and by Catawba College, Salisbury, N.C. in 1958.

DEAC ROSSELL is currently Film Coordinator at the Museum of Fine Arts, Boston, where he arranged their series of newspaper films "Dateline . . . Hollywood" in the Spring of 1975. He teaches film history at Tufts University in Medford, Massachusetts and contemporary film at Harvard University in Cambridge, Massachusetts. He spent five years as the film editor of the weekly Boston *Phoenix,* two years as the photography critic of the Boston *Globe,* and he has written widely on subjects in the arts for both newspapers and magazines, including *The National Catholic Reporter,* American Film Institute *Report, Cinema,* the Boston *Herald-Traveller,* and *American Film.* He spent two years as a field press representative for Jon-Carter & Company, handling accounts in New England for Metro-Goldwyn-Mayer Pictures, United Artists Pictures, Warner Brothers Pictures, and others. He has been a member of many film juries, including the 3rd U.S.A. Film Festival in Dallas, Texas, and in 1969 he produced 11 short films for Otto Preminger. Married to silkscreen artist Mickey Myers, he is a past member of the executive board of the Boston Visual Artists Union and is currently Vice-President of the Ford Hall Forum, the oldest public lecture series in America.

ROBERT RUTHERFORD SMITH is professor of communication at the School of Public Communication, Boston University. For the past decade he has been chairman of the Department of Broadcasting and Film. Before joining Boston University, he worked as a writer and director in numerous public and commercial stations in New York and the middle west.

Dr. Smith received the B.A. from the University of Buffalo, and the M.S. and Ph.D. degrees from The Ohio State University. He has served as an officer of the Broadcast Education Association and the Speech Communication Association and as a consultant to numerous broadcasters, publishers, and governmental agencies. His book, *Beyond the Wasteland,* is widely used as a text, and more than twenty of his articles have appeared in professional journals.

JAMES C. THOMSON JR., whose special interests are American–East Asian relations, the history of modern China, and the government-press relationship, is Curator of the Nieman Fellowships for Journalism and Lecturer on General Education at Harvard University.

From 1961 to 1964 Mr. Thomson was a Special Assistant in the Department of State. He then served for two years as an East Asia specialist on the national Security Council staff at the White House. Mr. Thomson who holds an M.A. degree from Cambridge University and the Ph.D. from Harvard (1961) joined the Harvard faculty in 1966 as an assistant professor of history, and became Lecturer on History in 1970. He was appointed Nieman Curator as of September 1972 and is concurrently Lecturer on General Education. He is an associate of the East Asian Research Center and has also been a Research Fellow of Harvard's Institute of Politics and a member of the faculty Council.

The author of *While China Faced West: American Reformers in Nationalist China, 1928–37* (1969) and of "Communist Policy and the United Front in China, 1935–36" (Papers on China, Vol. XI, 1957), he is co-editor with Ernest R. May of *American-East Asian Relations: A Survey"* 1972). He also contributed to *No More Vietnams? The War and the Future of American Foreign Policy* (1968), *Who We Are: An Atlantic Chronicle of the U.S. & Vietnam, The New Era in American Foreign Policy* (1973), and *Pearl Harbor as History* (1973). He has written articles and reviews for the *Journal of Asian Studies,* the *American Historical Review,* the *Atlantic Monthly, Foreign Policy* and numerous other publications. He is the editor of the quarterly *Nieman Reports.* Mr. Thomson received an Overseas Press Club award for magazine writing on foreign affairs (1968), and shared an "Emmy" for television coverage of President Nixon's trip to China on ABC-TV (1972).

WILLIAM WORTHY is director of the Afro-journalism program at Boston University, professor of journalism of its School of Public Communication, and professor of Afro-American studies in the Graduate School. He holds a Bachelor of Arts in sociology from Bates College. A correspondent of *The Baltimore Afro-American* since 1951, his overseas experience includes journalistic trips to China in 1957 and four trips to Cuba from 1960 to 1961 as well as a recent trip in 1977. He was the first U.S. correspondent admitted to North Vietnam in 1964. From 1969 to 1970, he was director of the Frederick Douglass Fellowships in Journalism, a one-year Ford Foundation funded training program for members of minority groups, including two trainees just paroled from prison. In the autumn of 1968, he was a Peter Edes Annual Visiting Lecturer in the Department of Journalism at the University of Maine. His awards include those from: Nieman Fellowship, 1956–57; Boston Press Club, 1957; Capital Press Club, 1957; Lincoln University (Missouri), Department of Journalism, 1960. His articles have been featured by such publications as *Life, Esquire, Ebony, New Republic, Village Voice, Christian Century, Ramparts,* Milwaukee *Journal,* Toledo *Blade,* New York *Post,* Boston *Globe,* Baltimore *Sun,* Des Moines *Registrar and Tribune, New Statesman* and *The Nation,* Hindustan *Times, Het Parool* (Amsterdam), *La Tribune de Geneve,* and *Mainichi* (Tokyo). Professor Worthy's recent book is *The Rape of Our Neighborhoods* (1976).

RELATED TITLES

Published by
Praeger Special Studies

PUBLIC BROADCASTING: The Role of the Federal Government, 1912–1976

George H. Gibson

POLITICS IN PUBLIC SERVICE ADVERTISING ON TELEVISION

David L. Paletz,
Roberta E. Pearson,
and Donald L. Willis

*MASS COMMUNICATION RESEARCH: MAJOR ISSUES AND FUTURE DIRECTIONS

Edited by W. Phillips Davison,
and T. C. Frederick Yu

*FREEDOM OF THE PRESS VS. PUBLIC ACCESS

Benno C. Schmidt Jr.

TELEVISION AS A CULTURAL FORCE

Edited by Richard Adler
and Douglass Cater

*THE FUTURE OF PUBLIC BROADCASTING

edited by Douglass Cater
and Michael J. Nyhan

THE MASS MEDIA: Aspen Guide to Communication Industry Trends

Christopher H. Sterling
and Timothy Haight

---

*Also available in paperback